CAMBRIDGE IBE
LATIN AMERICA

MW00831749

GENERAL EDITOR

EMERITUS PROFESSOR P. E. RUSSELL, F.B.A.

PROFESSOR OF SPANISH STUDIES, THE UNIVERSITY OF OXFORD

A social history of
black slaves and freedmen in Portugal
1441–1555

CAMBRIDGE IBERIAN AND LATIN AMERICAN STUDIES

already published

STEVEN BOLDY, *The novels of Julio Cortázar*

JUAN LÓPEZ-MORILLAS, *The Krausist movement and
ideological change in Spain, 1854–1874*

EVELYN S. PROCTER, *Curia and Cortes in León and Castile, 1072–1295*

DIANE F. UREY, *Galdós and the irony of language*

future titles will include

ROBERT I. BURNS, *Muslims, Christians and Jews
in the crusader kingdom of Valencia*

JOHN EDWARDS, *Christian Córdoba*

MAURICE HEMINGWAY, *Emilia Pardo Bazán:
the making of a novelist*

JOHN LYON, *The theatre of Valle-Inclán*

LINDA MARTZ, *Poetry and welfare in Hapsburg Spain:
the example of Toledo*

JULIÁN OLIVARES, *The love poetry of Francisco de Quevedo:
an aesthetic and existential study*

A. R. D. PAGDEN, *The fall of natural man: the
American Indian and the growth of historical
relativism*

FRANCISCO RICO, *The picaresque novel and the
point of view*

A social history of
black slaves and freedmen
in Portugal
1441–1555

A. C. DE C. M. SAUNDERS

MELLON POSTDOCTORAL FELLOW
CORNELL UNIVERSITY

CAMBRIDGE UNIVERSITY PRESS

CAMBRIDGE
LONDON   NEW YORK   NEW ROCHELLE
MELBOURNE   SYDNEY

CAMBRIDGE UNIVERSITY PRESS
Cambridge, New York, Melbourne, Madrid, Cape Town, Singapore,
São Paulo, Delhi, Dubai, Tokyo

Cambridge University Press
The Edinburgh Building, Cambridge CB2 8RU, UK

Published in the United States of America by Cambridge University Press, New York

www.cambridge.org
Information on this title: www.cambridge.org/9780521130035

© A. C. de C. M. Saunders 1982

This publication is in copyright. Subject to statutory exception
and to the provisions of relevant collective licensing agreements,
no reproduction of any part may take place without the written
permission of Cambridge University Press.

First published 1982
This digitally printed version 2010

A catalogue record for this publication is available from the British Library

Library of Congress Catalogue Card Number: 81–7716

ISBN 978-0-521-23150-3 Hardback
ISBN 978-0-521-13003-5 Paperback

Cambridge University Press has no responsibility for the persistence or
accuracy of URLs for external or third-party internet websites referred to in
this publication, and does not guarantee that any content on such websites is,
or will remain, accurate or appropriate.

Contents

List of plates	*page* viii
List of maps	viii
List of tables	ix
Preface	xi
List of abbreviations	xvi
Introduction	I
1 The slave-trade	4
From war to trade	4
Regulatory and fiscal institutions	7
The slaving voyage	11
The sale of slaves: corretores	17
Numbers and prices	19
The re-export of slaves	28
The place of the slave-trade in the Portuguese economy	31
Conclusions	33
2 Legal and philosophical justifications of the slave-trade	35
The legitimization of slave raiding and slave trading	36
Sin and servitude, civilization and Christianity	38
The promotion of Christianity among black slaves	40
Critics of the trade	42
Conclusions	45
3 The demography of blacks in Portugal	47
The distribution of slaves and freedmen in Portugal	50
Conclusions	59

page

4 The occupations of slaves 62
   Slave-ownership 62
   The employment of slaves 63
   Slaves in agriculture 69
   Nautical pursuits 71
   Slaves in the cities 72
   Slaves and the crown 80
   The place of slaves in the economy: conclusions 84

5 The life of the slave 89
   Baptism and slave children 90
   Clothing 92
   Shelter 96
   Food 97
   Language and education 98
   Sexual relations and marriage 102
   Festivities and pastimes 105
   Punishment and harsh treatment 107
   Disease and death 109
   Conclusions 110

6 Slaves and the law 113
   Juridical status 114
   Slaves in the courts 117
   Police legislation 120
   Theft 122
   Receiving stolen goods 123
   Assault and murder 125
   Prisons 128
   Incidence of black crime 130
   Conclusions 131

7 Fugitives, freedom and freedmen 134
   Fugitives 134
   Freedom: manumission 138
   Freedmen 141
   Conclusions 147

page

8 Blacks and Christianity   149
   Lay piety   150
   Blacks and holy orders   156
   Blacks and the Inquisition   158
   Conclusions   164

9 Race relations   166
   The white picture of black people   166
   The human reality   171

Conclusions   176
   Epilogue   178

Notes   180

Bibliography   224
   Manuscript sources   224
   Printed sources   236
      Primary sources   236
      Secondary sources   250
      Addenda   265

Glossary   266

Index   271

Plates

between pages 126 *and* 127

1 A Portuguese view of life in black Africa (detail from 'Livro de Horas de D. Manuel', f. 98v, early sixteenth century)
2 Black in attendance upon an aristocratic hunting party ('Livro de Horas de D. Fernando', month of May, early sixteenth century)
3 A black slave waits upon the family of a wealthy merchant at table ('Livro de Horas de D. Manuel', f. 5v, early sixteenth century)
4 Detail from a painting of the birth of the Virgin, showing a black serving-woman (Gregório Lopes, 'Nascimento da Virgem', sixteenth century)
5 Black minstrels playing shawms and sackbut (Mestre de Santa Auta, 'Santa Úrsula e o Príncipe Conan', *c.* 1520)
6 Detail from an Adoration of the Magi, showing a black king (Portuguese School, 'Adoração dos Magos', sixteenth century)

All these plates are taken from paintings and illuminations in the Museu Nacional de Arte Antiga, Lisbon, which kindly authorized their reproduction. Plates 4 and 6 are from paintings in the collection of the Duques de Palmela.

Maps

1 Western Africa, showing places mentioned in the text *page* 6
2 Residences of blacks mentioned in documents, 1441–1530 51
3 Lisbon in the later sixteenth century 56
4 Home ports of slaves and freedmen working on the boats on the Tagus in 1549, 1550 and 1555 73

Tables

1 Slaves shipped to Lisbon by the various captains of
  Arguim from 1499 to 1520   *page* 20
2 Slaves known to have been shipped from São Tomé
  to Lisbon between 1515 and 1534   21
3 Slaves known to have been shipped from Arguim and
  received alive in Lisbon between 1501 and 1520   22
4 Slaves purchased at Arguim, 4 May 1519–10 March
  1520   24
5 Population of Portugal, 1527–35   49
6 Numbers of slaves and freedmen in Portugal in the
  mid-sixteenth century   60
7 Owners of slaves who were baptized or were parents of
  children baptized in the Cathedral of Oporto, 1540,
  1544   64
8 Owners of slaves buried by the Misericórdia of Évora,
  1537–8 and 1547–55   65
9 Occupations in which blacks were involved in Lisbon
  during the 1550s   81

THIS BOOK IS DEDICATED TO
MY MOTHER AND FATHER AND TO MY TEACHERS:
PROFESSOR C. C. BAYLEY, DR J. R. L. HIGHFIELD
AND PROFESSOR P. E. L. R. RUSSELL.

Preface

The purpose of the present work is to study the social, economic, legal and intellectual developments associated with the growth of a community of black slaves and freedmen in Portugal during the first century of direct seaborne contact between Europe and black Africa. These developments were of profound importance because the form taken by relations between black Africans and white Portuguese in the fifteenth and sixteenth centuries was, with some modifications and exceptions, that which was to prevail throughout the Atlantic world until the nineteenth century, and we still suffer from its consequences today. The salient features of this system of relations were the Atlantic slave-trade and the relegation of black people to servitude or positions of inferior status in countries ruled by whites. The triangular slave-trade was organized by the Portuguese and it was in Portugal that considerable numbers of blacks first came to experience white domination and whites first decided what place blacks should hold in society.

True, that place was partly determined by traditions of slave-holding dating back to long before 1441 when the first of many blacks to be brought by ship directly to Portugal from western Africa were seized in a raid on Mauritania. Over the next hundred years, however, the distinct behaviour of blacks under slavery called for new responses to accommodate them to a society which had known mainly Moors and a few Canarian slaves in the Middle Ages. By the 1550s blacks appear to have displaced Moors as the principal ethnic group among the slaves who then constituted up to 10 per cent of the population of Lisbon and other towns. By that time too the expansion of the trade with black Africa had called forth a new topic of intellectual concern – the justness of the slave-trade – whereas Moorish slavery had been associated with concern for the justness of war, the chief means of acquiring Moorish slaves. In 1555 a scholar published the first attack on the evils of the trade and on the treatment of slaves in Portugal. The present study concludes at this point, when black slavery and the slave-trade had not only become recognizably important features of Portuguese society and the economy but had stimulated the sense of outrage which in the long run contributed so powerfully to the abolition of slavery. The opponents of slavery were not to triumph in Portugal for another two hundred years, when other conditions favourable to abolition appeared; during those centuries, however, the nature of black slavery in Portugal remained more or less as it was in the 1550s, as will be evident from occasional examples presented to show the extension of trends observable in the period under study.

The social history of slavery in Renaissance Portugal has been considered by Carvalho, Lopes, Brásio and Godinho in the course of larger studies, and I have made use of many of their findings in writing this book.[1] I have also benefited from the perceptions of historians of slavery working in different fields, and owe considerable debts to Heleno for his work on Moorish slavery in mediaeval Portugal, to Verlinden for his magisterial study of slavery in mediaeval Europe,[2] and to the historians of slavery in the Americas.[3] But ultimately the nature of the exposition which follows has been shaped by consideration of a large mass of documentary material, much of it hitherto unexamined, stored in archives scattered throughout Portugal. The ravages of time, negligence and natural disasters (such as the Lisbon earthquake of 1755) have deprived us of a great deal of documentary evidence, and hence some topics have not been treated as fully as could be wished, but on the whole far more has survived than I had dared to hope. I have tried to provide as much background information as possible to elucidate most questions relating to slavery; for general descriptions of the society and economy of Renaissance Portugal, however, I must refer the reader to other authors, and the same is true of the general history of Portuguese discovery and commerce in Africa.[4]

As regards nomenclature, I have employed the word 'black' to refer to all negroid people or people of mixed negroid and Caucasian descent, except where further definition was required. This more or less follows Portuguese practice, which usually described negroid people and their descendants as *preto* or *negro*. Both words meant black, but *negro*, the more common, was also the more offensive; it can be translated as 'nigger'. *Mulato*, meaning 'mule', came into widespread use only in the sixteenth century and described people of mixed descent. *Baço*, 'dark', could be used as a polite word for blacks, but it referred more specifically to mulattoes[5] and particularly to light-skinned mulattoes, who may also have been called *pardo*, 'dusky'.[6] Further distinctions by colour or parentage are not found in the period under study.

In the fifteenth century the word for slave was *mouro*, Moor, free Moors having to be designated as such, namely *mouros forros*, and black slaves were at first called *mouros negros*, blackamoors.[7] Except to some Portuguese, however,[8] the inconvenience of using a word with connotations of 'Muslim' to describe blacks who were mostly pagans and, when enslaved, willing Christians must readily have become apparent. Hence from at least 1459[9] the word *escravo*, simply designating servile status without any religious connotations, became predominant; as W. F. Oliveira has pointed out, the contemporaneity of the first influx of black slaves and the adoption of *escravo* does not seem purely coincidental.[10] Black slaves were thus *escravos pretos* or *escravos negros*; Moors, *escravos mouros* or *escravos brancos* (white slaves); and the use of the word could be infinitely extended to indicate the status of slaves of other races and religions brought back from overseas.[11] *Cativo*, 'captive', a mediaeval term, continued to have some currency as a word for slave,[12] but it is usually found qualifying *escravo*, to indicate a slave wholly in his master's power, as opposed to an *escravo forro* who had acquired a degree of freedom.[13] Some archaizers and humanists employed the mediaeval and Latinate *servo* in the same way as *escravo*, for the decline of serfdom meant that the word was less likely to be taken to mean 'serf'.

I have called all free blacks 'freedmen', since the term *forro* usually employed in the documents does not permit any precise distinctions between a freedman who had been manumitted and a black man who had been born free in Portugal. Probably most free blacks in this period had been manumitted. The terminology is considered at some length in Chapter 7.

Quite a few of the administrative titles of functionaries and of the names of institutions do not have an exact equivalent in English, so I have left them in the original Portuguese in the text. Definitions and descriptions will be found in the glossary. Names of persons appear in the modernized Portuguese form, except for Bastião, the standard Portuguese form of Sebastião until the reign of that unfortunate king. Similarly, the names of Castilians and other nationals, except for popes and a few scholars with Latin names, are given in the modern forms employed in their native countries. Where there are no common English equivalents for the names of peoples or geographical places, they appear in the local form or else, when a non-Roman script is involved, in the preferred transliteration. All translations of quoted material are my own, except when noted otherwise.

This study could not have been written without the economic backing of the Rhodes Trust and the Canada Council and without the help of many people in many places. I should like to thank the curators and staff of all the archives mentioned in the bibliography under the heading of Manuscript Sources, and especially those people whose kindness and forbearance eased the task of consulting documents in uncatalogued archives or when time was short. I owe special debts of gratitude to Dr J. Pereira da Costa, the director, and to Sras Alcina Fernandes and Lucília dos Reis at the Arquivo Nacional da Torre do Tombo; Sr João Caeiro at the Biblioteca Pública Municipal, Sr Alface at the Câmara Municipal and Sr António Pires Lucas, *provedor* of the Santa Casa da Misericórdia, all in Elvas; and Sr Fernando Magalhães and Sr Constantino Camelo Borges of the Arquivo Distrital in Évora. I should also like to thank the staffs of the following libraries not already mentioned in the list of archives: in Cambridge, the University Library; in Lisbon, the library of the Academia das Ciências; in London, the library of King's College, University of London; in Oxford, the library of the Ashmolean Museum, the Bodleian Library, the History Faculty Library, the library of Rhodes House, the Spanish Sub-Faculty Library and the library of the Taylor Institution; and the Bibliotecas Públicas Municipais of Aveiro, Santarém and Setúbal.

Dr Peter Bury, Dr Martin Cunningham, Dr Felipe Fernández-Armesto, Dr Nigel Griffin, Dr José Matoso, Anthony Pagden, Paul Sanders, Dr Paul Slack, Father Carmelo Solís, Professor H. R. Trevor-Roper and Dr John Vogt all helped in various ways to further my understanding of the nature of slavery in Portugal; and I am particularly grateful to Ronald Bishop Smith, Dr A. H. de Oliveira Marques, Professor C. R. Boxer and the late Dr Virgínia Rau for making their wide knowledge of Portuguese history and archives freely available to me while I was in Portugal. Cdr A. Teixeira da

Mota very kindly consented to read through and comment upon an initial draft of the first chapter. Above all, since this book began life as a thesis, I am indebted to Professor Peter Russell and Dr Roger Highfield, my supervisors at Oxford, for their patience and concern for sound scholarship. Last, but by no means least, thanks must go to my friends and parents for their encouragement and support.

A. C. de C. M. S.

Exeter College, Oxford
and West Jeddore, Nova Scotia
1976–1980

Abbreviations

Printed Works

Arch. Hist. Port.: *Archivo Historico Portuguez*

Bol. Bib. Univ. Coimbra: *Boletim da Biblioteca da Universidade de Coimbra*

Bull. Inst. Hist. Belge de Rome: *Bulletin de l'Institut Historique Belge de Rome*

Crón. Guiné: Gomes Eanes de Zurara, *Crónica de Guiné* (various editions: see Bibliography)

Descobs. Ports.: J. M. da Silva Marques (ed.), *Descobrimentos Portugueses*, in 3 vols.: vol. I; *Suplemento* (supplement) to vol. I (abbreviated as I, *sup.*); and vol. III (Lisbon, 1944–71)

Docs. Port. Moz.: *Documentos sobre os Portugueses em Moçambique e na África Central, 1497–1840 / Documents on the Portuguese in Mozambique and Central Africa, 1497–1840*, published by National Archives of Rhodesia (and Nyasaland) and Centro de Estudos Históricos Ultramarinos, vols. I–VII used (Lisbon, 1962–71)

Livros de Reis: *Documentos do Arquivo Histórico da Câmara Municipal de Lisboa. Livros de Reis*, published by Arquivo Histórico da Câmara Municipal, Lisbon (Lisbon, 1957–   )

Mon. Hen.: *Monumenta Henricina*, published by Comissão Executiva das Comemorações do v. Centenário da Morte do Infante D. Henrique, 14 vols. (Coimbra, 1960–73)

Mon. Miss. Af.: A. Brásio (ed.), *Monumenta Missionaria Africana. África Ocidental*, in two series: 1a sér., vols. I–VI used (Lisbon, 1952–5); 2a sér., vols. I and II used (Lisbon, 1958–63)

Ord. Af.: *Ordenaçoens do Senhor Rey D. Affonso V*, 5 vols. (Coimbra, 1792). The numbers following the title indicate the book (*livro*), law (*lei*) and sub-section of the law, viz., 4. 12. 3. (Most laws start with a descriptive preface, Pr.) A similar system of numbering is employed for the *Ordenações Manuelinas* (see below) and for D. Nunes de Leão, *Leis Extravagantes* (Lisbon, 1569).

Ord. Man. (1514); (1521): *Ordenações Manuelinas*, 1st and 2nd edns (Lisbon, 1514; and Évora and Lisbon, 1521). For numbers following, see above, *Ord. Af.*

Archives and Libraries

AD: Arquivo Distrital (District Archives), with name of town following; thus, AD Porto

AD Évora CM: archives of the *câmara municipal* (municipality) of Évora, housed in the Arquivo Distrital of Évora. Originais in notes refers to Colecção de Originais da Câmara, catalogue nos. 71–5

AD Porto, Notas: collection of notarial archives in the Arquivo Distrital of Oporto. The numbers which follow indicate the *maço* (bundle of documents) and the specific document within the *maço*

AGI Seville: Archivo General de Indias, Seville

AG Simancas: Archivo General, Simancas

AGU Coimbra: Arquivo Geral da Universidade, Coimbra

AHCM: Arquivo Histórico da Câmara Municipal (municipal archives), with name of town following; thus, AHCM Elvas

AHCM Elvas, Provizões: collection of Proprias Provizões, Alvaras, Cartas e Ordens Regias in the Arquivo Histórico da Câmara Municipal of Elvas

AHCM Lxa: Arquivo Histórico da Câmara Municipal, Lisbon, which houses the following collections:
 Ch. Cidade: Chancelaria da Cidade
 Ch. Régia: Chancelaria Régia
 Prov. Ofícios: Provimento de Ofícios
 Prov. Saúde: Provimento da Saúde

ANTT: Arquivo Nacional da Torre do Tombo, Lisbon, in which are the following collections:
 Bulas: numbers indicate *maço* and document
 C. C.: Corpo Cronológico, with numbers of *parte*, *maço* and document following
 Ch. Af. V: Chancelaria de D. Afonso V, Chancery books of King D. Afonso V
 Ch. Fil. I: Chancery books of King D. Filipe I
 Ch. J. I: Chancery books of King D. João I
 Ch. J. II: Chancery books of King D. João II
 Ch. J. III: Chancery books of King D. João III
 Ch. Man.: Chancery books of King D. Manuel I
 Ch. Seb.: Chancery books of King D. Sebastião
 Ch. Seb. e Hen.: Joint chancery books of Kings D. Sebastião and D. Henrique
 (From the reign of D. João III onwards there was a separate series of chancery books for pardons and legitimations, abbreviated here as Perdões e Legits., for Perdões e Legitimações. Thus Ch. J. III, Perdões e Legits., 12, f. 24 indicates Chancery of D. João III, Pardons and Legitimations, vol. 12, folio 24.)
 Col. S. Vicente: Colecção de São Vicente
 Cortes: the numbers following indicate *maço* and document. In the succeeding description, caps. esps. stands for capítulos

especiais, caps. ger. for capítulos gerais, being some of the chapters presented for consideration at the Cortes

Ctas Miss.: Cartas Missivas; numbers following indicate *parte* and document

Estrem.: Estremadura; by itself, Livro de Estremadura in the collection Leitura Nova

Frags.: Fragmentos; numbers following indicate *caixa, maço* and document

Gav.: Gavetas; numbers following indicate *gaveta, maço* and document

Inq.: Inquisition, in collection Santo Ofício

Leis: Numbers indicate *maço* and document

Núc. Ant.: Núcleo Antigo

Reg. Par.: Registo Paroquial

Arch. Prots. Badajoz: Archivo de Protocolos, Badajoz (notarial archives)

Arch Vat.: Archivio Vaticano, Rome, which contains Reg. Vat.: Registro Vaticano

BGU Coimbra: Biblioteca Geral da Universidade, Coimbra

Bib. Vat.: Biblioteca Vaticana, Rome, which contains Cod. Lat.: Codex Latinus

BL: British Library; the former British Museum Library

BM: Biblioteca Municipal, location following

BN: Biblioteca Nacional, Biblioteca Nazionale, Bibliothèque Nationale, according to the country; location follows, thus, BN Lxa, Biblioteca Nacional de Lisboa

BP: Biblioteca Pública, location following

BSG Lxa: Biblioteca da Sociedade Geográfica, Lisbon, which contains Res.: Reservados

GHC Porto: Gabinete de História da Cidade, Oporto (municipal archives)

Mis.: Misericórdia archives, location following

Other abbreviations

cod.: codex, *códice*

Lxa: Lixboa, i.e. Lisboa (Lisbon)

mistos: When referring to parish registers, indicates volumes which do not record only baptisms or marriages or funerals, but contain headings for two or three of these sacraments, and sometimes for confirmations as well

Núc. Not.: Núcleo Notarial (collection of notarial archives)

Núc. Par.: Núcleo Paroquial (collection of parish archives)

Pr.: see above, *Ord. Af.*

rs.: *reais.* The *real* (plural, *reais*) was both a coin and the fundamental unit of account during the period under study. See p. 26

xdo: *cruzado.* A coin and a unit of account. See p. 26

Introduction

All places are full of slaves. Captive blacks and Moors perform all tasks; Portugal is so crowded with these people that I believe that in Lisbon there are more men and women slaves than free Portuguese . . . Truly, when I first arrived in Évora I thought that I had come to some city of evil demons: everywhere there were so many blacks whom I so loathe that they may just be able to drive me away from here.

Thus the Flemish humanist Clenardus recorded some of his first impressions of Portugal shortly after his arrival there in 1535.[1] To a northerner such as he the very institution of slavery must have been somewhat surprising, but in southern Europe slaves drawn from trade with the lands around the Black Sea and from the continuous wars against Islamic states had been part of the social scene throughout the Middle Ages. What was truly striking about Portugal in the fifteenth and sixteenth centuries was the number of black slaves, forming one of the greatest concentrations of black people in any European society before our own time – though nowhere did they outnumber native Portuguese, as Clenardus whimsically supposed. Their presence was a consequence of the voyages along the western coast of Africa sponsored by the Infante D. Henrique (known in English as Prince Henry the Navigator) during the first half of the fifteenth century. In the 1440s his captains began to bring back black slaves, a trade developed and, a century later, black slaves probably outnumbered the Moors who had composed the bulk of Portugal's slave population in the mediaeval period. Thus Portugal became the first European society in modern times where black slavery was commonplace.[2]

The development of black slavery in Portugal and what this meant for both blacks and whites are the underlying themes of the pages which follow. There was hardly an area of Portuguese life – economic, social or intellectual – which slavery did not affect in some way. It

I

was a crucial influence on Portugal's historical role of discovery, since the possibility of acquiring slaves first brought the Infante D. Henrique popular support for his voyages to the south, and the desire to find new suppliers of slaves was undoubtedly a major reason for the continued exploration of the African littoral. Thereafter the slave-trade constituted the central commercial nexus between Portugal and most African coastal states, while the re-export of slaves to Spain and the Americas became an essential feature of the Portuguese economy.

In Portugal itself slaves were owned by the king, the nobility, the Church, artisans – even by simple working men. Some worked in the fields or crewed vessels in the oceanic or riverine trades, but the largest numbers were found in the towns and cities where they worked as domestic servants, labourers and petty tradesmen. The reasons for the employment of slaves have been debated since the sixteenth century; new evidence brought forward here concerning the demography and occupations of slaves qualifies the traditional assumption that slaves were imported to compensate for the loss of men to the colonies overseas. There was in fact no simple substitution of one form of labour by another; the northern provinces, which provided the most emigrants, had the fewest slaves. Rather, slaves were mainly employed in those areas where the local supply of free labour could not meet the demand created by development of the economy. This was the situation in Lisbon and the southern provinces for most of the period under study, but there are signs that toward the middle of the sixteenth century population growth was making slaves unnecessary, at least as far as Lisbon was concerned.

By that time, however, blacks had become a considerable group in Portuguese society, though not entirely of it. While the law frequently preferred the largely Christian and apparently more tractable blacks to the Moors, it still maintained a hierarchic social order which distinguished slaves and freedmen from freemen, that is, free whites. The blacks accordingly came to form a community of their own, speaking a distinct language (a hybrid form of Portuguese) and retaining African cultural traditions: even when they celebrated Christian festivals they did so with African songs and dances. After manumission, the freed blacks' poverty, occupations and experience of legal discrimination tended to approximate them to slaves, and the freed blacks of the religious confraternity of the Rosary came to provide leadership for the black community as a whole. The brothers not only promoted the interests of freedmen but also strove to facilitate the manumission of slaves.

Slavery was an accepted institution, but the enslavement of a new race of people and the novelty of a primarily commercial approach to acquiring slaves in West Africa called for some justification. The official response was that the slave-trade was an efficient way of bringing Christianity to pagan blacks, and most men seem to have been satisfied with this explanation. Some went so far as to suggest that Africans were bestial and therefore inherently servile. This argument soon dropped out of the official defence of the trade but lingered on in the popular mind as a belief that blacks were naturally good slaves. For instance, poets and playwrights depicted blacks as Sambo figures, none too bright, though humorous, loyal and possessed of some fighting spirit. While the authors showed some sympathy for ill-treated blacks, this portrayal implicitly justified the blacks' relegation to the lowest social orders.

From the mid-sixteenth century, though, a few moral theologians were disturbed by the cruelties of the slave-trade and the inequities of slavery in Portugal. These men rejected the notion that blacks were a lower form of humanity and thought that the slave-trade should be reformed or wholly done away with. The theologians' criticisms were the distant beginnings of the great abolitionist movement, but they had little immediate impact. Unfortunately, therefore, the present study cannot document a steady progress toward liberty for slaves in Portugal, but can only show the incorporation of blacks into the two lowest orders in Portuguese society and their reactions to that process of subordination.

I

The slave-trade

Vẽ grã somma a portugal
cadãno, tãbẽ aas ilhas,
he cousa que sempre val,
& tres dobra ho cabedal
em castella, & nas antilhas.

Every year a great number come to Portugal
and the adjacent islands; they are
something which is always valuable
and will triple your investment
if sold in Castile and the Antilles.

G. de Resende, *Miscellanea* (1554),
stanza lix, on black slaves

In the years under study the means the Portuguese employed to
acquire black slaves in Africa developed from warlike raids, similar
to those used to obtain slaves in Morocco and the Canaries, into a
regularly functioning seaborne trade.[1] Under the direction first of the
Infante D. Henrique and subsequently of the crown, this trade
expanded to provide slaves for markets not only in Portugal but
elsewhere in Europe and the Americas. The present chapter will
examine these developments, and will describe the complex institutional structure created to cope with the increasing numbers of black
slaves brought to Portugal and to obtain fiscal benefits for the
regulating authority.[2] This institutional history is admittedly somewhat dry in parts but it is the essential background to the story of
human relations which unfolds in later chapters.

From war to trade

The period in which the Portuguese relied upon warfare for the
majority of their black slaves was actually very brief: no more than a

few years in the 1440s. The first raid occurred in 1441, when the crews of two Portuguese vessels landed at the Río de Oro and carried off several of the local Berber people, the Idzāgen.[3] By chance, they also seized one of the Idzāgen's black slave women.[4] The reasons for seizing these people were the same as those which had moved the Portuguese to take Moors captive during the earlier campaigns in Morocco. The captives could supply strategic information and could also be ransomed or sold as slaves.[5] Further proof that western Africa had ample supplies of slaves and other booty appeared two years later, when a caravel returned to ransom a pair of aristocratic Idzāgen for ten black slaves and a little gold. Consequently, in 1444 and 1445, the merchants and nobles of the Algarve sent two massive expeditions against the Idzāgen. From the first came some 235[6] Idzāgen and black prisoners who were sold at auction in a field outside Lagos;[7] the second expedition was somewhat less successful.

These two expeditions marked the high point of the warlike approach to the acquisition of slaves. Raids on the now vigilant Idzāgen yielded fewer and fewer captives, while the Portuguese who attacked the black peoples south of the River Senegal were thrown back in ignominious defeat. Accordingly the possibilities of peaceful trade were investigated instead.[8] In 1445 Gomes Pires concluded the first transaction with the Idzāgen of the Río de Oro, who exchanged some of their black slaves for trade goods,[9] and after 1448 direct contacts were made with black princes who had numbers of prisoners of war and criminals for sale.[10] Trade with the Idzāgen was pursued at a permanent trading post or factory at Arguim, an island off the coast of Mauritania.[11] South of the Senegal, however, the trade was usually from ship to shore.

In the bull *Romanus Pontifex* of 1455 Pope Nicholas V ceded the conquest and, more importantly, granted a commercial monopoly of Atlantic Africa south of Cape Bojador to the Portuguese, who, assured of papal approval, proceeded to extend the slave trade ever further south along the western coast of Africa. In 1466 the island of Santiago in the Cape Verde group was settled as a base for trade with Upper Guinea. Five years later, Portuguese captains discovered the 'Mine' (that is, the Gold Coast), so called because gold brought down by African merchants from the interior was readily available there. In 1482 the fort of São Jorge da Mina was built as the Portuguese entrepôt in the gold trade and as a defence against European interlopers. Here slaves acquired further east along the coast in Benin

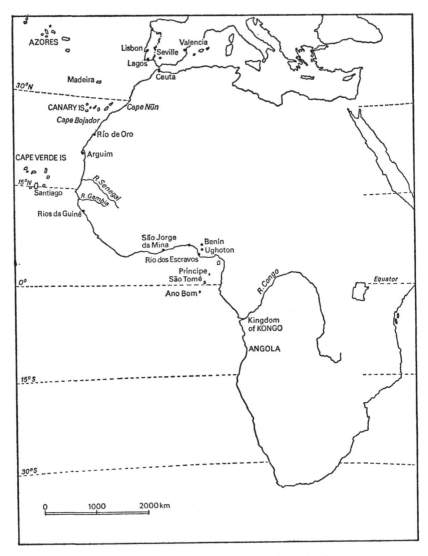

1   Western Africa, showing places mentioned in the text

and the Slave Rivers were among the goods exchanged for gold until the 1530s, when King João III declared that the sale of slaves by Christians to infidels was immoral.[12] After the definitive settlement of São Tomé in 1493, this island became the clearing-house for most of the slaves acquired in the coastal kingdoms of Benin and the Kongo. The Kongo had been discovered in 1483, and priests and artisans were sent there after 1490 to help its newly baptized ruler, the Mani Kongo, create a Christian kingdom. Within a few decades, however, the slave-trade superseded evangelization as the primary Portuguese interest in this black state.

Yet the distance of Benin and the Kongo from the principal markets for slaves, namely southern Europe and Spanish America, meant that slavers long preferred to draw slaves for export from Senegambia and the Rios da Guiné.[13] During the period under study, the Gulf of Guinea trade mainly provided slaves for Mina and the sugar plantations of São Tomé. Some slaves from the Gulf went to the American market but the South Atlantic slave-trade did not really come into its own until the 1550s, when a sugar economy based on slave labour developed in Brazil. The increasing demand for slaves in America was met by increasing trade with the kingdom of Angola, just to the south of the Kongo, and eventually by the flow of captives taken in the wars attendant upon the Portuguese colonization of Angola in 1575.[14] There was almost no recourse, though, to eastern Africa, which supplied black slaves to the Portuguese communities in Asia.

Regulatory and fiscal institutions

The African trades were a monopoly first of the Infante D. Henrique and then, after his death in 1460, of the crown; consequently all ships bound for black Africa, other than those fitted out by the prince or the king, required authorization. Authorization usually had to be bought from the royal or princely monopolists, who in addition levied special duties and imposts on all goods brought back from Africa. Of course, the monopolists did not personally perform these regulatory and fiscal activities but assigned the tasks to a bureaucracy which steadily increased in size and importance with the growth of the trade.

So far, little is known about the institutional arrangements created by the Infante D. Henrique, who directed the trade from his residence near Sagres in the Algarve. He did, however, delegate responsibility for the money spent in fitting out his ships for Guinea to the *vedor* and chief treasurer of his household, a man who was also entrusted with receiving the cargoes of gold, ivory, 'Moors, Mooresses, parrots and other things' on the vessels' return.[15] With the Infante's permission, royal vessels joined his own in exploiting the African trade. The royal ships were fitted out in Lisbon by the officials of the Casa de Ceuta, an institution originally intended to provide supplies for Ceuta after its capture in 1415.[16] The royal counterpart of the Infante's *vedor* was an official grandiloquently entitled the 'Receiver of all Moors and Mooresses and whatever other things which, God willing, may come to us [the king] from our trade in Guinea'. In his management of monetary expenditures and receipts the Receiver was subject to the authority of the *vedores* of the royal Fazenda and his accounts were audited by the royal *contador*.[17]

After the assumption of the commercial monopoly by the crown alone, the *vedores* of the Fazenda took over supreme financial control of the trade,[18] while the tasks of the Casa de Ceuta and the Receiver of Moors and Mooresses passed on to, or were divided among, other officials and institutions based in Lisbon. The *almoxarife* of the Armazém (that is, warehouse) da Guiné took charge of equipping vessels bound for Guinea,[19] and other *almoxarifes*, each with their own clerks and ancillary staff, looked after the supply of provisions and biscuits and the operation of the slave-trade. In 1486 all these officials were brought together within a mercantile complex known variously as the Casa da Mina e Tratos de Guiné, the Casa da Mina and the Casa da Guiné. Direction of this Casa was assigned to a factor, care of its finances to a treasurer, and settlement of disputes arising from the trade to the *Juiz da Guiné*.[20] After Vasco da Gama opened the sea route to the East, the factor also became the chief administrator of the Casa da Índia, especially created to supervise the Asiatic trades.

The department of the Casa da Guiné which handled the slave-trade was called the Casa dos Escravos. This Casa's buildings were in the Praça da Tanoaria, just to the west of the Armazém and Casa da Guiné, on the waterfront in Lisbon.[21] There were probably three units: a prison of one or two large rooms where slaves were kept after landing; the offices of the *almoxarife dos escravos* and his clerk at the front of the building; and the royal cooperage, also under the *almoxarife*'s direction.[22]

First appointed in 1486, the *almoxarife* came to play a key role in the organization of the African trades.[23] His principal duty was to oversee the management of the slave trade carried out in vessels belonging to or chartered by the crown, and to receive and sell the slaves on the ships' return. As was usual for *almoxarifes*, he also acted as a paymaster, giving slaves or their value in cash to persons designated by the king.[24] Secondly, since the main interest of private merchants who sought authorization to go to western Africa was in the slave-trade, the *almoxarife* was entrusted with the sale of permits to trade, the lease of trading monopolies of certain sections of the African coast, and the concession of the tax farms of the Cape Verdes and the islands in the Gulf of Guinea. Thirdly, he collected the *vintena*, a 5 per cent duty on all goods, including slaves, imported from black Africa.

The *vintena* and another duty, the *quarto* (quarter, or 25 per cent), were both special levies on goods brought from the coastline of Africa to Portugal or its island colonies. Both had been collected by the Infante D. Henrique,[25] though in the early years he had followed mediaeval practice and claimed only a fifth of the slaves taken in war, that is, in the descents upon the Idzāgen.[26] Under the royal administration of the trade, the *vintena* and the *quarto* on slaves were collected in the Casa dos Escravos, but only if these duties had not already been paid to the farmers of the customs of the Cape Verde and Gulf of Guinea islands which were clearing-houses for slaves acquired on the African coast.[27] The *quarto* was levied by dividing a shipload of slaves into four representative lots and taking one lot, the *vintena* by taking a twentieth of the shipload. Where numbers were too small to permit division into lots, the duties were levied in cash according to the value of the slaves.[28] By 1530, most slaves came via the islands, so the *quarto* and *vintena* yielded only 'very small' returns to the Casa da Guiné;[29] most of the revenue from slaves landed at Lisbon was raised in further duties assessed at the main customs house, the *alfândega*.[30]

These duties were the *dízima* and *sisa*, which were levied on all articles of commerce, not only on those from the overseas empire. The *dízima* was a 10 per cent duty on all goods entering or leaving seaports or frontier towns.[31] As an import duty, it applied to all slaves considered as merchandise to be sold in Portugal and was collected at all *alfândegas* in ports through which these slaves passed.[32] By 1534 the large numbers of slaves passing through

Lisbon necessitated a division of responsibility between the *alfândega* and the Casa da Sisa in the collection of the import *dízima*, with slaves from some overseas colonies going to the *alfândega*, those from others to the Casa da Sisa.[33] The *dízima* on the export of slaves from Portugal and the Cape Verdes does not seem to have been widely enforced until the reign of D. Sebastião, when the export of slaves to Castile and Spanish America had become a big business; an additional charge of 10 *xdos* per slave exported was also levied then.[34]

The *sisa* was a sales tax paid jointly by the buyer and the seller. It usually amounted to 10 per cent of the value of the article sold, but it could be a fixed sum. Thus each slave landed and sold in Lisbon in the early sixteenth century was subject to a *sisa* of 600 *rs.*, which was collected by the Casa da Sisa. In 1516, however, D. Manuel ordered that slaves sold by the crown should carry a *sisa* of only 300 *rs.* a head: clearly a measure to encourage purchases of slaves imported in royal vessels.[35] The treasurer of the Casa da Guiné was responsible for paying 150 *rs.*, half the *sisa*, on each slave imported and sold by the Casa dos Escravos; the other half was paid by the buyer – that is, if the buyer had not been exempted from paying his half, as yet another blandishment to encourage the purchase of the Casa's slaves.[36]

Exceptions and exemptions were typical of the whole system of regulation and fiscalization of the trade. Some contractors were allowed to export slaves without paying the usual duties and others enjoyed reduced rates of both import and export duty.[37] One important exception was the concession to customs posts in several Portuguese ports of the privilege of receiving slaves: trade was never wholly centralized in Lisbon. To be sure, Lisbon always received most of the slaves from Africa and in 1512 it officially became the sole port of landing.[38] Owing to special exemptions, however, Setúbal on the River Sado and the ports of the Algarve continued to receive black slaves throughout the sixteenth century.[39] The provincial customs collected duties such as the *vintena*[40] but, as a nod towards the policy of centralization, remitted the *sisa* they levied on the sale of slaves to the Casa da Sisa in Lisbon.[41] Evidently the crown was well aware that it did not have the means to prevent slave-traders from frequenting the smaller ports and therefore decided to secure some revenue from a trade which would have continued whatever laws the king decreed. To what degree this policy succeeded in diminishing fraud in the African trades is, unfortunately, not known.

The slaving voyage

Having considered the institutions which regulated the slave-trade, let us now examine how the trade itself was carried on. The vessels employed in the trade were the caravel and the *navio* (or *nau*).[42] The first was a single-decked, usually lateen-rigged vessel of 50–100 tons burden and could carry up to 150 slaves. A smaller version, the *caravelão*, of 20–25 tons,[43] carrying about thirty slaves, was used as a duty boat for the factories in Africa.[44] The *navio* of over 100 tons was a high-sided, three-masted roundship, square-rigged on the two forward masts and capable of carrying a large cargo.[45] In 1516 a royal official asserted that a *nau* of 100–120 tons had recently picked up no fewer than 400 slaves in Benin,[46] but *navios* bound from São Tomé to Lisbon normally carried only 100–150 slaves in addition to a large cargo of sugar.

Between ten and thirty officers and crew shipped aboard a caravel, and as many as sixty-one aboard a *nau*.[47] The officers included a captain or master, a pilot and an *escrivão* (scrivener), who was provided by the crown to oversee the trade, even when the vessel belonged to a contractor. The crew consisted of *marinheiros* (able seamen), *grumetes* (ordinary seamen) and, very occasionally, *pagens* (cabin boys).

By the early sixteenth century black seamen worked alongside whites on some ships. On the caravel *Santa Maria das Neves* which plied between Lisbon and Cantor on the Gambia in 1505 and 1506, seven of the fourteen ordinary seamen were black, as was one of the nine able seamen. There was no distinction between blacks and whites in terms of pay, and one black ordinary seaman was promoted to able seaman during his service abroad, making two black able seamen in the crew.[48] Further advancement for blacks was not contemplated: in 1517 blacks were barred from becoming captains of vessels on the run from the Cape Verdes to Guinea, and similar restrictions probably applied elsewhere.[49] The restraint on promotion applied to all blacks, free blacks being treated in the same way as the slaves whom masters, with royal permission, hired out as crew on ships bound for Africa. In such cases, the master received the wages due to his slave.[50] According to a French observer, the employment of slaves as crew altered Portuguese tactics whenever a caravel was attacked by French or English corsairs. The Portuguese apparently preferred exchanges of cannon-fire at long range to boarding 'because their whole crew consists of slaves, and, coming to close quarters, they fear lest they be betrayed by their bondsmen who are not only Moors and infidels but all kinds of Barbarians'.[51] Of course, the Portuguese may simply have wished to protect their cargo, which would have been endangered by fighting on board.

Many vessels also carried black interpreters to facilitate negotiations between the slave-traders and African princes and merchants. In the period of the discoveries, whenever the Portuguese encountered a new people, they seized some of the natives and took them back to Portugal in the hope that some of the captives already there might be able to understand the new people's language and to teach them Portuguese.[52] By the time of the Venetian Ca' da Mosto's first voyage to Guinea in 1455 there were many interpreters among the black slaves in Portugal. These interpreter-slaves were given food and wages aboard the slave ships, while each of their masters received one slave from every shipload in return for his slave's work as an interpreter. In theory, when an interpreter had gained four slaves for his master either in this way or independently he was freed. Ca' da Mosto claimed that many interpreters thus acquired their freedom.[53] But how common such manumissions were in practice is a moot point. Of the few surviving letters manumitting interpreters, none mentions acquisition of slaves for the master as a reason for granting freedom, though other documents indicate that interpreters were allowed to obtain and own slaves.[54]

Having taken on their cargo, the slaving vessels lay in Lisbon harbour for inspection by officials of the Casa da Guiné.[55] The inspectors were primarily concerned with checking for iron, arms and ship's stores, all of which were forbidden to be traded with infidels.[56] Permitted trade goods included cloth, old clothes and Moroccan garments; glass beads and shells; and metal ware, such as brass and copper bracelets (manilhas), barber's basins and chamber-pots. Some goods had a specialized appeal. Horses – or even just their tails – were prized by black kings as marks of rank,[57] the Idzāgen of the desert appreciated cereals and treacle;[58] and by the later sixteenth century the Gambian peoples had acquired a taste for wine.[59] Before then, however, wine was not very important in the trade. Once the inspectors had been satisfied that all was in order, the ship set sail for Africa, to begin trading.

Often a voyage would include several stops along the African coast.[60] At each stop the captain and interpreter, both scrutinized by the scrivener, would go ashore with trade goods and strike a bargain with the local ruler regarding the price of the slaves he had. Vessels trading with the Rios da Guiné sometimes made use of the services of *tangos maos* or *lançados*, white Portuguese who had settled among the blacks and adopted an African style of life. To ease the slaving captains' task, the *lançados* assembled slaves in prisons on the shore and continued to do so even after a decree in 1514 outlawed their activities.[61] Where there were legally established trading posts, as at Arguim and at Ughoton in Benin, royal factors performed a similar function. All purchases, including gold, ivory and slaves (described in Portuguese account books as *peças* or *peças de escravos*) were recorded by the ship's scrivener.[62]

The treatment of slaves collected at the royal factory on São Tomé prior to shipment elsewhere was regulated by a *Regimento* issued by King Manuel in 1519.[63] All slaves landed at São Tomé from Benin, the Slave Rivers or the Kongo were branded with a cross on their right arm. (This was later changed to a 'G', the *marca de Guiné*.)[64] One of the officers of the factory was detailed to look after the slaves, and the factor and *contador* were supposed to visit them frequently to see that they were in good condition. While awaiting shipment, the slaves worked on the island's plantations; if a slave showed particular aptitude, the king suggested that he should not be sent on to Portugal. Any slave who fell ill was to be kept on the plantation until he recovered.

D. Manuel also established minimum standards for the treatment of slaves aboard ship. He ordered that the slaves should have wooden beds, which were to be placed under a roof affording protection from the cold and rain. During the voyage the pilot had to give them adequate supplies of yams, *caroços*,[65] bananas and malagueta pepper to eat, besides sticks to gnaw in order to clean their teeth or assuage hunger pangs. The pilot was further instructed to prevent the crew from wasting the slaves' provisions. Bills of lading for slavers departing São Tomé for Portugal give an inventory of provisions similar to that contained in the royal *Regimento*; indeed, some slavers carried additional food, such as maize and biscuit, as well as antelopes to provide the slaves with meat. But how often all the king's stipulated

conditions were obeyed is unknown. And, unfortunately, the inde-
terminate measures of the principal foods, namely *pesos* of yams and
'sacks' of *avelana biscoitada*,[66] mentioned in the bills of lading make
exact computation of the quantity of food allotted to each slave
impossible.

Conditions for the slaves on board were harsh. Every ship carried
chains, manacles, neck rings and padlocks to secure its human
cargo.[67] Frequently (the *Regimento* notwithstanding) twenty-five to
forty slaves in that cargo were stowed on deck and left, scarcely clad,
to the mercy of the elements.[68] In 1540 an anonymous pilot recorded
that the women were usually put on deck and the men placed in the
hold so that the sexes could not see each other; when the sexes were
together, the women urged the men to assert themselves as warriors
and attack the crew.[69] If a slave died during the voyage, the scrivener
checked whether the victim had been marked as belonging to the
king or to a private party and entered the relevant information in a
special section of the accounts.[70] The corpse was then thrown overboard. Occasionally, living slaves suffered the same fate: during two
voyages from the coast of Africa in 1506 and 1507 one captain threw
suckling babies alive into the sea 'so that their mothers would not
die', and ordered a black man to be thrown overboard as well.[71]

Murderous captains aside, the normal mortality of slaves aboard
ship varied according to the distance from the point of embarcation
to the final port of landing. Bills of lading show that on the run from
Arguim to Lisbon in the years between 1501 and 1520, 1 to 5 per
cent of the total number of slaves carried on any one ship could be
expected to die, though losses occasionally ran to 18 or 25 per cent
on vessels heavily laden with slaves. The voyage from Arguim took
about twenty days to a month in good weather. Although data are
much scantier for the run from São Tomé to Lisbon, it seems – as
was to be expected – that the mortality was much higher during the
three to six months at sea. In the period 1525 to 1530 9 per cent was
a small loss and mortalities of 30–40 per cent were not uncommon.

Little is known about the slaves' reactions to life on board. There
is, however, a short description of a slave insurrection in a note
explaining the loss of thirty broken links of chain which the *nau Fieis
de Deus* had picked up along with the slaves at Arguim in 1509. The
few words convey a vivid picture:[72]

These links were thrown into the sea when the blacks on this ship rose and
sought to seize the said ship and to kill the crew; and according to the

testimony of the crew were lost as they were thrown by one side at the other during the quelling of the insurrection.

Save when ships were authorized to proceed elsewhere, or were blown off course to Spanish ports, they returned to anchor in the Tagus at Lisbon to be inspected for contraband and cleared by the officers of the Casa da Guiné. If the duties on the cargo had already been paid to the customs of the Cape Verdes or São Tomé, the owners of the merchandise were then free to dispose of it according to law and the terms of their contract with the crown; for instance, slaves might have to be taken to the *alfândega* to be assessed for the *dízima* and *sisa*. In all other cases, whether the ships belonged to contractors or the crown, all slaves aboard had to be cleared through the Casa dos Escravos, in the following manner:[73] the factor of the Casa da Guiné, the treasurer, the *Juiz da Guiné*, the *almoxarife dos escravos*, their clerks and the Casa's guards were all rowed out to the vessel to supervise the preliminary inspection. The crew and guards then assembled the slaves on deck so that the treasurer's clerks could list them in their accounts. After these formalities, the slaves were taken ashore to designated lodgings, usually in the Casa dos Escravos, where the *almoxarife* gave the treasurer a receipt acknowledging that he had assumed responsibility for them.[74] On the same day or the day after, the factor and treasurer of the Casa da Guiné, together with their clerks, went to the Casa dos Escravos and divided the slaves into various lots for the purpose of levying duty upon them.[75] The division was presumably made according to age, sex and physique, and whether the slaves belonged to contractors or the crown. The factor and treasurer evaluated each slave, and when they had arrived at a price their clerks noted it in their books and wrote it upon a piece of parchment which they attached to the slave's neck with a piece of string. The slaves were stark naked during the evaluation,[76] exposing their bodies to the appraisal not only of the official evaluators but of prospective buyers as well. These buyers inspected the slaves' mouths, made the slaves extend and retract their arms, bend down, run and jump and perform all the other movements and gestures indicative of good health and a sturdy constitution.[77] The *almoxarife* then had a receipt drawn up by his clerk which declared the number of slaves, their total value and the ship which brought them. (The Portuguese showed little interest in the slaves' nationality, but the Valencian registers which record the slaves received from Lisbon between 1479 and 1516 indicate that the majority of blacks were Wolofs from Senegambia.)[78] After the evaluation, the *almoxarife* in his capacity of *recebedor da vintena* levied the tax of one-twentieth of the value of the slaves as stated in the receipts and took payment in slaves or cash;[79] the *quarto* was probably collected in a similar manner. Contractors were then free to sell their slaves as they wished,[80] unless they chose to entrust this matter also to the *almoxarife*, who had experience in selling slaves belonging to the crown.

Before the centralization of the greater part of the slave-trade in Lisbon, lodging the king's slaves prior to sale appears to have been on a sort of putting-out system. During the Bohemian traveller Šašek's stay in Oporto in 1466, he was told that after the king's annual expedition to 'Barbary' (by which Šašek probably meant black Africa, as he was not very clear about African geography),

the women and children he [Afonso V] has had brought back he distributes amongst his cities to the citizens, who are obliged to keep them at their own expense. When the children are grown up, the treasury officials sell them as slaves, and many thousands of gold pieces are brought in by this trade and go to the privy purse.[81]

Vestiges of this custom survived in the practice of the Casa dos Escravos of entrusting the care of desperately ill slaves to private persons. Since at times slaves arrived 'so sick and ill-treated' – with bellies swollen from malnutrition, for instance[82] – that they could not be sold immediately, the *almoxarife* had orders to try to cure them. Once the slaves treated by the *almoxarife* had regained their health or were at least capable of being sold, they were brought before the factor and treasurer who evaluated them at prices low enough to move them from the Casa as quickly as possible, thus eliminating further outlays of money on their upkeep. But if a slave was so ill that a physician doubted his chances of survival, the factor and *almoxarife* found a private person who undertook to cure the slave in his own home and at his own expense. If the slave lived, his benefactor could buy him from the Casa at a fraction (normally half) of the price the slave would have fetched had he always been in good health.[83] As some people, however, were not beyond telling the *almoxarife* that the slave entrusted to them had died, when he was really alive and well, all contracts for the care of sick slaves stipulated that the *almoxarife* and his clerk must be allowed to verify that a slave entrusted to a private person was really dead, and that another dead slave had not been substituted for him.[84]

After the slaves imported on the royal account or collected from contractors in duties had been evaluated and were deemed to be healthy enough, the *almoxarife* took charge of their sale. At first he acted as the king's slave merchant, in addition to carrying out his other tasks, but from the 1520s the actual sale of the king's slaves was contracted out, the first contractors being two members of the foreign community in Lisbon.[85] Not all slaves were sold, however. Various senior officers and clerks of the Armazém and Casa da Guiné received a slave, or his value in cash, either as an integral part of their salary or as a perquisite.[86] The *almoxarife* also supplied the slaves whom the king gave away to favoured members of the court, or to religious institutions. The king gave away so many in 1513 that the then *recebedor dos escravos* complained that the Casa dos Escravos suffered an overall loss.[87]

The sale of slaves: corretores

Portuguese buyers had the option of acquiring slaves directly from the person responsible for the sale of the king's slaves or indirectly from slave-merchants. These merchants had in turn acquired the slaves whom they retailed from the crown or from the contractors of the slave-trade. João Brandão's unofficial census recorded some sixty to seventy slave-merchants in Lisbon during the early 1550s,[88] but the tax roll of 1565 reveals only three, all extremely prosperous.[89] Perhaps only these three were described in the roll as slave-merchants because they dealt exclusively in slaves, while Brandão included men who handled slaves along with other merchandise. The traders appear to have exhibited and sold their slaves openly in the streets of central Lisbon. As early as 1502 there was a square called the Praça dos Escravos in the Alfama and at mid-century the Pelourinho Velho, the square where criminals were punished, was the scene of auctions of slaves and other goods.[90] Doubtless the market-square served for slave auctions in other towns. Not all slaves, of course, were bought in public sales: private transactions could be negotiated with slave-owners or their representatives.

As Šašek observed, slaves were sold in the same way as horses, cattle or other livestock.[91] Commercial law regarded them no differently: the royal ordinances spoke of slaves as 'things' (*cousas*) alongside other animate and inanimate objects. Thus a 'barrel of wine, or of oil, or a slave, or an animal' could all be sold on approval, a fixed period being assigned for the purchaser to decide whether he was satisfied.[92] Defective animals could generally be returned to the seller, while buyers of slaves could claim their money back if the slave died from illness, or was found to be 'ill, crippled by illness, or lame' within a month after purchase.[93]

A surprising feature of the internal commerce in slaves in Portugal, where many transactions were recorded by notaries public, is the relative paucity of bills of sale for slaves in notarial registers. Admittedly, very few registers survive from the period under study, and none at all from Lisbon, the centre of the trade, prior to 1561; still, the global impression obtained is that Portuguese notaries, unlike their counterparts in Castile, where there was also a considerable trade in slaves, drew up very few bills of sale.[94] I have found only three bills of sale concerning slaves, and in two of them the transaction was conducted by representatives of the seller.[95] This suggests that these sales were recorded by the notary so as to ensure that all was above board and that the representatives' letters of procuration were in order.

The reason for the dearth of notarial evidence seems to be that many, if not most, sales of slaves involved a broker (*corretor*) whose records obviated the necessity of notarial bills of sale. The *corretor* collected a 2 per cent commission (paid jointly by the buyer and seller) at the same time as he entered an account of the sale in a book. This book was subject to the scrutiny of the public authorities and could be used to settle disputed sales,[96] but was probably regarded as the *corretor*'s private property; none of these books appears to have survived in public archives. The *corretores* who specialized in the sale of slaves were often connected with the sale of livestock as well, which would explain why there are few notarial records of sales of livestock.

Corretores practised their trade in most major towns and as the economy strengthened in the fifteenth century new *corretores* were added to existing groups, while fresh posts were created in towns where there had been no *corretores* previously.[97] In most places, the position was in the gift of the municipal council (*câmara*), but in Lisbon, which had the largest number of *corretores*, the crown had arrogated to itself all nominations to these lucrative posts by 1490. The following year D. João II forbade his nominees to collect a commission on sales of slaves imported by the Casa dos Escravos and by Bartolomeo Marchionni, an important Florentine contractor of the trade. This prohibition does not seem to have had a lasting effect.[98]

In the 1550s Brandão asserted that there were six or seven *corretores* of livestock in Lisbon who occasionally intervened in sales of slaves and another seven or eight who dealt exclusively in slaves.[99] These numbers may be slightly exaggerated: Brandão's contemporary, Cristóvão Rodrigues de Oliveira, who carried out a semi-official census for the archbishop of Lisbon, found that there were only twelve *corretores* in all. Certainly the tax roll of 1565 tends to support a lower figure, since it designates only six men specifically as *corretores dos escravos*.[100] On the other hand, there is strong evidence to suggest that Brandão was correct in estimating that each *corretor dos escravos* earned 50,000–60,000 *rs.* a year in commissions of 300–400 *rs.* on each slave sold.[101] This would mean that in the 1550s each *corretor dos escravos* intervened in the sale of 125–200 slaves a year. If, as seems most probable, there were six *corretores*, there were 750–1,200 slaves being sold in Lisbon every year at that time; if seven or eight, 875–1,600.

Numbers and prices

The exact number of black slaves landed and sold in Lisbon in the fifteenth and sixteenth centuries is unlikely ever to be known, because most of the commercial and fiscal records of the Casa da Guiné and the Casa dos Escravos were destroyed in the Lisbon earthquake of 1755. Hence one can only gain an approximate idea of the volume of the slave-trade from computations based on fragmentary official evidence and the estimates of reliable observers.

One thing that is certain is that the number of slaves acquired in Africa steadily increased between 1441 and 1555. The royal chronicler Zurara estimated that from 1441 to 1448 only 927 were brought from Mauritania and the Sahel.[102] By 1455–6, however, when trade had become the principal means of acquiring slaves, Ca' da Mosto reported that 800–1,000 slaves came from the same area every year.[103] Duarte Pacheco Pereira, referring to the turn of the sixteenth century, affirmed that 200–400 slaves came annually from the River Senegal, and 3,500 from all Upper Guinea, that is, the coast from the Senegal to Cape Palmas. But this was only when the trade was properly managed, which he implied was not the case when he wrote.[104] The slave-trade appears to have been subject to great

Table 1. *Slaves shipped to Lisbon by the various captains of Arguim from 1499 to 1520, as known from quittances and other information*

Period of office	Name of captain	Number shipped	Yearly average
1499, 10 May to 1501, 20 Dec.	Fernão Soares	668	259[a]
1505, 26 Mar. to 1508, 28 Aug.	Gonçalo da Fonseca	406	119[b]
1508, 24 Aug. to 1511, 23 June	Francisco de Almada	1,540	544[c]
1511, ? June to 1514, 18 July	Fernão Pinto	852	276[d]
1514, ? 18 July to 1517, ? Aug.	Estêvão da Gama	2,232+	744+[e]
1517, ? Aug. to 1520, 11 Aug.	António Portocarreiro	4,019	1,340[f]

Sources:

a. ANTT, Ilhas, f. 42, published in Freire, 'Cartas de Quitação', *Arch. Hist. Port.*, II (1904), 353 seqq.
b. ANTT, Ch. J. III, I, f. 51v, published in ibid., *Arch. Hist. Port.*, VIII (1910), 400 seqq.
c. ANTT, Ch. Man., 9, f. 53v, published in ibid., *Arch. Hist. Port.*, II (1904), 354.
d. ANTT, C. C., 2. 29. 64.
e. ANTT, Núc. Ant., 799, f. 508; 888; documents from C. C.
f. Documents from C. C.

annual fluctuations in volume, and evidence from various sources indicates that the first decade of the 1500s saw a decline in activity, for some as yet unknown reason.[105] As Table 1 shows, trade at Arguim fell to about 119 slaves a year between 1505 and 1508. In the following years, however, numbers increased; no fewer than 1,045 *peças* were purchased there between May 1519 and March 1520,[106] and the trade was still flourishing, though at a reduced level, in 1543.[107] Landings of slaves at Santiago in the Cape Verdes were also numerous after 1510: 565 slaves in the last six months of 1513, 978 in 1514, 1,423 in 1515 and 1,484 in 1528.[108] By the 1550s the Spanish government believed that enough slaves were brought to the Cape Verdes to allow an annual export of 2,090 to America.[109] Addition of the annual totals for Arguim and the Cape Verdes suggests that 3,500 is a reasonable maximum for the number of slaves taken from Mauritania and Upper Guinea in the sixteenth century, though it may have been high for the fifteenth.

Trade between the African mainland and the islands in the Gulf of Guinea seems to have expanded enormously in the sixteenth century, especially after 1512 when a Portuguese mission threatened the Mani Kongo with the cessation of all trade unless he supplied

Table 2. *Slaves known to have been shipped from São Tomé to Lisbon between 1515 and 1534*[a]

Year	Number of vessels involved	Number of slaves shipped	Received in Lisbon
1515	1	78	?
1518	1	70	?
1525	1	30	24
1526	2	281	195
1527	1	50	42
1530	1	160	111
1532	2	200	?
1533	5	530	?
1534	5	260	?

a. *Source:* documents in ANTT, C. C.

slaves.[110] Estimates of the number of slaves involved in the Gulf of Guinea trade are exceedingly high; perhaps the most plausible credits São Tomé with receiving some 6,300 slaves from the mainland between 1525 and 1527, that is, between 2,000 and 3,000 a year.[111] Other estimates of the Kongo trade in the next two decades are even higher, but these figures are based on the numbers of ships which carried slaves, and not on exact counts of the slaves aboard.[112] In any case, as Table 2 shows, very few of the slaves landed at São Tomé were sent on to Portugal: under 100 a year before 1525, and an average of 250 a year between 1526 and 1534.

Hence most slaves brought to Lisbon came from Upper Guinea, and from the possible 3,500 one must deduct several hundreds of slaves who stayed on in the Cape Verdes or were sent directly to the Canaries, Madeira, or the Azores.[113] Eventually, around 2,000 slaves probably arrived in Lisbon every year, though the number undoubtedly underwent fluctuations. This is the estimate of one of Pacheco Pereira's contemporaries, a Venetian named Lunardo Cha' Masser. He resided in Lisbon between 1504 and 1506, and his figures are usually reliable.[114] Official quittances show that some 300–700 out of the 2,000 arrivals passed through the Casa dos Escravos every year in the period 1490 to 1516, and some 800–900 in the years between 1525 and 1528.[115] These slaves appear to have been those brought directly from the coast of Africa or from Arguim, a hypothesis supported by a glance at Table 3, which gives the annual totals of slaves from Arguim landed at Lisbon during the early sixteenth century. The remainder of the 2,000 arrivals would have come from the Cape Verdes and São Tomé, where they had already passed

Table 3. *Slaves known to have been shipped from Arguim and received alive in Lisbon between 1501 and 1520, as shown by surviving bills of lading*[a]

Year of shipment	Shipped	Received
1501	145	143
1505	63	54
1506	177	?
1507	52	?
1508	86	45+?
1510	60	?
1511	102	97
1512	234	224
1513	442	432
1514	303	299
1515	301+?	589
1516	878	771
1517	864	853
1518	1,481	1,410
1519	1,939	1,884
1520 (to 11 Aug.)	342	339

a. *Source:* ANTT, C. C.

through customs; they therefore did not need to be cleared through the Casa dos Escravos. Their presence in Lisbon was due solely to a law of 1473 which required all slaves from the African posts to be brought to Portugal before they could be sold elsewhere. Some of these slaves were probably landed at the *alfândega*, and following customs clearance they would be sold by the shippers' agents or through the services of the merchants who farmed the contract to sell the king's slaves in Lisbon. Many others, however, never set foot in the city, but went on by sea to Seville and Valencia. In the early sixteenth century, these Spanish ports are known or reliably estimated to have received a number of slaves equal to or greater than the number landed at the Casa dos Escravos. (This is the strongest reason for not accepting the figures given in the quittances as the total number of arrivals: if no more slaves were brought to Lisbon than those landed at the Casa, there would not have been enough to supply both the home and foreign markets.)

Thus, some slaves were landed at the Casa, some were landed at the *alfândega*, and some were not landed at all, but re-exported to Castile and Valencia. To complicate matters further, not all of the slaves landed in Lisbon remained in Portugal. The Casa also seems to have re-exported slaves, as it could surely afford to do in 1519, for example, when the Arguim trade brought in 1,884 slaves. Consequently, the exact number of slaves actually landed and sold in Lisbon in any one year before the 1550s is a matter for conjecture.

Nevertheless, some trends in the numbers sold may be inferred from the few documents available. Somewhat over a half of the 2,000 or so slaves who arrived annually in Lisbon during the first two decades of the sixteenth century were probably sold there (see p. 30). In the 1530s, however, the export trade took precedence, owing to the rise of the American market. Around 1530 D. João III permitted direct shipments of slaves from the Cape Verdes and São Tomé across the Atlantic, a decision which had drastic repercussions on the numbers of slaves landed and sold in Lisbon.[116] More of the slaves taken from Africa were shipped directly to the Americas and, of the reduced numbers brought to Lisbon, a larger proportion was sent to Seville for re-expedition to the New World. In 1537 an unknown petitioner stated that exports to Castile and the Antilles had more than halved the revenues from the contract to sell slaves in Lisbon.[117] This downward trend was reversed towards the middle of the century. A greater flow of slaves from the coast of Africa, probably caused by the Mane invasions of Sierra Leone between 1545 and 1560, seems to have allowed shippers to send more to Portugal.[118] In 1552 Brandão reported that the previous four years had seen a vast increase in the numbers of slaves arriving in Lisbon; as mentioned above, his figures suggest that 750–1,200, maybe even 1,600, slaves were then being sold every year.[119] At this time, the annual number of slaves brought to Lisbon may have surpassed Cha' Masser's estimate of fifty years earlier. In 1578, a Florentine visitor, Sassetti, declared that the city received 3,500 slaves a year. This total, like the rest of his statistical information, may be exaggerated, but it does suggest that the Lisbon trade was still flourishing.[120]

To sum up: from the earliest seizures of slaves at the Río de Oro in 1441 until 1470, when trade in the Gulf of Guinea began, anything up to 1,000 slaves may have arrived in Portugal every year. There is not enough documentation from the next period, 1470 to 1490, to allow any conclusions to be drawn, but from 1490 to 1530 the evidence indicates that between 300 and 2,000 slaves were annually brought to Lisbon. The total number of arrivals may have declined during the 1530s, but had probably regained previous levels by the 1550s. Similarly, the number of slaves actually landed and sold in the city was quite high until the 1530s, and then slumped before

Table 4. *Slaves purchased at Arguim, 4 May 1519–10 March 1520, according to ANTT, Núc. Ant., 889*

The figures in column N1 indicate the number of male slaves in the age group, then the number of female slaves, and then the total number of slaves of both sexes in that age group. (c=Female slave and baby bought together as one *peça*. The baby's sex was not stated.)

The figures in column N2 indicate the number of male slaves in the age group expressed as a percentage of the total number of male slaves bought, then the number of females expressed as a percentage of the total number of female slaves bought, then the total number of slaves in the age group expressed as a percentage of the overall total of slaves bought. (Women with babies are included in the female percentages.)

Prices are expressed in Arguim *dobras*, where 1 *dobra*=about 225 *rs*. (Based on a transaction in 1508 where 10.75 *onças* of silver (worth 3,144 *rs*. in Lisbon) were traded in Arguim for gold worth 14 *dobras*: ANTT, Núc. Ant., 888, f. 34v; and see also f. 36. Godinho, *L'Économie de l'empire portugais*, p. 187, n. 4, calculates that the Arguim *dobra* was worth 460 *rs*. in 1514, but this higher value would make slaves cost as much in Arguim as in Lisbon, and is therefore improbable.) The top price of slaves was set at 15 *dobras*. Some slaves were bought for *fânegas* of wheat (1 *fânega*=100 kg): a *fânega* was worth 1 *dobra*.

Age group	Sex	N1	N2	Average prices		
				Mean	Median	Mode
3–7	male	20	3.59%	4.10	4	4
	female	23	5.35%	4.48	5	5
	both	43	4.36%	4.30	4	5
8–12	male	76	13.64%	7.18	7	7
	female	40	9.30%	7.08	7	8
	both	116	11.75%	7.15	7	7
13–17	male	106	19.03%	10.62	11	10
	female	77+1c	18.14%	11.58	11	10
	both	183+1c	18.64%	10.97	11	10
18–22	male	207	37.16%	13.41	15	15
	female	131+6c	31.86%	13.25	14	15
	both	338+6c	34.85%	13.35	14	15
23–27	male	94	16.88%	13.41	14	15
	female	57+7c	14.88%	12.61	13.5	15
	both	151+7c	16.01%	13.09	14	15
28–32	male	41	7.36%	11.17	12	15
	female	65+7c	16.74%	10.51	10.5	8
	both	106+7c	11.45%	10.75	11	15
33–37	male	9	1.62%	7.44	6	5
	female	7	1.63%	5.71	5	2
	both	16	1.62%	6.69	5.5	5

Table 4 (*cont.*)

Age group	Sex	N1	N2	Mean	Average prices Median	Mode
38–42	male	3	0.54%	3.33	3	not
	female	8	1.86%	4.00	4	applic-
	both	11	1.12%	3.82	4	able
Totals	male	557[a]		11.37	12	15
	female	408+22c[b]		11.02	12	15
	both	987[c]		11.22	12	15

a. Includes one male slave whose age was not stated, purchased for 8 *dobras*.
b. Includes one mother and baby, the mother's age not stated, purchased for 11 *dobras*.
c. The auditor found that 1,045 slaves had been purchased at Arguim during the period under consideration, but the additional slaves were probably recorded on the several folios which are now missing from Núc. Ant. 889.

My thanks are due to Dr A. M. MacKay, now of the University of British Columbia, who programmed the computer to analyse the above information and assisted me in the calculations.

rising again at mid-century. There is very little information about the slave-trade to the other port cities of Portugal, but what there is suggests that far fewer slaves came to them than to Lisbon. For instance, between 1490 and 1522 Lagos does not seem to have received more than a hundred slaves a year.[121]

The average price of black slaves remained fixed in terms of gold from 1457 to 1500, though it rose steadily in terms of the currency used to settle everyday transactions. Between 1500 and 1550, however, the price at least doubled according to both systems of reference. Although very little work has been done on the study of prices in Portugal and the economic conjuncture of the country in the fifteenth and sixteenth centuries has not yet been determined, the behaviour of the price of slaves seems to have followed the general trend of prices of goods brought to Portugal from overseas.

Most information on the price of slaves comes from documents stating the value of slaves who passed through the Casa dos Escravos. These records, however, do not usually indicate differences in price according to sex, colour or age and therefore it seems useful to refer to the scale of prices paid for slaves at Arguim, whence most slaves went directly to Lisbon. As Table 4 shows, in 1519 and 1520 the highest prices were paid for slaves between 18 and 27 years of age, the lowest for children under 7 and slaves over 38. Within each group, strong, healthy slaves fetched the highest prices. The price of prime male and female slaves was almost equal, indicating an equal demand for both sexes in Portugal. Slaves in good condition between the ages of 13 and 32 represented about 80 per cent of the total: hence the average prices, as calculated below, of slaves landed at Lisbon closely approximate the price of prime slaves. There is little information concerning the price of slaves bought and sold within Portugal itself, but presumably a slave who had spent some time in Portugal and had acquired a marketable skill could fetch a considerable sum of money.

Prices were expressed in *cruzados* (abbreviated *xdos*) and *reais brancos* (*rs. br.*), usually called simply *reais* (*rs.*). Prices expressed in *cruzados* provide a convenient standard, for the gold content of the coin remained constant from 1457 until 1538, and the coin was roughly equivalent to the ducats in use elsewhere in Europe. Nonetheless, prices in *cruzados* must be treated with care, for in the fifteenth century the value of the *cruzado* rose in terms of the *reais* in which wages and pensions were normally expressed and paid. In 1460 the *cruzado* was worth 253 *rs.*, but its value steadily increased to a maximum of 400 *rs.* in the early 1500s. From then until 1538 the coin called the *cruzado* was worth 400 *rs.*; thereafter the *cruzado* of 400 *rs.* became a money of account, distinct from the *cruzado* in coin, whose value rose to 500 *rs.* by 1559.[122] The Portuguese themselves generally preferred to assess the price of slaves in *reais*, and I have followed this practice in order to avoid stating rises in price in fractions of *cruzados*. (In the recapitulation at the end of this discussion I shall also give prices in *cruzados* so as to permit comparison of prices in Portugal and prices expressed in ducats elsewhere in Europe.)

During the first fifty years of the slave-trade, black slaves cost 12–13 *xdos*. In 1457, 12 *xdos* purchased a slave's freedom; in 1466 Šašek could have bought an 'Ethiopian' for 'twelve or thirteen gold coins of Portugal', and this was the price of slaves landed in Lisbon and other ports as late as the 1490s.[123] Since, however, the value of the *cruzado* in *reais* rose during the same period, the apparent stability in the price of slaves conceals a rise in terms of disposable income from a price of 3,036 *rs.* in 1457 to 4,800 *rs.* in the later 1490s.

By 1504 the average price of slaves in Lisbon had reached 5,300 *rs.*[124] It then climbed to 7,000 *rs.* by the end of the first decade of the 1500s[125] and to almost 8,000 *rs.* by the end of the second.[126] In

1530 the average price of a slave upon landing at Lisbon was still about 8,000 rs.[127] but prices rose during the next decade when fewer slaves arrived to meet the city's demand. By 1541 the Casa dos Escravos was selling slaves for about 15,000 rs., an average which, according to Damião de Góis, represented a range in price from 4,000 to 20,000 rs.[128] Brandão, writing in 1552, confirmed that the figure of 15,000 rs. for prime slaves from Guinea had been normal until recently[129] when, despite a massive influx of slaves, the price had leapt to 45,000 or 50,000 rs.[130] By 1578, however, prices had stabilized at between 15,000 and 30,000 rs.,[131] and in 1593 the government employed an average price of 20,000–30,000 rs. for computing the value of contracts in Guinea.[132]

The trend in prices may be readily grasped from the table below, which gives the date and the average price or range in prices first in *reais* and then in *cruzados*:

	rs.	xdos
1460	3,000	12
1500	5,000	12.5
1510	7,000	17.5
1520	8,000	20
1530	8,000	20
1540	15,000	37.5
1550	15,000	37.5
1552	45,000–50,000	112.5–125 (max. prices)
1580	15,000–30,000	37.5–75
1590	20,000–30,000	50–75

During the first half of the sixteenth century, the cost of slaves increased not only absolutely but also in relation to disposable wealth; nearly everywhere in the country income did not keep pace with prices. In the town and district of Loulé in the Algarve, for instance, 74.34 per cent of the taxpayers owned real and movable property worth less than 45,000 rs. in 1505, and sixty years later, in 1564, the percentage was virtually unchanged: 76.19 per cent.[133] Thus for these people the cost of a slave in 1505 (say 5,000 rs.) was equivalent to at least a tenth of the value of their total goods, while in 1564 (assuming a minimum price of 15,000 rs.), the fraction was a third or more. By the mid-sixteenth century, then, only a very rich minority in this small town, and probably in most of Portugal, could afford slaves.

The re-export of slaves

The rise in the price of slaves was partly due to inflation in Lisbon, which experienced the effects of the price revolution long before the rest of the country, where prices rose more slowly. Since most slaves were landed in Lisbon, they were evaluated at Lisbon prices. It is possible, too, that the rise in prices was the result of a growth in domestic demand for slaves, but as we have seen this could only have come from the wealthy minority in society. The most important cause of the vast increase in the price of slaves at a time when more slaves were coming from Africa than ever before was probably foreign demand. Godinho believes that external demand doubled the price of pepper between 1500 and 1560;[134] the same appears to be true of the price of slaves. The principal foreign markets were Spain and the Antilles, whose influence on the home market was already a cause for concern in 1537. As will be shown below, the great fluctuations in the price of slaves in the 1550s can be traced to arrangements to supply a very large number of slaves to America.

The re-export of slaves to foreign ports was almost as old as the Portuguese slave-trade itself. As early as 1462 one Diogo Valarinho was permitted to send black slaves from Portugal to Castile,[135] and four years later Šašek hyperbolically declared that the king of Portugal made more profit from selling slaves to foreigners 'than from the taxes levied on the whole kingdom'.[136] Although the Cortes of 1472–3 requested that Guinean and Barbary slaves not be exported, as they performed useful work in clearing land and draining marshes, D. Afonso V refused to restrict the export of slaves because of the better prices which he claimed were obtainable outside Portugal. He did order, however, that all slaves from Guinea should first be brought to Portugal before going elsewhere.[137] There is no evidence to suggest that his successors ever seriously considered interrupting the flow of slaves from their kingdom. Indeed, they made sure that they lost no revenue, for merchants who brought slaves to Lisbon to sell abroad had to pay the *sisa*, as if the slaves were to be sold in Portugal itself.[138] Portugal was the purveyor of slaves to the Early Modern world, as Venice and Genoa had been to the world of the later Middle Ages.

In 1470 the Portuguese chancery issued permits to allow 101 slaves to be exported. Most of the exporters were Castilian merchants whose names suggest that the valley of the Guadalquivir was the destination of many of these slaves.[139] Some slaves may have travelled by the overland route which ran from Lisbon, the port of landing, to Elvas and Badajoz on the border. Thence roads ran south to the Guadalquivir, north via Salamanca to Valladolid and the fairs of Medina del Campo, and east along the valley of the Tagus to Toledo. Slaves from Portugal are known to have been sold in all these cities. Most slaves exported went by sea, however; in fact, as early as 1510 the overland route was declared to be of very minor importance.[140] The slaves were shipped from Lisbon to all the ports of southern Spain from Seville to Valencia, and occasionally a slave would be sold from port to port, town to town.[141] One Wolof named Jerónimo went from Lisbon to Cartagena, and from Cartagena to Murcia. There he was bought by a canon who eventually sold him to the *batlle* of Valencia.[142]

The total number of slaves sent to Castile in any one year is not known, but it must have been considerable, for by 1565 Seville had 6,327 slaves out of a total population of 85,538. Most of these slaves appear to have been black.[143] Much more is known about the number of slaves sent to Valencia, thanks to the survival of the registers recording the tax levied on all sales of slaves in that city. Before 1489 only a few score, at most, of slaves were sent directly from Portugal to Valencia in any one year, but then Bartolomeo Marchionni, the Florentine contractor of the slave-trade, evidently decided that the city would prove to be a good market. From 1489 to 1497, he and other merchants sent no fewer than 2,100 black slaves to Valencia, an average of 233 a year. Numbers declined in the first decade of the sixteenth century, but then increased to an annual average of 348 between 1509 and 1516.[144] Although prices in Valencia and Seville followed the same trend as in Lisbon, they were always somewhat higher, justifying the Portuguese monarchy's interest in sending slaves there.[145]

Further east lay Barcelona, where prices for black slaves were even higher in 1500 than in Valencia; there is as yet no information regarding Portuguese involvement in the slave-trade there.[146] Further away still were the markets of Italy, where black slaves appeared in increasing numbers after the Turks effectively ended the flow of slaves from the Black Sea countries in 1453. Evidence suggests, however, that most blacks in Italy were acquired from North African merchants who in turn acquired these slaves from central Africa, via the trans-Saharan route.[147] While some slaves from Portugal were sent to Porto Pisano, Florence and Genoa, on the whole Italy does not appear to have been an important market for the Portuguese.[148]

There are no accurate figures giving the number of blacks re-exported from Portugal to the rest of Europe, apart from Valencia. For the first quarter of the sixteenth century, however, one may allow Castile a slightly higher annual import of slaves than Valencia – say 400–500. Bearing in mind that a few slaves brought to Lisbon also went on to Italy and Flanders,[149] this would mean that about 800–1,000 of the 2,000 or so slaves brought to Lisbon at this time were re-exported. The majority, though, probably remained in Portugal. But during the second quarter of the century, the balance between the number of slaves landed in Portugal and the number sold abroad seems to have shifted in favour of the latter, leaving a smaller proportion for the domestic market.

The increase in the number of slaves re-exported was, as the petitioner of 1537 pointed out, mainly the result of the expansion of the Spanish American market.[150] The first important shipment, of some 250 black slaves, to Spanish America occurred in 1510, and from 1518 Charles V granted licences permitting the importation of thousands of blacks into his trans-Atlantic colonies. Licensees made arrangements with Portuguese contractors who acquired the slaves in Africa and cleared them through Lisbon before shipping them on to Seville.[151] From Seville the slaves were re-exported once more, this time across the Atlantic. Around 1530, however, D. João III decided to shorten the slaves' journey (and thus cut down the mortality at sea) by allowing slaves to be sent directly to the New World from the Cape Verdes and São Tomé.[152] This lowered the total numbers brought to Lisbon, but many slaves still made the long voyage from Africa to America via Lisbon and Seville.

Official Spanish government figures for the number of slaves sent to America are not available for the period before 1577. In that year 2,511 slaves went to the New World, while the next eight years saw from 514 to 2,039 slaves cross the ocean every year, making an average annual export of 1,424 slaves for the years 1577 to 1585 inclusive.[153] Probably fewer slaves crossed the Atlantic in the early years of the trade than in the 1580s, and perhaps the licences to send slaves to America give a fair estimate of the maximum number expected to cross in one year: 1,000 in 1528, 3,000 in 1552.[154] There is no way of knowing how many more slaves were shipped across the Atlantic without official authorization.[155]

In any event, the number of slaves officially sent to America constituted a considerable percentage of the total number – say some 5,000 – taken from Upper Guinea and the Kongo every year. Furthermore, prices paid for slaves were extremely high in the New World: by 1530 slaves cost 50–70 *pesos* (36–51 ducats) in the Antilles and a staggering 100–150 *pesos* (72.5–109 ducats) on the Main. In 1556 a Spanish royal decree fixed prices at 100 ducats in Hispaniola and at 150 ducats in Peru.[156] The expansion of the American market must, therefore, have had the effect of driving up prices in Portugal and the other countries supplied by the Portuguese slave-trade, as long as the number of slaves taken from Africa did not increase appreciably. In 1552, news that Spain was considering sending 3,000 slaves a year to America, more than half the annual total taken from Africa, would have caused prices in Lisbon to soar to American levels, as Brandão observed. The lower prices in the second half of the sixteenth century were probably due to an increase in the number of slaves available in Africa as a result of the Imbangala and Portuguese invasions of Angola.[157]

The place of the slave-trade in the Portuguese economy

It is very difficult, because of inadequate documentation, to estimate the importance of the slave-trade and the duties levied upon it to the finances of the crown, and thus, more generally, to the economy of Portugal. The principal sources are estimates made by contemporary observers, and not state papers, though these provide a valuable check upon the observers' accuracy. However, the official documents, namely quittances to *almoxarifes dos escravos*, are the only source of information regarding the money raised from the sale of slaves by the Casa dos Escravos. These slaves were, as has been stated above, those imported by royal vessels, those collected in duties and some of those imported by the contractors. Between 1486 and 1493 sales of slaves brought an average annual return to the Casa of 1,944,037 *rs.*, and between 1511 and 1513, of 2,695,658 *rs.*[158] Such sums accord well with Cha' Masser's estimate that the slave-trade brought the crown 2,000,000 *rs.* in 1506.[159] Unfortunately, the Casa's income from the sale of slaves in later years is not yet known, nor can the value of slaves imported and sold by contractors be calculated with any accuracy.

Still, a good deal is known about the amounts of money which the contractors paid to the Casa for the privilege of farming the trades and customs of Guinea, albeit the figures given in the documents pose certain problems of interpretation. Presumably the sum which a contractor paid to the Casa dos Escravos represented a considerable percentage of the profit which the crown expected him to make, after all expenses and duties had been paid (unless the duties were included in the price of the farm). But what proportion of the contractor's profit came from the sale of slaves – as opposed to gold, ivory and other products – is unknown. It seems likely, though, that the expansion of the slave-trade played a large part in the steady growth of the contractors' profits (as evidenced by the increase in the crown's revenue) over the years.

In 1469 Fernão Gomes leased the trade of all Guinea south of Sierra Leone for 200,000 rs. a year, and in 1473 added the trade of Arguim for an additional payment of 100,000 rs. a year.[160] Thirty years later, in 1490, Bartolomeo Marchionni paid 1,100,000 rs. for the trade of the Rio dos Escravos alone; we can assume that this trade was mainly in slaves.[161] Between 1511 and 1513 the various West African customs and coastal trades (excluding Mina and Arguim) which were farmed out to contractors were worth some 4,200,000 rs. a year to the Casa dos Escravos.[162] By 1531 the total value of the same customs and trades, plus that of Arguim, was some 12,750,000 rs.,[163] and in 1559 a French observer, the Chevalier du Seure, estimated that Arguim and the other farms brought 34,706,000 rs. to the crown. Obviously, the increasing slave-trade to America (apart from monetary inflation) had a great deal to do with the rise in value of the West African trades. Just how much is uncertain, for the most important trade in 1559 was that of São Tomé, which besides slaves exported an 'infinite quantity of sugars'.[164]

Compared with the Portuguese crown's other sources of income from overseas, the West African trades – other than the Mina gold trade – were not of primary importance in the early sixteenth century. Between 1511 and 1513, as we have seen, the crown could expect 2,695,658 rs. from the sale of the king's slaves and another 4,200,000 rs. from the contractors – say 7,000,000 rs. every year. Now, in 1506 Cha' Masser estimated that the spice trade with India was worth 400,000 ducats annually, though expenses lowered this to some 35,000–40,000 ducats (14,000,000–16,000,000 rs.). The Mina gold traffic yielded 120,000 ducats (48,000,000 rs.) before expenses.[165]

In 1559, however, the situation wore a new aspect. Heavy charges caused by the defence of the trade routes severely reduced the value of the Indian trades, and similar charges brought Mina's value down to some 14,070,000–18,760,000.[166] Meanwhile the value of the slave-trade and the other trades of West Africa had advanced to 34,706,000 rs. annually by mid-century.[167] Of course, this sum was probably reduced by the costs of maintaining ships to protect Portuguese slavers and other vessels from French and English privateers. All the same, it seems safe to conclude that the Guinea trades, of which the slave-trade was a major component, provided an increasingly important share of the crown's revenue. None of the overseas trades, however, matched the crown's income from taxation and monopolies in Portugal itself: 69,200,000 rs. in 1506, 234,500,000 rs. in 1559.

Conclusions

After the 1440s, when slaves were seized in warlike raids on the coast of Mauritania, the Portuguese acquired their black slaves mainly by trade with African princes and merchants. Since trade with western Africa was a royal monopoly, private merchants had to seek a licence to go there, and the crown established the Casa dos Escravos in Lisbon to regulate and draw fiscal benefits from their activities. The number of slaves taken from Africa in vessels belonging to merchants or the crown cannot be calculated with any precision; it is possible to arrive at estimates of the annual volume of the slave-trade, but one should bear in mind that there were probably considerable fluctuations in the supply of slaves from year to year. It is generally true, however, that the number of slaves acquired each year steadily increased from the middle of the fifteenth century to the middle of the sixteenth. Estimates of up to 3,500 slaves per annum from Upper Guinea, and of at least 2,000 more, on average, from the Kongo and Angola, appear reasonable for the period 1510 to 1550. Not all these slaves came to Portugal: the yearly arrival was probably about 2,000, mainly from Upper Guinea, during the first half of the sixteenth century. And of these many were re-exported, first to Spain and later to the Spanish colonies in the New World. The American demand was particularly strong after 1535 (presumably because of the conquest of Peru), with the consequence that by the 1550s only some 750–1,200 (at most 1,600) slaves were sold each year in Lisbon. Foreign demand had the additional effect of driving up prices within the whole system until massive new sources of slaves appeared in the

1560s and 1570s as a result of migrations of peoples in Africa and the Portuguese conquest of Angola. In Lisbon, the average price of slaves more than doubled between 1500 and 1540, and the price of the best slaves reached American levels at mid-century. This price rise put slaves beyond the reach of most Portuguese, but the crown had never been concerned primarily with domestic demand. Indeed the policy of re-export favoured by the kings of Portugal showed concrete returns, for it encouraged an increase in the volume of the slave-trade, and this increase brought more revenue to the royal coffers: between 1511 and 1559 the revenue from the western African trades in which slaves were one of the principal commodities almost quin-tupled. Meanwhile revenue from Mina and the East remained static; this was equivalent to a decline in real income, given the inflationary conjuncture of the period.

Legal and philosophical justifications of the slave-trade

There is no doubt that the Portuguese saw and could be moved by the suffering caused by slavery: in 1444, for instance, the first slave auction at Lagos was interrupted by the common folk who were enraged at seeing the separation of families of slaves, and even Zurara, the royal chronicler, declared his sympathy for these unfortunates.[1] An uneasy conscience did not, however, lead the crown and other slave-merchants to favour the abolition of slavery, because that would have diminished their revenues; rather, it had the opposite effect: it prompted them to embrace arguments which justified slavery, the acquisition of slaves by war and trade and the enslavement of West Africans in particular.

Abolition of slavery was more or less unthinkable, since the institution was traditional and customary in the Iberian peninsula, as in most of the Mediterranean world. Furthermore, custom rested on the solid foundation of the most authoritative works of law, religion and philosophy: Roman and canon law, the Bible and the Aristotelian corpus all permitted slavery and considered it to be part of the universal social order. These works also provided a traditional sanction for the means employed to acquire slaves: by the end of the Middle Ages most commentators on Roman and canon law were agreed that the appropriate authorities in any country, Christian or infidel, could reduce prisoners of war and criminals to slavery; that children of slaves were slaves themselves; and that slaves could be bought and sold like chattels.[2] Both slavery and the slave-trade could thus be defended by recourse to authority. Finally, to justify the enslavement of the blacks and Idzāgen, the Portuguese crown's official propagandists declared that these West Africans were primitive peoples whose enslavement in Portugal brought them the inestimable benefits of Christianity and European material civilization.

The crown's justifications did not win complete acceptance. Indeed, from the middle of the sixteenth century, some moral theologians were openly critical of them. Although the theologians did not question the legality of slavery as an institution, they pointed out that the official arguments did not really take into account the peculiar conditions of the western African slave-trade and were therefore invalid. Nonetheless, the Portuguese government remained convinced that the slave-trade was not only lucrative but also legally and philosophically justifiable. Consequently, the king and his ministers did nothing to oppose the creation of a black slave community in Portugal.

The legitimization of slave raiding and slave trading

When the Portuguese enslaved Moorish, Idzāgen and black prisoners of war, they did so in the knowledge that their actions were in accordance with the laws of war prevailing in Christian Europe. Originally all prisoners of war could be enslaved, but by the thirteenth century there was a general European consensus that Christians could enslave only infidels, provided that the infidels had been taken in a just war.[3] Legists considered a war to be just if it met certain conditions; only two of these need concern us here, namely that the war have a just cause and that it be declared by the sole competent public authority. In most wars the relevant authority was a prince without a secular overlord, though where battle for the faith was concerned, some thinkers held that the pope alone had the declaratory power.[4] Generally, however, war against the infidel appeared such a good cause that a sovereign prince was deemed competent to attack states ruled by unbelievers whenever he pleased.[5] He might then seek papal approval of his actions, so as to enjoy the considerable material and spiritual benefits conferred upon warriors in a papally authorized crusade.

The Portuguese kings evidently believed they had sufficient authority to declare war on infidels, because they launched both the attack on Ceuta in 1415 and the first raid on Mauritania in 1441 without specific permission from the pope. Still, that permission was promptly sought and obtained after the initial attacks had proved successful. Hence any doubts about the legitimacy of enslaving the earliest prisoners taken quickly disappeared when the wars were recognized as crusades and therefore indisputably just.

Technically speaking, the pope was supposed to be assured that there was a just cause to attack the infidel before granting a bull of crusade. Canonists disagreed about what these causes were. Some, such as Innocent IV and Augustinus Triumphus of Ancona, held that the pope had no absolute right to declare war on non-Christians outside the lands 'consecrated' by Christ during his lifetime or those once held by the Christian empire of Rome. He could, however, 'punish' them for crimes against natural law.[6] To the mediaeval mind these crimes included cannibalism, sodomy, incest and bestiality (that is, living like beasts in ignorance of European customs).[7] Similarly unnatural were refusal to allow Christian missionaries to proselytize and the worship of many or simply non-Christian gods.[8] Aquinas did not accept that the Church had the power to punish those who had never embraced the faith, but agreed that the pope could punish those who impeded proselytization.[9] The extreme view was advanced by thinkers such as Cardinal Hostiensis and Egidio Colonna (Aegidius Romanus), who asserted that Christ's coming signified that the whole world had been taken away from the infidels and given to the faithful. Hence any war against the infidels was licit to force them to recognize papal supremacy.[10]

Hostiensine arguments, which required no proof that the infidels were sinning against natural law, were naturally the most popular among the Portuguese lawyers who framed the *supplicae* for the bulls of crusade. However, as de Witte has observed, they could have employed almost any argument, since there is no evidence that the papacy seriously considered the larger juridical and ethical problems arising from contact with infidels in Africa.[11] The curia merely approved whatever the Portuguese requested. In 1442 D. Henrique wished to elevate the raids on West Africa to the status of a crusade, so that he could both legitimize the war and attract troops with the promise of spiritual indulgences; his wishes were granted in the bull *Illius qui*.[12] Ten years later, the Portuguese sought confirmation that they could enslave infidels seized in the crusade. The pope responded with *Dum Diversas*, which allowed them to conquer and reduce to perpetual slavery all 'Saracens and pagans [i.e., blacks] and other infidels and enemies of Christ' in West Africa.[13]

By 1452, however, relations between the Portuguese and the peoples of West Africa were almost entirely limited to peaceful trade. This new mode of acquiring slaves also seemed to need justification, since it involved trading with infidels defined in previous bulls as enemies of Christendom. Once again, the Portuguese requested authorization from the pope, who, according to canon law, had the power to permit such commerce, provided that good cause was shown. Good causes were duly adduced: profits from trade supported crusading armies; furthermore, the slave-trade brought many blacks to Portugal where they became converts to Christianity. In 1455 Pope Nicholas V indicated his approval of these reasons in the bull *Romanus Pontifex*, which gave the Portuguese a monopoly of all trade in Africa south of capes Nūn and Bojador. As the bull also confirmed their exclusive right to conquer the same area, henceforward the Portuguese could rest assured that any slaves taken by war or trade in West Africa had been acquired perfectly legally.[14]

Sin and servitude, civilization and Christianity

While slavery's immediate causes were war or trade, many thinkers subscribed to the Augustinian doctrine that its ultimate cause lay in the divine punishment of sin.[15] Alvarus Pelagius, for instance, held that 'servitude was introduced after sin and on account of sin' so as to provide a way to order an imperfect world.[16] Sin thus became the defect in personality which Aristotle had sought in order to explain why some people were natural slaves.

Zurara was the main Portuguese exponent of the idea that West Africans were slaves because of sin. In one passage he noted that the blacks were slaves of the Idzāgen because the blacks were of the sinful race of Ham, who had been cursed by his father Noah.[17] Ham had committed the sin of looking upon his father's nakedness while the latter was drunk, for which Noah condemned Ham's son Canaan and his descendants to be slaves forever (Gen. ix. 22–5). (The belief that Ham's descendants had been cursed with blackness as well as servitude was, interestingly enough, not a Christian tradition, but part of Portugal's Jewish and Muslim inheritance.)[18] Elsewhere the chronicler followed scholastic philosophers in asserting that the sinfulness which reduced men to the status of natural slaves was a matter of conduct. Aquinas, commenting on Aristotle, had observed that man was free because he was reasonable, but sin fettered freedom and, by sinning, man could fall into the 'slavish state of the beasts'.[19] Following on from this, Egidio Colonna set forth various criteria for bestiality in his *De Regimine Principum*. Man, he said, was distinguished from the beasts by his food, his clothing, his speech and his means of defending himself. But man could not fully manifest his humanity in these four ways unless he cooperated with his fellows in society. Consequently, if a people did not live peaceably under government and had no laws, they were more bestial than human, and the more bestial they were, the more naturally servile.[20] Zurara was familiar with Colonna's thought, and clearly had it in mind when he described the Idzāgen and their black slaves. They were, he said, in a state of perdition 'of their bodies by living so like beasts, with no law of reasonable creatures; nor did they know what bread, wine, clothing or houses were; and what was worse, because of their great ignorance they had no knowledge of good, only of living in bestial sloth'. In sum, the royal chronicler considered the West Africans sinful, bestial and, because of that, naturally servile.[21]

To further justify the enslavement of these people, Zurara contended that slavery brought them positive benefits. First, they could become Christians for, despite their bestiality, they were men with souls which could be saved from the sin of infidelity.[22] Indeed, one black boy seized in 1445 was educated so well in reading, writing and Christian knowledge that, the chronicler averred, 'there are many Christians who do not know these things so perfectly'. Second, they enjoyed a higher form of material existence: in Portugal both Idzāgen and blacks came to know bread, wine, clothing, houses and the other appurtenances of civilized life.[23]

Three of Zurara's arguments almost disappeared from later Portuguese treatises justifying the enslavement of black Africans. The uncanonical origin of the tradition that blacks descended from Canaan seems to have caused the tale of Noah's curse to be used mainly as an explanation of why blacks were black, rather than of why blacks were slaves.[24] Further, as the exploration of Africa proceeded, the Portuguese saw that the criteria of bestiality could not be applied so easily to the blacks as to the nomadic and miserably poor Idzāgen, with whose life Zurara had been best – though still imperfectly – acquainted. Blacks ate well, drank palm wine, lived in houses and had recognizable legal systems, states and kings. In fact, Ca' da Mosto noted that only the Barbacins and Serers did not have kings, which he believed was for the very good reason that a king would sell their wives and children into slavery, as happened elsewhere.[25] Even the lack of clothes was understandable, because of the heat: a Portuguese captain sent to the Kongo gave this explanation,[26] which was accepted as held truth by Garcia de Resende in his poem, the *Miscellanea*, published in 1554.[27] The worst that Barros, the royal chronicler of the sixteenth century, called the blacks was 'barbarous'; he did not think they were bestial.[28] In any case, the charge of bestiality could be employed only to justify the enslavement of people in Africa, not the continued servitude of blacks living in a civilized manner in Portugal. Once they had forgone bestial conduct, they remained slaves by convention alone, that is, as a result of *Dum Diversas*, which allowed the Portuguese to enslave West Africans in perpetuity.

There was accordingly no extensive development of the arguments that divine punishment had relegated blacks to natural slavery or that blacks lived bestially or even that blacks brought to Portugal experienced an immense improvement in their conditions of material life. True, these ideas never completely disappeared, but by the sixteenth century the paramount justification of the slave-trade was that enslavement was an effective method of bringing blacks to a knowledge of Christianity.[29]

The promotion of Christianity among black slaves

Although the dispatch of missionaries to the kingdom of Kongo in 1490 gave clear evidence of Portuguese evangelical intent, active steps to ensure the conversion of black slaves landed in Portugal were not taken until seventy years after the first slaves had arrived, and even then do not appear to have been entirely effective. As late as 1493 King João II owned unbaptized slaves who retained their African names of Tanba, Tonba and Baybry. D. João's slaves were given a new suit of clothing called 'clothes of victory' if they did convert, which must have been an incentive, but otherwise there does not seem to have been much pressure upon them to do so.[30]

D. Manuel was the first king to bother about the spiritual welfare of blacks in Portugal; and his professed concern may have had less to do with any particular interest in the blacks themselves than with a diplomatic campaign demonstrating his egregious piety, so that the pope would grant him increased control over the Church in Portugal and overseas.[31] In 1513 the king wrote to Pope Leo X that, much to the distress of his royal conscience, many of the blacks brought to Lisbon from Guinea died before they had received baptism. He therefore requested that the vicar of the church of Nossa Senhora da

Conceição in Lisbon should be empowered to administer the sacrament to those blacks who were willing to receive it. Furthermore, he
asked that captains of slave ships bound for Lisbon might be permitted to baptize, on the vicar's behalf, slaves who were in danger of
dying. Leo's *Eximiae Devotionis* granted these requests and ordered
that a font be erected in the church of the Conceição exclusively for
the baptism of slaves.[32] D. Manuel then proceeded to make the
necessary arrangements but, in the long run, the programme does
not seem to have been markedly successful: in 1553 the royal secretary, Pedro Carneiro, complained of the large numbers of slaves
landed and sold in Lisbon without ever having been baptized,[33] and
six years later the king gave the vicar of the Conceição an annual
pension and dispensed him from making do with the few *cruzados* he
received for baptizing newly landed slaves.[34]

Efforts to create a Christian population among the blacks who had
spent some time in Portugal or who were born there produced somewhat better results. In 1514 D. Manuel ordered all masters to have
their adult black slaves baptized within six months of their landing,
on pain of losing the slaves to the crown. There was, however, a
qualifying clause: a slave over 10 years old was allowed to decline
baptism, and the master was not held responsible if the slave adhered
to that decision after having been admonished by clergy. On the
other hand, all slave children under 10 had to be baptized within
one month of their arrival. Slave children born in Portugal were to
be baptized at the same time as other new-born infants in their
parish.[35] Although parish registers indicate that the baptism of slave
children was customary, it is doubtful whether the ordinance was
ever rigidly enforced. Indeed, in 1568 the archbishop of Lisbon found
it necessary to order all masters who owned slaves over the age of
7 to have them baptized.

He also decided to do something about the generally low standard
of religious instruction received by blacks: the Council of Trent had
just ended and its resolutions to disseminate Catholic doctrine were
still fresh in the good bishop's mind. Henceforth no slave was to be
baptized unless he knew the paternoster, the Ave Maria, the Com-
mandments and the Articles of the Faith. Priests were to ensure that
all Christian slaves in their parishes knew these fundamentals. Slaves
who did not know the basic dogma were required to attend classes in
church and could not receive any sacraments until they had mastered
their religious education.[36] Here Portuguese practice differed from

that in Castile, where many slaves who did not know their catechism were rebaptized after the Council of Trent.[37] In both countries, however, the post-Tridentine level of religious knowledge among slaves was probably not much greater than it had been before.

Apart from these poorly educated Christians, there were some slaves who were outright infidels, usually Muslims who strenuously refused baptism. During the fifteenth century the law compelled both black and white Muslims to wear a red crescent stitched to the shoulder of their outer garments.[38] After 1497, when all free Jews and Muslims were supposed to have been expelled or converted to Christianity, the clothing regulations seem to have been relaxed, doubtless to convince foreign visitors of the unalloyed purity of Christian orthodoxy in Portugal. Muslim slaves still existed, however, and the clothing laws were reintroduced in 1537 by D. João III,[39] though without much effect: in 1563 the Church authorities in Lisbon complained that the Muslims of that city did not bother to wear the crescent.[40] A ban on owning Muslim slaves in Lisbon or within 20 leagues of it was enacted only in 1621 and was not extended to the whole kingdom until 1641.[41] Thus for two centuries there may have been a few black Muslims living in Portugal besides the black Christians whom the Portuguese exhibited as justifications of the slave-trade.

Critics of the trade

Although the crown had stepped up its efforts to convert the black infidel to Christianity and by the mid-sixteenth century had started to baptize slaves in the royal trading posts in Africa,[42] some thinkers began to have serious doubts about the legitimacy of the slave-trade.[43] Not only did they question whether the slaves had been justly acquired, according to Roman and canon law, but some of them also challenged the official justification that the trade was an effective means of propagating Christian belief. These critics were mostly Spaniards under the influence of Las Casas and Vitoria, who had drawn attention to the plight of the American Indians. Since Spanish America was one of the principal destinations for slaves from western Africa, it is not surprising that Spanish legists and theologues should concern themselves with the justice of the means used to acquire the black slaves who often replaced a dwindling Amerindian work-force.

Nonetheless, the first published and, for its time, most complete attack on the slave-trade was contained in the *Arte da Guerra no Mar* brought out in 1555 by a Portuguese, Fernão de Oliveira. While Oliveira mentioned neither Guinea nor blacks by name – perhaps because slaves came from many parts, perhaps to avoid censorship – he obviously had the West African slave-trade in mind. As a military theorist, he was familiar with the laws of war, and knew that war waged merely to acquire slaves was not just. Consequently, he attacked the theories justifying the slave-trade at their weakest point: the tacit assumption that slaves purchased by the Portuguese had been reduced to slavery legally according to Roman and canon law. He asserted, correctly, that this was not so: rather, the vendors of slaves (the African merchants and princes and the *tangos maus*) acquired them by robbery, rapine and other unjust means.[44] Unlike some later thinkers, he saw very clearly that without buyers there would be no sellers, and that the trade by its very existence engendered the deplorable slave hunts which African wars had become. In furious indignation Oliveira damned his countrymen for being the 'inventors of such an evil trade', which involved 'buying and selling peaceable free men, as one buys and sells animals' with all the methods of a 'slaughterhouse butcher in a stockyard'.[45] Worse, not only the Africans themselves but their children, born and baptized as Christians in Portugal, were enslaved. If enslavement were really an act of Christian piety, these unfortunates should be freed after serving a term fixed by law.

In his view, the justificatory argument derived from the conversion of the slaves was only a 'pious wash' (*cor piadosa*): if the purchase of slaves had not been in the Portuguese traders' own interest they would never have engaged in it and nothing would ever have been heard of evangelization. Furthermore, once the blacks were in Portugal, they were forced to obey their masters' commands, not those of God and the Church. The slaves were not allowed to go to church to hear mass or the gospel, so they did not even know what a church was for. They did not keep Sundays or holy days, but were sent to the river or fountain for water and upon other errands. Indeed, the service of their masters was placed so far above the service of God that if the slaves were ordered to wound or kill someone or to commit some other sin, they would not hesitate to do so. Oliveira was forced to conclude that apart from being legally wrong, the slave-trade could never satisfactorily promote the conversion of the slaves. Only preaching the faith, presumably in Africa itself, could do that.[46]

Similar misgivings about the slave-trade were expressed by other men, both in Spain (where Las Casas privately shared the same views)[47] and in Portugal. Few were as radical as Oliveira, however. For instance, in 1556 Las Casas's friend Domingo de Soto queried the justice of wars between black Africans, but he merely counselled masters with an uneasy conscience to sell their slaves who had been taken in such wars.[48] The Spanish Dominican Martín de Ledesma, who taught theology at Coimbra, was somewhat more resolute. Although in his *Secunda Quartae* of 1560 he accepted that slaves could be bought from black Africans, he ordered all those who owned slaves captured through trickery of Portuguese traders to set them free immediately, on pain of eternal damnation. Like Oliveira, he did not find conversion a sufficient justification even for legal trade, since blacks should accept the gospel freely after having heard it preached, not under duress. Finally, he declared that Aristotle's doctrine of the natural slave applied only to wild men living without any social order, a description which he evidently did not think was applicable to black Africans.[49] Still others entered the lists: Tomás de Mercado, Bartolomé de Albornoz, the Portuguese Carmelite Amador Arrais, the Spanish Jesuit Luis de Molina...[50] All expressed their doubts, more or less profound, about the legality of the enslavement of blacks in Africa.

The Portuguese government's response was negligible. Álvares de Almada says that the crown ordered slave-traders not to buy slaves from African merchants who had acquired them by robbery or in slave raids, and that some traders did in fact obey this prohibition. Faced with a conscientious trader, however, the African merchants had a tendency simply to kill the slaves whom they would have sold; thus on the whole the traders thought it best to buy the slaves whatever their source.[51] Whether this story was true or not, the trade carried on, and the government continued to justify it as a means of Christianizing the blacks. To lend further substance to this claim, in 1623 King Filipe III decreed that all Portuguese slave ships should carry a priest to attend to the spiritual needs of the human cargo.[52]

Conclusions

The methods used to acquire slaves were defended by an appeal to the pope's supreme power to regulate dealings between Christians and infidels. For the first fifteen years the Portuguese claimed to be waging a just war authorized by the pope against the infidel in Africa and they enslaved the black prisoners they took, as was allowed by the laws of war. After 1455 papal permission to trade with the infidel enabled the Portuguese to acquire slaves by peaceful commerce with African princes and merchants. The primary justification advanced for the enslavement of blacks was that it brought them to the faith of Jesus Christ, and insofar as Christianity implied civilization to most Europeans, the blacks were thus raised to a higher level of material existence as well. Zurara, the earliest chronicler of Portuguese activity in Africa, was particularly insistent on the civilizing effect of slavery, but as the Portuguese became more aware that Africans did not live as much like beasts (who were by definition servile) as Zurara had thought, more was said about the Christianization of slaves and less about civilizing them. The stress on Christianization was reflected in King Manuel's efforts to have black slaves baptized as soon as possible after their arrival in Portugal.

Although in 1485 the Portuguese told the pope that profits from the slave-trade helped to finance war against the Muslims in North Africa,[53] material gain was never officially adduced as a reason for acquiring slaves: Barros even asserted that profit had been of no interest to D. Henrique's captains.[54] But the evidence suggests that the principal motivation of the slavers themselves was far from the disinterested evangelization professed by the Portuguese monarchy. The extreme rapidity with which the noblemen and merchants of Lagos organized a fleet in 1444 to scour the Mauritanian coastline for slaves, as soon as that had been shown to be a commercially attractive proposition, indicates that gain was not far from their minds. And the blunt Venetian Ca' da Mosto flatly stated that he went to trade in Guinea in 1455 because of the colossal profit to be made 'among these new people, turning one *soldo* into seven or ten'.[55] Men such as these may have swallowed the official justification as a placebo to soothe the occasional twinge of conscience, but it was enough for them that the slave-trade was customary and extremely lucrative.

By the mid-sixteenth century, however, some thoughtful and

humane men began to have difficulty reconciling the official justifications with the conditions in which the slave-trade actually operated.
Fernão de Oliveira denounced the disparity between the evangelical
ideal and the reality of a slave population which, when not openly
infidel, was only imperfectly Christian. Oliveira also struck at the
weakest point in the theoretical defence of the slave-trade: the un-
justifiable supposition that slaves purchased in Africa had been
legitimately reduced to slavery in the first place. Although the cry
was taken up by Spaniards already concerned about the treatment
of the American Indians, the Portuguese crown paid them little heed
and continued to claim that enslavement was ultimately beneficial
for the slaves' souls.

The critics of the trade were not in a strong position: children of
their time, none of them stood against the institution of slavery itself.
Moreover, they appeared divided among themselves. Only Oliveira,
Arrais and Mercado saw that the slave-trade would have to be
eliminated, not just reformed, in order to end its abuses.[56] Molina,
on the other hand, endorsed the trade, if properly run, as a means of
bringing Africans to Christ. Thus the critics could be, and were, dis-
missed as wrangling schoolmen. In any case, as J. H. Plumb has
pointed out, not until European employers began to improve conditions for free working men of their own race did they begin to con-
template the abolition of black slavery.[57] The interests, and especially
the crown interests, vested in the slave-trade were so great, the
profits from it so attractive and slaves so convenient to so many, that
for most men a 'pious wash' was sufficient justification.

3

The demography of blacks in Portugal

The financial returns gained from Portuguese participation in the slave-trade and the re-export of slaves to Spain and America are obvious, and the employment of slaves on the previously uninhabited Atlantic islands was needed to remedy a labour shortage; but the economic advantages derived from importing slaves into mainland Portugal are not quite so clear. Certainly those Portuguese who looked at the importation of slaves from an economic, rather than a theological, point of view disagreed about the usefulness of employing slaves in Portugal itself. The argument was conducted mainly on the grounds of population: some thinkers held that the Portuguese population was inadequate and that slaves were a necessary addition to the workforce; others that the population was sufficient and that slaves were superfluous.

The first school had the longer pedigree. From the Infante D. Pedro in 1436 onwards, many Portuguese and foreigners had claimed that Portugal suffered from a lack of people.[1] Yet only in the 1530s did Count Giulio Landi of Piacenza state the corollary implicit in this observation: slaves were needed in Portugal to do many tasks which in more populous lands were performed by freemen.[2] D. Pedro's comments had formed part of an attack on overseas colonization. In the seventeenth century this argument was taken up by Manuel Severim de Faria, a canon of Évora cathedral and an early economist. He blamed the continuing shortage of manpower on emigration to the empire and concluded that slaves were imported to make up the deficiency.[3]

The number of emigrants is impressive. Emigration to India is believed to have depleted the population by about 2,400 men every year in the first quarter of the sixteenth century, dropping to between 1,000 and 1,500 by mid-century. Then massive emigration to Brazil and the Atlantic islands began, involving some 3,000, perhaps even

47

5,000, people a year.[4] Such an exodus would have severely strained a population of little over a million, whose natural increase could have been at best 10,000 people annually and was probably far less, given the birth- and death-rates of the time.[5] After considering these figures, recent historians such as Costa Lobo and Lúcio de Azevedo concluded that the import of 1,000 or more slaves a year was a direct response to the labour problems caused by massive emigration.[6]

This, however, was not the view of all sixteenth-century Portuguese, and in fact the first complaints about the superfluity of slaves appeared in the second half of the century, precisely when emigration to Brazil was increasing. In 1562 the Cortes of Lisbon received a petition from a group 'zealous for the common good' who were of the opinion that it had been an error to bring so many slaves to Portugal. Slaves, the zealots claimed, wasted the available food supplies and forced those whose work was now done by slaves into lives of laziness, vagabondage, robbery or prostitution.[7] In 1589 Amador Arrais declared that there had never been enough food for the native Portuguese, let alone for slaves, and shortly afterwards he was echoed in this opinion by Duarte Nunes do Leão.[8] If anything, these arguments imply that emigration was a response to the importation of slaves, which deprived freemen of food and jobs. The frequent re-enactment of laws against vagrancy, some of which attempted to deal with the problem by shipping sturdy beggars overseas, also seems to indicate that there was a shortage of employment which could only have been aggravated by the use of slave labour.[9]

A middle ground between the diametrically opposed positions in this debate appears in the work of Severim de Faria. Upon closer reading, his argument suggests that slaves were not needed everywhere but only in some parts of Portugal. He notes that there was no absolute shortage of free labour: the northern provinces were overpopulated, in terms of the arable land available, so every year northerners had to look for work elsewhere. This point was also made by Nunes do Leão and is corroborated by demographic evidence (see Table 5). But the southern provinces, though underpopulated, could not provide acceptable employment: short leases, uncertainty of tenure and the overweening power of the great landowners made the Alentejo unattractive to a man wishing to make a life for himself as a small farmer, and life as a day labourer on one of the southern latifundia held few charms. Therefore the northerners went to the cities and to Lisbon in particular, making increased demands on the

Table 5. *Population of Portugal according to census and other demographic data, 1527–35*

Province/Kingdom	Hearths	Population (hearths × 4)	Area (km²)	People/km²
Entre-Douro-e-Minho	55,099	220,396	6,680.96[a]	33.0
Trás-os-Montes	35,616	142,464	11,355.21[b]	12.6
Beira	66,800	267,200	18,053.78[c]	14.8
Estremadura	65,412	261,648	15,232.30[d]	17.2
Entre-Tejo-e-Odiana (Alentejo)	48,804	195,216	32,622.77[e]	6.0
Algarve	8,797	35,188	5,071.60	6.9
Total	280,528	1,122,112	89,016.62	12.6

North and south compared

Region	Hearths	Area (km²)	Percentage of population	Percentage of area
North of Tagus	222,927	51,322.25	79.47	57.65
South of Tagus	57,601	37,694.37	20.53	42.35

Sources of population data: Returns of 1527 census, ed. A. Braamcamp Freire, in *Arch. Hist. Port.* III (1905), 241–73; IV (1906), 93–105, 330–63; VI (1908), 241–84; VII (1909), 241–90. Also used: BL, Add. MS. 20: 959 (population of Beira); F. de Almeida, *Historia de Portugal*, III, 243–7; Lobo, *Historia da Sociedade*, pp. 28–32; Santarém, *Documentos, Parte 1a*, p. 93.

a. *Distritos* of Viana do Castelo, Braga and Porto (less the *concelhos* of Amarante, Baião and Marco de Canavezes); plus the *cancelhos* of Castelo de Paiva and Espinho.
b. *Distritos* of Bragança and Vila Real; plus *concelhos* of Amarante, Baião and Marco de Canavezes.
c. *Distritos* of Castelo Branco (less *concelhos* of Sertã and Vila de Rei), Guarda and Viseu; plus the *concelhos* of Arganil, Góis, Oliveira do Hospital, Pampilhosa da Serra and Tábua.
d. *Distritos* of Aveiro (less *concelhos* of Castelo de Paiva and Espinho), Coimbra (less *concelhos* of Arganil, Góis, Oliveira do Hospital, Pampilhosa da Serra and Tábua), Leiria, Lisbon and Santarém (less *concelhos* and portions thereof south of the Tagus); plus *concelhos* of Sertã and Vila de Rei, and area of Belver, north of Tagus.
e. *Distritos* of Beja, Évora, Portalegre (less area of Belver), Santarém (less *concelhos* and portions thereof north of the Tagus) and Setúbal; plus area of Olivença, currently, and illegally, held by Spain.

country's agricultural regions, such as the Alentejo, which supplied Lisbon with much of its bread grain.[10] But since Portuguese industry was underdeveloped, there were not enough good paying jobs in the cities, nor could the courts of the nobility accommodate all the migrant labourers. Hence many of the native Portuguese emigrated to seek their fortunes overseas. Meanwhile slaves were imported to do the jobs the emigrants had refused to do, for instance in the fields of the south where Faria as a canon of Évora saw blacks and mulattoes hard at work.[11] At bottom, his argument is a great deal more subtle than those of his predecessors who were simply concerned with the size of the free population: he saw that the root cause of both the inward flow of slaves and the outward flow of free emigrants lay in the defective organization of the Portuguese economy.

If Faria's analysis is correct – and modern economic historians such as Magalhães Godinho believe that it is[12] – one would expect to find more slaves in southern Portugal than in the north. But if large numbers of slaves were found in the populous cities and the north, then the complaints of Arrais, Leão and the petitioners of 1562 become readily understandable. No research, however, has been undertaken in order to determine where slaves were actually most numerous. To resolve this problem I made an extensive study of parish records and other demographic material which might provide an idea of the size and distribution of the slave population in Portugal. The results are set out below. (The distribution and size of the population of freedmen are also treated here, so as to assess the overall importance of the immigrant workforce created by slavery.)

The distribution of slaves and freedmen in Portugal

The general picture of the black population has had to be constructed from a mass of local records, because the one source concerned with the population of all Portugal, namely the census of 1527–31, did not enumerate slaves nor did it distinguish freedmen from other freemen in the enumeration.[13] Very little is known about even the white population before the census, for there are almost no formal demographic records from the fifteenth and early sixteenth centuries. Consequently the best that could be done to illustrate the distribution of blacks between 1441 and 1530 was to draw a map indicating the places where blacks were said to live (see Map 2). In the 1530s, however, new sources of information appear: parish registers of births, marriages and deaths, and lists of people buried by the Santa Casa da Misericórdia.[14] (Although the Misericórdia was essentially a religious brotherhood dedicated to performing works of charity, it undertook the funerals, not just of charity cases and its own brothers, but of people from all walks of life.) These records are often incomplete, and many have been lost, but enough remain to indicate in some detail where blacks lived in the mid-sixteenth century.

Yet it must be admitted that the parish and Misericórdia records have certain grave limitations. Since they were kept by Christian institutions, there is no mention of obdurate pagans or Muslims or

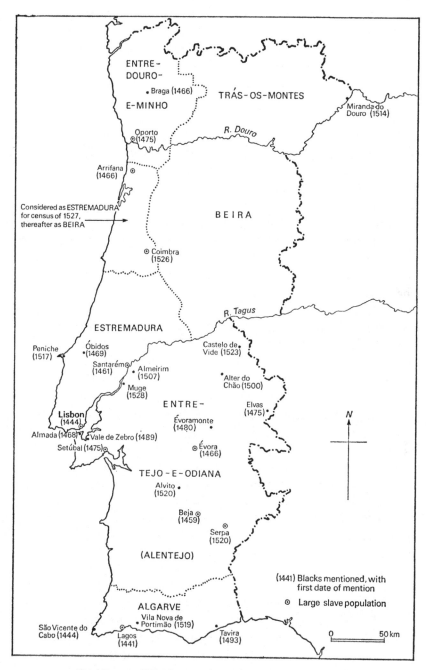

2 Residences of blacks mentioned in documents, 1441–1530

even of slaves whom their masters failed to have baptized. Furthermore, the race of a slave or freedman appears to have been of secondary importance to the priests and clerks who kept the registers. (It is hard to say why this should have been so. Perhaps the writer was lazy, or else race meant less to him than status.) Hence in dealing with these registers the frame of reference had to be widened to include all slaves and freedmen, not just blacks. In four of the largest samples considered,[15] slaves and freedmen whose colour was not stated formed by far the largest group, with blacks in second place and Moors or 'white slaves' a very poor third. This order suggests that blacks formed a majority of the group whose colour was not stated, but final judgement must be reserved.

In any case, the number of slaves recorded in the registers is, strictly speaking, an imperfect reflection of the number of slaves in the parish or town, since the birth- and death-rates of slaves and freedmen are unknown.[16] Still, one cannot afford to speak too strictly when dealing with the documents of a pre-statistical age, and for purposes of reaching a rough estimate of the population of slaves and freedmen in Portugal it seems reasonable to accept a working hypothesis that their birth- and death-rates were about equal to those of the rest of the community. There is some justification for doing so, at least as far as mortality is concerned, since (as the following chapter shows) the poor whites who formed the majority of the population, slaves and freedmen were all engaged in the same occupations and suffered much the same occupational hazards. We are on more uncertain ground with the birth-rate, for black slave women were less protected from casual violation than were most free women, though white serving women were also subject to advances from their masters.[17] Whether the slave birth-rate was higher or lower than that of the white population cannot be calculated from the evidence available, so on the whole I have preferred to use obituary registers rather than registers of births.

Starting with the three northern provinces of Beira,[18] Trás-os-Montes and Entre-Douro-e-Minho, the data suggest that before 1530 the slave population was confined to localities on or near the coast, though some slaves were found in major towns inland (see Map 2). This pattern seems to have persisted at least until the mid-sixteenth century. Slaves remained extremely uncommon in rural districts north of the Douro. For instance, none appear in the registers of nine villages and towns in the province of Entre-Douro-e-Minho and in the three surviving sixteenth-century registers from Trás-os-Montes.[19] This is not to say that there were never any blacks in the country districts of the north, for traces of their presence linger in the folklore of inland Trás-os-Montes,[20] but their numbers seem to have been unimportant.

The populations of slaves and freedmen in the coastal towns were more substantial. The smaller ports, such as Monção on the river Minho, Póvoa de Varzim, Vila do Conde and Azurara, all had a small slave population, usually constituting no more than 2 per cent of the entries in the parish registers.[21] These slaves were probably brought back by seamen returning from the West Africa run. Oporto, however, was better supplied. The city was a slave market of some note in the 1460s,[22] and even after the slave-trade had been concentrated in Lisbon, the occasional shipload of slaves was forwarded to Oporto.[23] In the 1540s baptisms of slaves and their children accounted for up to 6 per cent of the baptisms recorded in the registers of the Sé (Cathedral), while the children of freedmen represented only 0.2 per cent. If these percentages are applied to the population of Oporto as shown in the census of 1527, the calculations indicate some 700 slaves and a mere twenty-four freedmen (surely too low) in an urban population of 12,000.[24] Slaves lived with their masters on the hill in the Rua de São Miguel, the Rua Nova das Flores and the Rua Chã, that is, in the commercial quarter. Few lived on the waterfront in Miragaia:[25] merchants and tradesmen evidently owned more slaves than fishermen did.

Riding south from Oporto in 1466, Šašek found numerous black and white slaves in Arrifana,[26] and later sources show that there were slaves in Aveiro as well. Unfortunately, most of the demographic material for these places dates from after 1575, when a storm closed the harbour bar of Aveiro and the region's economy went into decline. There are no records of slaves in Arrifana in the 1590s and only 2.6 per cent of the burials undertaken by the Misericórdia of Aveiro in that decade were of slaves. Even before 1575, however, there were next to no slaves in the parishes inland from the Aveiran lagoon.[27]

Still further south, in Coimbra, the municipal by-laws indicate that there was a sizeable population of slaves in the city well before 1530. But here again there are almost no parish registers older than the very late sixteenth century, so the numerical size of the slave population cannot be estimated. At mid-century a few slaves (up to 1.5 per cent of the entries) are mentioned in the registers of the larger country towns near Coimbra, such as Penela and Condeixa-a-Nova. Further inland in Beira, however, slaves seem to have been a rarity in country towns and villages, though there were some in the cities and larger centres, such as Castelo Branco and Covilhã.[28]

The records of Estremadura and the lands south of the Tagus reveal a far greater and more widely dispersed population of slaves. Here, too, there were many slaves in the ports and in the larger cities, but within a few decades after the first black slaves were brought to Portugal they could also be found well inland in rural districts. Some were definitely employed in agriculture: as early as 1461 there were blacks working in the olive-groves around Santarém.[29] The lower Tagus valley supplied a good deal of Lisbon's grain and during the fifteenth and sixteenth centuries production increased, in part thanks to reclamation of marshes and fertile water-meadows (the *lezírias* of the Tagus).[30] Slaves may have taken part in the work, for the usefulness of slave labour in clearing the land and draining marshes was remarked upon by the Cortes of 1472–3.[31] By the mid-sixteenth century, the towns and villages on either side of the Tagus from Abrantes to the sea held considerable numbers of free blacks and slaves. For instance, from 1540 to 1560 children of slaves accounted for 3.76 per cent of all baptisms in Ameixoeira, just outside Lisbon; and between 1585 and 1589, slaves and their children formed 7.6 per cent, children of free blacks amounting to 3 per cent of all candidates for confirmation in this village. On the south bank, slaves and their children constituted up to 6 per cent of the total number of people baptized in Aldeia Galega (now Montijo) every year in the early 1570s.[32] The slaves worked on farms owned by noblemen and citizens of Lisbon, and some were boatmen who ferried produce to the metropolis itself.[33]

Lisbon was not only the largest city but also the largest single concentration of slaves in the kingdom. The city's growth appears to have been extraordinary, the population rising from somewhere between 35,000 and 60,000 in 1484[34] to about 100,000 in 1552.[35] The slave population also gave rise to comment long before any attempt was made to estimate its size. Both Münzer in 1494 and Bronseval in 1532 marvelled at the numbers of slaves in the Portuguese capital, and Clenardus whimsically suggested that they outnumbered the whites.[36] This was hardly the case, for, after making a parish by parish census in 1551–2, Rodrigues de Oliveira decided that there could be only 9,950 slaves, that is, 9.95 per cent – say 10 per cent – of the city's total population.[37]

Oliveira's estimate cannot be thoroughly checked because so few parish registers survive and the Misericórdia records were destroyed in the earthquake. The earliest records of the Sé reveal no baptisms of slaves,[38] but this was probably a result of snobbery: the canons of the cathedrals of Évora and Elvas also seem to have been curiously reluctant to baptize slaves, though both cities had large slave populations. Slaves owned by priests and other officials of the cathedral were baptized in Santa Cruz do Castelo instead, along with the slaves of courtiers and humanists attached to the nearby Palácio da Alcáçova. (See Map 3 for the location of parishes.) In the 1550s almost a quarter (24 per cent) of the baptisms at Santa Cruz were of slaves.[39] Many slaves – about 5 per cent of the entries in the register – were baptized in São Vicente de Fora, and even more were buried there: about 15.5 per cent of all funerals in the church in the mid-sixteenth century. In the 1560s, slaves accounted for 2 per cent of the entries in the baptismal and funerary registers of the parishes in the Alfama, not only in well-off São Tiago, but in lower-class São Pedro and Santo Estêvão as well. Records from the populous and wealthy parishes in the valley and on the waterfront date from the later sixteenth century and, like those of the Sé, mention few baptisms and burials of blacks. In two of these parishes, however, the number of weddings involving free blacks and slaves was extremely high: 5.5 per cent of all weddings celebrated in the church of Conceição Nova between 1569 and 1574 involved slaves, while in 1594 weddings involving free people of colour and slaves accounted for no less than 25.3 per cent of the total in Santa Justa. (In the latter case the number of weddings between slaves equalled the number between freedmen.[40]) All in all, Oliveira's figures are plausible, and 9,950 slaves in a population of 100,000 in 1552 could fairly easily increase to an estimated 15,000 in a population of 100,000 or more in 1633.[41]

As far as free people of colour are concerned, they and their children provide less than 1 per cent of the entries in the records of births and deaths, though over all their numbers may have constituted 2 per cent of Lisbon's population, just as they constituted 2 per cent of the city's taxpayers in 1565. Free blacks tended to congregate in the parishes on the two hills to the west and east of the

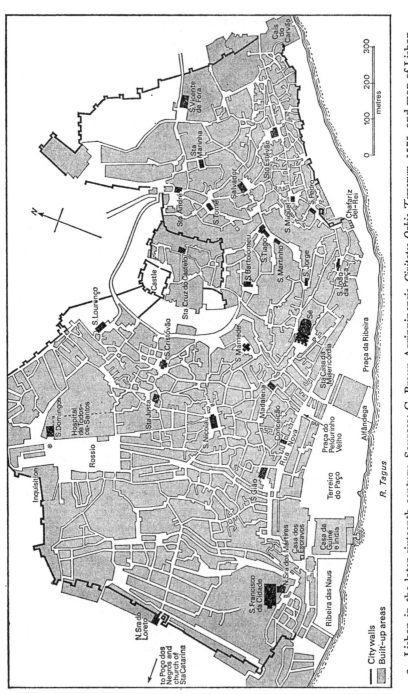

3 Lisbon in the later sixteenth century. Sources: G. Braun Agrippinensis, *Civitates Orbis Terrarum*, 1575, and map of Lisbon drawn by João Nunes Tinoco, 1650 (copy in AHCM Lxa)

city, presumably because they could not afford the higher rents in the central parishes.

Blacks were in many parts of the Alentejo (or, as it was called then, Entre-Tejo-e-Odiana) long before 1530, and it is safe to say that they were everywhere in the province by the mid-sixteenth century. In 1466 Šašek asserted that there were some 3,000 black and Moorish slaves in Évora, the second largest city in Portugal, capital of the Alentejo and the preferred residence of the later kings of the dynasty of Avis. This figure would represent about 16 per cent of the city's population, which Resende put at 18,000 by the end of the fifteenth century.[42] Such a percentage is not wholly improbable, but later and more reliable evidence suggests that the numbers were actually much lower. The census of 1527, for example, found that Évora had a population of only 11,252 inhabitants within the walls and a total of 14,168 within the municipal limits. The census-takers did not count slaves, but between July 1547 and December 1555 slaves formed about 9.4 per cent, and freedmen 2 per cent, of all the people whose funerals were undertaken by the Misericórdia.[43] Similar numbers of slaves and freedmen also appear in the parish records, the parish of São Pedro having perhaps the largest slave population.[44] This quarter, like Santa Cruz in Lisbon, was near the royal palace, and many slaves belonging to courtiers would have lived there with their masters. If the percentages obtained from the local records reflect the true proportion of slaves to free persons in society, there would have been at least 1,400 slaves and 280 freedmen in Évora by the middle of the sixteenth century.

The records of other towns in the Alentejo reveal comparable percentages. Black slaves had lived in the border city of Elvas since 1475,[45] if not longer, and by the 1530s 2.19 per cent of all funerals performed by the Misericórdia were of slaves. At mid-century, in the years between 1546 and 1555, the figure had risen to 4.52 per cent, while the percentage of freedmen buried had grown from 1.10 to 1.92.[46] In 1527 Elvas had a population of 9,416 people within the municipal limits, so in the 1530s there may have been about 210 slaves and 100 freedmen, and perhaps double those figures in the 1550s. Elsewhere in the northern Alentejo slaves accounted for 2 to 4 per cent of the entries in the parish registers of Borba, Estremoz, Arraiolos and Olivença, and for 7 to 10 per cent in Montemor-o-Novo.[47]

Although slaves lived mainly in the towns of the inland Alentejo, this did not preclude their employment in agriculture. Alentejan towns, including those of considerable size, were not primarily centres of commerce and industry but dormitories for landless labourers who went out to work on the nearby estates. Even in a city the size of Évora the purely urban employment of slaves as street vendors was opposed (albeit unsuccessfully) on the grounds that slaves were needed in the fields.[48]

Of course, not all slaves in the Alentejo were farm labourers. It was already the custom in the 1470s for masters who lived in villages in the hinterland to send their slaves into Setúbal to look for work in the salt-pans along the estuary of the Sado.[49] The first parish registers show that there were large numbers of slaves in the towns associated with the salt industry. In the 1570s 8.73 per cent of all baptisms in the parish of Santa Maria da Graça, the mother-church of Setúbal, were of slaves, while the figure was 5.33 per cent in the parish of Santa Maria do Castelo, in Alcácer do Sal. In neither parish did baptisms of freedmen amount to more than 1 per cent of the total.[50]

Slaves in the Algarve appear to have lived mostly in the communities of the coastal plain. This was the main agricultural region, with fruit orchards and nut-groves forming in parts a man-made forest,[51] and it is understandable that more slaves should work there, rather than inland in the Serra do Monchique, whose pastoral economy required a considerably smaller workforce. The extent to which slaves were employed in the coastal belt is shown by the confessional roll of the rural parish of Moncarapacho, near Tavira, the Algarve's major town and port. The roll is a unique document, since no others from the 1540s have yet been found.[52] It provides solid evidence that slaves constituted some 10 per cent of the total population of Moncarapacho, a percentage which could hardly be guessed from the parish registers.[53] Hence there is a good chance that the late sixteenth century records of deaths from Vila Nova de Portimão and Lagos, where slaves were respectively 7 per cent and 10 per cent of the total dead, may indicate the actual ratio of slave to free in those towns.[54] An estimate that in the 1550s at least 10 per cent of the population of the Algarve was slave appears reasonable:[55] this represents a figure of 3,500 slaves in all.

Conclusions

This survey, though not complete, is sufficiently extensive to enable certain important conclusions to be drawn regarding the size and distribution of the population of slaves and freedmen. In terms of numbers, it seems safe to say that slaves and free blacks were everywhere a distinct minority and that more lived in the south than in the north. Even if one does not accept the hypothesis that the parish and Misericórdia records reflected the relative sizes of the free and slave populations, the percentages of slaves and freedmen found in the registers of southern Portugal are quite striking when compared with those found in registers of the north. If one does accept the hypothesis, it then appears that by the mid-sixteenth century the largest numbers of slaves, about 10 per cent of the local population, were found in Lisbon, Évora and the Algarve. Elsewhere in the Alentejo, and in Estremaduran towns neighbouring Lisbon, they may have constituted some 5 per cent, give or take a few percentage points. In the north, only the slave population of Oporto approached this figure; in other northern towns slaves may have been 1 or 2 per cent of the population, and there were almost none in the countryside. In all parts of Portugal freedmen were a tiny fraction of the community – perhaps 1 per cent, and never more than 2 per cent, where slaves were common, much less elsewhere. Calculations based on these figures and on the assumption that the national population as revealed in the census of 1527–31 had not increased significantly by mid-century are shown in Table 6. (The figures may appear exact, but they are all approximations.)

32,370 slaves, 2,580 freedmen: say 35,000 in all. This is the minimum number, because non-Christian slaves were not taken into account, but it is unlikely that there were many more blacks, for most of them, unlike the Moors, became at least nominal Christians. Thirty-five thousand is not a very impressive figure: only 2.5 to 3 per cent of the national population.[56] On the other hand, the local concentrations of slaves, of up to 10 per cent of the population, were quite high for sixteenth-century Europe. Traditional Mediterranean economies do not appear to have been able to absorb very many slaves. In Sicily, for instance, a kingdom which had ample opportunities for acquiring slaves through the trans-Saharan trade and by raiding in the Mediterranean, slaves constituted no more than 4 per cent of the population.[57] And Domínguez Ortiz believes that there

Table 6. *Numbers of slaves and freedmen in Portugal in the mid-sixteenth century*

1. Approximate population of slaves by provinces (to nearest 5)	
Entre-Douro-e-Minho	2,730[a]
Trás-os-Montes	645[b]
Beira	1,265[c]
Estremadura	13,730[d]
Entre-Tejo-e-Odiana (Alentejo)	10,480[e]
Algarve	3,520[f]
Total	32,370

a. 6 per cent of population of city of Oporto (700 slaves); 1.5 per cent of pop. of *termo* of Oporto, and of pop. of all other towns and their *termos* represented in Cortes (2,030 slaves), from ANTT, former Armario 26, maço 3, doc. 2, 'Lugares que vem aas Cortes, e os Vezinhos, que tem: anno de 1535', published in Visconde de Santarém, *Documentos, Parte 1a,* pp. 88–9. A multiplier of 4 persons per *vizinho* is used here, as throughout this study.
b. 1.5 per cent of pop. of all towns, cities and their *termos* represented in Cortes. Ibid., p. 88.
c. 1.5 per cent of pop. of towns and *termos* represented in Cortes. Ibid., p. 89.
d. 9,950 slaves in Lisbon and *termo*, from Oliveira, *Sumário,* p. 95; 5 per cent of strictly urban pop. of Aveiro and towns south of, and including, Tomar, represented in Cortes (1,255 slaves); 1.5 per cent of pop. of *termos* of the same towns, plus 1.5 per cent of remaining pop. of Estremadura shown in census of 1527 (2,525 slaves), Santarém, *Documentos, Parte 1a,* pp. 90–1.
e. 10 per cent of pop. of Évora and *termo*; 5 per cent of pop. of the rest of the Alentejo, as shown in the census.
f. 10 per cent of pop. as computed by Lobo, *Historia da Sociedade,* p. 31.

2. Approximate population of freedmen (to nearest 5)
Let freedmen be 0.5 per cent of the total population where at least 5 per cent was slave, and 1 per cent of the population where 10 per cent was slave; then

Oporto, excluding *termo*	60
Lisbon and *termo*	995
Towns in Estremadura, excluding *termos*	125[g]
Évora and *termo*	145
Alentejo, excluding Évora and *termo*	905
Algarve	350
Total	2,580

g. These are Aveiro and the towns south of, and including, Tomar, which were represented in Cortes.

were only about 100,000 slaves in Spain, a mere 1.25 to 1.5 per cent of the total population of seven or eight millions.[58]

Little has been said so far about the balance of the sexes in the slave population, mainly because there are few samples big enough to provide reasonable figures when considered in detail. However, the funerary rolls of Évora and Elvas indicate a slight preponderance of male slaves over female, and there are three men for every two

women in the confessional roll of Moncarapacho.[59] Thus the balance
of the sexes in Portugal corresponds to what is known about the
balance in shipments from Africa: although the Portuguese tried to
ship equal numbers of men and women,[60] men seem to have pre-
dominated somewhat in shipments from Arguim and most other
posts (see Table 4, p. 24). The relative numbers of freedmen and
women are harder to assess, because the freed community was so
small. In Évora, the Misericórdia buried the same number of
freedmen as freedwomen, in Elvas, slightly more men.[61] The only
large sample of a freed population, indeed of a free black population, comes from the Lisbon tax roll of 1565 where the estates
of 169 black women and only 44 (or perhaps 46) black men
were assessed. The majority of women may indicate that in the
capital masters preferred to free women rather than men, as later
happened in Bahia, in Brazil, where two women were freed for every
man, even though there were more men in the slave population.[62]
It may also indicate a disproportionate number of women among the
slave population of Lisbon, but there is as yet not enough information from parish records to confirm this.

To sum up: we have seen that most slaves seem to have lived in
the valley of the Tagus and the agricultural provinces to the south.
This bears out the essentials of Faria's argument. Nonetheless, the
presence of slaves in the northern cities and particularly in Lisbon
is not accounted for by his theory, and requires a more detailed
investigation of the ownership and employment of slaves; in short,
of the role of slavery in the Portuguese economy.

4

The occupations of slaves

Slaves were owned by people of almost every class in Portugal and were employed in almost every sector of the economy. Their employment answered a range of economically rational and irrational demands. On the one hand, there were slaves who did not increase the productivity of the society to which they were brought: these slaves were the personal servants and retainers of royalty and the nobility, who bought them for purposes of display and conspicuous consumption. On the other hand, slaves helped to extend the workforce in the fields and on the waterways, and earned or saved money for their masters in the exercise of gainful occupations in the towns and cities.

Slave-ownership

Except for beggars, people of all classes, from labourers to kings, owned black slaves. Even prostitutes, who were not allowed any free servants, could have slave girls in their houses.[1] And, though there is no confirmatory evidence, it is probable that free black Christians in Portugal, like those who worked as interpreters in the African forts and trading vessels, could own slaves if they wished to do so.[2]

Only Muslims and Jews were limited in their choice of slaves, because the law forbade unbelievers to have Christians subject to them.[3] But before 1497, that is, while there were still large Islamic and Hebrew communities in Portugal, no very active effort was made to convert incoming slaves to Christianity, so Jews and Muslims had little difficulty in acquiring slaves. Nor did they experience many problems in retaining them, since for most of the Middle Ages Portuguese law did not encourage slaves of infidel masters to espouse the Christian religion: Jews and Muslims were too useful as slave-merchants for the Christians to circumscribe their property rights too narrowly.[4] In 1457, for instance, D. Afonso V decreed that an infidel's slave who became a Christian did not thereby become a freeman until three months after his conversion, and then only if he had not been sold to a Christian master.[5] Not until 1490, when anti-Semitic feeling was on the increase, did the Cortes protest that the Jews (who were said to be the owners of 'many slaves, both white and from Guinea') took advantage of this last clause. Jewish masters whose slaves had converted to Christianity would make an arrangement with some 'bad Christians' who would purchase, or say they had purchased, the slaves, but would leave the slaves in the Jews' employ. The representatives thought this alleged state of affairs was disgraceful, and persuaded D. João II to order that henceforth Jewish masters had to free immediately any of their slaves who became Christians.[6] Either this law was not enforced, or the Jews owned unswervingly non-Christian slaves, for in 1494 Hieronymus Münzer found some extremely rich Jewish merchants in Lisbon living (as did their Christian compatriots) 'entirely off the labour of their slaves'.[7] After 1497, when the free Muslims and Jews resident in Portugal were forcibly converted to Christianity, these New Christians joined other Christians in the unrestricted right to own slaves.

Such widespread ownership of slaves was rare in Europe outside the Iberian peninsula, and even the Castilians were surprised that relatively poor Portuguese were slave-holders.[8] Labourers and seamen could own slaves because Portugal was so heavily involved in the slave-trade. Anyone in the trade could easily acquire a slave, and sick slaves could be purchased cheaply from the Casa dos Escravos.[9] Still, slaves usually cost a fair amount and were thus particularly associated with the aristocracy and the more comfortable classes. Brandão asserted that only the 7,000 clerics, courtiers and foreigners in Lisbon could generally afford slaves.[10] This was somewhat of an exaggeration for, as Tables 7 and 8 show, merchants and tradesmen could also afford them. In Évora a few members of lower income groups, such as servants and shepherds, owned slaves, but not very many. Most slaves were owned by the aristocracy, priests and religious institutions, government officials and professional men.

The employment of slaves

The nobility employed – or underemployed – large numbers of slaves solely as domestic servants. Clenardus noted that when a gentleman

Table 7. *Owners of slaves who were baptized or were parents of children baptized in the Cathedral of Oporto, 1540, 1544*[a]

Owner	Male	Slaves Female	Total
Nobility			
status imputed (Señor)[b]	–	3	3
widow of nobleman	–	1	1
	–	4	4
Religious			
religious house (Santa Leira)	–	1	1
	–	1	1
Government			
contador	1	–	1
escrivão (notary)	–	1	1
	1	1	2
Professional men			
doutor, bacharel (lawyers)	–	2	2
	–	2	2
Tradesmen			
merchants	–	5	5
tanoeiro (cooper)	–	1	1
sapateiro (shoemaker)	–	1	1
	–	7	7
Total slaves whose masters' status or occupation is mentioned or can be known	1	15	16
Total slaves who were parents of children baptized in the cathedral	5	27	32

a. *Source:* AD. Porto, Reg. Civil, Porto (Sé: N. Sra da Assunção), baptismos, 1 (1540–72).
b. The priest officiating at some baptisms wrote in Castilian.

of Évora sallied forth on horseback, two slaves marched in front, a third carried his master's hat, a fourth his cloak (in case of rain), a fifth held the horse's bridle, a sixth the gentleman's silk slippers, a seventh his clothes-brush, an eighth bore a cloth to rub down the horse while his master attended mass or chatted to a friend, while a slave bearing his master's comb brought up the rear.[11]

Clearly these slaves served no real economic purpose, but were merely symbolic of the slave-holder's wealth. Even as servants they were superfluous, since service in the courts of the nobility was a popular occupation for free whites. Indeed, the Cortes of 1439 declared that the country was in a bad way because most of the

Table 8. *Owners of slaves buried by the Misericórdia of Évora, 1537–8 and 1547–55*[a]

| Owner | Slaves | | |
	Male	Female	Total
Nobility			
stated to be noble (*dom, dona,* etc.)	3	3	6
known to be noble	7	7	14
	10	10	20
Servants of nobility			
vedor of *meirinho mor*	1	–	1
amo (head of household)	1	–	1
violeiro (guitarist)	–	1	1
trombeiro (trumpeter)	–	1	1
	2	2	4
Religious			
Cardinal D. Henrique	4	–	4
inquisitor	2	–	2
prior, prioress	1	1	2
religious house (Santa Clara)	–	1	1
priests	5	1	6
bacharel da Sé (canon lawyer)	1	–	1
	13	3	16
Servants of religious			
daughters of Cardinal's housekeeper (*ama*)	1	–	1
criado of Cardinal	2	–	2
	3	–	3
Government and judiciary			
vereador (town councillor)	1	–	1
juiz dos orfãos (in charge of orphans' funds)	–	1	1
provedor	–	2	2
chanceler	1	–	1
almoxarife	–	1	1
escrivão, tabelião (notaries)	3	1	4
	5	5	10
Professional men			
doutor, bacharel, licenciado (lawyers)	–	4	4
físico (physician)	1	–	1
curador (healer; possibly a trustee or guardian)	–	1	1
humanist (Garcia de Resende)	1	–	1
	2	5	7
Tradesmen			
craveiro (maker of horseshoe nails)	1	2	3
merchant	1	1	2
ourives (goldsmith)	–	3	3
sapateiro (shoemaker)	2	2	4
pedreiro (stonemason)	–	1	1
trapeiro (rag-and-bone man)	2	–	2
ferrador (farrier)	2	–	2

Table 8 (*cont.*)

Owner	Male	Slaves Female	Total
Tradesmen			
tintoreiro (dyer)	I	–	I
serralheiro (locksmith)	I	–	I
carreteiro (carter)	–	I	I
barbeiro (barber)	–	I	I
pichaleiro (tinsmith)	I	–	I
parteira (midwife)	–	I	I
	II	I2	23
Agriculturalists			
lavrador (farmer; wealthy peasant)	–	3	3
pastor (shepherd)	–	I	I
	–	4	4
Total slaves whose masters' status or occupation is mentioned or can be known	46	41	87
Total slaves buried by the Misericórdia in these years	129	117	246

a. *Source:* AD Évora, Mis. 476, Livº de Receita e Despeza da Mizericordia de Evora do An. D. 537 and Mis. 761, Livro dos Defuntos, 1547–56.

people did not want to work on the land but went off to 'enjoy themselves' as servants.[12] Some servants worked on terms which were, at least temporarily, not appreciably better than those of slaves: the *criados a bem fazer* served for their clothing and keep alone, in the hope of preferment.[13] Hence the nobility's real need for domestic slaves was often very slight. But in the aristocratic society of the Iberian peninsula, possession of a large retinue was the principal means of demonstrating wealth and power, which conferred honour and prestige.[14] And, since slaves were costly, possession of a large retinue of slaves was an exceptional indication of wealth and power. Slave-holding became a mark of nobility: in 1560, for instance, a Portuguese priest in Mozambique remarked that the principal men among the blacks thought it 'an honour to have many wives, as it is held among us to have many slaves'.[15] 'Many', however, should not be thought of in Brazilian or West Indian terms: a large retinue was measured in tens, not hundreds.

Such numbers of slaves working exclusively as servants were rarely found outside houses of the nobility, except in religious institutions. Charitable and monastic foundations commonly included slaves in their domestic staff. One of the Infante D. Henrique's first acts after the first large shipment of slaves had landed was to send a slave to the monastery of São Vicente do Cabo, near Sagres, and during the following century slaves served in religious foundations in Elvas, Santarém, Setúbal and Lisbon, among other places.[16]

Institutions employed slaves, not for reasons of conspicuous consumption, but from necessity. Offerings of slaves were solicited and accepted by religious houses because they were frequently hard pressed for alternative sources of labour. Some houses were too poor to pay the high initial price of a slave or even the considerably lower annual wages of free servants. The abbess of one convent wrote to the queen, begging, 'for the love of the Lord God give us a pair of slave women as alms, because we are spending the pittance we have entirely on hired girls'.[17] Others had difficulty in attracting free servants. The houses could offer few of the chances of secular preferment which made freemen so willing to serve the nobility, while freemen infected with the ideals of an aristocratic society considered much of the work performed by servants in religious foundations to be menial and beneath their dignity.

Hospitals in particular often had to employ slaves, since work near the sick and dying was dangerous as well as menial. This may be why D. Manuel provided an annual supply of slaves for the hospital of Todos-os-Santos in Lisbon and for other hospitals in the empire.[18] Although the slaves were generally sold to raise funds, some remained to perform the unpleasant work scorned by free servants. In 1504, for instance, Todos-os-Santos had a staff of twenty-six people, of whom six were slaves. The four male slaves were assigned only the most menial physical labour, such as sweeping the floors, changing the bed linen and emptying the patients' chamber pots; the two women helped a free washerwoman clean the bed linen and the patients' clothes.[19]

Apart from being a mark of nobility, and a means of acquiring drudge labour, ownership of slaves could be a profitable investment. Slaves could replace or supplement free labour in the master's own business venture, whether that was a country estate or an urban workshop. Otherwise, masters could hire out their slaves' services to other men. A third option was to permit the slave to carry on a remunerative trade by himself, on condition that part or all of his earnings be paid to the master. The second and third options were particularly attractive to the poorer nobility and people of quality, since they allowed the master to make a profit from manual labour or petty trade without incurring the social stigma attached to direct personal involvement in these occupations.[20] In fact, slaves employed in these ways might be the only source of income for a person of quality. Later sections of this chapter will examine how slaves were set to work to earn money for their masters.

Slaves were not always diligent or reliable workmen, nor could their masters be depended upon to punish them for damaging or trespassing on other people's property. Hence public authorities enacted legislation to restrict or regulate the employment of slaves in occupations where they could impair the interests of free members of the community. There was, however, hardly any legislation regulating the conditions of labour for slaves. The nature and the hours of the slave's employment depended almost entirely upon his master. Slaves of the nobility might have a leisurely existence: as Clenardus remarked, they were often just a 'useless rabble . . . who would do anything rather than learn the mechanical arts'. On the other hand, the Flemish humanist could see little difference between beasts of burden and the slave girls whose daily round was to fetch water, go to market, clean the clothes, tidy the house and dispose of the garbage.[21] Poorer masters and mistresses, such as genteel widows in Lisbon, drove their slaves hard both as servants and as workers. Before one of the widows' slaves could go out in the morning to purchase the goods he would sell in the streets during the day, he had to tidy the house and put on the fire for his owner's breakfast.[22]

Slaves were supposed to have every Sunday off and apparently several feast days were also days of rest: Brandão and the episcopal constitutions both assumed that the working year for slaves and freemen was about 270 days.[23] But the rule seems to have applied only to work outside the house for, according to Fernão de Oliveira, nearly all masters expected their slaves to perform domestic tasks on Sunday. And only New Christian masters had to be particularly circumspect, since they could be denounced to the Inquisition as observers of non-Christian Sabbaths in cases where an Old Christian master might suffer no more than disapproving remarks from his friends or a reprimand from his confessor. In 1541, for example, several neighbours denounced the New Christian Alonso Barreira of Santos for making his black slaves dig his garden and orchard on the Sabbath, a practice which the neighbours said 'looked bad'. On one occasion Barreira had even dragged the slaves away from church, at which time they were heard to complain, 'It's the Lord's day today, we don't have to work'.[24]

Slaves in agriculture

Apart from clearing the land, as was mentioned in the previous chapter, slaves were employed in a wide range of rustic chores. The simplest way of employing slaves in country districts was to send them out into the woods and scrublands to gather nuts, berries, herbs and honeycombs. These natural products formed an important part of the diet of rural slaves (and of poor people too), and any excess could be sold to their masters' profit.[25] Another vendible product was esparto grass, which grew wild in rocky places in the Algarve. Black slaves of both sexes joined the other harvesters who scoured the wastelands, cutting the grass and binding it into sheaves which were later sold to manufacturers of rope and matting.[26] During the summer months some slaves in the southern and central provinces spent their nights guarding fields, vineyards and olive-groves, while others tended flocks and herds. Slave herdsmen were in fact quite common, because the long hours and monotonous way of life made herding unattractive to freemen.[27] (Elvas, for instance, suffered from such a lack of shepherds that the city fathers had to offer incentives to attract Castilian herdsmen from across the border.)[28] Come the autumn, slaves worked with other farm-hands to bring the harvest in. Around Coimbra, they laboured in the vineyards, picking the grapes and driving the animals laden with wine and must to the cellars.[29] Further south, the Algarvian blacks were renowned for their skill in the operation of the olive presses and in the manufacture of olive oil.[30]

The tasks assigned to slaves at the rural hospital of Caldas da Rainha are fairly typical of the division of labour on an estate run with slaves. The women worked as domestics, while the men ran a small farm whose produce fed the patients and nursing sisters. One slave woman baked all the bread, two others cooked the rest of the food and two more washed the clothes and linen. Two male slaves tended a herd of cows and a flock of goats, which provided meat and milk for the kitchen. Fruit and vegetables came from a garden looked after by another male slave who was also in charge of distilling water for use in medicines. Any further necessities were fetched from town in a cart driven by a slave.[31]

As the foregoing examples show, in many tasks slaves worked on their own. Some undoubtedly performed their tasks with care, but municipal legislation suggests that without supervision others worked negligently or ignored the consequences of their actions. The city council of Coimbra, for instance, forbade slaves to operate commercial olive presses; management of the presses was considered a position of trust, requiring an oath of office, and the councillors had a low opinion of slaves' sense of responsibility.[32] They would not even allow slaves to tend flocks of sheep in the olive-groves on the banks of the Mondego, presumably because they feared the slaves might let the sheep damage the trees.[33] Slaves who stayed out overnight to tend livestock or guard crops were particularly troublesome. In Coimbra, slaves and farmhands who were ostensibly guarding their masters' fields spent the night pillaging those belonging to other men; and as early as 1461 the councillors of Santarém complained that blacks sent to guard the olive-groves let their cooking-fires blaze out of control. Angry property-owners subsequently forced the municipal councils of these and other towns to ban slaves from spending the night in the fields during the growing season and to punish them severely for starting fires.[34]

Quantitative information about slaves in agriculture is unfortunately minimal, since no account books have yet been found from an estate run with slave labour; there were no cadastral surveys, and the wills of slave-holders do not normally indicate the area of land they owned. Hence correlations between the number of slaves and the area of land owned must await the more detailed researches of an agrarian historian. For the time being, the most that can be said is that the numbers of slaves on any one estate were usually quite small. The confessional roll of Moncarapacho indicates that no household there had more than four slaves, or more than six slaves, freedmen and free servants (criados) all together. Estates were larger in the Alentejo, but slave-holders' wills show that the landed nobility rarely owned more than fifteen slaves. The ten female and seventeen male slaves owned by Diogo Lopes de Sequeira at the time of his death in 1530 constituted a considerable holding, commensurate with the wealth he had acquired as governor of India between 1518 and 1521. Not all the slaves, however, were on Sequeira's estate at Alandroal or employed as field-hands: three men were in the Algarve and four women were definitely household slaves.[35] Farms in Estremadura apart from Ribatejo were fairly small in area, and what evidence there is suggests that a farmer might have one or two slaves as herdsmen or farm-hands, but seldom many more.[36] There is in fact nothing to indicate that slaves were employed in large-scale plantation agriculture. And, where they were employed, slaves were seldom the only source of labour; rather, they extended the regular workforce of hired hands and indentured servants.

Nautical pursuits

Not only did slaves man the ships plying between Lisbon and Africa, but they were also crew aboard smaller vessels on the rivers and coastal seas of Portugal. This recourse to slave seamen was of long standing: as early as 1286 a charter assumed that the fishermen of Póvoa das Paredes, near Leiria, would be assisted by their Moorish slaves.[37] During the period under study, the sheer numbers of slaves serving on the boats which carried passengers and freight on the rivers Douro and Tagus necessitated legislation to define the conditions of their employment.

The manners of ferrymen as a group were proverbially unruly,[38] but those of slave boatswains (arraíses) in charge of ferries were viewed with greater suspicion than usual. In Oporto it was said that the slaves extorted money from passengers and committed other misdemeanours. Hence in 1521 the city council prohibited slaves from serving on boats on the Douro unless they were accompanied by their masters or other experienced white boatmen. (Interestingly enough, women crew on the ferries suffered the same accusations and restrictions: they had to serve with experienced boatmen or with their husbands.)[39] The Lisbon authorities, on the other hand, were haunted by the fear that slave ferrymen would help other slaves to escape, in defiance of a law of 1284 which forbade slaves to cross the Tagus without their masters' permission.[40] There seems to have been little cause for concern, however, until 1534, when several Moors escaped from gaol in Lisbon during an uproar created as a diversion by their fellow inmates and disappeared without a trace. D. Fernando de Castro, the governor of the Casa do Cível, assured King João III that the Moors made the attempt because they knew they could count on assistance from the 'many Moors, blacks and Indians [working] as boatswains and hands on the lighters and skiffs which are in [Lisbon] and Ribatejo as far [upriver] as Tancos'. After consultations with the watermen of the city to determine what steps could be taken to prevent further escapes,[41] masters were required to post a bond of 100 xdos to guarantee the good behaviour of any of their slaves who served on river craft. The money itself was not required, merely a statement of intent on the part of the master or of a wealthy friend or patron to pay, should the slave take himself or others to freedom in North Africa. Freedmen were considered no better than slaves and had to find a patron to stand surety for them.

The bonds posted between 1549 and 1556 still survive, and a sample from the years 1549, 1550 and 1555 yielded much information about slave boatmen and their masters.[42] All of the ninety-six slaves were men and the vast majority (seventy-one) were black, with East Indians the second largest group (fifteen). There was only one white, that is, Moorish, slave: clearly Moors were not trusted. The slaves' home ports were towns and villages on both sides of the Tagus as far up as Abrantes (beyond Tancos), though the largest concentration of slave boatmen was on the south bank of the Mar da Palha, the estuary (see Map 4). Fifty-five of the eighty-six masters had some connexion with the river and shipping, but twenty-two of the thirty-four guarantors are known to have drawn their money from other sources. The forty-nine masters who were themselves boatmen, boat-owners and fishermen probably employed their slaves on their own vessels, though the bonds left open the option of hiring slaves out to other captains. (Only four of the masters mentioned were fishermen, because the scheme did not embrace the fishing villages below Lisbon and Almada.)

Slaves probably continued to work on the boats of the Tagus throughout the later sixteenth century, for though the watermen's guild refused in principle to accept slaves, the guild made an exception if the slaves had authorization from the city: that is, if bonds had been posted.[43] There does not appear to have been any loophole, however, in the total prohibition enacted in 1587 by the council of Oporto against slaves and women serving on ferries across the Douro.[44] In the northern city there were always enough free whites from the overpopulated hinterland to fill a position from which slaves had been excluded – and competition from white freemen may well have been the reason why women and slaves were first restricted in, and finally excluded from, the trade of boatman.

Slaves in the cities

The cities, particularly Lisbon, provided the most diversified opportunities for masters who wished to make money from their slaves'

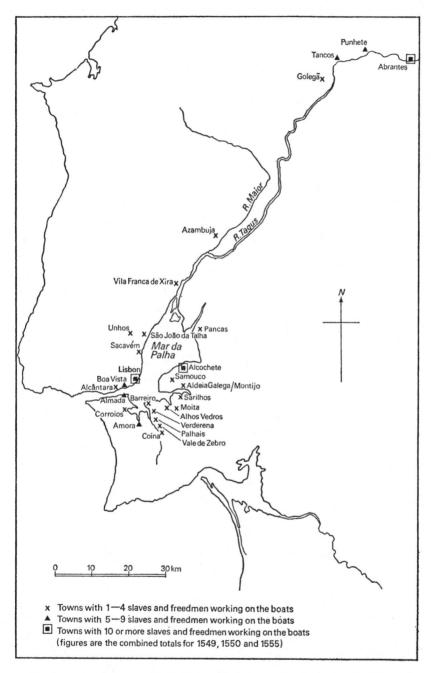

4 Home ports of slaves and freedmen working on the boats on the Tagus in 1549, 1550 and 1555

labours, whether by employing the slaves directly, hiring them out, or allowing them to carry on a modest business of their own.

Those masters whose slaves worked under their direct supervision were chiefly artisans and other self-employed men. Most slaves belonging to guildsmen probably worked as occasional labour, outside the guild structure, but some craftsmen appear to have treated their slaves as apprentices and to have accepted other men's slaves in that capacity. Of course, apprenticeship implied that the slaves could work their way up in the guild hierarchy; and if an artisan's slaves became master-craftsmen with their own workshops, the artisan slave-holder would profit from their businesses as well.

Guild reactions to these possibilities varied, generally in relation to the size and social status of the guild concerned. Smiths and shoemakers, for instance, do not seem to have had any objections to teaching black slaves and freedmen their craft.[45] These occupations were neither very prestigious, having been associated often enough with Moors and Moorish slaves in the Middle Ages,[46] nor particularly exclusive: according to Rodrigues de Oliveira, there were more shoemakers in Lisbon than men of any other trade.[47] The smaller trades, on the other hand, were more concerned about their prestige and exclusiveness. Thus in 1575 the hosiers (*calceteiros*) and jerkin-makers (*jubeteiros*) of Lisbon amended their charter so as to require authorization from the city and the slave's owner before a slave could be examined for admission as a full member of their mystery.[48] At that, the hosiers were relatively broad-minded, for they could at least envisage the possibility of a slave as a master-craftsman. Not so the sword-makers of Oporto, whose charter forbade slaves to rise above the rank of journeyman,[49] nor the goldsmiths and lapidaries of Lisbon, who allowed slaves only to serve as drudges in the forges, working the bellows and aiding the smiths to hammer out the precious metal. The goldsmiths may not have been moved wholly by a desire to preserve their own dignity: they claimed that they debarred slaves even from apprenticeship 'because of the thefts and errors [slaves] could commit in a profession of such importance and which requires such great exactitude and neatness'.[50] Similar doubts regarding slaves' sense of responsibility led the *pasteleiros* who made meat pies and pasties to ban slaves. All these examples of discriminatory legislation affected slaves in general, rather than black slaves in particular. Religion, not race, was the grounds for any further discrimination: the piemen, for instance, singled out Muslim and *mourisco* slaves as particularly undesirable and refused to let free *mouriscos* join the trade. Free and Christian blacks, mulattoes and Indians, however, were specifically permitted to be examined as master-piemen.[51]

Slave-owners who were not self-employed, such as seamen, labourers and stone-masons, sometimes persuaded their employer to take on their slaves as well, so that master and man worked side by side in the same or different capacities.[52] In these cases, the master pocketed the combined wages, his own and his slaves'.

A master who was not himself a working man or tradesman could send his slaves out into the streets, sometimes even to other towns,[53] to sell goods or hire out their services. The work of women slaves hired out in this way was often an extension of their domestic employment: there were slave washerwomen, for instance, and slave women were responsible for removing much of the garbage and excrement from houses in the larger cities. Municipal ordinances occasionally placed more strictures on slaves who earned money for their work than on those who simply worked for their masters. In Lisbon, women slaves and other domestics were allowed to carry refuse and, during the hours of darkness, excrement from their masters' houses down to the river in any container they wished; only in the day-time did they have to carry excrement in *canastras* – tall wicker baskets with lids which concealed the basins inside. Slave women who earned money for the same tasks had to use *canastras* both day and night.[54]

The municipalities left the washerwomen's customers to worry about standards of cleanliness and hygiene, and washerwomen themselves gave rise to relatively few problems: it was their friends who worried town councillors. In both Coimbra and Évora the city council had to forbid men from hanging about on the riverbank and paying court to the slaves and other women who were trying to wash clothes.[55] The problem was more serious in Coimbra, where the husbands and lovers of white Muslim and *mourisco* slave women not only dallied on the banks of the Mondego, but sometimes concealed themselves in the bushes and then sprang out to mistreat and rob the other washerwomen. The council, assuming collusion between the male and female Moors, determined that the white slave women should wash their clothes beside the bridge, where they could be seen by passers-by. By contrast, free white Portuguese or black slaves or freedwomen could wash their clothes wherever they liked: yet another instance of blacks being considered more trustworthy than Moors.[56]

Male slaves were usually hired out to perform heavy physical labour. In Lisbon they carried baskets of meat and fish in the market[57] and, at least until the 1550s, were concerned with unloading fish from vessels berthed at the river's edge.[58] In the second half of the sixteenth century, however, the job of unloading the catch was reserved for whites only.[59] Presumably blacks continued to earn a living as stevedores (mariolas), for whom there was a fluctuating demand according to the number of ships in harbour.[60] Blacks also found work on building sites and in public works. Then, as now, the possibility of private profit to be made in public works proved attractive to certain municipal officials. To prevent this abuse, in 1517 the king forbade the councillors of Lisbon from contracting for their own slaves, servants and pack animals to be used in works approved by the city.[61] The crown itself tried to set a good example: very few of the king's slaves helped to build the royal palaces, while none is mentioned as having laboured on the great monastery and church at Belém.[62] Freemen and their slaves were hired instead. Loosely connected with the building trades were the black pinceis or caeiros (whitewashers), both men and women, of whom about fifty roamed the streets of Lisbon in the 1550s looking for work.[63]

According to the evidence available, more male slaves worked as manual labourers than as petty traders – regatões – who hawked goods through the streets. They were, however, involved in the sale of bulky or heavy goods, such as charcoal for cooking-fires and straw for bedding, floors and stables. Both charcoal and straw came to Lisbon by water, and blacks were among the men who unloaded the vessels and drove the carts which delivered the goods to houses in the city.[64] By 1544 there were so many black and mourisco slaves and freedmen in this line of trade that the city council decided upon separate treatment for them should they be found selling straw or charcoal with false measures. A slave or freedman accused of defrauding customers of petty sums (under 600 rs.) by selling at short measure was given a summary trial in the council, rather than in the royal courts, which tried free whites. And if the slave or freedman was found guilty, he received a public lashing over and above the statutory fine for this crime.[65]

Some charcoal was also sold by black women from stalls in the

Terreiro do Paço, the main square beside the Tagus,[66] but most women slaves were associated with the trade in snacks, provisions and water. Fetching water from the nearest municipal fountain was a tiresome task, bearing the stigma of menial labour, so many city-dwellers preferred to buy water from the *negras do pote*, who carried great jars (*potes*) of water on their heads. (In Lisbon they were forbidden to display their pots on the ground, for fear that dust might contaminate the water.)[67] In the 1550s each *negra do pote* earned 40 rs. a day; 20–25 rs. of this went to her master, and the woman kept the remainder to buy food for herself while at work. At night she returned to her master's house to have dinner and rest.[68]

Water-sellers and the men who drew water for them added further elements to the confusion at the Chafariz del-Rei, the main municipal fountain: fights and even deaths occurred there because so many people wanted to fill their jugs at the six spouts. Finally, in 1551, the *câmara* decided to impose a policy of segregation. The first spout was assigned to male slaves and freedmen of all races, black, mulatto, Indian or otherwise; they could also use the second spout after galley-slaves had finished filling water-barrels there for the fleet. Free white men used the third and fourth spouts, women slaves and freedwomen the fifth and white women the sixth.[69]

The pages of Brandão's census include some short but colourful sketches of the life of other black *regateiras*, as women street vendors were called. Early in the morning the black women who sold rice pudding, couscous and chickpeas from pots which they carried on their heads began to cry their wares along the Lisbon waterfront. Soon they were surrounded by children newly wakened from their beds and clutching money extorted from their parents by means of sobs and tears. Many parents must have agreed with the demographer that a nourishing breakfast for a child was worth the price, for the black women's wares were quickly sold. Almost as popular a snack, though with a different clientele, were stewed prunes, particularly loved by the homeless and unwell who lacked stoves to cook the fruit which they believed had medicinal value. Brandão observed that the black women always kept the prunes well covered with freshly laundered cloths and he commended this attention to cleanliness.[70] Black *regateiras* sold other snacks, such as cooked beans and *aletria* (pasta), besides more essential supplies such as olive oil and seafood.[71] Although Brandão makes no special mention of them (he occasionally forgot to state all the races employed in a trade), it can be assumed that black *regateiras* sold vegetables, fruit and fish in Lisbon as they did in Évora and Elvas.

Whether purveying goods or services, slaves were rarely without free white competitors.[72] While the removal of garbage in Lisbon seems to have been principally the concern of black women, the municipal legislation suggests that other people were also engaged in this noisome work, and other evidence shows that not all water-sellers were *negras do pote*: there were Galicians, Beirans and other migrant workers as well.[73]

Sometimes the government intervened to limit competition from slaves, but most bans and restrictions on black *regatões* and *regateiras* were usually repealed or allowed to lapse. Lisbon, probably the first city to have a considerable black population, was also the first to try to drive black *regateiras* off the streets. In late 1514 or early 1515 the city fathers protested to King Manuel that many of the black women who hawked fruit and other goods were 'unreasonable' [*desarrazoadas*] and insulted ladies of birth and wealth. On the strength of these and other (unspecified) charges the council believed that the city would be better off without black *regateiras*. D. Manuel, probably aware of the effect such a ban would have on slave-holders' incomes, was not so sure, and compromised by restricting the women's freedom of movement. After 23 February 1515 black women, slave or free, could only sell their wares from their masters' doorsteps or from the doors of other people who had come to an agreement with the *regateiras*.[74] Since free black women were sorely affected by this law, the Confraria de Nossa Senhora do Rosário, the black people's religious confraternity, protested to the king. D. Manuel was well disposed towards the brotherhood, and exempted free black women who were married or widows from the restrictions.[75] This exception seems to have been the thin end of the wedge: although the legislation of 1515 was not repealed, it is clear that by the 1550s, when Brandão wrote his description of the city, black slave women were again crying their wares in the streets.

Why the Lisbon authorities allowed the discriminatory legislation to lapse is not so clear. However, the experience of Évora and Elvas, which passed similar laws, suggests that many of the poorer people, and not just the rich people who owned the slaves, benefited from having slave *regateiras* in the streets. Elvas banned black and Moorish women, both slave and free, from being *regateiras* in 1537, but repealed

the law five years later as 'prejudicial to the people and good government'.[76] In May 1584 Évora tried to limit the occupation to married
women of good reputation, and slaves were allowed to sell only their
masters' produce. The law was repealed in three months, the council
having found that the poorer classes had been unable to buy fruit and
vegetables cheaply, because the city was not as well supplied as
before.[77] The council also found that it was more convenient if
regateiras sold their goods in the market-place rather than from their
own doorsteps, though freedwomen were permitted to obtain a
licence to do the latter.[78] True, the economic and demographic
situation of these Alentejan cities was not analogous to that of Lisbon,
for neither experienced the massive influx of free men and women
looking for jobs – including, presumably, the job of *regatão* or
regateira – that the capital did. But the very growth of Lisbon's
population may have made it necessary to countenance, if not encourage, an increasing number of slave or free street vendors and
market-women who were known to be able to distribute provisions
effectively and cheaply.

Masters who bought slaves to profit from their labours could expect
a reasonable return on their investment, even when the master and
slave had agreed to share the proceeds. Slaves hired out as labourers
yielded the lowest returns, since the wages for manual work were low
and do not appear to have risen appreciably during the first half of
the sixteenth century. In the early years of the century a male slave
employed as a labourer in the Lisbon area earned 30–35 *rs.* a day,
and a woman slave 15–20 *rs.* a day.[79] In the 1550s drudge labour
and the *negras do pote* were still earning 30–40 *rs.* a day, as shown in
Table 9. Nonetheless, a regularly employed slave labourer could
bring his master 8,100–10,800 *rs.* – the cost of a slave – during the
course of a working year of 270 days. *Regatões, regateiras* and stevedores on the waterfront earned considerably more. Brandão claimed
that in the 1550s these slaves could expect at least 100 *rs.* a day –
27,000 *rs.* a year. Sweetmeat sellers might make far more: they
earned over 200 *rs.* a day, and worked 300 days a year, since they
had to cater for the sweet tooth of holiday crowds on the less solemn
feast days. From these earnings one should probably subtract the cost
of the slave's keep – 3,250–5,400 *rs.* if the slave was to be maintained
at all adequately in food and clothing (see p. 98) – and, in the case
of *regateiras*, the initial cost of the goods which they retailed. But even

if the *regateiras'* takings were split fifty-fifty with their masters, there seems no reason to doubt the assertion made by a Capuchin friar who visited Lisbon in 1633 that a master could not only live, but live well on what his or her slaves earned.[80]

Slaves and the crown

In owning and employing slaves, Portuguese nobles and commoners followed the example set by their king, the royal family and princes of the blood. All the royal palaces seem to have had their complement of slaves – not only the great urban palaces of Évora and Lisbon, but the rural ones as well, such as Sintra, Almeirim and the near-by Paços da Ribeira de Muge and Paços da Serra.[81] Exactly how many slaves the crown owned is uncertain. In a list of 4,920 people at the court of D. João III, 1,337 may be classified as servants, but of these only three out of eight *varredores*, who swept the floors, were specifically described as being slaves: an improbably low figure.[82] There were more slaves than that in the households of D. João's brother, Luís, who owned some eleven blacks and Moors,[83] and of his queen, D. Catarina, who was the possessor of fifteen female and five male slaves.[84] It seems reasonable to suppose that a few hundred slaves worked as permanent maintenance staff in the royal palaces or as servants in the ambulatory household of the king and members of his family. Certainly there were too many slaves for the king and his family to supervise directly, so slaves were placed in the care of various court officials whom the slaves assisted in the performance of their duties.[85]

Slaves were thus found serving in various capacities at court. Each palace had a maintenance crew of sweepers and carpenters[86] among whom there were usually some black slaves working alongside free whites. Slaves also assisted the gardeners in the vegetable patches[87] and orchards[88] which supplied the palace kitchens, and they watched over the herds of cattle, sheep and goats which provided meat and milk for the great banquets.[89] There were slaves not only in the palace kitchens, but in the smaller kitchens set aside for the use of the various households.[90] A slave with special cooking skills might be highly prized, as was the confectioner named Domingos de Frorença (Florença?) whom D. João III gave as a present to his queen in 1526.[91] The stables were an important part of any ambulatory court,

Table 9. *Occupations in which blacks were involved in Lisbon during the 1550s*

Occupation	Total nos. (Oliveira)	in the trade (Brandão)	Nature of workforce (Brandão)	Estimated earnings (rs.) (Brandão)	Earnings per year (rs.)
washerwoman	324	1,500 blacks ⎫ 3,500 in all ⎭	black and white women	300 per week	15,600[a]
negras de canastra	—	1,000	black women	30 p.d.	8,100[b]
basket-carriers in fish and meat markets	—	100	black and white youths	40 p.d.	10,800[b]
whitewashers	52 women	50	black men and women	'much money'	—
charcoal: stevedores and sellers[c]	—	150–200	black and white men	up to 120–40 p.d., usually 100 p.d.	27,000[a,b]
negras do pote	41 women	1,000	black women	40 p.d.	10,800[b]
regateiras[d]					
rice	27	⎫	black and	150–200+	45,000[a,e]
couscous	23	⎬ 50	white	p.d.	
chickpeas	—	⎭	women, slave and free; also youths		
stewed prunes	—	50	black women	100–20 p.d.	30,000[e]
beans and *aletria*	28 (sellers of *aletria* only)	—	black women	up to 120–40 p.d., usually 100 p.d.	30,000[a]
olive oil	—	50	free and slave women	—	—
seafood	—	200	black women	—	—
old clothes and jumble at Rossio fair each week	—	50+	white, black and Moorish women	1,200 per fair	62,400[f]
workers on the waterfront	—	300+	black and white men	100 p.d.	27,000[a]
Total workers	495	6,500–6,650			

(Note: the *rice/couscous/chickpeas/stewed prunes/beans* group is bracketed as "200 in all".)

a. Not actually stated by Brandão, but calculated from his figures.
b. Said to be, or calculated from, a working year of 270 days.
c. Oliveira notes 39 *carvoeiros*, but these are probably charcoal burners.
d. Oliveira mentions 660 to 670 *regateiras* on the waterfront, 900 at the city gates.
e. Working year of 300 days, excluding Sundays.
f. Improbably high figures.

and there were no fewer than eighty-eight stable lads (*moços da estrebaria*) in D. João's household. Most stable lads were free whites or North African Muslim slaves with skill in horsemanship, but some blacks worked in the stables too.[92]

Many of the slaves in the royal households were domestic and body-servants, under the command of the stewards (*reposteiros, guarda-repostes*) or, in the queen's and princesses' households, the *guardas das damas* who enforced the almost Muslim seclusion in which the Portuguese kept their women.[93] These slaves appear to have been well treated and were employed in positions of trust. For instance, slaves frequently served in the apothecary's store, *botica*, which was part of every noble household.[94] Only in 1565 were slaves debarred from working in *boticas* in any capacity where they would be handling medicines.[95]

Women slaves in attendance upon the queen and princesses were treated almost as if they were free maids of honour. They wore clothes of the finest materials and apparently had several changes of clothing: when four slave women belonging to the Infanta D. Beatriz were transferred after their mistress's death in 1506 to Queen D. Leonor's care, two pack animals were needed to carry their belongings. Each of these slave women rode a mule, and they were accompanied by four muleteers, a stable lad and a chaperon in the form of a woman who baked bread. An esquire was in charge of the party, which must have resembled the progress of four high-born ladies.[96] As with her other ladies, the queen arranged marriages for her slave women. In 1556 Queen D. Catarina sent two of her slaves, Catarina da Cruz and Clemência, to be married off in Brazil; these two were probably white or mulatta, the colours held to be most attractive, but the queen may have married off her black women as well.[97]

Male slaves at court do not seem to have been so fortunate. Only one black man appears to have risen above the physical labour exacted from his brothers: D. João III's wise fool, João de Sá, known as Panasco. Panasco suffered a good many jests on the subject of his colour, but gave as good as he got. 'Happiness for a Portuguese cavalier', he asserted, 'consists of calling himself Vasconcelos, owning a country estate with 600,000 *rs.* in rents, and being simple-minded and good for nothing.' Born a slave in Portugal, he was freed later on, and D. João awarded him the habit of the order of Santiago, no small honour. Eventually, however, the strain of a life spent being treated merely as a laughing-stock seems to have told upon this witty, clever man, for in his old age he took to drink.[98]

In addition to serving at court and in the departments of state attached to it,[99] slaves were employed about the king's business in the Casa da Guiné e Índia and the complex of royal industries concerned with the production of the arms, ships and provisions essential for overseas trade and conquest. At the beginning of the sixteenth century each of the two treasurers (one for Guinea, one for India) at the Casa was allowed a staff of two freemen and two slaves to run errands and to shift the crates and bales of merchandise which the treasurers wanted to inspect. In the 1550s Brandão noted that the factor of the Casa had a staff of four freemen and two slaves, while the treasurer of India had two freemen and one slave. Each official received money from the crown to pay the wages and living allowances of his staff.[100]

The extent to which the king's own slaves worked in the royal industries poses a problem. There are, unfortunately, no records concerning the largest royal industry, the shipyards of the Ribeira das Naus on the riverside near the Casa da Guiné. Somewhat more is known about the arms and munitions factories. During the reigns of D. Manuel and D. João III the Casa da Pólvora, or powder-works, employed no more than two of the king's slaves, probably as sweepers, at any one time.[101] The naval foundry associated with the royal armoury certainly employed numbers of blacks during the reign of D. João II, for when Hieronymus Münzer visited it in 1494, 'There were so many blacks working at the forges that you might believe them to be Cyclops and the shop the cave of Vulcan.'[102] Whether all were the king's slaves is not certain. Some twenty years later, between 1517 and 1525, the almoxarife of the armoury was responsible for only five slaves belonging to the king.[103] If the slaves Münzer saw were not mostly on hire from their masters, but belonged to the crown, then the number of king's slaves employed at the foundry would seem to have decreased during the reign of D. Manuel.

Such a decrease occurred in another royal industry, the Fornos Reais, or Royal Ovens. Situated at Vale de Zebro, on the south bank of the Tagus (see Map 4, p. 73), they made ship's biscuit to provision the fleets sent overseas. During the reign of D. João II, from 1489 to 1496 to be precise, there were considerable numbers of slaves at the ovens: the almoxarife had in his charge no fewer than nineteen black men and women and eleven white slave women and their children.[104] Judging from later practice, the women would have been engaged in winnowing wheat and sifting flour while the men worked in the mill or kneaded dough and baked biscuit. Evidently the original plan was to run the industry almost entirely with slave labour, for the total workforce never greatly exceeded thirty people during the first third of the sixteenth century. By 1513, however, the number of king's slaves was down to a mere six men and one woman, all black, and remained at that level.[105] The male slaves were mainly employed in the mill, the woman was probably a cook. All the other tasks had been taken over by wage labourers and their indentured servants and black slaves. The hired slaves worked only at the less skilled jobs, carrying sacks of wheat, sawing and stacking firewood for the ovens, unloading hay for the carthorses. A few black slave women were hired to help the other women workers to winnow and sift. These black men and women received the same wages as other labourers: in 1526 a decision to lower the blacks' wages but not the whites' was shelved in favour of an over-all reduction in labourers' wages.[106] Since so few blacks were employed, very little money would have been saved by discriminating against them, and more drastic measures had to be taken. But the decision shows that a tendency towards discrimination did exist.[107]

While not conclusive, the evidence suggests that D. Manuel and D. João III limited the participation of their own slaves in royal industries, and favoured the employment of their free subjects instead. Furthermore, the more highly paid jobs went to free whites, rather than to freemen's slaves. This employment policy was probably a response to rapid population growth in the Lisbon area during these two reigns. Since much of the work in supplying the royal fleets was of an episodic nature, D. Manuel may well have decided to take advantage of the increased numbers of white labourers, who could be hired for the day or the week, rather than maintain a large, permanent staff of slaves. He may even have been moved by a concern to provide his white subjects with work, by substituting them for slaves whom he could sell at a profit abroad.

The place of slaves in the economy: conclusions

A striking feature which emerges from this study of the place of slaves in the economy is that no occupation was exclusively associated with slaves. While slaves may have been very common in certain branches of manual labour, they usually worked alongside free whites and thus may be considered as no more than an extension of the existing workforce. In the rural parish of Moncarapacho, for instance, where most of the working men must have been employed in agriculture, slaves constituted 10 per cent of the population, but 6 per cent was still composed of free *criados*. Furthermore, slaves were found not only on the estates of the nobility, but as servants in their courts as well, and service in the courts was definitely a preferred occupation for free whites.

This coexistence of slaves and free labourers in various sectors of the economy suggests that there was little to choose between free and slave labour in terms of flexibility. Sometimes the employment of free labour was actually more advantageous. For episodic work, as at Vale de Zebro, free labourers taken on as required were preferable to a permanent workforce of slaves, since the slaves cost a good deal to buy and had to be maintained whether there was work for them to do or not. Freemen, notably the *criados a bem fazer*, could also be profitably employed in long-term work: pay-rolls indicate that masters not only hired out *criados*, but could claim their entire wages as well.[108]

If slave labour did not automatically recommend itself over free, the reasons for the recourse to slaves must have been specifically related to the employers' preferences or to local economic conditions. Unfortunately, Portuguese masters have left almost no statements as to why they bought slaves, and conclusions are not easily drawn from the fragmentary demographic and occupational evidence at our disposal. The task is certainly not facilitated by the scarcity of secondary studies on wages, prices, unemployment and migratory labour. Any explanations of the employment of slave labour must accordingly be couched in general, and tentative, terms.

First of all, some men, particularly noblemen, bought slaves in order to be fashionable, as a matter of conspicuous consumption; black servants added a touch of exotic elegance to a palace or manor-house. But conspicuous consumption alone cannot account for the large numbers of slaves in Portugal. Secondly, some men may have preferred slaves to freemen, because slaves were more directly under the master's control and could be compelled to perform tasks which free labourers declined. A free woman was unlikely to see much point in hawking goods around the streets for her master's, rather than her own, benefit; and free servants seem to have rejected dirty work, as in the hospital of Todos-os-Santos. Thirdly, in some places, *criados a bem fazer* were scarce, and paid servants were more expensive than slaves.

As a rule, slaves would be cheaper and freemen more reluctant to accept dirty work only in those places where there was a shortage of free labour, that is, where the population density was low. This was particularly the case in the lands in the valley of the Tagus and to the south, which were called upon to increase their agricultural production to provision the growing cities and the fleets bound for overseas. Here, as Clenardus remarked, slaves were everywhere, and he then suggested why this was so: free labourers were hard to find, demanded high wages and rejected menial labour.[109] The labour shortage affected both the towns and the countryside, as is evident from Elvas's attempts to find herdsmen and from the difficulties encountered by Elvas and Évora when they tried to dispense with slave *regateiras*. Hence men turned to slaves to perform the tasks elsewhere entrusted to freemen. The southern nobility employed slaves on their estates and also in their palaces, since there may not have been enough free servants to swell retinues to the desired size.

Of course, at least as far as agriculture was concerned, the demand for slaves varied in different parts of the southern provinces according to local conditions and the availability of other forms of labour. The coastal Algarve's need for slaves was especially pressing, since its irrigated fields required year-round attention and were far away from Beira, the source of the migrant labourers called *ratinhos*. In most of the Alentejo, on the other hand, only one crop could be raised a year, and labour was therefore more seasonal. A large gang of slaves would be idle or underemployed for much of the time, unless they were found something else to do. For instance, the slaves from country districts who were sent to work in the salt-pans of the Sado were probably filling in slack periods during the agricultural year. Some landowners may therefore have preferred to own a few slaves and have recourse at harvest time to *ratinhos* from nearby Beira; this would explain why *ratinhos* were found in the Alentejo.[110] The presence of large numbers of slaves in the country towns of the Tagus valley was probably due to the proximity of Lisbon, which drew off freemen but demanded a constant supply of produce from market gardens and the fertile fields of the *lezírias* (water-meadows).

Whatever the local variations in the demand for, and consequently in the density of, the slave population, there were enough slaves in the Algarve and the Alentejo to diminish the south's attractiveness to free labour. In the Algarve, Romero Magalhães has shown that the extensive use of slave labour kept free wages down, while in the Alentejo manual labour took on the stigma of servility. The council of Elvas, for instance, wished to try and punish wage labourers suspected of petty theft in the same summary way as slaves.[111] Unpleasant working conditions led to an outflow of native Algarvians and Alentejans to Lisbon and overseas, leaving their places to be filled by migrant labourers and slaves.[112] Thus to some extent the employment of slaves in the southern provinces created a self-perpetuating demand.

Slaves were much less common north of the valley of the Tagus. Some worked on farms in the coastal belt as far north as Coimbra, probably because the work was unattractive to freemen who could easily go to Lisbon. In the overpopulated regions of Entre-Douro-e-Minho and inland Beira, landlords had little difficulty in obtaining agricultural labour at low wages and thus had no need for slaves.[113] The presence of a few slaves in larger centres of population may be attributed to conspicuous consumption on the part of noble and wealthy masters.

Lisbon presents a special case. By far the largest city in the kingdom, with an assured supply of migrant free labour, it was nonetheless home to a very large number of slaves. If Oliveira's figures are accepted as substantially accurate,[114] then in the middle of the sixteenth century Lisbon was a city of 100,000 inhabitants, including 9,950 slaves and some 2,500 unemployed – namely 2,000 women 'without trades' and 552 men described simply as 'poor'. Brandão also speaks of 1,000–2,000 beggars.[115] Slaves do seem to have put freemen out of work; certainly the level of unemployment among women (15.3 per cent), who were engaged in the same sort of domestic labour as many slaves were, was far higher than that among men (3.7 per cent). But if all the slaves were removed and all the unemployed or beggars given work, some 7,400 jobs would have gone unfilled. In other words, slaves made up for a definite shortage of labour, though there were somewhat more of them than necessary. Since most slaves performed a useful economic role, very few sections of the working population objected to their presence in the city. By 1572 only eight of the 105 guilds had limited or excluded the employment of slaves and these guilds were either very small, very prestigious, or justifiably mistrustful of slaves' reliability.[116]

Annual unemployment figures do not exist for the fifteenth and early sixteenth centuries, so there is no ready test for determining whether some of the city's slaves were always superfluous to requirements or not. But it is possible to construct, by way of hypothesis, a picture of the evolution of the Lisbon labour market which synthesizes the known facts. From the reign of D. Afonso V, as Lisbon grew on the wealth first from Africa and then from India, a demand for labour was created which could not be met by natural increase of the city's population or by immigrant labour from the countryside. The manpower problem was doubtless aggravated by the drain of people to conquer and settle the empire. Therefore Lisbon needed slave labour, and in the early years of the sixteenth century slaves were a good bargain, the price of a slave – 5,000–8,000 rs. – being equivalent to or less than a year's wages for a manual labourer. But a turning-point was reached about the middle years of the century. By that time, population growth in the Portuguese countryside could produce a more than adequate supply of free labour for Lisbon.[117] So much is indicated by the stagnation of manual labourers' wages, which had hardly increased since the beginning of the century, and by the fact that, as Brandão observed, employing a free maidservant was cheaper than employing a slave. Thus, he said, only wealthy men owned slaves; poorer folk made do with hired girls and commercial washerwomen.[118]

At a time when the free population was expanding, the continued employment of slaves for reasons of convenience, prestige or profit could only cause unemployment to rise, especially among the ranks of unskilled working men (hence the few complaints from the guilds). This would explain the level of unemployment noted by Oliveira in the 1550s, the increasingly frequent re-enactment of the vagrancy laws and the spate of complaints, beginning with the petitioners of 1562, against the importation of slaves. From the mid-sixteenth century onwards, emigration was a response to the lack of opportunities available for freemen in Lisbon and, given the overpopulation of the north and the poor working conditions in the south, probably in Portugal as a whole. Slavery might have created a self-perpetuating demand in the south, but that demand, taken within the context of the entire Portuguese economy, simply exacerbated the shortage of jobs for freemen.

5

The life of the slave

In many respects the life of black slaves resembled that of the white lower classes. Blacks dressed, ate and worked in much the same way as whites, were taught to speak the same language and answered to the same Christian names. They were expected to conform to the same legal, religious and moral codes. Subjection to a master did not differentiate slaves so clearly from white commoners as might be imagined. Many members of the lower classes were subject to a master and depended upon him for their food, lodging, clothing and medical care. Furthermore, the master's powers of corporal punishment extended over all persons in his household. Even wages did not constitute a clear distinction between free labourers and slaves, because some white servants did not serve for money and some slaves could keep a little of the money they earned in the streets.

Rather than subjection *per se*, it was the degree of subjection that distinguished slaves from free servants. Slaves were servants for life: unless sold or freed, they could not leave their master for a new one. This was because, by law, they were their master's possessions. The legal implications of this status will be considered more fully in the next chapter, but as far as the daily life of slaves was concerned, it meant that their bodies were far more under their masters' control, and more open to physical and sexual abuse, than those of free servants were.

Their African cultural inheritance further distinguished black slaves from white commoners. Although not, perhaps, as completely as in Brazil, elements of African culture survived in Portugal and influenced blacks' adjustment to European civilization. Many blacks spoke a form of Portuguese whose morphology and syntax had been amended to suit people accustomed to African languages. African music and dances flourished at the slaves' own gatherings and were performed by blacks at Portuguese festivities. Together with the disabilities of servile status, this amalgamation of African and European culture gave a characteristic tenor to the daily life of black slaves and set them apart as a community distinct from lower-class white society.

Baptism and slave children

Black slaves imported from Africa were supposed to be baptized when they entered Portugal or shortly thereafter; those who were born in the country were supposed to be baptized in their local parish church. Of course, some adult slaves preferred to remain infidels, and some masters took no steps to encourage Christianity amongst their bondsmen. All the same, most black slaves, both children and adults, probably became at least nominal Christians. Their names were entered in the baptismal registers together with those of free children.

The slave's Christian name usually seems to have been chosen by his owner. Although slaves might acquire a nickname,[1] very few of their baptismal names were at all out of the ordinary, nor did they serve to hold the slave up to ridicule.[2] For instance, of a group of five male slaves purchased for Queen Catarina in 1550, four received the name António and one Fernando, while four women bought at the same time were all named Maria.[3] One of the master's own names might become the name of his or her slave: thus the daughter of Catarina, a slave belonging to one Guiomar Silveira, received the name of Guiomar, and a slave child was christened Afonso after his mother's owner, Maria Afonso. Occasionally slave parents were conceded the right to name their own children. Thus a slave child born in Olivença in 1562 was named Juliana, after her aunt, Juliana Pires.[4] Slaves' surnames were seldom recorded; when they appear, the name is frequently that of the master.[5]

Baptized slaves always had godparents, though the number allowed varied according to the diocese.[6] While there are some instances of blacks, both slave and free, standing in this capacity,[7] godparents were usually white. Sometimes they were relatives of the master,[8] but more often they were simply friends of the master or the slave. Although the master might allow a slave's child to have the same godparents as his own son,[9] for the master himself to stand as a godparent was extremely rare. A point of social status may have been involved here, because it was equally rare for a slave to have a member of the gentry as a godparent.[10] Godparents were mainly people from the lower classes: tradesmen and their wives, or servants. In some towns kindly widows who liked children became godmother to more than one slave child[11] and, as with white children, the midwife frequently assumed responsibility for the religious education of the child she had delivered.

Most slave children were born out of wedlock. So much is clear from the parish registers, where the priest made a note concerning the child's illegitimacy[12] or merely gave the mother's name, without mentioning the father's. Very occasionally the father was indicated, if he was another slave or a lower-class white man; but masters were never named in this capacity. The omission of the father's name may have been due to simple lack of concern on the part of the priest, genuine ignorance, or the reluctance of married men to admit adultery to a priest or to a jealous wife who could take steps to end the liaison. António Carneiro, for instance, who was the king's secretary between 1509 and 1522, appears to have fathered a child upon a black slave woman, whom his wife promptly sent to Málaga to be sold. (That was not the end of the story. The woman's new master wrote to Carneiro when the child was about three years old and said that various Portuguese had remarked upon the striking resemblance between the secretary and the boy – who had been called Juan Antonio Carnero accordingly!)[13]

White fathers who for some reason could not afford to acknowledge their slave offspring sometimes found ways of retaining an indirect connexion with them. Every now and then slips of the priest's pen suggest that a father who was not officially recognized as such would stand as godfather to his own child. Of course, such evidence is not conclusive. More convincing is the concern shown by a *cavaleiro fidalgo* named Francisco de Lemos for a child of a mulatta woman whom he did not own. His paternity of the child is uncertain, for he did not declare it openly. Nonetheless, he bought the mother's freedom from her master and provided generously in his will for both her and her boy, whom he ordered to be taught to read and write.[14]

A very few masters not only recognized their children by slave mistresses, but went on to obtain decrees of legitimation for them from the crown. The masters who did so were mainly clerics or members of the gentry, wealthy men who wanted an heir of their own flesh, regardless of colour.[15] The birth of these children was obviously a time for rejoicing, but Clenardus noted that in most houses the birth of a slave child was greeted warmly. Whether or not he was the father, the master of the household often became fond of his slaves' children, and affection for a slave born or brought up in the house was frequently cited as a cause for manumission.

To be sure, the birth of a slave child might be welcomed solely for pecuniary reasons. Clenardus also observed that some masters made a considerable profit from the sale of home-born slaves and that they encouraged their slave women to lie with healthy black slaves, rather than – an anti-clerical gibe – with the parish priest. He likened these masters to pigeon breeders or owners of stud farms.[16] Giambattista Venturino, who visited Portugal in 1571, came to a similar conclusion about the role of women slaves in the duke of Bragança's palace at Vila Viçosa. They were treated, he said, 'as herds of horses in Italy are', the object being to produce as many offspring as possible for sale at 30–40 scudi each. Nor was the practice perhaps uncommon: Venturino asserted that there were 'many of these flocks of women in Portugal and the Indies'.[17] In the absence of detailed quantitative evidence the allegations are hard to prove,[18] and it may be that the two foreign observers mistook the casual sexuality of a slave-owning society for an organized commercial enterprise.[19] Still, there was nothing to prevent masters from raising slave children for sale. While the Portuguese customarily sold slave women together with children at the breast, no law forbade the separation of mothers and older children. Transactions which divided slave families are known to have occurred from the time of the first large landing of slaves at Lagos.[20]

Clothing

Black slaves in Portugal wore European clothing. Quite apart from the fact that the Portuguese held that such clothing was necessary if a slave was to lead a proper Christian life,[21] slaves needed warm clothing if they were to survive the Portuguese winter, which can be unpleasantly cold.[22] What slaves wore depended on what they did and who their master was. To be sure, as Zurara noticed, blacks and Idzāgen preferred bright colours: if the clothes provided for them were dull they picked up brightly coloured rags and stitched them to their garments.[23] Masters, of course, were not bound by their slaves' wishes, and work clothes for menial servants have tended to be drab in all ages. Some slaves of the nobility and the crown had the opportunity to wear brilliant livery, but even at court men's clothing was often sombre.[24]

There is very little information concerning the dress of slaves not belonging to the crown. An early sixteenth-century illumination, which portrays a prosperous merchant and his family seated at table and being waited on by one black slave while another stands with a bowl in the kitchen, indicates that male slaves wore much the same clothes as lower-class whites: a shirt, covered by a knee-length smock. The slaves in the picture do not wear shoes (see Plate 3). Styles changed over the years, and when a commoner's black slave was admitted to hospital in Oporto in 1596 he was wearing a cap (*carapuça*), a shirt, knee breeches (*calções*) of coarse burel – but still no shoes.[25] Throughout the century women slaves' clothes probably resembled the cook's in the early illumination: a long dress and a shawl or headscarf.

Since a noble acquired prestige from the number and appearance of his followers, free or slave, he made sure that they could be recognized by dressing them in livery. When he died, they received mourning clothing, sometimes no more than a black hood and cape.[26] Institutions such as the Hospital de Todos-os-Santos also dressed their slaves in livery. The hospital at Caldas even provided its slaves with a suit of Sunday best in which to go to church.[27]

The fullest descriptions of slaves' apparel are found in royal accounts and clothing orders, which show that the attire of the crown's slaves varied according to their occupation and place of employment. Heavy manual labour in a royal industry necessitated sturdy work clothes, such as those worn by slaves at the Royal Ovens at Vale de Zebro in the first quarter of the sixteenth century.[28] These clothes were provided by the *almoxarife* of the ovens, who bought up poor quality cloth in bulk and had it made into garments by the local tailor. The slaves in the *almoxarife*'s care received their main suit of clothes in autumn or winter, when clothes were most needed, though minor articles such as shoes and belts were replaced throughout the year, as they wore out. The male slaves wore shirts made of canvas, *fustão* (a mixture of cotton and wool), *estopa* (a material of unwashed wool) or the like. Over the shirt was worn a doublet, often made of burel. Only one clothing order mentions the wearing of *calças*, the long hose so typical of mediaeval and Renaissance fashion;[29] most others refer to *calções* or *calças bragas*, which were probably 'whole hose': breeches and stockings sewn together.[30] Shoes were made from cow leather but must have been quite thin, for the slaves who worked in the mill wore them out every three months or so. At Vale de Zebro the mill slaves also wore a smock (*camisão*) made of white or off-white cloth which would not show the flour marks; the miller, a freeman, had a work suit of the same material. In cold weather the slaves wore white caps with ear flaps (*carapuças de orelhas*) and a variety of jerkins called by different names – *cotões com mangas, pelotes, jaquetas* – but all probably more or less the same. The senior slaves were issued with capes as well.[31] Only one woman slave worked full time at the ovens, and her clothing consisted of a blouse of *estopa* or *fustão* and a long dress (*sainho*) made of coloured cloth, taken in with a belt at the waist. She covered her head with a headscarf, in West African style (see Plate 4), or with a *beatilha*, a cloth in the form of a nun's veil. In 1514 the *almoxarife* issued her shoes with wooden soles whose upper part could be replaced when worn out, but later she wore leather shoes, as the men did. By 1526 she also had a white smock (*brial*) to work in.

Whereas the clothes worn by the slaves at Vale de Zebro were usually made out of Portuguese cloth, the clothing of slaves at court was made out of both domestic and imported fabrics. To take the court of D. João II, for instance (and slaves at the courts of D. Manuel and D. João III wore much the same garments),[32] sweepers wore shirts of *estopa*, domestic linen or other Portuguese cloth and doublets of black *fustão*, but hose, jerkins and hoods of thick woollen Bristol cloth or black *antona* (from Southampton).[33] Their outer garments, such as capes with or without hoods, were made of the same material as their hose and jerkins.[34] As opposed to the slaves at Vale de Zebro, who often wore white, undyed cloth, the male slaves at court wore black, according to the fashion there. The women slaves probably wore brighter colours, but the clothing orders normally mention only the types of materials used, which were the same as those used in clothing the men: *estopa* or domestic cloth for blouses and *antona*, *palmilha*, Bristol or Irish cloth for underpants, dress and belt or girdle.[35] Clothing orders for slaves at the courts of later monarchs normally indicate only the cost of the cloth, rather than its nature, but most slaves' garments continued to be made of relatively cheap material, whether foreign or domestic.

Naturally, there were some exceptions. Slaves who performed responsible duties or who were highly visible at public functions wore clothes whose opulence reflected favourably upon their royal master. For instance, the black crier who worked in the Royal Treasury in 1493 was distinguished from his less important companions by having shirts of Breton linen, a doublet made of camlet and a black bonnet (*barrete*).[36] The best-dressed slaves of all seem to have been the women in attendance upon the queen and her ladies. In 1551 one of these slaves, a black woman called Maria de Noronha, wore a long dress made of sandy-coloured Perpignan cloth over which she slipped a bodice or doublet (*gibão*) of black camlet, and covered her head with a small mantilla which matched her dress. She also had a green *vasquinha*, a long dress taken in with many pleats at the waist, which could be worn over all her other clothing. When going outside she wore a blue hooded cape and a hat, both decorated with black ribbons, and on cold days she draped a heavy mantle over her shoulders.[37]

In all these cases the slaves wore clothing more or less equivalent to that of free whites engaged in the same work. Their clothing was likewise subject to the restrictions of the sumptuary laws, which were principally concerned with the wearing of silks.[38] These laws were strictly enforced: in 1548 and 1549 two slaves were arrested, one for wearing an old hat with a taffeta lining, the other for wearing satin knee breeches, also lined with taffeta.[39] Indeed, the silken liveries of slaves serving masters enlisted in D. Sebastião's fatal expedition to Morocco in 1578 were commented upon with some surprise as departures from the norm.[40]

Even under these laws the cost of dressing a slave varied considerably, since the range of fabrics permitted to be worn was still quite large. The simple work clothes worn by male and female slaves at Vale de Zebro cost the *almoxarife* 700–1,000 *rs.* per slave every year, excluding any outlays on heavy overclothes. Despite the inflation of prices, these simple clothes did not have to cost considerably more in the mid-sixteenth century, for in 1553 the clothes of a male slave who served the queen's ladies cost only 1,410 *rs.*[41] Nonetheless, most male slaves at court sported outfits which cost at least twice as much, apparently because of the higher cost of imported cloth. For instance, in 1535 a suit of clothes (without a cape) for a sweeper cost 2,360 *rs.* In the 1550s a full suit of clothes for a male slave at court might be worth anything from 3,000 to 4,497 *rs.*,[42] but the usual sum seems to have been the 3,640 *rs.* it cost to outfit two slaves who served in the queen's stables. A cape cost some 2,000 *rs.* more.[43] Unfortunately, far less is known about the price of court dresses for women slaves. All that can be said is that in the 1550s the garments of a woman who cooked for the shepherds at the Paços da Serra cost 2,112 *rs.*,[44] while

Maria de Noronha's splendid outfit required an outlay of 6,680 *rs*. To sum up: the annual expenditure on a slave's clothes might represent a third to a half of the original purchase price of the slave, though simple work clothes cost much less.

Shelter

Although it is probable that most masters kept their slaves in fairly close proximity to themselves, some allowed their slaves to lodge elsewhere. One slave who lived apart from his master on a farm near Tavira in 1472 was said to be 'guarded by God', but many men doubted such slaves' honesty and eventually the authorities came to the conclusion that God's care was not enough.[45] In various places legislation (considered at greater length below; see p. 124) was enacted to prevent slaves living on their own without supervision. One response, found in Moncarapacho, was to allow a slave to live in a completely separate house with an indentured servant, technically a freeman.[46] Most masters, however, lodged their slaves in quarters in or adjoining their own home. At Vale de Zebro, for example, the slaves were housed in the *almoxarife* or *provedor*'s dwellings, though sometimes the slaves who worked in the mill spent the night there.

Once again, royal accounts and clothing orders provide most of what is known about sleeping accommodation for slaves. At Vale de Zebro, the slaves slept on beds made of pine boards. In 1526 each bed had a canvas mattress stuffed with straw, two coverings made of burel and two blankets (*mantas da terra*), costing 1,216 *rs*. in all. Except for the woman, the slaves slept more than one to a bed, as was common among the poor and servants.[47] Even at court slaves, including the queen's attendants, often slept two to a bed, though not all did.[48] The sleeping arrangements for court slaves, however, were more comfortable than those at Vale de Zebro and cost considerably more. In 1554 the bed of two of the queen's sweepers cost no less than 5,040 *rs*. Although this bed was made up on a reed mat on the ground, it had a wool-stuffed mattress, sheets of Brabant cloth, a shaggy wool blanket, a striped Alentejan blanket and a bolster.[49]

The better-off and more considerate masters probably gave their slaves similar accommodation, but sleeping arrangements for slaves could be very poor indeed. In 1537 Clenardus took his three slaves with him when he travelled from Évora to Braga and remarked upon the various conditions they encountered. On the first night out, he says, 'My slaves, who at home were accustomed to soft beds [*stratis mollibus*], at length inquired of the innkeeper where they were to sleep and were compelled to spend the night upon a mat.' The next night, at Montargil, was worse: Clenardus slept on his baggage while the slaves slept under the stars. Happily for all four, they found better inns after they had crossed the Tagus.[50]

Food

Clenardus delighted in amusing his humanist friends with tales of the uncouth dreadfulness of Portugal; hence his comment that some masters fed their slaves upon hunger may not have been wholly serious.[51] Yet there may have been more to it than mere banter. A law of 1538 which forbade slaves to beg, whether they had their masters' consent or not, suggests that masters existed who could not or would not feed their slaves properly.[52] This hypothesis is supported by frequent complaints that slaves stole grapes, fruit and other food; evidently some slaves not only had to beg but to steal in order to get enough to eat.

At least royal and institutional masters assumed the responsibility of maintaining their slaves in food. The charity hospital of Todos-os-Santos in Lisbon gave the same meal to all its staff, slave or free. All ate together in the hospital refectory, where stories from the lives of the saints were read to them during the course of the meal. There were only two meals a day, as was customary in Portugal at this time, but the helpings were generous: about half a kilogram of bread and half a litre of wine at a sitting, and a ration of about a third of a kilogram of meat and the same amount of fish a day.[53]

The account-books of Vale de Zebro show how much it cost to feed a slave in this way.[54] In 1514 the *almoxarife* received 5 *rs.* every day to provide food for each of the seven slaves in his care. Since the slaves also had a wheat allowance, the total 35 *rs.* would have been spent on meat, fish and vegetables. In 1515 a whole lamb or kid could be bought for 25–30 *rs.*, so the slaves may have eaten fairly well, provided the *almoxarife* did not embezzle the funds. A slave's allowance of 1.31 kilograms of wheat a day would have cost between 2 and 4 *rs.*, according to the price of wheat at the time.[55] In addition, four slaves who worked in the mill each received half a *canada*, that is, three quarters of a litre, of wine a day; this portion cost 3 *rs*. Thus the basic cost of feeding a slave at the Royal Ovens ranged from 7 to 9 *rs*. a day, and up to 12 *rs*. if wine was included. Royal orders from the first third of the sixteenth century confirm that 7, 10 or 12 *rs*. were commonly allocated to provide a day's meals for a slave,[56] the same as for some free servants.[57] Later allocations were higher, as inflation affected the economy. In 1537, for instance, the daily ration for a slave who worked in the royal *Tapeçaria*, or carpet-works, cost 20 *rs*.[58]

The diet of slaves at Todos-os-Santos and Vale de Zebro was healthy, and quite sufficient to maintain a slave employed in hard physical labour. The slaves and servants at Todos-os-Santos each consumed 6,871 calories a day, mostly bread, but with a good balance of protein from meat and fish. And at both the hospital and the Royal Ovens, the yearly wheat allowances per slave, of 420 and 487.2 kilograms respectively, were more than double the 200 kilograms which Braudel has estimated were the yearly average consumption of a person living in the Mediterranean area.[59]

As the royal account-books show, maintaining a slave properly even in the essentials of food, clothing and bedding cost a fair sum. At Vale de Zebro, the annual outlay in the early sixteenth century on a slave's food and clothing ran from about 3,250 to about 5,400 *rs*., and a bed for two slaves cost 1,216 *rs*. All these prices had risen, perhaps doubled in the case of food, by mid-century. Consequently it is easy to understand why a master who maintained his slaves in the royal manner should seek to find them employment – that is, if he thought of slaves as a commercial investment, rather than as status symbols. To keep a slave like Maria de Noronha, who earned no money for her mistress but whose expenses must have run to about 20,000 *rs*. a year, was clearly an exercise in conspicuous consumption.

Language and education

Slaves received not only food and clothing from their masters, but a new language as well. Most blacks learned Portuguese in Portugal, though some may have been familiar with a form of it as a trade language in their western African homeland. As with any group of people learning a foreign tongue, levels of competence varied: there were blacks who had little or no standard Portuguese and, at the other end of the scale, blacks who, having been born in Portugal or having spent a long time there, could not only speak, but read and write standard Portuguese as well.

The lowest level of competence was represented by the blacks described as *boçal*.[60] This word, if anything like the Castilian *bozal*, meant 'a black who could only speak an African language'.[61] The term is fairly rare in documentary descriptions of slaves, as is only to be expected, since a slave was unlikely to escape his master's wrath for long if he did not know a modicum of Portuguese. Nonetheless, in 1568 the number of slaves who did not yet speak the language fluently was sufficient for the archbishop of Lisbon to recognize that an interpreter might be needed by priests administering the last rites to dying slaves.[62]

Interpreters may also have been needed because the speech of some blacks who were not *boçal*, but had spent a long enough time in Portugal to gain a moderate linguistic proficiency, was not readily understood by educated churchmen and other whites.[63] In 1553, for instance, the inquisitors of Lisbon had to call in a Wolof interpreter, for they could not understand the way a Wolof defendant spoke Portuguese, even though he had lived in the city for five years. Fourteen years later, the speech of a black cook at the Jesuit house of São Fins was reported to be almost incomprehensible, though he too apparently spoke Portuguese.[64]

According to João de Barros, such difficulties arose because blacks simply 'barbarized' the language.[65] There is, however, strong evidence to suggest that in fact many of them spoke a non-standard, if fairly regular, Africanized form of Portuguese which whites did not always find easy to comprehend. Certainly from 1455 onwards black characters in poems and plays were presented as altering the sounds and constructions of standard Portuguese in a distinctive and reasonably consistent way. This manner of speaking was referred to as *fala de Guiné* or *fala dos negros*, that is, 'Guinea-speech' or 'black-speech'. Castilian authors also portray blacks as speaking a similar form of Portuguese, a parallelism which (discounting literary plagiarism) indicates that such a language actually existed.[66] If Castilians had merely wished to make blacks speak in a comic manner, there seems no reason why they did not make them speak a form of Castilian instead.[67] Besides this, the most important evidence in favour of the belief that the *fala de Guiné* of literature accurately reflected the speech patterns of blacks in Portugal is its strong morphological and syntactical resemblance to Portuguese-based creole tongues spoken by blacks in West Africa and the offshore islands today.

Standard Portuguese grammar is simplified in both *fala de Guiné* and in the black creole tongues; for instance, uninflected infinitives do much of the work of other tenses; *a mi* (me) replaces *eu* (I); gender and number go by the board, and possession is frequently indicated by simple juxtaposition of owner and thing owned. Furthermore, pronunciation is altered to make words easier for black Africans to say: final consonants, especially r, s and l, are often omitted, but may be retained by the addition of a final vowel; consonants in clusters also seem to pose problems which are avoided by reducing the cluster to one consonant only or by inserting a vowel between the consonants; v is sometimes replaced by b, while there is confusion of r and l, and d and r sounds; diphthongs are simplified, and there is even more omission of syllables than in normal Portuguese speech.[68] Many of these features can be found in the following passage in *fala de Guiné* from Gil Vicente's *Clerigo da Beyra* of 1527; a translation into standard Portuguese is provided for comparison.[69]

Fala de Guiné	*Standard Portuguese*
Elle rize: – 'Porque boso nam guarday	Ele diz: – 'Porque não guardais vós
rinheyro que boso bebee?'	o dinheiro que vós bebeis?'
Jeju, Jeju! moladeyro	Jesu, Jesu! o esmoler
'sa riabo aquella home!	é o diabo aquele homem!
Quando a mi morê da fome	Quando eu morrer de fome
nunca busucay sua rinheyro.	[or, correctly, Se eu morresse de fome]
	não buscaria o seu dinheiro.

He says: – 'Why do you not save / the money you drink away?' / Jesus, Jesus! the almoner, / that man is the devil! / If I were dying of hunger / I would not seek his money.

There is some question of where this black form of Portuguese actually originated. Some scholars of linguistics believe that it developed on the west coast of Africa as a trading language to facilitate contacts between Portuguese and blacks. More recently, others have suggested that it was a simplified form of Portuguese taught to African interpreters and other blacks in Portugal itself.[70] Unfortunately, there is still not enough evidence to confirm or disprove any theory of evolution. Nonetheless, as far as Portugal is concerned, *fala de Guiné* could maintain or develop reasonably consistent rules only in those places with large slave populations: primarily the cities, with which the authors who reported the language were most familiar. This in turn suggests that *fala de Guiné* should be viewed as a hybrid language peculiar to an urban, alien minority not yet fully integrated into the surrounding society.[71]

Blacks who from birth and upbringing in Portugal or simple isolation from other blacks were more thoroughly conversant with Portuguese culture were more likely to speak fluent Portuguese. But in the middle of the sixteenth century these fluent speakers were still few enough in number to be designated by a special word. They were called *ladinhos*, the term also used for Moors who could speak Portuguese well: João Pinto, a religious fanatic who denounced several of his fellow slaves to the Inquisition, was described as an 'homem preto ladinho'.[72] The effect of upbringing was most clearly apparent in the case of mulattoes, who often seem to have been fluent speakers. When a mulatto character appeared on stage he did not speak *fala de Guiné*,[73] while in real life the mulatto playwright Afonso Álvares spoke, wrote and taught Portuguese, and knew Castilian besides. Álvares never used *fala de Guiné* in his plays, though he did present Moors speaking a simplified form of Portuguese.[74]

The number of blacks, free or slave, who could write their own names, let alone plays, must have been very small. Nonetheless, the Inquisition records show that there were a few who rather than simply making their mark actually signed their depositions. João Pinto, for instance, had a rather flashy signature. He also claimed to be able to read a Book of Hours in his possession.[75] No law forbade teaching slaves to read or write, and the Portuguese did not think that black men were inherently uneducable, or else they would not have undertaken to educate the sons of the Kongolese nobility (see below, p. 157). But most slaves did not have to be literate to perform their work, so most masters did not bother to teach them, though they might not oppose the slaves' picking up some learning by themselves.[76]

One master who did educate his slaves (but not, perhaps, in reading and writing) was Clenardus, who taught Latin to his three black slaves so that they could assist him in his school in Évora. As Clenardus himself never learned to speak Portuguese well, his method of teaching corresponded to the modern system of total immersion in a language. He spoke to his class entirely in Latin, and in the early stages one of his blacks mimed actions corresponding to his master's commands. Later on, he would ask the slaves simple questions in Latin to which they would reply (though not always in perfect accordance with the grammatical rules of Priscian).[77] When he came to write a Latin grammar, he included these dialogues and entitled the book the *Grammatica Aethiopica* in honour of his assistants. Since his method gave rapid results,[78] in the summer of 1537 he was called to Braga to found another Latin school there. Among its two hundred pupils, he noticed some black faces among the white: perhaps black slaves of white pupils, perhaps free blacks, he does not say.[79]

Sexual relations and marriage

Black slave women could expect no effective legal protection against sexual assault. Although the statutory punishment for raping any woman was death, royal consent was required before sentence could be executed upon a man convicted of raping a slave woman or a prostitute. Given a law which virtually assumed that slave women were common whores, magistrates were unlikely to give much attention to complaints lodged by slave women.[80] Even the law forbidding sexual intercourse between Christians and unbelievers was not enforced when a Christian master raped or seduced an infidel slave.[81]

Among slave women, blacks were held to be the least desirable. Only white, that is, Moorish, women slaves were considered so attractive that a master might want to keep them exclusively for himself. After 1521 a master could sue any man who seduced a white woman slave who had been guarded as if she were a free woman of the master's family; the law said nothing at all about blacks.[82] Similarly, the episcopal constitutions of Évora and Lisbon only forbade priests to possess white women slaves. Evidently the bishops did not believe that black women were beautiful enough to lead their priests into temptation.[83]

Be that as it may, negroid women did not escape the attention of white philanderers. Perhaps mulattas, being lighter-skinned, were the most sought after, as is indicated in the prose plays of Jorge Ferreira de Vasconcellos (fl. 1535–55),[84] but the charms of black women were not neglected. Indeed, some men seem to have become sexually fixated upon black women, to the exclusion of whites. One such was Álvaro Afonso, the *inquiridor* of Serpa in the Alentejo during the reign of D. Manuel. Although Afonso was entrusted with making inquiries into the state of crown lands and rights, his obsessive longing for black women interfered with the execution of his duties. If a black woman happened to pass by the chamber where he was listening to testimony, he would rush out after her, and when he returned was so tired (from his exertions?) that he would sign the deposition without reading it – that is, when he did not fall asleep and let the notary sign for him. After a day of remarkable silliness, when he capered around the town square wearing a dunce's cap and blowing on his rod of office as if it were a flute, he absconded to Castile with a black woman, leaving his wife and children behind.

Afonso was cashiered in 1520, probably more for dereliction of duty than for his love of black women.[85] There is no evidence that any white man suffered for his affairs with blacks. The Portuguese generally regarded white men lusting after black women as no more than a joke, as witness Gil Vicente's plays which twitted unfaithful husbands[86] and the gentry in the audience for their amours with black women.[87] But the law dealt more seriously with black women who had responded to white adulterers' attentions. In Vila Nova de Portimão a slave named Inês was sentenced to twenty lashes at the *pelourinho* for having had an affair with a married man called João Fernandes. Luckily for Inês, her master obtained a royal pardon for her after squaring the matter with Fernandes's wife. Few slave women, however, had masters who were willing to pay 4,000 *rs.* for a pardon.[88]

Vicente may also have thought that the amorous designs of the black men whom he depicted lusting after white women were amusing because the blacks had no hope of obtaining satisfaction.[89] If he did, he was mistaken. In the later sixteenth century, the crown prosecutor of Oporto noted a paternity suit which a white girl had filed against a white youth, who bought her off with a promise of 650 *rs.* The youth refused to pay, though, when he saw the child: a little mulatta girl with curly hair.[90] Landi, too, knew a merchant and his wife in Évora who both obtained sexual satisfaction from black slaves.[91] Vicente's laughable impossibility became so possible, in fact, that by 1617 there was a law on the books in Elvas which forbade any free white woman to have a male slave for a friend, and expressly forbade her to welcome him in her house, night or day.[92]

A few interracial marriages did occur between people of free status (see p. 146), but whites and blacks usually found their spouses within their own distinct racial communities. Marriages between slaves and between slaves and freedmen were recognized by the Catholic Church,[93] and records of such marriages are found in the parish registers of most of the larger slave-owning centres.[94] Since the number of slaves in any one household was generally small, slaves often found their partners among the slaves belonging to another master. In these cases, the slave spouses seem to have been allowed to visit each other on occasional nights.[95] The same visiting rights presumably applied when a slave was married to a freedman.[96] Both whites and blacks witnessed the weddings. Most of those whose names were written down by the priest were white and lower-class friends of the black couple or relatives and friends of the master. The master himself was often not present.

Despite these instances, the number of marriages between slaves during the greater part of the period under study was not commensurate with the size of the slave population. Liaisons between slaves were normally casual affairs, though some slaves formalized their union by exchanging vows without a church ceremony. These common-law marriages (*casamentos a furto* or *de pública fama*) were popularly held to be binding.[97] Eventually, inspired by the Council of Trent, the bishop and chapter of Lisbon decided to find out why so few slaves married in church. Their investigations showed that some slave couples were unaware that they could marry with benefit of clergy, but that most had been forbidden to do so by their masters. The bishop therefore decreed that slaves who knew the fundamentals of the Christian religion could lawfully marry even if their masters opposed the union. Furthermore, a master fell into mortal sin if he treated his slaves worse after their wedding than before or attempted to separate them entirely.[98]

The later sixteenth-century parish registers of Lisbon indicate that the bishop's fulminations had the desired effect. But in a different diocese, that of Évora, compromises were struck which would have invalidated any good intentions on the bishop's part. The parish priest of Santa Maria do Castelo in Alcácer do Sal was called upon several times in the 1570s to perform marriages involving slaves and freedmen. As the priest noted, if the slaves had received permission to marry from the diocesan chancery, he was bound to perform the ceremony according to the Council of Trent. Nonetheless, several masters tried to stop the marriages, since they claimed that they would not be able to sell a slave who was married.[99] In these cases the priest proceeded with the ceremony, but admonished the slaves that they remained subject to their master, who was entitled to sell them. Sometimes the slaves consented to this condition, sometimes the master's protest was merely set down in the marriage register.

Festivities and pastimes

Slave spouses may have met each other at work in the city streets and in the fields, but there were other occasions to meet when they could not be accused of neglecting their masters' business. These were festivities sponsored by the crown or municipal authorities and festive gatherings which (given the chance) the slaves organized by themselves in their free time.

State occasions during the Middle Ages were often marked by the participation of the subject peoples. When an important ambassador came to town, when a procession was held to signalize a happy event, when a royal marriage was celebrated, the Moors and Jews of the area were commanded to come and perform their exotic songs and dances.[100] Alien forms of music seem to have held a fascination for the Portuguese.[101] Hence it followed naturally that the newly-found African peoples should be called upon in their turn to perform at these affairs. As early as 1451 a German ambassador noted blacks and Canarians among the dancers at the celebrations in Lisbon in honour of the marriage by proxy of the Infanta D. Leonor to the Emperor Friedrich III. The blacks provided various forms of entertainment: in 1451 some engaged in mock battle with a war-elephant,[102] and in 1521 the black brothers of the Rosary presented a short play (*entremês*) when King Manuel entered Lisbon with his new queen;[103] their musical skills, however, were most in demand.

Sad to say, very little is known about black songs and dances in Portugal before the seventeenth century.[104] None of the songs which playwrights gave their black characters to sing were written down, and they were probably just popular songs of the day. Gil Vicente does have one black who enters 'singing in the language of his land',[105] but this may have been a comic song in *fala de Guiné*. As far as black dances are concerned, I have only encountered mentions of the *mangana*, which a satirical song of the late fifteenth century said the slave-trader Fernão Gomes da Mina danced better than any other.[106] The music for the *mangana* apparently had a sad sound, and the dance was popular until well into the sixteenth century.[107] There must have been other dances, probably similar to the *undul*, *guineo*, *ye-ye* and *zarembeque*, all of which, together with the *mangana*, were danced by blacks in Castile during the sixteenth century.[108] The steps and nature of all these dances are not known, but the *guineo* was danced very quickly, with agile movements.[109]

Some blacks played musical instruments, which generally appear to have been of the European type, though with African cognates.[110] Drums were particularly associated with blacks: for instance, black drummers welcomed Cardinal Alexandrino's party to Vila Viçosa and Évora in 1571.[111] So also were flutes, which several Portuguese remarked were played very sweetly in various parts of Africa.[112] Indeed, when Álvaro Afonso tootled on his rod of office, he was said to be playing a 'negro pipe'.[113] Hence blacks were formed into wind bands,[114] one of which may be seen in Plate 5, where blacks are shown playing a sackbut and different kinds of shawm. Another instrument associated with blacks was the guitar: a woodcut of a black guitarist was used to decorate the frontispiece of several plays.[115]

Blacks sang, danced and played instruments at their own gatherings, held during their time off work. Unfortunately, most of what we know of the blacks' festivities comes from legislation forbidding them, but at least we know what blacks liked to do when given the opportunity. In the middle of the fifteenth century, for instance, the blacks of Santarém frequently obtained permission from their masters to celebrate Sundays and religious festivals by inviting other blacks to a feast. In 1461, however, the town's representatives to the Cortes objected to this practice because, they claimed, the slaves stole the lambs, ducks and hens which were eaten, and pilfered money from their masters to buy bread and wine. Worse, these gatherings enabled blacks to lay plans for escape. The town council had therefore forbidden masters to allow their slaves to hold parties, and the ruling was approved by the king in Cortes.[116]

While local custom elsewhere may have prevented blacks from gathering together, there were no more formal laws to this effect until 1559, when all blacks, both slave and free, were prohibited from holding dances and meetings in Lisbon and in an area 1 league (4.5 km) about the city.[117] Four years later the *corregedor* of Colares – about 25 km north-west of Lisbon – broke up a *festa dos negros* where the blacks had elected a king and hanged a scarecrow from a gibbet.[118] The reasons underlying this renewed concern about blacks in groups are hard to fathom, for no explanations were given for the Lisbon ruling and the *corregedor* at Colares acted because he found the blacks' activities an 'offence to Justice' – a phrase which can bear various interpretations. Perhaps whites in Portugal were disturbed by news of the slave revolts troubling São Tomé since the 1530s, but if so no one seems to have committed his fears of a slave insurrection to paper. Furthermore, according to the Lisbon law, blacks who were dancing were subject to fines twice as heavy as those imposed on blacks who were standing and watching, though the latter would seem to have been in a better position to hatch plots against whites. Probably the reasons for the new moves against black gatherings were much the same as those given by the representatives of Santarém a century before: prevention of robberies, escapes and other misdemeanours. In Lisbon, the authorities may also have been worried about the inconvenience caused to whites who could not easily pass through narrow streets blocked by a street party.

The white masters' and authorities' conceptions of public order and a properly functioning society limited the slaves' other recreations as well. In Lisbon, no one was allowed to race horses along the riverside, in the Rossio or elsewhere in the city. Racing horses was apparently a favourite pastime of youths and slaves, for both groups received special mention in this edict.[119] In Évora, no working man or slave was allowed to play ball during working hours.[120] The usual penalty for breaking these municipal laws was a fine, though slaves could be whipped instead, if their masters refused to pay. Workmen caught playing ball with black slaves in Évora had to pay twice the fine that was due had they been playing with white freemen. This law appears suspiciously segregationist in intent, but was probably meant only to protect slave-holders' interests, as it discouraged whites from distracting blacks away from their masters' business; certainly none of the other laws regulating sport took heed of race. Nor was there social prejudice against commoners of both races playing games together. One pair of gamblers pardoned by King João III consisted of a mulatto slave and a white youth, and black and white stable lads from the court occasionally met in the evenings to play cards for wine and grapes, a legal form of gambling.[121]

Punishment and harsh treatment

Dances and games provided a welcome respite from the daily round, which for some slaves was governed with an iron hand. If he chose, the master of the household could impose a stern regimen on all subject to him, for the law assumed that masters required powers of corporal punishment to maintain order in their houses. Thus a master could strike with impunity any person in his house, whether his wife, child, free servant or slave, and could beat them with a rod until the blood flowed.[122] Free servants could not be punished in any other way, but slaves could, which created an important distinction between free and slave domestics. Slaves, like the master's children, were more immediately subject to his discipline: a man could imprison both his children and his slaves to cure them of bad habits, though private gaols were otherwise illegal.[123] But whereas family feeling customarily tempered the punishments meted out to children, custom sanctioned harsh punishments and constraints on slaves. They could be loaded with chains, lashed with whips and burned with drops (*pingos*) of hot fat or wax applied to their naked flesh.[124] The only limit on a cruel master was that he could be tried for murder if a slave died as a result of punishment; the law offered slaves no protection against cruelty.[125]

Besides physical mistreatment, slaves might also suffer verbal abuse intended to convince them that they were the lowest of the low, mere beasts in human form. Blacks, like Moors and Jews, were often called 'dogs' or 'bitches': *cão, cadela, perro, perra*.[126] From calling slaves animals, it was a short step to treating them as such. Slaves were branded as if they were cattle when they were shipped from Guinea, and were branded again after each subsequent sale, in Lisbon or elsewhere. The crown branded its slaves on their arms, but other masters could be more unfeeling: one slave who fled from Évora in 1559 had been branded on both cheeks.[127]

The poet and playwright Francisco Sá de Miranda suggested that this practice was not uncommon, but no statistical data exist on the incidence of facial branding.[128] Nor is it known how often slaves were whipped, imprisoned or otherwise abused. Hence no exact conclusions may be drawn as to the severity of Portuguese slavery in this regard. There was, however, a general agreement among Portuguese and foreign observers that black slaves were treated less harshly than Moorish slaves were. Although Zurara's claim that he never saw a black or an Azenūg slave in chains may be taken with a grain of salt, blacks, unlike Moors, do not seem to have been kept shackled as a matter of course, only as a punishment.[129] According to Landi, this was because the Muslim Moors, as resentful prisoners of war and enemies of Christendom, were considered a threat to the peace, while the Christian blacks were not.[130]

Disease and death

The counterpart of callous masters were those who made an effort to maintain their slaves in reasonable physical condition and provided them with medical treatment when they fell ill. Home remedies were the usual standby, but professional assistance might be sought to cure severe maladies. On several occasions the *almoxarife* of Vale de Zebro took a slave to a barber–surgeon to have a tooth pulled. He also secured medicine and a doctor to look after slaves suffering from a range of ailments: pleurisy, a blow on the head, an injured foot and a cancer.[131] Slaves belonging to the crown or the wealthy nobility doubtless received better medical treatment than those belonging to poorer men, as doctors' fees were relatively high. One physician charged Diogo Lopes de Sequeira 2,000 *rs.* for attending a slave who had been wounded in Lisbon; while in 1552 the queen paid a surgeon 1,000 *rs.* for dressing a slave's head wound.[132]

Almost no slaves were treated in the charity hospitals, a puzzling fact, for these institutions did not exclude black people[133] or slaves on principle.[134] The explanation of the small number of slave patients probably lies in the hospitals' regulation that only the indigent could be admitted for care.[135] Evidently in most cases hospital administrators must have assumed that a master wealthy enough to buy a slave was also wealthy enough to pay a physician to look after him at home.

For some illnesses neither home remedies nor professional treatment sufficed. The numerous epidemic diseases and fevers indiscriminately called the plague (*peste*) were virtually incurable given the medical knowledge of the time. All that could be done was to isolate the infected, be they slave or free, from the well. In 1506, for instance, slaves were among the persons barred from entering Évora if they came from a place where plague was raging,[136] and other towns took similar precautions. The insanitary towns were natural breeding grounds for disease, and none suffered more than Lisbon, where epidemics ran riot among a large population packed several families to a house along narrow, dirty streets. Accordingly, in 1520 King Manuel determined that a permanent pest-house be built in the western suburb of Alcântara so that infectious cases could be isolated from the rest of the citizens. However, when the Casa da Saúde was completed in 1523, considerations of class and status took precedence over effective control of disease: the pest-house was reserved for slaves and working men only, while infected people of quality remained secluded in their own homes.[137]

Some years earlier, in 1515, D. Manuel's concern for public health had led him to ensure that all slaves in Lisbon received some (though not necessarily Christian) form of burial. The king noted that callous slave-traders and masters simply left their dead slaves to rot on dung-hills and middens, or else buried them in such shallow graves that the dogs dug them up and ate the corpses. Lest the rotting bodies corrupt the atmosphere, D. Manuel ordered that a pit be dug and filled with quicklime in order to serve as a communal grave for dead slaves.[138] The pit, which gave its name to the present Lisbon street, the *Poço dos Negros*, was on the western side of the city, outside the Santa Catarina gate and near the area where many slave corpses had been found unburied. Another, adjoining pit, the *Poço Novo*, was dug in 1594,[139] and similar arrangements may have existed in Elvas (the *Poço Seco*) and elsewhere.[140]

Most Christian slaves, however, received a full Christian burial. In 1513 the *almoxarife* of Vale de Zebro made sure that a dead black slave who had worked in the mill had a shroud and a funeral complete with candles and a mass with wine and bread.[141] The many funerals noted in the parish and Misericórdia registers would have been equivalent to this one. Where the Misericórdia was called upon to undertake a slave's funeral, the master offered alms to cover the ceremony and the grave-diggers' fees.[142] Municipal authorization was sometimes necessary for a slave to be buried inside the city,[143] but usually there were no objections to burying slaves in churchyards and even in the churches themselves.[144] Indeed, by the 1530s, people expected slaves to have Christian burials: in Aveiro some citizens went so far as to inform the Inquisition of a priest who had refused to conduct the funeral of a slave.[145]

Conclusions

As Braudel has pointed out, people in service, including slaves, were among the privileged of the working classes in sixteenth-century Europe for, unlike those without regular employment, they were assured of maintenance in food, clothing, shelter and other physical necessities.[146] Yet there were obvious variations in the adequacy of the maintenance provided: because the crown and charity hospitals fed and clothed their slaves extremely well, it does not thereby follow that all Portuguese masters did. Documentary evidence suggests that some slaves were dressed poorly and had to supplement their diet by begging or stealing. Since most masters were nobles or wealthy men who could afford to keep their slaves well, there may be some supposition that they did so; but to transform that supposition into a certainty requires a great deal more statistical information in the form of household accounts. This information is not, and is unlikely to become, readily available.

Somewhat more quantitative data exist on the abuses to which slaves were subject because of their status. The parish registers show that before the Council of Trent masters prevented most slaves from marrying: the numbers of marriages celebrated correspond in no wise to the total numbers of slaves in the parishes, and the overwhelming majority of slave children were born out of wedlock. (After Trent, the masters' opposition may have continued, but there was a striking increase in the number of marriages between slaves.) Yet the statistical information is not complete. The registers do not record how many children were fathered by slaves, as opposed to masters and other whites. Nor can we tell how many of the mothers had been victims of rape or whether some masters tried to organize slave-breeding. There is still less information on the regularity of punishments and the incidence of harsh treatment, merely an over-all consensus among contemporary observers that black slaves were treated less severely than Moors.

On the whole, despite a generalized attempt to integrate black slaves into the Portuguese Christian community through baptism and the provision of decent funerals, their conditions of everyday life seem to have been sufficiently distinct to have given the blacks a feeling that they had more in common with people of their own race and status than with lower-class whites. Although there were seldom many slaves in one household, most slaves lived in close proximity to one another in villages, towns and cities, so that black slaves (and freedmen too) had frequent opportunities to meet at work or play. Shared experience of servitude seems to have led to the development of a feeling of community. This black community was linked by friendship and marriage and in some places by a common language, a hybrid form of Portuguese. The existence of a separate language suggests not only that the community embraced people from different tribes, but also that in the places in question contacts between blacks and whites may have been limited. Communal spirit found its expression, and African traditions were preserved, in gatherings and dances.

Some municipalities strove to limit these social events because the blacks were then obviously outside their masters' control and could easily hatch conspiracies to steal or to escape. In fact, the subordination of slaves in society could not be left to masters alone, because so many slaves spent their working days outside their masters' direct supervision. Hence slaves were brought within the jurisdiction of royal and municipal law.

6

Slaves and the law

The development and refinement of Portuguese slave law during the period under study was partly due to a general preoccupation with codifying Portuguese law but was mainly a response to the problems created by the massive influx of black slaves from western Africa. To be sure, when blacks first arrived in Portugal in the middle of the fifteenth century, they came to a society which already had a recognized place for slaves. That society was hierarchic, with the king at the top, slaves at the bottom, and the various ranks of churchmen, nobility and free commoners in between. The law maintained this order by assigning privileges and disabilities to each person according to occupation, sex, age and descent. Naturally, since slaves were in the lowest rank, they suffered the greatest disabilities and the fewest privileges: in fact, the law was mainly concerned with restricting their activities and guaranteeing their masters' control over them. So much is clear from the body of legislation which articulated later mediaeval Portuguese society, namely the ordinances, statutes and widespread customs which, shortly after the arrival of the blacks, D. Afonso V collected and promulgated in his *Ordenações Afonsinas*. The institution of slavery and the limited legal rights allotted to slaves were also assumed in the law codes which D. Afonso and later monarchs declared were supplementary to royal law: canon law, Roman law (with the glosses upon it by Accursius and Bartolus) and local customs.

This whole corpus, however, proved inadequate to cope with all the problems created by the advent of black slaves. It is evident from the paucity of royal laws concerning slavery that the servile population had not been very large in the later Middle Ages; presumably its regulation had been left to local customs and the arbitrament of municipal magistrates.[1] Furthermore, the slaves were predominantly Muslims, as is apparent from the use of the word *mouro* as the synonym for 'slave' in the relevant legislation. Blacks, however, could not be treated in exactly the same way as Moors, for they behaved differently in servitude. Then again, there were many more of them, in many parts of the country, so the regulation of slaves could no longer be regarded as a minor aspect of the law, to be dealt with on an *ad hoc* basis. Consequently, new laws were enacted by the municipalities and the centralizing monarchy (which could not stand aside if it were to maintain its claims to comprehensive judiciary power). While these laws responded to the interests of various groups in white society, the slave-holders, being for the most part wealthy men and aristocrats, were the principal influence on local and royal councils. Hence they usually succeeded in overturning or amending any laws which inconvenienced them.

Most of the royal legislation on slavery from the reigns of D. João II and D. Manuel was included in the *Ordenações Manuelinas*. A first edition of this work appeared in 1514, but it was superseded by the edition of 1521, which remained the definitive Portuguese law book for the rest of the century. Unlike the *Ordenações Afonsinas*, the new *Ordenações* provided a slave code capable of meeting most of the contingencies arising in a slave-owning society. Of course, there were some deficiencies which became apparent as time passed; these were covered in supplementary legislation. The *Leis Extravagantes*, edited by Duarte Nunes do Leão, is a collection of these laws up to 1569, a date which serves as a terminus for this study of slave law. Like all post-Afonsine legislation, the new *Ordenações* and the *Leis Extravagantes* recognized the changes in the racial composition of the slave population by referring to slaves as *escravos*: *mouro* had acquired the more limited meanings of 'Muslim' or 'Moor'.

Juridical status

Both Portuguese and Roman law considered the slave not simply as a thing, but as a man who, having been deprived of his natural freedom by the law of nations, was treated as a thing for some purposes.[2] Both codes also stressed the dependence of the slave upon his master. Thus Accursius in one of his glosses upon the *Institutes* pronounced that 'A slave is he who, being part of someone's property, owes his master perpetual service.'[3] This definition was assumed by Portuguese law when it declared that a freeman was one who, subject to the law of contract, was able to choose his own master, the obvious corollary being that a slave was a man whose master was chosen for him.[4] The full implications of these two definitions were worked out in legislation which assimilated slaves sometimes to moveable property, sometimes to dependent minors, sometimes to free commoners, but always ensured that slaves enjoyed the least possible civil rights in any circumstances.

Treatment of the slave as a chattel was most apparent in commercial law where, as we have seen (p. 17), he was the only human thing (*cousa*), alienable at his owner's pleasure. Slaves and inanimate objects or animals were interchangeable in commercial transactions. As objects, slaves could be left as securities for a debt or, in time of war, for a ransom.[5] They could also be pawned to raise money. For instance, on 17 April 1545 Justa Falcoa of Lisbon pawned her black slave Maria to Ambrósio Correia of Évora for 10,000 rs., redeemable on 31 August. Any money Maria earned for Correia during the time she was in pawn was to be deducted from the sum owed by Falcoa, who assumed responsibility if Maria ran away or died.[6]

On the other hand, the law recognized the humanity of slaves by according them the fundamental human right to live unless found guilty of a capital offence by due process of law. Both the Roman and Portuguese codes prescribed death for anyone, masters included, who murdered a slave.[7] Popular sentiment backed up this legislation, for citizens were not loath to come forward to denounce men who killed slaves and to assist judicial inquiries initiated when slaves died in suspicious circumstances.[8]

There is, however, no evidence that anyone was ever executed for killing a slave.[9] Yet one should not assume, as some authors have, that this lack of retributive justice betokened legal discrimination specifically against slaves.[10] In fact, it was typical of legal discrimination against the lower classes in general: very few people were executed for killing any working man, slave or free. Instead of rigidly enforcing the *lex talionis* for such homicides, the crown preferred to extract some advantage to itself. The death penalty was retained chiefly as a threat to force murderers to accept exile in the dangerous and unhealthy fortresses in Morocco, which were chronically in need of new men for their garrisons, or to encourage them to pay a considerable sum for commutation or remission of their sentences. For instance, in 1451, an esquire who murdered a Castilian *criado* was not put to death, but required to serve in Ceuta for six years.[11] Frequently the crown managed to extract both military service and monetary

composition from an offender. A representative case was that of
Fernão Nunes of Funchal, in Madeira. In the spring of 1488 Nunes's
black slave, Cumba, died after he had lashed her and subjected her to
pingar. His neighbours promptly denounced him for inflicting excessive punishment. Rather than face the courts, Nunes fled and joined
an expeditionary force sent to aid the defenders of Fort Graciosa,
near Larache in Morocco. In November 1489 this service to the
crown won him commutation of his death sentence to three years
exile in Ceuta; and three months later his exile was remitted in
exchange for a gift to the crown of 9,000 *rs*.[12] During the fifteenth
century 8,000 or 9,000 *rs*. appears to have been the usual composition
paid by murderers of slaves for remission of their exile to North
Africa, the composition paid by murderers of *criados* being only
slightly higher, at 10,000 *rs*.[13] Ultimately the deterrent to killing
members of the lower classes was not the death penalty but considerable trouble and expense, in addition to the possibility of ostracism
by one's neighbours.

Recognition that slaves were human beings implied that they were
members of society, but their rights were severely restricted. In many
ways their civil status resembled that of the most disadvantaged free
persons, dependent children. Minors under the age of 14 and slaves
were not considered to be citizens of the town in which they lived.[14]
Nor could they be called upon to testify in court, though a judge
might determine that special circumstances justified accepting their
testimony.[15] Neither a child nor a slave could make a will or act as
tutor or guardian to an orphan who was a minor, even if named as
such in a will.[16] Their property rights were similar: by Roman law, a
dependent child of any age was merely the administrator of goods
given him by his father and of any proceeds realized from that
administration, while the slave was in the same position *vis-à-vis* any
goods entrusted to him by, or which he earned for, his master. The
master might allow the slave to set aside a *peculium*, some money or
goods for personal use, but the master was in fact the legal owner of
this property.[17]

Only when there was a possibility that the slave might become free
did his rights begin to approximate those of a free and independent
adult. Portuguese custom provided that, with his master's consent, a
Christian slave could buy his freedom with his *peculium*, as if it were
his own exclusive possession. And though slaves and minors could not
usually initiate legal actions, slaves who believed themselves to be

wrongfully held in servitude had the right to seek a legal ruling on their status, even in periods normally given over to judicial holidays.[18] They had, moreover, the right to appeal against an unfavourable ruling, but in these cases they might find it difficult to obtain support for their cause. For example, in 1536 the king authorized João, a mulatto, to appeal against an unfavourable ruling on his freedom, on condition that he find someone to stand as surety. The surety was to undertake to surrender João (or his monetary value) if the decision went once more against the would-be freeman. Unfortunately, João could not find a guarantor and so remained a slave.[19]

Slaves in the courts

As human beings, slaves were legally responsible for their acts, and therefore slaves who committed a crime were tried in the royal and municipal courts. If convicted, the slave was punished by public officers or else a pardon could be bought for him, should the master deem himself better served in this way. At all stages of the proceedings, every effort was made to safeguard the master's interests in his slave.

Slaves' trials were usually heard very rapidly in order that the master might not lose his slave's labour for an appreciable length of time. Delays could occur in the higher, royal courts when a slave was being tried for a serious offence, but even here the crown attempted to act with all due speed, as in 1536, when D. João III ordered that the case of a slave who had been held three years awaiting trial for the murder of another slave should be heard as soon as possible.[20]

The authorities assumed responsibility for punishing criminal slaves because masters alone could not be relied upon to take effective action. This problem was clearly stated by the *procuradores* of Lagos at a Cortes of the late fifteenth or early sixteenth century. The municipal representatives claimed that the many slaves in their town did much damage to vineyards, gardens and orchards by stealing fruit and vegetables, but masters responded in different ways to their slaves' misdemeanours. Some masters made restitution, but did not whip the slaves – which was hardly likely to discourage them; others beat them soundly, but even then the slaves did not desist. The only remedy, the king was told, lay in standardization of punishment: all slaves who stole produce should be whipped at the post (*picota*) in public by royal officers of justice, because only then would the slaves be 'ashamed' of their misdeeds.[21]

When King Manuel established a formal scale of punishments for criminals, he placed slaves in much the same category as free servants and labourers. Fundamentally, there were two scales of punishment: one for people of quality and another for the lower classes, except when a crime was so heinous that the same punishment was inflicted on all who committed it.[22] People of quality included the aristocracy, wealthy commoners, such as merchants with over 100,000 *rs.* in capital, and the privileged, such as magistrates and their families or masters and pilots of royal vessels. No person of quality could suffer a 'degrading punishment' for a crime: he was exiled to the African colonies or Brazil instead. The 'degrading punishments' (*penas vis*) were reserved for the lower classes and included whipping and the *baraço* and *pregão*.[23] Whipping usually involved twenty lashes at the post (*pelourinho* or *picota*); the *baraço* was a noose worn around the criminal's neck at the time of the sentence; the *pregão*, public proclamation of the crime and sentence by the hangman. Lower-class criminals could, of course, also be sentenced to exile.

If a law provided no specific punishments for offenders who were slaves, slaves who broke that law suffered the same punishment as lower-class freemen. Where the usual punishment was a fine, however, the slave's owner had the choice of paying it or seeing his slave whipped, whichever option seemed preferable to him. And when the usual punishment was exile overseas, the slave did not receive this sentence, which could jeopardize the master's hold on his property. There was at least one attempt to exile a black slave to Africa, but it was impeded by the slave's master. In 1475 Pedro Vaz, an arch-deacon of Elvas, informed the king that his black slave João, held for assisting another man to escape from gaol, had been sentenced to work on the fortifications of Asilah for two years. The archdeacon pointed out that while João was in Asilah he could flee to the Moors, thus occasioning loss both to his master and to God and little service to His Majesty. D. Afonso V agreed that the exile would be better commuted to a fine and henceforth temporary exile to Africa was apparently not contemplated for slave criminals.[24]

Yet exile was the customary means of removing serious criminals from contact with law-abiding people, since the gaols were used mainly to detain debtors or prisoners awaiting trial. Sentencing judges therefore had to find other means of secluding slave criminals.

One alternative was banishment within Portugal itself, to one of the towns which served as a sanctuary for freemen who were wrongdoers. Thus in 1539 the court of *Suplicação* sentenced António, a slave who had wounded a woman slave, to a year's banishment in Castro Marim in the Algarve.[25] More commonly, though, the authorities seem to have had recourse to the mediaeval expedient of sending convicted slave criminals to Castile to be sold there; the money from the sale provided compensation for the injured party or for the master in return for the loss of his slave's services.[26] Sale of blacks to Spain as a punishment appears to have been practised at least from the beginning of the sixteenth century, when it is mentioned in a poem in Resende's *Cancioneiro Geral*.[27] After 1551 there was a third option. D. João III, concerned about the shortage of rowers in the galleys, authorized the *Provedor dos Armazens* to purchase slaves who had been condemned to be sold outside Portugal. The price of the slaves was determined by two expert evaluators.[28]

Most sentences passed by the royal courts could be commuted or remitted in exchange for a cash payment, officially described as a gift toward some pious or publicly useful cause. Such pardons were usually bought after the offender had made a private settlement with the injured party, and in the case of slave offenders their masters made the settlements and put up the money required. This was in accordance with mediaeval Portuguese judicial practice: for example, a pardon for theft was granted to a Canarian slave in 1439, a few years before the first large shipments of blacks arrived from West Africa.[29] Since the crown was anxious to profit from the administration of justice, masters encountered little difficulty in obtaining commutations or remissions of almost any sentences imposed upon their slaves, from the most usual, a public whipping,[30] to the most severe, death. A benevolent master evidently believed that he would be better served by a grateful slave, though quite possibly he also felt himself to be in the position of a seigneur who had a duty to support and protect his retainers, in this instance his slaves.

In determining the cost of the pardon, the appellate judges appear to have taken into account the seriousness of the crime, the master's ability to pay, and mitigating factors such as the master's services to the crown and the age, fidelity, industry and general good behaviour of the slave. In the fifteenth century, the recent conversion of the slave also stood in his favour. Thus in 1468 the king's chaplain, who owned a black slave found guilty of having robbed a muleteer in Almada, asked D. Afonso V to pardon the slave not only because the stolen goods had already been returned, but also for the sake of Christ's passion and death, as the slave had become a Christian since committing the crime.[31] Such conversions appear suspiciously expedient and in later years, after large numbers of black slaves had been baptized in Africa or in Portugal, a new soul won for Christ became less of a novelty to sway judges' hearts to compassion and the plea of recent conversion was seldom employed.

Police legislation

Insofar as the law's function is to maintain public order, it is as much concerned with preventing as with punishing crime. In Portugal, preventive legislation included, among other things, restrictions on the bearing of arms and the imposition of a night-time curfew. Slaves suffered more restrictions than freemen did, for in principle no slave was allowed to bear arms, least of all after dark. But, as always, exceptions were made so as not to cause inconvenience to slave-owners. And since experience suggested that blacks were less of a threat to public order than Moorish slaves were, the two races received different treatment in law.

In the first half of the fifteenth century, the crown clearly indicated its desire to keep weapons out of the hands of the then largely Muslim slave population. In 1402 D. João I prohibited the carrying of arms by Muslims, Jews and foreigners in the city limits of Lisbon, and in 1442 this law was extended to the entire kingdom.[32] These restrictions, however, conflicted with the wishes of the aristocracy, who believed an armed retinue was a necessary symbol of their power, not to mention a protection against private enemies. Not wishing to offend its most powerful subjects, the crown compromised, as in 1459 when the *procuradores* of Beja protested that disturbances and public danger were caused by black and Moorish slaves carrying arms in the retinues of their noble masters. These lords were so powerful that the local justices could take no action against them, and therefore the *procuradores* besought the king to forbid slaves to bear arms. D. Afonso V replied that while it was true that slaves, as foreigners, should not carry arms, they could if they were pages of noblemen – a decision hardly calculated to gratify the *procuradores*, but which satisfied the nobility.[33]

Gradually the law gave in to the demands of other masters who wished to live in the aristocratic manner and have armed slaves, as may be seen from a series of laws passed by the *câmara* of Oporto and the crown. In 1475 the *câmara*, though it believed that black slaves were unruly when armed, allowed a master who feared personal enemies to obtain a licence to arm his slaves. Some twenty years later, in 1497, the law was relaxed to enable any slave to bear arms in his master's presence, and in 1521 D. Manuel made this the law of the land. Finally, in 1559, unaccompanied slaves were permitted to carry arms while going on their master's orders from the palace, or any other place where the master was, directly to the master's lodgings.[34]

These instances apart, a slave outside his master's supervision was forbidden to bear arms; slaves were thus distinguished from freemen, who could wear a sword or dagger at all times, subject only to the curfew laws.[35] But if a slave was found wearing side-arms, the penalty was not very great: a fine of 500 *rs.* or a whipping, should the master decline to pay the fine.[36] However, carrying weapons against which a person with a sword had little defence was regarded more seriously: a law of 1557 which sentenced freemen caught bearing a small arquebus to perpetual exile or servitude in the galleys prescribed the death penalty for slaves.[37]

If no slave was completely trusted with weapons, blacks were much preferred to Moors, perhaps with good reason. For instance, D. João III observed that in Évora most robberies, knifings and killings were committed by white (that is, Moorish) slaves. Therefore, to make sure that the slaves themselves were punished, he ordered that the sole penalty for white slaves apprehended while carrying a weapon was a public whipping. Their masters were not allowed to make monetary composition instead, as they could when armed black slaves were arrested.[38]

Black slaves were even more clearly favoured by the curfew laws, which forbade anyone, free or slave, to be out and about without a lamp from the curfew bell until clear sunrise.[39] Freemen and black slaves caught breaking the curfew incurred relatively light fines of 60–200 *rs.*, depending on whether the offenders were armed or not.[40] But in Lisbon, Évora, Elvas and the precincts of the royal court an unarmed white slave, whether Muslim or Christian, was subject to fines of 500 or 1,000 *rs.* merely for being abroad after dark. The Évoran law specifically exempted black slaves from its provisions.[41]

Security was especially stringent in the vicinity of the court, wherever that happened to find itself. In 1525, D. João III commanded that all white Muslim or *mourisco* slaves found with weapons in the court should be whipped and lose their ears. He added that if they were found there after eleven o'clock at night, they should be hanged, whether they had been armed or not.[42] Although Nunes do Leão noted that this last, particularly draconian, provision was not usually enforced, the body of legislation shows that the Portuguese believed that their Moorish, but not their black, slaves were addicted to crimes of violence and were capable of directing that violence against the state.[43]

Theft

On the whole, however, petty theft was the crime most often committed by slaves. At the time when the blacks began to arrive in Portugal, all slaves accused of theft were tried in the royal courts. These cases could take some time, for the *Ordenações Afonsinas* made no distinction in the matter of larceny between defendants who were free commoners and defendants who were slaves; thus they all received a full trial with the right of appeal should the verdict go against them.[44] As the slave population grew, and more and more slaves appeared before the courts, many slave-holders came to believe that the delays occasioned by the due process of law were excessive and contrary to their interests. Therefore, in 1472–3, the slave-holders' representatives in the Cortes pressed for an accelerated form of legal procedure in cases of petty theft committed by slaves. The *procuradores* informed D. Afonso V that 'the blacks as a nation are evil thieves' who often stole trifles, but were nonetheless imprisoned and held for long periods until their trial could be heard by a royal judge. Thus the masters suffered the loss of their slaves' services and a loss of money in paying the gaoler for the slaves' maintenance. The victims of the robbery, on the other hand, often received belated and insufficient compensation. The *procuradores* proposed that henceforth slaves who stole things of small value should be summarily tried in the local *câmara*, that is, before the town magistrate and the councillors in assembly. If found guilty, the slaves were to be whipped, without recourse or appeal against the sentence, and could not be released from prison until restitution of the sum stolen had been made. After 1475 this method of dealing with slaves who stole goods worth between 60 and 300 *rs.* was enforced in the Algarve and, by 1504, throughout Portugal.[45]

To further discourage slaves from committing petty thefts, the *Ordenações Manuelinas* of 1521 decreed that slaves were to receive harsher corporal punishments for stealing goods worth less than 400 *rs.* than did free commoners. (It may be noted that inflation had raised the money value of what were considered petty thefts.) If a slave stole goods worth between 100 and 400 *rs.*, then he was not only whipped with *baraço* and *pregão* but he also had his ears cut off. Free commoners who committed the same crime did not lose their ears.[46] For more serious thefts, which carried severe penalties, freemen and slaves were punished in the same way.[47] In these cases slaves were still subject to imprisonment and full court trials, with the right of recourse and appeal to a higher court.[48]

Receiving stolen goods

To provide themselves with things which free persons had, slaves needed money, which they often obtained by stealing and selling goods belonging to their masters. Hence laws were enacted, primarily at the municipal level, to prevent slaves from finding a purchaser for stolen goods. Interestingly enough, these laws frequently applied to free wage labourers (*mancebos de soldada*) as well, which indicates that not only did slaves and labourers behave similarly, but that the authorities viewed the two groups in much the same light. Several acts passed by the *câmara* of Coimbra between about 1514 and 1523 are typical of this legislation. At first the council forbade everyone to buy anything from slaves except firewood, hay and straw which the slaves' masters sent to market. In July 1519 any slave living with his master, but without his master's written permission to act as a purchaser, was specifically prohibited from buying anything save the allowed three categories of goods from another man's slave. Finally, in August 1519, everyone was ordered not to buy firewood, grass or straw from any slave or *mancebo de soldada*. Evidently some enterprising slaves had stolen and sold even these bulky goods. The slaves were certainly enterprising for, as the law noted, other slaves had hired out their masters' beasts for riding or ploughing without their masters' consent, and often with subsequent injury to the horses or mules. The *câmara* therefore decreed that only slaves who could show a licence provided by their masters were allowed to enter into commercial transactions.[49] As the sixteenth century wore on, similar legislation was enacted so often and in so many towns as to suggest that it was not very effective and that many people did not care whether a slave or servant had his master's authorization to buy or sell.[50]

Some slaves sought solace in alcohol for their restricted lives or else went to a tavern or hostelry for a bite to eat and jovial company. These carousals were frequently paid for in stolen goods: in 1461 the *procuradores* of Santarém complained that 'the blacks are very great drunkards and they steal in order to drink'.[51] The crown's response was to amend the laws which forbade Jews and Muslims to be served in taverns; discrimination on the basis of social status was added to discrimination on the basis of religion.[52] Thus in 1502 D. Manuel decreed that any taverner, vintner or innkeeper in the city limits of Lisbon who sold wine or food to any slave, black or white, Christian or infidel, had to pay a fine of 500 *rs*.[53] Similar measures were enacted in other towns, but again the repetition of these laws every few decades suggests that they were more honoured in the breach than in the observance, though the occasional prosecution is recorded.[54] Perhaps abuses crept in because in some cities certain categories of slaves were allowed to buy drink. In Évora and Oporto, for instance, a slave was served if he brought a jug or other container to be filled with wine for his master's table. Moreover, in Évora those slaves whom their masters had established in separate dwellings (*moradias*) were given leave to eat and drink where they wished.[55]

This practice of establishing slaves in residences apart from their masters was the subject of some controversy, since restriction of the practice, as many townspeople wanted, ran directly counter to the interests of slave-holders, who wanted the utmost freedom to place their slaves in gainful employment wherever they chose. The townspeople's fundamental grievances were that slaves living on their own tended to commit thefts and other crimes or else made their homes receiving-houses for goods stolen by other slaves. As early as 1475 the *procuradores* of Setúbal claimed that slaves whom their owners had sent to work in the city or in the salt-pans of the Sado turned the houses they inhabited into dens of thieves. The slaves stole both by night and by day, breaking into houses and wine warehouses, stealing the goods of muleteers while their mule trains rested for the night, and raiding orchards and vegetable gardens. Since these slaves belonged to powerful persons the ordinary people could not take action against the robbers, despite the fact that the Infante D. Fernando (1433–70), Grand Master of the Order of Santiago, which governed Setúbal, had forbidden anyone to rent houses to slaves. Once more, D. Afonso V's ties with the powerful persons led him to decline to take any action in this case.[56]

The controversy was finally resolved not by forbidding slaves to live apart from their masters, but by forbidding them to live in houses on their own and by restricting their ability to offer hospitality to fellow slaves. In 1530 the *câmara* of Loulé, in the Algarve, accused women slaves who lived in lodgings of accepting stolen goods from other slaves; therefore the councillors ordered that no one, and especially none of these slave lodgers, was to give another man's slave food, drink or shelter overnight in his or her home. Elvas and Évora also promulgated laws of this type.[57] In Lisbon the crown was not willing to place such restrictions on free, white, Old Christian householders, but in 1545 D. João III forbade slaves in lodgings to entertain other slaves. Furthermore, no slave in Lisbon was to live in a house by himself without supervision.

Suspicion also fell upon freedmen, because of their close contacts with the slave community. In 1544 the *procuradores* of Lisbon requested D. João to force all freed men and women to live with their former masters, wherever they might be. The king refused to discriminate against the freed population in this way, but he did order freedmen not to entertain slave friends in their houses, nor to receive money, clothes or other things from them.[58] In 1542 the *câmara* of Beja, however, forbade more than one freedman to live or lodge in the same house and appended the usual prohibition against freedmen entertaining slaves in their dwellings.[59]

Assault and murder

The Portuguese seem to have believed that such laws, in conjunction with police legislation and masters' powers of discipline, would usually suffice to keep the slave population in order. Except for one instance, which will be considered shortly, no exceptionally severe punishments were inflicted upon slaves who committed crimes of violence. In fact, as far as minor cases of assault were concerned, legal theory held slaves to be of diminished responsibility on a par with women and children. In response to a request of the Cortes of Montemor-o-Novo in 1477, the regent, Prince João, decided that when children under 15 or slaves wounded each other with sticks or stones, they were not liable to the statutory fines for drawing blood and for carrying sticks or stones. After 1510, most of the new town charters granted by D. Manuel absolved women, children under 12 or 15 (according to the town) and slaves from the *pena de arma* for drawing blood in a fight or quarrel, though the *Ordenações Manuelinas* specified that the law exempted these people only if they drew blood in fist fights or with sticks and stones.[60]

In practice, however, a slave who committed one of these offences was treated as if he were a free commoner. He was punished in the same way, and had the same right to a pardon. Thus in 1533 Manuel Gomes, a sailor from Alcácer do Sal, had to pay for two pardons for his black slave António. After paying out 2,000 *rs.* in May, Gomes spent a further 1,000 *rs.* in October because in the meantime António had beaten Francisco, a slave belonging to one Pedro Cubelos, over the head with a stick. The *Ordenações* notwithstanding, Cubelos had successfully initiated an action against António, though he eventually pardoned him in September.[61] The law regarded slaves and lower-class free commoners who inflicted injuries with metal weapons as equally responsible in theory and as a rule treated them no differently in practice.

The equivalent treatment of slaves and free commoners in these cases of assault suggests that while the magistrates did not believe that slaves deserved lighter penalties than freemen, neither did they perceive a threat of insurrection behind every violent act committed by a slave, a threat which had to be countered by repressing such acts with harsh and exemplary punishments. Indeed, the authorities showed no signs of panic fear respecting a servile rebellion even when fairly large groups of blacks armed with striking or cutting weapons were involved. Irritation at their rowdiness and a desire to prevent its recurrence were the prevailing sentiments. In 1461, for instance, the *procuradores* of Santarém complained that the black slaves who came into town in their time off brought along clubs to have fights with the locals; the *câmara* had therefore decided that any slave found with a weapon should forfeit it and be locked up until his master paid a fine for his redemption. D. Afonso V approved the council's action, but allowed the slaves to carry knives without points, for dining.[62] Legislators reacted sternly only when brawlers or other criminals, slave or free, were armed with crossbows or guns, that is, with lethal weapons.[63]

1 A Portuguese view of life in black Africa

2 Black in attendance upon an aristocratic hunting party

3 A black slave waits upon the family of a wealthy merchant at table

4 Birth of the Virgin, showing a black serving-woman (detail)

5 Black minstrels playing shawms and sackbut

6   Adoration of the Magi, showing a black king (detail)

In part, the relative equanimity with which Portuguese authorities viewed slaves armed with clubs or swords was probably due to a realistic perception that a slave revolt could not possibly succeed, given the small size of the slave population. But in part it was also due to their recognition that brawling, though deplorable and punishable, was a fact of Portuguese life and was especially typical of retainers, whether slave or free. There was good reason to regard slaves as retainers, for in many ways slaves and free servants of the same master behaved so similarly as to be indistinguishable. In feuds, both groups identified themselves with their masters' interests. For instance, in 1539 Fernão Carvalho, a *cavaleiro fidalgo* resident in Setúbal, was at odds with his brothers-in-law, Diogo and António Reboredo. During the course of the vendetta, Carvalho's slave Jerónimo and four slaves belonging to Carvalho's father-in-law (who was evidently not of his sons' party) went off and attacked a slave belonging to António de Mendonça, since it was alleged that Mendonça was helping the brothers Reboredo. When the differences between the major rivals had been settled, Carvalho exerted his influence with the judiciary to obtain a pardon for Jerónimo.[64]

That slaves and free servants considered each other to be members of the same extended family appears even more clearly from the spontaneous way in which they came to each other's assistance when danger threatened. In 1492, while Bastião Fernandes, a *criado*, was passing by the gaol of Évora, he saw officers of the law trying to hustle two slaves inside. One of the two slaves belonged to Bastião's master. Bastião thereupon drew his sword and in the ensuing *mêlée* one of the slaves escaped.[65] Similarly, in 1557 António Gomes, a black slave, intervened with a halberd to try to prevent the law from seizing one of his master's *criados* while this man was at work building a house in a village near Barcelos. Gomes apparently always carried the halberd with him, and both he and Bastião were fully pardoned: so much for the laws concerning the bearing of arms by slaves and for the statutory death penalty for obstructing officers of justice.[66]

Legal treatment of slaves as if they were lower-class free commoners extended so far as to provide the same punishment for members of either group who killed another member of the lower classes: all murderers were to hang.[67] Of course, the sentence was usually commuted, to the crown's or the slave-holder's benefit. Thus free commoners were frequently exiled and slaves were sold in Spain or to the galleys.[68]

Yet if magistrates were prepared to alter or commute the sentences imposed on violent or even murderous slaves out of deference to the powerful men who were the slaves' masters, that same deference led them to regard any acts of servile insubordination as extremely serious (that is, of course, if the masters cared to bring such acts to their attention, which was not always the case: see p. 159). A slave who threatened his master with a weapon was whipped through town with *baraço* and *pregão* and had one hand cut off. If he wounded his master he was executed, but not mutilated. And if he actually killed his master or his master's son not only were both his hands chopped off, but he was torn with pincers or hooks before he was hanged from the gallows.[69] Amputation of the hands was no idle threat, as two grisly entries in the accounts of the *câmara* of Elvas reveal. On 12 September 1504 the *câmara* purchased a chopping block and a cleaver 'to do justice on the hands of a black man'.[70] These laws clearly show that however much slaves felt themselves to be retainers, and however much their masters viewed them as such, the ultimate sanction of the relationship was naked force, backed up by the state.

According to an ancient Roman law, if one slave killed his master, all the other slaves in the house were sentenced to die with him.[71] This savage law did not find acceptance in later Rome nor in Portugal, but obviously some punishment was required to discourage slaves from plotting against their master. The punishment inflicted upon at least one group of slave conspirators was sale in Castile. In the late 1530s, after a Moorish slave had murdered D. Rodrigo de Eça, witnesses inculpated D. Rodrigo's other slaves. The murderer was hanged, the other slaves condemned to be sold in Castile, and royal justice ensured that this sentence would be carried out by threatening to confiscate the slaves if D. Rodrigo's heirs did not sell them. Only one slave was spared: a lad of 9 or 10 for whom the murdered man's widow interceded, declaring that she knew he was innocent since he 'loved her family as [if he were] a son'.[72]

Prisons

Imprisonment was not generally employed as a punishment in Portugal during the period under consideration. Rather, gaols served to detain criminals awaiting trial or who had not yet paid a fine or debt, and it was in these capacities that slaves were found in gaol. Masters were responsible for paying their slaves' fines, but many were

not willing to do so. Hence in larger centres, such as Lisbon and
Évora, where the gaols were constantly crowded, the authorities
decided to relieve the pressure by whipping and releasing those slaves
who were being held for petty offences and whose masters would not
pay their fines.[73] Different local conditions, however, prompted
different responses. Toward the middle of the sixteenth century the
municipal councils of Coimbra and smaller towns, where there was
more room in the prisons and, perhaps, a shortage of revenue,
decided to sentence convicted slave criminals to a fine or a month in
prison.[74] Evidently the councillors hoped that masters would be
moved, by the threat of losing their slaves' services, to pay the fines.

While in gaol, prisoners had to pay for their upkeep. When a slave
was imprisoned, his master was required to pay the gaoler a certain
sum to cover the daily food consumed by the slave; in 1503 the sum
was 15 rs., but by 1520 it had been reduced to 12 rs. Even if the slave
died in prison the master had to pay any bills for maintenance that
were still outstanding,[75] and if the slave was acquitted of the charges
against him, he could not be released until all his bills had been
paid.[76] Occasionally a master refused to pay for his slave's upkeep.
In these cases the Santa Casa da Misericórdia undertook to look after
the slave, as it looked after prisoners too poor to provide for themselves.[77] The Misericórdia supplied prisoners in its care with food
twice a week. On Sunday they were given enough bread to last until
Wednesday, a portion of meat and half a *canada* (0.75 litres) of wine.
On Wednesday they received bread to last until Sunday and another
half *canada* of wine. The officials who looked after the prisoners'
rations also paid the gaolers for cooking the meat.[78] In short, the diet
of slaves in prison was not much different from, and cost about the
same as, that of slaves outside. After sentence was passed or the slave
acquitted, the Misericórdia claimed compensation from the master
to meet the cost of having maintained his slave in prison. If the
master refused to pay, the slave was sold at public auction to raise the
funds required.[79]

Conditions in gaol could be very unpleasant, since some gaolers
withheld the food ration and others forced prisoners to work for
them.[80] Together with the fear of punishment, these annoyances led
many prisoners, slaves included, to attempt to escape. Although the
law ordained harsh penalties for prisoners who escaped, especially
for those who broke down doors and cut through manacles, pardons
were easy to obtain and cost relatively little – about 800 to 1,000 rs.

Slaves benefited as much from royal lenience as did other would-be escapers. Thus in 1551 a pardon was granted to António, a black slave who had filed through a leg-iron and removed two stones from the Avis gaol wall before being overheard by the warder.[81] There were many other such pardons.

Incidence of black crime

The numerous laws and protests of *procuradores* to various Cortes reveal that white Portuguese believed that their black slaves had a marked proclivity to petty theft, and were unruly when under arms, though less violent than the Moors. Very little quantitative judicial information has survived from the period in question, but what evidence has come to light suggests that this was a fair assessment, at least as far as non-violent crime was concerned. Petty crime was rife among the slave population: in 1530 the *câmara* of Loulé noted that out of nineteen persons fined for trespass, damage and theft of crops in July of that year, no fewer than eleven were slaves.[82] Serious crimes, on the other hand, were much less common among slaves. The most important information regarding serious crime comes from three letters written in 1535 and 1536 by D. João III, then in Évora, to D. Fernando de Castro, governor of the Casa do Cível in Lisbon, with respect to what should be done about criminals held in the Casa's gaol.[83] Out of a total of 97 prisoners mentioned in the three letters there were:

			Percentage of total prisoners
blacks:	slaves	3	3.1
	free	3	3.1
mulattoes:	free	3	3.1
	status undecided	1	1.0

The percentage of slave criminals is about the same as the previously calculated percentage of slaves within the Portuguese population as a whole; this seems to indicate that however given black slaves were to petty theft, they were no more inclined to commit major offences than were Portuguese whites. (The free people of colour, however, appear statistically over-represented. This imbalance may mean that there was an objective basis to the contention of those masters who said they did not wish to free their slaves because freedmen were commonly criminals. See p. 147.) One black slave was held for murder, and a black freedwoman for battery, but whether the

Portuguese had good reason to believe that their black subjects were less violent than their Moors cannot be determined from the data in these three letters. In any case, eleven slaves in Loulé and eleven people of colour in Lisbon hardly constitute a significant numerical sample and, obviously, only massive new documentation can really confirm whether the popular prejudices against slaves and freedmen were justified.

Certainly some slaves were on the right side of the law: they were employed to enforce it. As early as 1516 Jorge Fernandes, a black slave, served as part of the watch led by his master, the *meirinho* Lionel Quiroz, of Frois (?Flores) in Beira. The *recebedor* of the royal chancery paid Fernandes a living allowance (*mantimento*) of 400 *rs.* a month, which his master received in his name.[84] The Cortes of Torres Novas of 1538, however, determined that no *meirinho* or *alcaide* could employ his own or another man's slave as an officer of justice, on pain of a fine of 20 *xdos* and six months' suspension from office.[85] Nonetheless, the practice continued, thanks (as was usual under the *ancien régime*) to the possibility of acquiring a licence to do so. Thus in 1552 among the men of António de Carrança's watch in Lisbon was Carrança's slave António, who had been given a licence by the *câmara*.[86] Later, by a decree of 1568, this licensing power passed from the *câmaras* to the *desembargadores do paço*, the royal judges who granted pardons and privileges in the name of the king.[87]

Conclusions

The juridical status of the slave essentially derived from the fact that he was the only human being who was classified for some purposes as a thing. Still, his inherent humanity, and hence his membership of society, was recognized by assigning him minimal civil rights similar to those of dependent children and by bringing him under the jurisdiction of the law. Portuguese law prescribed generally the same procedure for crimes committed by or against slaves as in cases where the crimes were committed by or against lower-class free commoners. Slaves and free commoners had the right to a trial; their punishments for assault and grand larceny were similar; and if they were murdered, the penalty was theoretically death, in practice exile or monetary composition. Differences in procedure occurred chiefly in matters relating to petty theft (to which slaves apparently had a propensity) and when treatment of the slave as if he were a free commoner would impair the slave-holder's interests or his authority over the slave. Hence slaves had to live in supervised housing and could not frequent taverns, received a speeded-up trial for petty thefts[88] and were subject to punishments chosen to suit their masters' pleasure. The effect of this body of legislation was to define slaves as commoners with peculiar disabilities. Portuguese society was therefore not marked by an abrupt division between slave and free, but by a gradual increase of legal disabilities in classes toward the lower end of the social hierarchy.

The blurred division between slaves and lower-class freemen was in sharp contrast to (and a consequence of) the clear distinction in law and practice between the privileged classes and those who served them. The very definition of a freeman as one who could choose his own master reveals that the principle of order within Portuguese society was not the subordination of slaves to all freemen, but the subordination of all servants, free or slave, to their masters. Hence masters were granted exceptional disciplinary powers over their servants. Of course, free servants and slaves differed in degree of subjection: disobedient servants could be thrashed until the blood ran, while slaves were subject to further corporal punishments; and a free servant who took up arms against his master suffered only the penalties for assault, while a slave could be punished with death or mutilation. But slaves and servants who attacked each other were regarded as more or less on a par.

The emphasis on service betrays the essentially seigneurial structure and outlook of Portuguese society, an outlook which explains various features of the treatment of black slaves. Both their masters and the law tended to view them as retainers. Slaves were therefore allowed arms to protect their masters. In return, some masters assumed the responsibility of the overlord to protect his dependants: these masters concealed slaves who had committed a crime from officers of the law, subverted local magistrates' efforts to convict slave criminals and, when these tactics failed, bought pardons for their slaves from the offended parties and the crown. Slave retainers repaid their masters' generosity by identifying themselves with their households, aiding their masters' other servants who were in trouble, and fighting on their masters' behalf in vendettas. The law was accordingly disposed to consider acts of violence committed by slaves as the normal turbulence expected of retainers, and not as potential insurrection. Moors, who unlike blacks were generally not Christians, and therefore deemed to be less integrated into society, were regarded with far greater suspicion. Nonetheless, their masters' influence seems to have mitigated the force of the draconian laws enacted against them.

In sum, the legal treatment of slaves in Portugal was indelibly marked by the fact that the extreme subordination of the slave to his master occurred in the context of a seigneurial society. On the one hand, the slave was burdened with special disabilities and restrictions intended to preserve his master's interests and dominion over him. On the other hand, where the master's interests were not directly affected, the law placed slaves in much the same category as free retainers. Furthermore, the respect accorded masters as seigneurs could enable slaves to escape the full punishment for infractions of the slave code or other crimes. From the slave's point of view, however, too much depended on his master's goodwill and influence over the judiciary; the slave's natural human desire to make the principal decisions affecting his own life was denied. Hence freedom, even if only to choose one's own master, became a thing to be prized.

7

Fugitives, freedom and freedmen

Na verdade homens que prendem catiuos com cadeias, & lanção braga a
escrauos, não sabem o que fazem. fazeis aos coitados mal sobre mal, &
desejão fugir se podem, he graça.

Truly, men who bind captives with chains, and weigh down slaves with
shackles, don't know what they are doing. Force the poor creatures to
suffer hardship upon hardship and they seek to flee if they can – it's a
mercy.

J. Ferreira de Vasconcellos, *Comedia Vlysippo* (pre 1561), ed. B. J. de Sousa
Farinha (Lisbon, 1787), act II, scene vii, p. 150.

A slave could recover his freedom in two ways: he could run away
from his master, an unlawful act, or he could wait until his master
decided to free him by due process of law. Although a few fugitives
may have succeeded in their aim, most stood little chance, for those
who escaped being apprehended in Portugal could be extradited
from neighbouring Castile. France, the nearest Christian free soil,
was too far away, while flight to Muslim North Africa involved a
difficult sea voyage requiring knowledge of navigation. Thus manumission remained the most assured means for a slave to obtain his
freedom. Freedom, however, was a dubious prize. Not only could it
be revoked legally (and illegally), but the legal and economic position of freedmen in Portuguese society was usually not good. Still,
the freedman enjoyed the feeling that he was no longer always at his
master's beck and call, and he had at least a possibility of bettering
himself. Such were the attractions of freedom.

Fugitives

During the Middle Ages legislation to deal with the problem of
fugitive Moorish slaves varied according to the locality.[1] Only in the

reign of D. Duarte (1433–8) did there appear a standardized system which discouraged the assistance of runaways and provided incentives for their capture by private persons. These laws were later expanded, with some modifications, to cope with black runaways. Thus anyone who captured a fugitive could claim a reward from the master and employ the slave as his own servant until the sum was paid.[2] But whereas the reward for apprehending a Moor was 1,000 rs., it was only 300 rs. for the arrest of a black.[3] No reason was given for this discrepancy: perhaps blacks, being more easily obtainable, were worth less, perhaps slaves who resembled Europeans were more highly prized. Both explanations would account for D. Manuel's decision to maintain the lower rate for blacks, while awarding 1,000 rs. for the retrieval of an Indian slave.[4]

Kindly souls who sheltered or assisted fugitive slaves were also subject to harsh punishments. By Duarte's laws, such people became the temporary slaves of the person who arrested them.[5] Furthermore, if they could not pay a heavy fine[6] they were forced to work off the debt as slaves of the fugitive's master, except when this would lead to a Christian being subjected to a Jew or Muslim; then they became slaves of the crown.[7] D. Manuel commuted the punishment for Christians who assisted runaway slaves to perpetual exile in São Tomé, probably because of the courts' reluctance to impose slavery as a punishment on free whites. Jews and Muslims, however, were still subject to enslavement, and Jewish or Muslim slaves who helped others to escape had their ears cut off as well.[8]

The combination of incentives and threats appears to have had the desired effect, for there are numerous instances of private persons arresting runaway slaves.[9] Nonetheless, further legislation was required before masters could count on the swift return of their apprehended slaves. During the fifteenth century many slave-catchers simply left runaways in the care of the local authorities, who threw the slaves in gaol and made no attempt to inform their masters that they had been caught. This meant that much time and money might be wasted looking for a slave who had already been caught. In 1498, therefore, D. Manuel ruled that all runaways should be brought before the judge or magistrate of the principal town of the district (almoxarifado) in which the slave had been arrested. The judge was empowered to give the slave thirty lashes to force him to reveal the name of his master, who was then notified, the slave being kept in gaol until the master sent someone to collect him.[10]

There was no secure place of refuge for a fugitive slave in Portugal. As early as 1355, and probably much earlier, slaves were denied the right to seek sanctuary in churches.[11] They were not alone in this exclusion: various types of criminals, Jews and Muslims were also denied sanctuary. All, like runaway slaves, could be dragged from church by the legal authorities and wounded, or even killed, if they tried to resist.[12] Nor could slaves, Jews or Muslims find asylum in the *coutos*, the towns of refuge, since these were for criminals only.[13]

Crossing the Castilian border did not necessarily increase a runaway's prospects of freedom, for three reasons. First of all, the return of runaways found in Castile to their masters in Portugal and of runaways found in Portugal to their masters in Castile was customary. Local authorities often arrested fugitive slaves who had come from across the border, holding them until their masters acquired warrants for the slaves' extradition and sent agents to bring them back.[14] Although slaves were never specifically mentioned in the various extradition treaties concluded by the two kingdoms between 1271 and 1569, Portuguese masters had no trouble in obtaining Castilian royal warrants to extradite their fugitive slaves. This was probably because the treaties did provide for the return of thieves, and in Castilian law slaves were considered thieves who 'stole themselves'.[15]

Secondly, the governments of both countries allowed masters to send slave-catchers after fugitives whom the authorities had failed to apprehend. Even if a master did not want a troublesome runaway back in his household, he would not let the slave go free. Instead, he would nominate an agent to catch the slave and, when the slave was found, to sell him. This procedure was well established by the mid-sixteenth century, to judge from the number of documents relating to it in the notarial archives of Badajoz.[16] Indeed, selling slaves who had escaped to Castile became so common that in 1565 the Portuguese crown decided to levy a duty of 10 *xdos* on these sales, the same as it had begun to levy on normal export sales of slaves.[17]

Thirdly, even when a slave successfully avoided the local authorities and his master's agents, he might fall into the hands of some unscrupulous Castilian who would try to re-enslave him and sell him. One Portuguese master, for instance, instructed his agent to search for a runaway in the market of Peña Guillén, near Toledo, and in other towns where slaves were sold.[18] All in all, runaway slaves did not stand much chance of finding freedom in Castile, nor of successfully crossing that kingdom to reach France.

North Africa was a more secure destination for runaways, since the Muslims refused to return fugitive slaves to Portugal, but this direction of escape also presented difficulties. The greatest of these was simply getting there. Although obtaining a boat might be fairly easy, for no very close watch was kept upon the docks, only sea-faring slaves in the Algarve and possibly Lisbon were likely to know the way to Africa.[19] The pathetic story of four blacks from Peniche, a fishing port just south of Coimbra, illustrates the point. In 1516 this little band stole a boat and headed south for freedom. However, after a voyage of scarcely more than 100 nautical miles they decided that they had arrived in their own country, beached the boat and walked inland. They had in fact gone no farther than Setúbal, and were recaptured in the Alentejan village of Souto Redondo.[20]

A lesser inconvenience was that slaves who managed to reach North Africa had to become Muslims if they were to enjoy the full benefits of freedom. For some slaves this was no hardship, as is shown by the records of two cases tried in 1553 by the Inquisition in its capacity of prosecutor of all would-be apostates. Two Wolof slaves, both called Bastião, were apprehended in Lisbon while planning to escape. Since their destination was North Africa, they were haled before the inquisitors. Each confessed that he had known something of Islam in his native land – not much, but considerably more than he knew of Christianity in Portugal – and that he intended to live as a Muslim and a freeman when he reached North Africa.[21]

On the other hand, conversion to Islam was repugnant to successful fugitives who had become sincere Christians during their stay in Portugal. Fortunately for them, they could take advantage of a mediaeval Portuguese and Castilian custom whereby escaped Moorish slaves who gained Muslim soil could return to the Christian kingdoms as freemen.[22] Strictly speaking, the rule only applied to Muslims, but it was extended in the later fifteenth century to include *mouriscos* and other converts as well, provided royal authorization was obtained.[23] Thus Pedro, a black who had escaped with several others in a boat from Tavira to Morocco, returned to Portugal so that he could live as a Christian and was granted his freedom in 1495.[24] A striking extension of the custom to cover fugitives in pagan lands occurred in the case of João Garrido, an interpreter who jumped ship in his homeland of Guinea. As soon as he was safely out of reach of Portuguese slave-catchers, he petitioned to return to Portugal to serve as a freeman in his trade. D. João II freed Garrido and allowed him to bring back whatever merchandise, gold and slaves he chose, duty free.[25]

Freedom: manumission

Slaves did not always have to go to such lengths to win their freedom. Manumission was an accepted practice in a country where freedom was legally considered to be the natural state of men. Furthermore, the experience of the mediaeval centuries during which Moorish prisoners, employed as slaves by the Christians, were ransomed and freed must have gone far to establish the conception of slavery as a condition that need not be permanent. There is no evidence that the Church officially encouraged masters to free their slaves, but the influence of Christian doctrine tended in that direction, as is clear from the inclusion of manumission among the pious acts that masters willed to be done after their death.[26]

The fundamental legal instrument which gave a slave his freedom was the *carta de alforria*, or letter of manumission. This could be granted by the master himself, usually to take effect during his lifetime, or by his heirs or assigns after his death, if the master had made provision for freeing the slave in his will.[27] Both will and *carta de alforria* could lay down conditions which the ex-slave had to fulfil; having done so he was given an unconditional *carta de alforria* (called in Castile a *licencia de libertad*),[28] which was recognized throughout Christendom.[29]

Under the general heading of conditional manumissions may be placed manumission by purchase, that is, where a slave was required to put up a certain sum of money in exchange for his freedom, in the same way that Moorish prisoners ransomed themselves. As a rule, the price of freedom seems to have been equivalent to the market price of a slave, though the would-free freedman might have to pay considerably more in duties and incidental expenses. In 1552, for instance, Margarida, a black woman of Oporto, had to pay 10,000 *rs.* for her *carta de alforria*, and twenty-five years later Francisco de Cor Baço, an Indian man of Évora, paid 25,000 *rs.*, plus 100 *rs.* notarial fees.[30] In addition, Francisco would probably have had to pay a tax of 2,500 *rs.*, that being 10 per cent of the purchase price, to the municipal council. This duty was a continuation of a similar levy on the ransoms of Moorish prisoners.[31] The duties on ransoms were ended in 1529, doubtless to facilitate prisoner exchanges, and before that the Manueline charters of some towns, such as Lisbon, Silves and Santarém, had exempted Christian slaves from paying duty on purchased manumissions. However, in other places, of which Évora was one, all slaves who bought their freedom had to pay 10 per cent of the agreed composition.[32]

Even if a slave worked as a street vendor and shared the profits with his master, he would still have had to work for many years to raise the money needed to purchase his freedom: it is not surprising that Margarida was in her forties and Francisco in his fifties, relatively old people for the time. Accordingly, a slave's father, mother, or husband who was free and could therefore save money more easily sometimes provided the necessary cash.[33] Sometimes too, a free white Portuguese who had fathered a child on a slave woman paid the master for his child's freedom.[34] The master himself might help the slave financially. Thus while Estêvão da Gama of Elvas did not free his slave Pedro in his will made in 1553, he authorized Pedro to purchase his freedom and left him 4,000 rs. for the purpose.[35]

Since money was hard to come by, a slave could occasionally persuade his master to accept his services as a freedman over a certain time instead.[36] The services did not have to be rendered to the master himself: in 1546 Maria Afonso, a widow living in Évora, granted a carta de alforria to Domingos her slave on condition that he serve one Simão Nunes, with whom Maria was staying, for ten years. Nunes was to treat Domingos as an indentured free servant and to provide him with bed and board, shoes and clothing. As Domingos was only 8 years old, it seems hardly likely that he himself bargained with his mistress for his freedom, though his mother Antónia may well have done so.[37]

Such negotiations may have lain behind the clauses in wills which freed slaves if they served the testator's heirs for some years. The heirs who benefited from the former slaves' services could be relatives, friends or religious institutions, and the period of service could be fixed or variable. Fixed terms could last from three to six years in the case of adult slaves and up to twenty for children, while variable terms usually lasted until the death of a human heir.

Of course, the initiative to free the slave on these terms could have come from the master himself, for wills granting conditional freedom make no explicit mention of contractual negotiations or agreements. That conditional manumission was in some cases entirely due to the slave-owner's initiative seems apparent from the testamentary conditions imposed by pious ladies who were determined to make respectable women out of their slaves. For example, D. Maria, D. Manuel's queen, freed only those of her slave women who married or took religious vows.[38]

Even with all these qualifications, the documents given to slaves were called *cartas de alforria*, and all freedmen, whether their freedom was conditional or unconditional, were commonly called *forros*. A more exact, if less frequently employed, terminology described the conditionally free as *forro* (quit) and real freedmen as *livre* (free). Thus D. Fernando II, the duke of Bragança, could command that 'the slaves whom my father had made quit (*forrados*), may be free (*livres*)', while *cartas de alforria* which conceded complete freedom made a freedman 'forro e livre isento', that is, exempt from conditions.[39]

Another term sometimes encountered is *meio forro*, half-quit or half-free. Applied to Moorish captives, it usually meant that they had not entirely paid their ransom.[40] It had another meaning, however, more applicable to black slaves. If a slave was owned by two or more people, one of the masters could free what was considered to be his fraction of the slave.[41] Usually there were only two masters involved, a husband and wife, whose joint consent was required for their slave to become wholly free.[42] Therefore if one spouse freed the slave, he was said to be *meio forro*. This status, half-slave and half-free, could be extremely frustrating. In 1501 António, a *meio forro* of Santarém, became so angry with his master that he took him to court on the grounds that the master had promised to honour his late wife's will, which freed the slave, but had in fact done nothing at all. The master then seems to have stolen some of António's clothes, but denied that he had done so. There was an argument; the master struck António; António uttered a blasphemy, and was haled into court for it. The blasphemy was pardoned, but nothing more is known of the suit for manumission.[43]

Such complications and psychological stress were avoided when the slave was freed unconditionally. Unconditional manumission seems to have been at least as common as conditional. Of 137 slaves mentioned in thirty-eight wills between 1447 and 1562, seventy-six slaves were freed outright, twenty-four were freed conditionally and thirty-seven were not freed (though of those who were not freed, two had been freed by the testator but were sold by his executors). Conditions were more likely to be imposed when the slave was freed by a *carta de alforria* during his master's lifetime: of sixteen *cartas* dated between 1446 and 1577, nine freed the slave outright, seven conditionally. (The paucity of *cartas de alforria* is related to the scarcity of notarial records during the period under study, since the sample was taken primarily from those *cartas* drawn up by notaries; there may have been, as in Castile, *cartas de alforria* which were not registered with a notary and which have not survived.)[44]

The professed reasons for freeing a slave were more or less the same in both conditional and unconditional letters of manumission. The slave's devotion to the master and years of faithful service were commonly adduced, as was the love the master bore toward a slave born and raised in his house. Throughout the period under consideration the crown and princes of the blood preferred to free slaves who had been converted to Christianity, but not all masters concerned themselves with their slaves' religion, at least in the fifteenth century.[45]

Whatever the professed reasons, some masters simply wished to be free of the burden of maintaining an aged or infirm slave. In 1490, for instance, Lopo Gil of Elvas freed Jorge, a black slave who was crippled in one leg,[46] and the 50- and 60-year-old men and women who received *cartas de alforria* (five out of the sixteen in the sample), though possibly hale and hearty, had evidently come to the end of their useful working lives as slaves. Without assistance from their ex-masters or relatives these freed people would find it hard to lead a decent life.

Freedmen

In any case, the prospects of an unassisted freedman were not good. Poverty represented a particular threat to the many freed people who, because they had been domestic servants and menial labourers, had not learned a profitable skill during their years of slavery. The Lisbon tax roll of 1565 indicates that, of the 213 free black taxpayers, 167, or 78.4 per cent, were in the lowest taxable category, that is, they had an estate worth less than 2,500 *rs.*, excluding the beds they slept in and the clothes they wore. The tax roll of Loulé in 1564 tells a similar story: only two out of fourteen free blacks and mulattoes owned an estate worth more than 5,000 *rs.*[47] The records of the Misericórdias of Évora and Elvas also suggest that there was widespread poverty among the free people of colour in those towns, judging from the numbers of freed blacks who could not afford to pay the cost of their burial.[48]

The poverty of the destitute was reflected in their clothing. In July 1555 the Misericórdia's charity hospital in Évora admitted a middle-aged mulatto freedman dressed in what the admissions clerk could only describe as 'rags' (*farrapos*). In January of the same year – and January is a cold month – the hospital admitted a 70-year-old free black wearing only an old burel doublet, a ragged shirt, ragged breeches and broken leather shoes; he died in February.[49]

And if poverty, or the threat of it, was not enough to contend with, freedmen also had to cope with a legal system which did not regard them as the complete equals of free white men. True, their juridical status was immensely better than that of slaves: they automatically became citizens, *vizinhos*, of the place where they were freed;[50] they were entitled to a regular trial for most crimes and their testimony was acceptable as a matter of course; they could act as the legal agent of a freeman;[51] and they could own, alienate[52] and bequeath property.[53] They were, however, placed in a subordinate position with regard to their former master. D. Afonso V ordered that freedmen show respect toward their former master by seeking judicial authorization before taking legal action against him, and D. Manuel required freedmen to defer to the master's parents and children as well.[54] These requirements put freedmen in the same position as the master's own adult children and thus, though circumscribing the freedmen's liberty, may be considered as a way of incorporating foreign elements into the system of deference peculiar to Portuguese society. More seriously demeaning to the freedman's status was the fact that his liberty was precarious: his freedom could be revoked if he showed ingratitude towards his former master during the master's lifetime.[55] A clause in *cartas de alforria* usually declared that the gift of freedom was irrevocable, even in cases of ingratitude, but in strictly legal terms this clause was invalid.[56]

Most seriously demeaning to the freedman's status as a free man were the police regulations which approximated the 'freed slaves' (*escravos forros*), as they were often called in such laws, to slaves proper. Freedmen, as we have seen, were forced to give security for their conduct as boatmen on the Tagus and they were not allowed to gather or hold dances in the streets of Lisbon. Such regulations were usually designed to prevent freedmen from aiding and abetting slaves in robberies and other criminal acts; this was why many towns did not permit freedmen to entertain slaves in their lodgings.

If freedmen themselves were convicted of some crime, their trial and punishment might differ from that inflicted upon Old Christian freemen. For example, black freedmen who were found to have falsified the measures while selling charcoal and straw in Lisbon were given the same summary trial and punishment as slaves.[57] Freedmen might even be returned to temporary slavery: in 1536, Bastião, a free black who in galloping a horse along a street had knocked down and crippled a girl, was sentenced to serve her father as a slave until he had made financial restitution. Fortunately, Bastião was able to find the money.[58] (Usually debtors were only required to pawn some of their goods or to find sureties to make good the debt.)[59] Furthermore, if sentenced to exile, free blacks apparently had to post a bond to guarantee that they would return, as New Christians had to do.[60] All in all, the position of free blacks in Portuguese society was roughly equivalent to that of New Christians and *mouriscos*: technically freemen, all three groups were constantly made aware of the fact that they had been subject peoples; they were suspected of collusion with criminal slaves, Jews or Moorish slaves or pirates, as the case might be; and they were denied the full rights of Old Christian freemen.

The burdens of a freedman's existence could, however, be mitigated by an understanding judge or a kindly former master. While doing nothing to ease legal discrimination against freedmen, the higher courts realized that many free people of colour were poor and therefore might be driven to commit some petty crime; consequently freedmen sometimes found that their sentences had been reduced, a debt forgiven or the cost of a pardon diminished.[61]

Some masters tried to provide against their freedmen becoming paupers and criminals. Where the freedmen were too old or unlikely to be able to look after themselves, a kindly master might ensure that they were sheltered and cared for. The Infanta D. Beatriz, for instance, left money to maintain three old freedmen in hospital.[62] Where, on the other hand, the freedmen were still able-bodied, the former master might give them something to help them make a start in their new life. A gift of a suit of clothes was the minimum; some money was considerably more helpful.[63] Freedwomen were given money as a dowry should they wish to marry or to become nuns (occasionally on condition that they do so) and sometimes some bed linen as well for a trousseau.[64] Gifts of money were often considerable

– some 10,000 *rs.* or 20,000 *rs.*, enough to buy a house or lodgings –
and at times were specifically earmarked for this purpose.[65]

The most substantial gift of all was a house or land bequeathed to
the freed person in his former master's will. Frequently, though, the
property reverted to the master's relatives or to other whites upon
the death of the freedmen. Thus in 1510 Isabel Lourenço of Elvas
freed her slaves João and Engrácia and left each of them lodgings
and the joint usufruct of two plots of land and two vines; but upon
the death of both freed people the property went to other heirs.[66]
Presumably the master normally made the bequest in this way
because the ex-slaves were old and unlikely to have children and
heirs, in which case their holdings, like those of lower-class commoners, would eventually escheat to the crown at their death.[67] But
this was not always so. Álvaro Luís, a cleric of Sintra, believed that
his freedman Tomé might father children by a lawful marriage, yet
in that eventuality the children were to inherit only the orchard and
vine which he gave to Tomé along with a house (at the time a stable),
household furniture and a pipe of wine; otherwise all – except, it may
be supposed, the contents of the pipe – had to be returned to Luís's
estate at Tomé's death.[68] In short, there seems to have been some
reluctance to bequeath property to freedmen, as compared to, say,
criados.[69]

Still, while they lived, these freedmen had in their orchards, fields
or vines the means of a modest sustenance. The tax roll of 1565
reveals that some of the wealthiest free blacks in Lisbon lived in the
parish of Nossa Senhora do Loreto, outside the western walls; this
was an area that was not built up and where they could raise
vegetables in their gardens for sale in the city. No fewer than eight
of the twenty-three free blacks who lived in this parish owned their
own houses. Similarly, one of the few freedmen in Loulé in 1564 who
was relatively well off, with an estate worth 45,000 *rs.*, was a black
market gardener (*hortelão*).[70] Other rural freedmen had to live as
best they could. In 1515 one Pedro Lourenço, a black man, is known
to have made a reasonable living chopping logs and selling them to
the Royal Ovens at Vale de Zebro, but many freedmen must have
had to hire themselves out as agricultural labourers.[71]

It is impossible to say how many freedmen in Portugal worked on
the land and how many in urban occupations, but the demographic
records suggest that most freedmen lived in towns of some size.
Admittedly the large population samples from big towns enable a

small percentage of freedmen to be detected far more readily than do the scanty records of small towns and villages. Nonetheless it would not be surprising if the greater opportunities for employment in the big towns exerted a powerful attraction, drawing free blacks away from the countryside. Certainly in 1544 the *procuradores* of Lisbon complained about the large numbers of free blacks from other towns and villages who had come to seek work in the city.[72]

In Lisbon, freedmen, like slaves, worked as boatmen on the river, and some shipped out as sailors or interpreters in the West African trades.[73] Free black women resident in Lisbon were able to make considerable sums of money working in unstated occupations at Mina: in 1565 two of them had estates worth 10,000 rs. and 60,000 rs.[74] In the city itself, Brandão's descriptions of the workforce engaged in various occupations in the 1550s suggest that free blacks worked in much the same manual and menial occupations as did black slaves (see Table 9, p. 81). This conclusion is also borne out by the tax roll of 1565.

Freedmen who had already learned a trade while still slaves were clearly in a better position after manumission than the unskilled, and hence a thoughtful master would occasionally secure his freedman an apprenticeship in some trade, such as shoemaking.[75] The attitude of white artisans towards admitting black freedmen into their guilds is unclear for, apart from the piemen of Lisbon who explicitly welcomed blacks, most guild regulations do not mention freedmen. Other evidence, though, indicates that some of the less prestigious trades accepted black freedmen. In 1565 three of the wealthiest blacks in Lisbon were all guildsmen: a locksmith, a cushion-maker and a tailor.[76]

Throughout Portugal one occupation which lay open to free blacks, especially to black women, was that of innkeeper. Apparently very few whites wished to take up the profession,[77] and occasional attempts to fill the need with slave innkeepers were opposed in Cortes, since the law forbade slaves even to eat or drink in hostelries, let alone keep them.[78] Hence no one objected to the desire of free blacks to become innkeepers. In the 1550s Rodrigues de Oliveira noted a street named the Beca da Estalagem da Negra in the parish of Santa Justa in Lisbon,[79] while Jakob Cuelbis recorded that during his travels in Portugal and Castile in 1599 he stayed in several inns with black landladies.[80]

All the same, the way for free blacks, as for other lower-class persons, to advance to a position of social respectability did not usually lie in trade but in the patronage of the Church or of a respected person, or a combination of the two. In 1544, for instance, a black named António received his licence to practise as a surgeon in Oporto, and thereby the right to be called *mestre*, master. Mestre António had been raised in the house of Mestre João, also a surgeon, who had taken a liking to his freedman and taught him what he knew.[81] Ecclesiastical patronage helped the mulatto playwright Afonso Álvares to establish himself in the world. Álvares, whose mother may have been a black slave who worked in a bakery,[82] grew up in the household of D. Afonso de Portugal (d. 1522), the humanist bishop of Évora, where he acquired a good education and mastery of Portuguese and Castilian. He then became a teacher of grammar in Lisbon and married the daughter of a pack-saddle maker (*albardeiro*).[83] From 1531, the date of his *Auto de Santo António*, which was commissioned by the canons of São Vicente de Fora, he supplemented his income by writing plays based on the lives of the saints. These plays, though in the tradition of Gil Vicente, demonstrate a greater knowledge of European dramatic fashions than those of the earlier playwright; Álvares is also considered superior to Vicente in his range of poetic metres, though not in invention of plots.[84] The official honours paid to Panasco, D. João III's wise fool, have been remarked upon in an earlier chapter; other blacks who took minor orders or became priests will be considered in the chapter which follows. As can be seen, none of these blacks rose very far socially, but they did acquire positions of some respectability.

In terms of day-to-day social intercourse, black freedmen seem to have found fairly ready acceptance, especially among the lower classes of Portuguese society. Poor blacks and poor whites mingled easily; they played games and enjoyed social evenings together; and some whites seem to have thought nothing of offering to share a bed with a black visitor from out of town, or of accepting a black's hospitality.[85] The Lisbon tax roll of 1565 shows that there was no distinctively black ghetto in the city and that blacks took lodgings in the same houses as whites. Interracial friendships developed, and a black's fellow tradesmen and their wives would stand as godparents to his children.[86]

Members of the two races intermarried, either in church or by common law. It was more usual, however, for poor white men – labourers, mostly – to marry black or mulatta women, than for black men to marry white women.[87] I have in fact encountered only one certain reference to a black man apart from Afonso Álvares marrying a white woman,[88] though a few other records which indicate the man's colour but not the woman's may also refer to interracial marriages of this sort.[89] Most free blacks married other blacks, free or slave. This pattern of marriages may reflect the blacks' natural preference for people who shared a similar background, but it also suggests that there was, even among the poor, some prejudice against the blacks.

Yet whatever the extent of their prejudice, the Portuguese did not translate it into laws forbidding manumission, probably because the number of free blacks was never so great as to pose a serious threat to the livelihood of the whites. Masters did not free their slaves in large numbers. Some masters refused to cause their family material loss by letting go of such a valuable piece of property; others, such as André de Resende (?1500–73), simply disliked a slave so much that they refused to grant him his freedom.[90] Fernão de Oliveira tells us that quite a few masters shared the views of another member of the Resende family, Garcia (?1470–1536), who refused to free any of his slaves because, he said, most freedmen were beggars or thieves.[91] Resende's remark points up the difference between Portugal and colonial Brazil: in the latter country free people of colour were needed to fill the positions of minor responsibility which could not be entrusted to slaves, but which white men were not numerous enough (and maybe too proud) to take.[92] In Portugal, however, there were sufficient whites to fill these positions; hence there was little economic pressure upon a master inclining him to free his slaves.

Conclusions

The search for freedom could prove to be disillusioning. Many Portuguese were on the look-out for fugitive slaves so as to claim a reward, while escape overland to Castile could lead to recapture and resale as a slave. Escape to North Africa was not easy and convinced Christians might find it hard to live among Muslims. Fortunately these fugitives could return to Portugal to live as freemen. Manumission was not as common as would appear from reading the wills of wealthy masters who could generally afford to free some slaves, though it was an accepted practice. Once free, moreover, freedmen usually found themselves among the poorest classes of a society in which there was little social mobility. Assistance in the shape of gifts of money or property from their former masters was often needed for freedmen to lead a bearable existence. The patronage of a master or the Church was almost essential if a freedman was to advance in society.

Toward the middle of the sixteenth century there were signs that, as the free white population grew, the Lisbon municipal council wished to limit competition from free blacks for the dwindling supply of jobs in the city (see pp. 125, 145). D. João III, however, seems to have thought that the freed population was not large enough to pose a serious threat, an opinion which apparently was shared by most lower-class Portuguese both in Lisbon and elsewhere. On the whole relations between poor whites and poor blacks were friendly. Similar conditions of employment and equally restricted prospects of social advancement tended to give white and black *criados* and labourers a degree of fellow-feeling.

Yet the free blacks could never completely share the outlook of the poor whites for, if equally poor, the two groups were not equally free. Although conceded the juridical status of freemen, freedmen were, like *mouriscos* and New Christians, set apart from the Old Christians in police regulations. These laws were based on the assumption that black freedmen had more in common with black slaves than with free whites, and that they would therefore aid and abet slave criminals and runaways. This was probably true to some extent, but these laws, together with the prejudice that some Portuguese had against blacks, must have gone far toward reinforcing the sense of community among blacks, both slave and free. Perhaps this sense of solidarity was most clearly shown in the number of marriages between slave and freed blacks, but it also had an institutionalized manifestation in the black religious fraternity of the Rosary, which will be considered in the next chapter.

8

Blacks and Christianity

Of the black, brown and tawny Moors brought back to Lagos in 1444 and 1445, Zurara says that four were given to churches and monasteries. One of them was simply sold to buy ornaments for the church which received him,[1] but another, a boy, grew up serving the monastery of São Vicente do Cabo and eventually became a Franciscan friar or lay brother.[2] These examples illustrate the Portuguese Church's various attitudes towards Africans. The Church had no objection to buying and selling slaves as if they were chattels – indeed, in 1446 the bishop of the Algarve fitted out a caravel for the slave-trade[3] – nor to their employment as servants. But the Church also saw Africans as men with immortal souls to be baptized and guided in the way of a Christian life. There was no question of withholding the sacraments from them.

On the other hand, until the Council of Trent the ecclesiastical hierarchy did not attach a high priority to fostering the spiritual life of slaves. In fact, the crown, moved by reasons of state as much as by genuine piety, was more concerned than the Church to evangelize the non-European community in Portugal. D. Manuel determined that all slaves except adult objectors should be baptized, and he also promoted the admission of blacks and others to holy orders. Unfortunately, the religious education of slaves was not organized but was left to those masters and parish priests who might take an interest in the slaves' spiritual welfare. Hence, though slaves were baptized and received the sacraments, they were sometimes woefully ignorant of the articles of the faith. (Admittedly, the doctrinal knowledge of most peasants and working people was probably not much greater.)

Nonetheless, most blacks seem to have embraced or managed to follow the Christian *lei*, or way of life. (In Portugal Christianity was considered a law which governed all aspects of one's existence.) Many took part in religious celebrations, while some formed lay brother-hoods and a few took holy orders. To be sure, Inquisition records show that there were blacks who through ignorance or adherence to their former beliefs and practices deviated from the Christian moral code and religious dogma. But the heterodox were quickly reconciled with the faith, once it had been properly explained to them. On the whole, Christian and African moral codes were not incompatible and Catholicism offered an attractive channel for expression of the blacks' religious feelings.

Lay piety

All aspects of religious life that were open to white laymen were open to blacks. As has been noted previously, blacks were customarily baptized and given a Christian burial. Confirmation rolls indicate that black slaves and freedmen were among the parishioners con-firmed in the faith by visiting bishops. And they could marry in church and attend mass, though sometimes their liberty to do either of these things was impeded by their masters.

They also took part in lay activities organized by the Church – religious festivals, for instance. Here similarities between Portuguese and African practices encouraged black participation. In 1466 the Bohemian Tetzel remarked upon dancing in the churches as one of the strange customs of Portugal.[4] This custom was both readily comprehensible and appealing to blacks, in the light of their own traditions. Unfortunately, there are no descriptions of black religious festivities prior to 1633, when a Capuchin friar described how the blacks of Lisbon celebrated the day of Our Lady 'ad Nives' (5 August), but the account probably holds good for earlier celebra-tions. On the day in question, the blacks donned their native dress of loincloths or skirts and tied ornamental bands around their heads, arms and chests. So attired, they marched and danced, some in African fashion, through the streets to the sound of castanets, drums, flutes and African instruments. A few of the men carried bows and arrows, while the women bore on their heads baskets full of wheat given to them by their masters. Still singing and dancing, they entered the conventual church of São Francisco da Cidade and paraded two or three times round it, before stopping to hear mass. Then they left their offerings of wheat and danced away.[5]

Blacks were involved in another organized form of lay piety, the religious fraternity. There were many of these *irmandades* or *confrarias* throughout Portugal. While primarily dedicated to the cult of some saint, they usually functioned as friendly societies as well and often acted as lobbies for special interest groups. An important fraternity which extended its charity to people other than its own members was the brotherhood of Our Lady of Mercy, generally called the Misericórdia. Founded in Lisbon by the dowager queen D. Leonor in 1498, other branches followed rapidly, both in Portugal and overseas. No fewer than sixty-one branches had adopted the Lisbon rule (*compromisso*) by the time of D. Leonor's death in 1524.[6] The brothers concerned themselves with charitable acts, such as visiting prisoners, healing the sick, providing food, clothing and shelter to travellers and the needy, and so on. Men joined the brotherhood with their entire families, including *criados* and black slaves, as is clear from the register of brothers in Évora and the surrounding district for the period 1499–1556.[7] Free blacks, both men and women, and their families were allowed to join by themselves.[8] (In this the Misericórdia of Évora was more broad-minded than the Misericórdia of Bahia, in Brazil, which always refused to accept people of colour and even whites married to men or women of colour.)[9] Blacks do not seem to have been allowed to play any role in the direction of the Misericórdia of Évora: they merely benefited from the security of membership.[10]

Blacks were, however, allowed to take part in the government of their own confraternities, which were usually dedicated to the cult of Our Lady of the Rosary. These represented the black community's variation on the special interest group fraternities formed by members of different trades throughout Portugal and by the communities of foreign nationals in Lisbon. The creation of such bodies was welcomed (when not actively promoted) by the crown, which saw them as institutional channels through which it could negotiate with and regulate the groups concerned. The earliest black confraternity was probably that of Lisbon, whose *compromisso* of 1565 claimed it had been in existence by 1460,[11] though another account states that the first fraternity of the Rosary, of white or black men, was not founded until 1484.[12] Neither source is completely reliable; all that can be said with any certainty is that the Lisbon brotherhood appears to have been in existence for several years before 1494, when it was first referred to in a royal letter.[13] By the middle of the sixteenth century other groups had been formed in Évora (in 1518) and Lagos (in 1555), and overseas in São Tomé (in 1526).[14] Possibly some of the branches mentioned during the second half of the century in Elvas, Leiria, Mugem, Funchal, Setúbal and Alcácer do Sal were functioning before the 1550s either separately or perhaps in association with whites who also formed brotherhoods of the Rosary.[15]

These fraternities were associated with houses of the Dominican order, which had promoted devotion to the rosary during the later Middle Ages. It is understandable that blacks should wish to have a club of their own, to defend their interests and to promote social life and festivities under the cover (as it were) of religion, but why they should have been attracted specifically to the rosary is hard to say.[16] An active policy of proselytization by the Dominicans, who provided several of the Infante D. Henrique's confessors and were involved in overseas missions, may be one reason.[17] Otherwise, the semi-magical, almost talismanic nature of the rosary itself may have appealed to Africans accustomed to fetish objects. Certainly the spiritual indulgences and privileges obtainable by belonging to the brotherhood and saying the rosary were considerable, including plenary indulgence once during a brother's lifetime and again in articulo mortis.[18] This magical aspect also approximated the organization to the secret societies characteristic of many African tribes. Indeed Pedro de Azevedo suggested that the brotherhoods were actually a screen for the practice of pagan rituals after black secret societies had been banned in Portugal, but he never published the documentation which he promised and I have found none to substantiate the claim.[19] D. João II and succeeding monarchs seem to have been convinced of the blacks' piety, and it would be surprising to find heterodoxy in organizations so closely associated with the inquisitorial Dominicans.[20]

By the second half of the sixteenth century the brotherhoods could have had little opportunity to practise magical rites, for they were then clearly subject to white tutelage. So much appears from the twenty-eight chapters of the compromisso of the Lisbon body, confirmed by the crown on 2 December 1565. At that time the fundamental governing council consisted of a judge (juiz), two mordomos and a clerk (escrivão), who met every Sunday and holy day, morning and afternoon, to transact business. There were also a procurador geral who gave legal counsel and a juiz conservador, a high government official nominated by the king to ensure adherence to the brotherhood's regulations. In this task he was aided, especially in matters concerning religious orthodoxy, by the prior of São Domingos.[21] The *juiz conservador*, the prior and the *procurador* were presumably all whites, while it was a rule that the clerk be a white man. He was charged with overseeing the daily business of the brotherhood and had the right to expel brothers for disobedience.[22] He could be reinforced in his tutelary role, if need be, for a king, prince, duke, count, marquis or cardinal who wished to be a *mordomo* was automatically elected for life and could provide a deputy to carry out his functions. No noble seems to have taken up the option by 1565, probably because the post was unpaid.

Thus the offices of judge and *mordomo*, while open to whites, normally went to blacks. Elections to the governing body were held on the Sunday after Saint Isabel's day (8 July). All the brothers, each bearing a lighted candle and telling his rosary, met and filed quietly through the streets to the monastery of São Domingos. After hearing mass they retired to a room provided for them and elected their officers, under the clerk's scrutiny. No one could be re-elected until three years after his term expired, except for the clerk, who therefore enjoyed the administrative benefits of continuous tenure of office. The black officers had, moreover, to be freemen. Although black slaves could join the fraternity, they could not hold any position in it; nor could other members who were free or slave mulattoes, Indians or white *mouriscos*. (The exclusion of mulattoes is characteristic of a society which classified its slave and freed population primarily by colour, rather than by racial origin.)[23] Until 1578 only married and reasonably prosperous free blacks could be elected. By that year, however, few brothers answered the description, so it was decided that the prior of São Domingos could, after consultation with the brothers, nominate the most suitable unmarried free blacks as *mordomos*. The nominees were not allowed to decline the honour.[24]

Prosperous *mordomos* with enough money to support a family had doubtless been preferred because they would have less incentive to embezzle the brotherhood's funds. This preoccupation with financial probity is clearly apparent from the numerous, strict and detailed instructions in the *compromisso* relating to the annual transfer of the money chest, books and appurtenances in the brotherhood's chapel and room to the incoming officers.[25] Taken along with the lack of qualified men, the preoccupation attests to the general poverty of the brothers. Such was only to be expected from what is known of the occupations of the thirty-nine brothers in 1565. The *compromisso* lists only a few, but there were an embroiderer, a tailor, a stone-mason, five labourers, a ship's caulker and three seamen. These trades were hardly lucrative, so the men in question would accordingly have little cash to spare for the upkeep of their fraternity.

Most black brotherhoods were badly off, and hence all constantly sought new ways of raising funds, over and above the begging for money which most fraternities were licensed to do.[26] The crown assisted them to some extent, but rarely gave them monetary pensions similar to those granted white brotherhoods of the Rosary. An exception was the 500 rs. in gold which, from the time of D. João II, the Lisbon brotherhood received from every caravel returning from Mina.[27] Usually royal assistance was more indirect, in the form of authorization to seek revenue from sources not generally open to fraternities. For instance, in 1521 D. Manuel permitted the brotherhood of Évora, described as 'very poor', to collect alms in kind from donors' wine cellars and threshing-floors. The same king allowed the Lisbon brothers to sell candles to the crew and passengers of ships bound for Mina and Guinea. The candles were blessed on Candlemas (2 February) and given to the ships' captains to sell on the brothers' behalf.[28]

Funds were needed first of all for the maintenance of the cult, both to pay priests to hold masses and to buy church furnishings for ostentatious ceremonies. Every Sunday morning the Lisbon brothers attended a sung mass in their chapel in São Domingos amid a blaze of light. Everyone in the chapel held a lit taper, and important moments during the ceremony were marked by the lighting of more candles until every candle possible was lit at the raising of the host. Then, their black skins contrasting with their long white cloaks, the officers went forward to take Communion: a stunning sight, provoking devotion, as was its intent. On the Sunday following All Saints', the mordomos erected a bier in the church of São Domingos and had vespers sung for the departed souls with much burning of candles and ceremonial decoration. On the Monday a mass was sung with litanies, after which the brothers brought offerings of bread, wine and fish to the priests who were under contract to the brotherhood. The feast of Our Lady of the Rosary was an occasion for especially costly decoration of the chapel – the mordomos were admonished to enter all the expenses in the accounts.[29]

Secondly, funds were needed because the Rosary acted as a mutual aid and burial society for its members. If any brother fell sick or was otherwise in need, he was helped from the alms box, while if a brother or his wife died, all the brothers, each holding a burning candle, went with the priests to fetch the body and bring it to the church where the funeral service took place. The brotherhood paid for the funeral of penurious brothers, but in those cases mass was said, not sung.

The black fraternity had, however, a broader view of its own interests than simply the physical or spiritual well-being of its members: it also considered itself, and was accepted by the crown as, the spokesman for the interests of the free black community as a whole, and for black slaves in matters relating to their freedom. We have already seen how the Lisbon brotherhood defended the rights of free black *regateiras* in 1515; six years later it intervened on behalf of black women married to interpreters and seamen. While their husbands were away on voyages to Africa, these women were often molested by men of the watch (*homens do alcaide*) and even by other men who came by night and demanded entry on the pretext that the women were concealing fugitive slaves and stolen goods in their houses. Once admitted, the intruders ransacked the house, stealing things and 'affronting' the women. On hearing these complaints put forward by the officers of the Rosary, D. João III agreed that no one should enter the women's dwellings without a proper search warrant, but since he imposed no penalty it is uncertain whether the abuse was remedied.[30]

The brothers had somewhat more, if still limited, success in their representations concerning freedom and manumission. According to the charter of the brotherhood of São Tomé in 1526, a charter based on the existing privileges of the Lisbon body, the brothers could demand and oblige masters to free any black slaves who were members of the fraternity.[31] They could also seek to secure the freedom of slaves who were not members but had been freed by testamentary manumission: the brothers' services were required in these cases, because some heirs and executors refused to carry out the testators' wishes. This was a continuing problem which D. João II and D. Manuel attempted to solve by giving the brotherhood the right to take legal action against recalcitrant executors and heirs.[32] The latter, however, put up a strong resistance, and in 1518 D. Manuel capitulated to them by deciding that the brotherhood could not take legal action until the heirs had been provided with security equivalent to the value of the slave. If the case failed, the heirs could either keep the security or have the slave returned.[33] This ruling, which made the manumission of slaves considerably harder to obtain, appears to have led the brotherhood to concentrate only on the cases which it had a fair chance of winning, so as not to deplete its funds.

The later chapters (later probably in a chronological as well as an ordinal sense) of the Lisbon *compromisso* suggest that the brotherhood became more selective in lending its support to all slaves seeking their freedom, not just those who had been freed by wills. Chapter xxii forbade any officer to accept money from an external source (that is, from the slave himself) for the purpose of freeing a slave, unless the matter had been discussed and approved by the entire governing council. The following chapter noted that the brotherhood was often importuned by *meios forros* for funds wherewith to purchase their complete freedom. The brothers decided, however, that they were not obliged to provide such slaves with financial assistance, nor to demand their liberty in the courts, but merely to speak in their favour. An exception was to be made when the brotherhood was particularly indebted to a slave. Even so, the *meio forro* could not expect an outright gift of more than 500 *rs*. – a paltry sum – lest the brotherhood be defrauded by an unscrupulous master. The brothers had evidently adopted a policy of hard-headed realism as a result of long experience with slave-holders who broke their promises. Yet they did not harden their hearts against the slaves; their fight to ease the manumission of slaves continued until well into the seventeenth century.[34] New brotherhoods continued to be founded to represent black people's interests, and the organization spread to Brazil. There, unlike in Portugal, the fraternities tended to be created on a tribal basis, doubtless because there were many more blacks, and hence more people from one tribe, in any one place.[35]

Blacks and holy orders

Profound religious devotion could be expressed in a desire to take holy orders, but for some time devout blacks found even minor orders difficult to obtain. First of all, in accordance with canon law, no slave could take orders, since his master would continue to have a claim upon him.[36] Furthermore, the requirement that ordinands be the children of a lawful Christian marriage was an impediment to the ordination of blacks who had been born in Africa, and indeed to many born in Portugal.[37] Dispensation from this requirement was obtainable, but not at all common for blacks before 1518.

This year marks a turning point in the Church's attitude toward the induction of black priests. The best-known event is the elevation of the Mani Kongo's son, D. Henrique, to the bishopric of Utica *in partibus infidelium*. He was permitted to reside in the diocese of Funchal which at that time included the kingdom of Kongo.[38] D. Henrique's elevation owed much to the efforts of King Manuel who saw in it a means not just of promoting Christianity but of extending Portuguese influence in Africa. Similar considerations led the king to petition Leo X to allow other Christian Ethiopians (that is, blacks), Indians and North Africans then living in Portugal also to become priests. The request was granted in the little-known but extremely important papal brief *Exponi Nobis*. Henceforth these non-Europeans could be invested with full holy orders, regardless of the circumstances of their birth. However, in accordance with D. Manuel's wishes, Leo agreed to limit the new priests' freedom of action: they could preach, celebrate mass and administer the sacraments only when they returned to their homelands or to other infidel parts where there were no parishes. And on no condition were they to hold a benefice or be responsible for any ecclesiastical property, such as a chapel.[39] Thus at the same time as D. Manuel ensured the promotion of Christianity and Portuguese influence, he managed to reserve the temporal benefits of the Church for white Portuguese.

Among the first, probably the first, to profit from the papal brief were Bishop D. Henrique's countrymen, the BaKongo sent to Portugal by their aristocratic parents to be instructed in Portuguese culture and the Christian religion. Their earliest mentors were the canons regular of the order of Saint John the Evangelist, the so-called 'Loios' or 'Blue Canons'. From 1488 black Kongolese frequented their houses of Santo Eloi in Lisbon and São João at Xabregas and, in later years, the houses of other orders elsewhere.[40] In 1534 Pedro, one of these BaKongo, was dispensed from the impediment of birth in Africa to infidel parents and was granted minor orders in the cathedral of Évora.[41]

But Pedro was accompanied by blacks and mulattoes who were far from being aristocratic Kongolese. Some, like André Freire, who took minor orders in 1535, were the children of an illicit union of a master and his slave; others, like one João, ordained in 1533, were the children of unmarried slaves. These ordinands had to provide clear proof that they were freemen. This was why in 1538 Manuel, a black man, was assisted at his investiture by his former master's son, who showed Manuel's letter of manumission to the ordaining bishop, and generally stood in lieu of a relative during the ceremony.[42]

Very few blacks and other former slaves were admitted to holy orders and they did not advance rapidly within the secular Church. Of 1,137 men who took minor orders in Évora on 29 March 1533, there was only one child of slave parents and one freedman, and of 334 on 21 September 1538, two sons of unmarried slave parents – the son of a cleric and his slave, and Manuel, mentioned above.[43] By 1555 none of these, or any other black, had taken higher orders.[44] Some may have been ordained elsewhere, in Lisbon for instance, before going overseas, but the figures do not indicate that great numbers were being trained in Évora for missionary work.[45]

In Portugal itself the only way an ordained black could legally follow his vocation was as a member of a monastic order, where there were no benefices nor cures of souls. Yet the number of blacks who could aspire to become full monks or nuns is uncertain: when, in 1493, the Infanta D. Filipa gave her freedwoman Maria da Cunha the option of marriage or taking religious vows, she did not expect Maria to be anything more than a lay sister, a *freira conversa*.[46] Mulattoes seem to have fared better both as regular and secular churchmen and could even secure the administration of church property. In 1553, Isabel Borges of Beja freed her mulatto slave João Fernandes, left money for him to be trained as a priest (*clérigo*), and endowed a chantry chapel of which she constituted João and his white father the administrators.[47] Two years later, the prior of Alcochete, António Mendes, was described by a witness before the Inquisition as a mulatto.[48] If this was so, Mendes had reached the most responsible position in society of any person of black African ancestry in Portugal at the time.[49]

Blacks and the Inquisition

During the course of the sixteenth century the orthodoxy of all Portuguese Christians, black and white, came under the scrutiny of the Inquisition. Although D. Manuel had asked for an Inquisition in 1518, the papacy did not accede to the request until 1531. The Inquisition then established was more directly responsible to the papacy than was the Spanish one and ceased to function in 1535. In 1536 D. João III obtained the concession of an Inquisition of the Spanish type, though still hemmed in with papal restrictions. It was suspended between 1544 and 1547, after which date it followed a similar course and was similar in nature to the Spanish Inquisition. Originally based in Évora, the Inquisition established several tribunals in other cities, but later the number was reduced to three, in Évora, Coimbra and Lisbon. Of these the most important in terms of the number of people denounced and tried was that of Lisbon, and accordingly most of the cases dealt with below come from there, from the years before 1560.[50]

Blacks frequently appeared before these tribunals as witnesses, for the inquisitors had few reservations about taking the word of black informers as evidence. Unlike judges in secular courts, they accepted the testimony of a slave, even against his master or another free person. In fact, they often called upon slaves belonging to a suspect to confirm the evidence of other witnesses.[51]

Hearsay from slaves was also taken into account, so a slave who had a grudge against his master could easily get even with him by denouncing him, or making sure that he was denounced, to the Inquisition. Such a case occurred in Lisbon in 1541. Vicente, who seems to have been a mulatto, told one witness that his master's family observed Jewish sabbaths and that they fled from the house when the priest came to take the confessional roll. Now Vicente had been locked up for four or five months previously for having drawn a knife upon his master and was subsequently sold to some Castilians, so he clearly had no cause to love his owner. As Vicente was leaving with the Castilians another witness heard him cry out that his master's family were Jewish dogs who should be burned.[52]

Fear of being denounced drove some masters to kill their slaves to stop them from telling what they knew: in 1541 and 1542 two masters from Setúbal were accused of just this crime.[53] Yet a slave had very little to gain by denouncing his master, for when the goods of a convicted heretic were confiscated, slaves were included: there was no question of manumission.[54] Therefore only blacks who really loathed their masters were likely to deliberately inform on them.

Blacks themselves were denounced to the Inquisition for sins involving moral or sexual deviance, such as bigamy and homosexuality, as well as on charges of religious deviance – blasphemy, heterodoxy and witchcraft. Given the customs of some African peoples it would seem logical that blacks might be tempted to commit what, in Christian eyes, was the sin of bigamy. However, the influence of African *mores* on bigamists of African descent is hard to prove, since before 1560 the only black bigamists known from the records were mulatto or *baço* (dark), that is, people who had grown up in Portugal. Mere geographical separation could have been the main reason why Bastião Rodrigues, a mulatto or *baço*, forgot his lawful wife in Elvas and took up with a common-law wife in Lisbon, just as it caused a white man in Lisbon and his *baça* wife in Oporto to take new partners. Still, African traditions may have prompted António Lopes, a free mulatto, to marry no fewer than three girls in the region of Santarém. There is no record of the mulattoes being brought to trial, but the white man was sentenced to five years in the galleys, with a secret instruction that he be pardoned after two.[55]

Homosexuality was also punished by time in the galleys. The Inquisition kept a special book, called the Book of the Evil Sin (*mau pecado*) listing all those denounced as homosexuals. Among them was one Bastião, a free black who lived in Palhais (see Map 4, p. 73). Somewhat effeminate in appearance, he had been subject to the attentions of a white paederast while growing up and later had affairs with other white men. He was denounced in 1557 by a white who (apparently ignorant of Bastião's sexual preferences) had let the black man share his bed for the night after Bastião had come to Lisbon to sell grapes. Since this was the second delation, Bastião was apprehended, tried and sentenced to be whipped in the prison of the Inquisition before being sent to the Algarve to serve for ten years in the galleys.[56] Bastião steadfastly maintained that no anal intercourse had been involved, since the penalty for this was death at the stake, with infamy on all the bugger's descendants (if any).[57] But in practice the penalty was not death: eight years later another free black who had committed buggery was also sentenced to the galleys.[58]

The background to most blacks' appearances before the inquisitors was an abject ignorance of Christian doctrine, the result of masters' negligence in giving their slaves religious instruction.[59] Bastião, the homosexual, for instance, knew how to cross himself, to say the paternoster and Ave Maria in Latin, and some of the creed in Portuguese, but others knew even less and still others nothing at all. Whether knowing the articles of the faith would have curbed the physical drives of bigamists and homosexuals is a moot point, but it might have spared some blacks from being denounced and arrested on charges of religious deviation. To blacks who had received little more of Christianity than baptism, the religion could appear to be a meaningless and alien ritual, not to be taken too seriously. Thus one black girl in Setúbal was reported for encouraging a young boy in her care to lean out of the window and make the sign of the horns as the Holy Sacrament was passing by.[60]

This was blasphemy; worse than that in the inquisitors' eyes (though understandable even to them in view of the blacks' ignorance of the faith) was retention of previous beliefs and practices after baptism. Blacks who retained Islamic beliefs were particularly suspect. Before 1560, the majority of those denounced for this reason were Wolofs, which is not surprising, since the proximity of the Wolof kingdoms of Senegambia to North Africa had exposed them to considerable Muslim influence by the beginning of the sixteenth century.[61] Two Wolofs were denounced to the Inquisition of Lisbon for non-Christian beliefs in 1549; three more (and one Fula) in 1552; and two more in 1554.[62] The informer in 1552 and 1554 was another black, João Pinto, the perfervid convert. Most of the Wolofs denounced had expressed their belief in the superiority of the customs of their homeland – an understandable assertion, but one which implied that a non-Christian religious law was better than a Christian one. One man added that Christians were unclean because they did not wash before prayers and because they laundered their clothes with urine.[63] Another, called Francisco, told João Pinto that God had no son but that Christ was Muhammad's servant whom the latter used to trick the Christians. Francisco's lack of belief in Christ's divine paternity was shared by António, whom Pinto also denounced.[64] Although both Francisco and António were arrested and tried, only António's trial records exist in their entirety.[65]

Under questioning, António declared that he had been truly converted since he had last talked to João Pinto. But he still knew nothing more of Christianity than how to say a paternoster and an Ave Maria, which he had learned from a serving lad after a priest had told him that he was destined for perdition since no one had taught him the faith. His story is that of a man caught between two worlds, mindful of the Islam of his boyhood, but disturbed by the feeling that Christianity might be true, and wishing for some authoritative decision – which the inquisitors provided. Raised as a Muslim with the name of 'Amaçambat', he had received a good grounding in Islamic theology. Accordingly he had found it hard to believe that God was the crucifix, since man cannot see God (though he had taken off his cap to the icon, as he did to everybody), nor that God was in the host, chalice or images. When the inquisitor explained that God was not in these objects but was present in the Sacrament, António readily assented, declaring that this was what he had suspected. He was reconciled with the faith at the *auto da fé* of 27 August 1553, where he publicly abjured his sins and was sentenced to wear a penitential habit and to suffer imprisonment at the Inquisition's pleasure. His time in prison was short, for he was released on 20 November into his master's custody on condition that he be sent to the Inquisition's college to learn doctrine every Sunday. Nor was his master allowed to sell him without the inquisitors' leave, on pain of excommunication and confiscation of the slave or his value.[66] A short prison term followed by compulsory religious education seems to have been the standard punishment for heterodox blacks: the two would-be fugitives mentioned on p. 137 were treated in the same way.[67] Evidently the inquisitors, however harshly they dealt with moral lapses, were prepared to show understanding toward black slaves who, through lack of instruction, still retained a sympathy for Islam.

The attitude of the Inquisition and secular authorities toward formerly pagan blacks who retained beliefs and practices considered to be sorcery in Portugal is not clearly known, nor can the African, pagan component of black sorcerers' practices be precisely defined. The reason for these lacunae is insufficient evidence. To judge from the number of sorcerers held in municipal gaols, most cases of malefic sorcery (*feitiçaria*) appear to have been tried in the secular courts. But no trial records survive, and the few pardons available do not indicate whether the severity of the Manueline ordinances regarding sorcery was usually moderated when formerly pagan blacks were the culprits.[68]

The Holy Office was interested only in heretical sorcerers, which apparently meant those who invoked devils.[69] Two blacks were accused of this sin before 1560, but their cases were treated so differently that no assessment of the Inquisition's attitude towards black sorcerers is possible. One was Filipe da Cruz, a free black from Setúbal, who was said to have declared that he had given his little finger, which had a lump on it, to Satan, so that he now kept company with devils.[70] The inquisitors made no attempt to secure corroborative evidence, so Filipe was not prosecuted. The other was Beatriz, a black slave from Évora who, called as a witness in another trial for invocation of devils, condemned herself by admitting she knew one spell. The inquisitors held her for interrogation from 24 October 1551 until May 1552, when she died in prison.[71] Her spell was meant to bind a man in love to a woman and consisted of tying knots in one of the points (*atacas*) of his hose, while keeping one's eyes fixed on the star nearest the moon and murmuring an incantation.[72] In October she said that the words of the spell were simply, 'Through here you must enter and through here you must leave', but on 13 April she confessed that they constrained Beelzebub (*Barzabu*) to enter and leave in this way, and on 4 May that the words bound the man's genitalia by the power of Satan and Beelzebub. In April she also said that she had learned to speak with devils from a sorceress in Madeira who had shown her the images of her parents in Guinea in a basin of water, but in May she retracted these statements and further denied that she had ever slept with devils – to which she had never previously confessed. Beatriz herself said she had been delirious in April, and it appears that after six months in prison her health was failing and she was ready to tell the inquisitors what she thought they most wanted to hear: that she had invoked the powers of Satan. The most plausible elements of this story are that she made knots in cords to bind men to their mulatto mistresses or white wives, in return for food or drink or favours, as she claimed; there does not seem to have been any doubt in her mind that the spell worked. The rest of the story, her dealings with devils and so on, was probably suggested to her by her questioners or by recollections of stories she had heard. The inquisitors themselves seem to have been puzzled and in the end must have decided to reconcile her with the Church, for she was buried by the Misericórdia and hence, presumably, in consecrated ground.[73]

Although Beatriz claimed in October that she had learned her spell from an old black woman in Beira, and in April from the free black washerwoman-cum-sorceress in Madeira, neither the spell nor her other stories provide striking evidence of distinctly African forms of magic. Rather, her magical beliefs and practices seem to represent an amalgamation of European and African traditions. For instance, she said that she had invoked devils by standing at the centre of a cross scratched on the ground (an *encruzilhada*) and calling, 'Soma-tambra'. These words, she averred, were African; but the *encruzilhada* is part of Portuguese magical tradition.[74] Furthermore, while the devils she invoked may have been African, she evidently believed in the power of Satan and Beelzebub (as did Filipe da Cruz). Such an amalgamation of magical beliefs could have occurred through the relatively easy mixing of blacks with superstitious white commoners. However, to construct a general theory about the nature and development of the magical beliefs held by Portuguese blacks from one or two case histories seems as presumptuous as to determine inquisitorial attitudes towards black sorcerers from the same evidence, and will not be attempted here.

Conclusions

The beliefs and practices of the few blacks arraigned before the Inquisition should not be considered as typical of the religious life of the black community as a whole. Numerous other Inquisition records concerned with suspects who were not black show that prior to 1560 more blacks denounced or were overheard to denounce culpable acts than actually committed them. Most of the black community appears to have been reasonably orthodox. Even those who were heterodox had accepted some Christian beliefs and practices – Beatriz, for instance, believed in Satan and António, the former Muslim, said some Christian prayers – or were willing to become Christians. This willingness to follow the Christian way of life distinguished blacks from North African Moorish slaves, who usually remained fervent Muslims.

The reason for the blacks' acceptance of Christianity is probably related to the nature of paganism which, unlike Islam, was permeable to new cults, provided the new gods gave visible proof of their power. Now, most of the western African peoples were fundamentally pagan. The Wolof were the most Islamized, but Ca' da Mosto observed that only the upper classes were strongly attached to Islam; Muslim and pagan beliefs intermingled in the religion of the commoners. For a pagan the efficacy of the Christian God in providing the Portuguese with a high standard of living was very impressive indeed. No less a figure than the Wolof Damel of Kayor was prepared to admit as much (though, being a Muslim, he did not think highly of the Christians' chances in the afterlife), while the pagan Mani Kongo was quite overawed by the power of the new god.[75] Thus when pagans were removed from their own societies, where the weight of tradition supported pagan beliefs, and taken to Portugal as slaves, they had few inherent objections to embracing Christianity.

Their conversion to a Christian way of life was doubtless aided by the various features which Portuguese Catholicism shared with pagan religions, such as common prayer, the cult of saints (who could be seen as minor gods or tutelary spirits), the direction of worship by priests and religious processions with dancing in the churches.[76] Even the shadow side of Christianity, the belief in witchcraft and devils, was easily understood, and some blacks made their contributions to magical practice and belief in Portugal.

A further (and quite possibly the major) inducement to espouse Christianity was that conversion was the key to social acceptance, advancement and influence. The Christian slave received better treatment in law and doubtless at the hands of his master than did the Moor; he certainly had a better chance of being freed. The blacks who took minor orders escaped the jurisdiction of the secular law and may have proceeded to the monkhood in Portugal or the priesthood overseas, thus winning some respect. And the sincere Christianity of the brotherhoods of the Rosary gained them the king's favour and hence the power to protect the rights of the black community. To be sure, the brothers' success in obtaining laws which favoured free blacks and the manumission of slaves must be qualified by the apparently widespread lack of compliance with those laws. Still, even if the concrete political results were small, they were not to be despised in terms of the encouragement which they gave to black people who otherwise might not have had any spokesmen at all. The brotherhoods' mere existence affirmed that someone was concerned with blacks as people and that someone was prepared to fight for their freedom. It is unlikely that a purely secular group composed of black people from the two lowest estates in Portuguese society could have acquired the same respectability and hence the influence which the brothers enjoyed as a consequence of their pious observances.

9
Race relations

During the Middle Ages, Portugal's slave population had been predominantly Moorish, but by the mid-sixteenth century it was predominantly black and, as we have seen, legal and social adjustments had been made to cope specifically with blacks. By that time too, the outlook and culture of Portuguese whites had been significantly affected by the existence of a black servile class as an integral part of society. Folklore recognized the blacks' abiding presence in songs about blacks and in fairy tales where even giants were presumed to have black servants.[1] There were allusions to blacks in everyday figures of speech and wise saws,[2] while artists painted blacks as usual participants in *genre* scenes, both secular and religious (see Plates 2, 3 and 4).

The image of the black which had grown up in the white mind received its fullest expression in the comments of historians and travellers and in poems and plays featuring black characters. Documentary evidence shows that this literary picture was founded upon accurate observation of the behaviour of blacks in Portugal. Yet the interpretation which the whites placed upon the observed facts, namely that the blacks' actions were those of an inherently servile people, is clearly no more than a rationalization and justification of slavery and the status quo. Further examination shows that the blacks' behaviour is best explained as a reaction to their oppressed social position.

The white picture of black people

Most Portuguese seem to have thought that blacks as a people were innately inferior to whites in physical beauty and mental ability and, moreover, that they were temperamentally suited to a life in slavery. The first recorded impressions of the blacks' outward appearance were far from appreciative, though as time passed the occasional voice was raised in the blacks' favour, albeit in tones of qualified approval. To begin with, the Africans' very colour was against them: traditionally, black, and especially the word *negro* which was used to describe the people, signified misfortune and sadness. In fact, it was held to be the skin colour of the devils in hell.[3] Furthermore, by European standards, the blacks' facial features were unattractive: when Gil Vicente wished to describe ugly peasant women he endowed them with dark skins and broad noses.[4] These strains of ugliness and devilishness appear quite clearly in Zurara's record of the first landing of black captives at Lagos in 1444. He notes that the blacks were 'so deformed in their faces and bodies, that they almost seemed . . . images from the lowest hemisphere'. (To the blacks he opposed other, Idzāgen, captives of 'reasonable whiteness, beautiful and comely'.)[5] The European physiognomy remained the standard of beauty in the sixteenth century, but some whites began to make distinctions, favouring some African peoples over others. Duarte Lopes, for example, who was a merchant in the Kongo between 1578 and 1582, declared that the blacks of Nubia and Guinea had 'deformed' faces, but allowed that the Bantu BaKongo had full and subtle faces, without thick lips. Indeed, 'except for the black colour, their appearance is like that of the Portuguese'.[6]

No one, however, dissented from or even qualified the opinion that in mind and temperament all blacks were clearly adapted for servitude. Zurara may not have been referring to the blacks specifically when he described the captives landed in 1444 as loyal and obedient, not inclined to escape nor to committing the sin of venery, though somewhat vain about their apparel. He could well have been talking about the Idzāgen, whom Ca' da Mosto says were considered better slaves than the blacks.[7] Nevertheless, later authors speak of blacks in much the same terms. Barros, for instance, who thought that blacks in Africa were barbarians, averred that, brought to Portugal, they were 'good people, faithful, Catholic, serviceable and who helped us in our necessities'. They had, besides, enough warlike spirit to be useful as soldiers, and he recommended that the Portuguese recruit a black guard, as the Sharif of Morocco had done.[8] Similar notions were expressed by the Italian travellers Landi and Sassetti, who probably did no more than repeat what their Portuguese hosts had told them. According to Landi, blacks were often very good and most faithful slaves, but of an 'undeveloped and dull intellect' which suited them almost naturally to their servile rank. (It may be remembered that Ledesma, in his critique of the slave-trade, took pains to dispel the belief that blacks were natural slaves: see p. 44 above.) Sassetti also deemed the blacks more apt for manual than intellectual labour, though he observed that those from Cape Verde were very quick to learn, good players of the lute and especially good men-at-arms.

Not that black slaves were without defects. Landi noted that unless blacks were kept hard at work and occasionally disciplined with the lash, they could easily fall into bad habits. This belief was perhaps the origin of the folk saying, 'Work is good for a black'.[9] Another proverb, translated by Sassetti as 'Egli ha più fantasia che un Nero' ('He is more fantastical [or extravagantly conceited] than a black'), shows that the Portuguese thought that blacks gave themselves airs.

Hence blacks were not the most highly prized slaves. In Landi's opinion, this distinction fell to mulattoes, most of whom had been born in their masters' houses. They were excellent in all service, which they performed so willingly that in consequence they were often manumitted. Sassetti commended the Asiatics – Japanese, Chinese and Indians – on their intellect.[10] But the blacks were certainly better liked than the 'good for nothing, rebellious and fugitive' Moors, who were thought to be evilly inclined and great robbers, rendering little service to their masters.[11] Furthermore, blacks willingly submitted to what Barros termed the 'evangelical yoke', while the Moors remained Muslims, sworn enemies of the Christian religion which informed Portuguese civilization.[12]

Recognition of the blacks' acceptance of Christianity is implied in paintings of the Adoration of the Magi where, from the first third of the sixteenth century, the mage Balthasar was portrayed as a black man far more often than before.[13] Plate 6 offers a particularly fine example.[14]

The blacks of literature exhibit the same range of behaviour as was remarked upon by Barros and other racial theorizers. Figures representing blacks entertained the public from 1455, when a 'black king' from Sierra Leone performed a song in rudimentary *fala de Guiné* to accompany a dance at the wedding of the Infanta D. Joana.[15] Thereafter black characters appeared with some frequency in Portuguese poems and plays, the black being definitively established as a stock character of the stage by Gil Vicente in the 1520s. Black stereotypes speaking *fala de Guiné* fitted without difficulty or incongruity into a form of comedy which consisted to a large extent of the manipulation of stock characters, some of whom, notably the rustic simpleton, the Moor and the gypsy, also spoke dialectal forms of Portuguese.

Most of the blacks depicted in poems and plays were male, and most of them were loyal and dutiful slaves. Some of them, however, were rascals, slaves whose masters had evidently not cured them of 'bad habits'. Many of the males, and all of the less common female figures, displayed *fantasia* or conceit, the females in sharp complaints directly to their owners, the males in impertinence to other people.[16]

Several stage blacks showed the qualities which the Portuguese appreciated in their slaves. Bastião, in the *Auto de Dom Fernando*, was so loyal and obedient to his owner that, charged with protecting the daughter of the house from amorous suitors, he fulfilled his duty so faithfully that he even refused one suitor's offer to purchase him his freedom.[17] Furnando, in Sebastião Pires's *Auto da Bella Menina*, called up his fighting spirit to protect his master, the Menina's lover, from the retinue of her outraged father.[18] But the blacks' bellicosity was never directed toward winning freedom or exacting revenge upon whites. Vindictive Moorish characters appeared on stage, but no vindictive blacks.[19] While stage blacks might have disagreements with their masters, they were generally good-humoured, suggesting that they were satisfied with their place in society. Most blacks in poems and plays sang a song or played an instrument, and even the less dutiful ones were cheerful.[20]

The less dutiful slave is exemplified by Fernando or, as he called himself, Furunando in Gil Vicente's *Fragoa d'Amor* of 1524. Furunando met the goddess Venus on his return from gorging himself at the grape harvest in Tordesillas. He was immediately smitten with love and offered to take the goddess home with him to the Alfama in Lisbon, where he would maintain her by stealing clothes, money and more grapes. To win her heart he sang her a popular ballad in *fala de Guiné*. The goddess then asked him if he was a Christian, which Furunando affirmed; as proof, he recited a paternoster, which came out as 'pato nosso' ('our duck'). His suit was rejected, but he returned later in the play to take advantage of Cupid's magical smithy which reforged anyone who entered it into the person he wished to be. Furunando wished to be given white skin and European features, so that he would be 'handsome'. Cupid granted his wish, but the former black man still spoke *Guiné*. This was a disaster, he complained, for now when he made advances, white women would laugh at him and black women would think he is mocking them.[21]

No less than his more obedient cousins, Furunando embodied several common white prejudices about blacks. He was not very bright, as witness the impossibility or failure of his schemes. His proclivity to theft, especially of fruit, was a defect noted often enough by *procuradores* and municipal councillors. And his admiration for Venus's beauty and dislike of his own colour merely confirmed the Portuguese belief that blacks were ugly. Thievishness as part of a laughably simple-minded rascality was also attributed to blacks by António Ribeiro Chiado, while blacks with an unrequited desire for white women appear later in the century in the poems of Fernão Rodrigues Soropita.[22] But the superficiality of blacks' religious knowledge, which Vicente introduced into two plays, did not become a standard component of the 'wayward black' stereotype.[23] Evidently whites were aware of the problem, but the inquisitorial censors forbade advertising it, as an implied criticism of the Church's missionary efforts.

Furunando's attitude to Venus was certainly forward, and other blacks, including the dutiful ones, could be openly rude to people who were not their masters. Bastião, in the *Auto de Dom Fernando*, called one of the suitor's servants a 'little turd' (*merdinho*).[24] But the male blacks usually assumed an ingratiating, placatory tone when answering for their faults to their masters. Black pride is more evident in the female figures, who reply boldly. The outspoken female slave first appears in a poetic dialogue or short comic sketch (*entremês*) by Henrique da Mota in the late fifteenth or early sixteenth century. Here a Kongolese woman defended herself against her priestly owner's accusation that she had overturned a barrel of wine. When he threatened to hand her over to the law, she said she would then tell all about his own offences, presumably his sexual relations with her.[25] Her literary descendant is Luzia, of Chiado's *Auto das Regateiras*.[26] Luzia actively complained of her mistress's incessant stream of commands which were couched in the most offensive terms, and was rebuked for having too much *fantasia*.[27]

Playwrights generally made free blacks resemble the Furunando type, perhaps to indicate that blacks' bad habits flourished when unchecked by slavery. The black prince of Benin in Vicente's *Nao d'Amores*, for instance, desired a white girl, but she rejected him as a 'dog'.[28] The freedman Furunando in the same author's *Clerigo da Beyra* made a great show of his religiosity, reciting a hopelessly garbled paternoster as proof, before making off with the belongings of a rustic simpleton who had gone for a swim. Besides being a thief, he is also described as a great liar.[29] More similar to Luzia, however, is the black herbalist doctor, Mestre Tomé, of the *Auto de Vicente Anes Joeira*. Driven to distraction by a dim-witted rustic who purchased all the wrong drugs because he could not understand the doctor's *fala de Guiné*, the doctor provides a rare example of a black man calling a white man ignorant in a play.[30] Such a characterization of lower-class whites was, of course, perfectly consonant with the social ideology of the age.

The attitudes and behaviour of whites toward blacks appear in no very favourable light in these plays. Furunando the freedman complained that he had a master who chained him, several blacks were threatened with being whipped or tortured with drops of hot fat, and almost all, slave and free, were called 'dogs'.[31] Usually the slaves complained behind their masters' backs. But one character, the mulatto slave Solis in Henrique Lopes's *Cena Policiana*, addressed a moving appeal directly to his white interlocutors who he believed were mocking him:[32]

Solis: You have quickly touched me upon my colour but I also spin delicately.
Teodosio: I don't catch your drift.
Solis: I want you to know that I can feel.

The human reality

By placing such complaints in the mouths of stage blacks, white authors showed that they believed that their fictional characters were accurate representations of flesh and blood people. To be sure, documentary evidence confirms that the descriptions of blacks' behaviour by historians and travellers and the depiction of it in poems and plays closely correspond to reality. However, if the whites were accurate observers, their assessment of the motives behind the blacks' actions is suspect. Fundamentally, they believed that blacks as a people were inherently ignorant and servile. These innate characteristics moved blacks to behave as they did and thus made it unthinkable for them to be accommodated in society in any but the lowest classes. The blacks' disposition to theft and *fantasia* was troublesome but, as poems and plays suggested, was less serious than simple-minded and childish, and merely indicated the blacks' need for a master to direct and control them.

Of course, the Portuguese belief that distinct aptitudes and behaviour were inherent to each of the subject peoples was false. The skills which were assumed to be evidence of mental aptitudes had been learned in the slaves' own homelands. Blacks were considered ignorant because very few African accomplishments other than musical and martial ability were regarded at all highly in Portugal. Greater intelligence was imputed to Asiatics because they had skills which the Portuguese admired: Indian cabinet-makers, for instance, were much in demand. Similarly the mulattoes who, because of their upbringing, were thoroughly conversant with Portuguese customs, were supposed to be more gifted intellectually than were blacks from Africa. The various ways in which the subject peoples behaved in servitude was not the result of racial differences but of differences in the conditions surrounding their enslavement. Moors often made poor slaves because they were prisoners of war who looked upon slavery as a temporary condition from which they would be released by a ransom paid from North Africa or even by armed intervention by Barbary corsairs. They were, moreover, hereditary enemies of the Portuguese, from whom they were separated by severe religious differences. The blacks, on the other hand, could not expect to be released from slavery by external means, and therefore had to make the best of a bad situation. (The same was probably true of the Asiatics.) Coming to terms with life in Portugal was perhaps less difficult for blacks than for Moors because they lacked any traditional enmity towards the Portuguese and their religious beliefs were permeable to Christianity.

By embracing Christianity they aligned themselves with the great mass of Portuguese. In fact, much of their behaviour closely resembled that of lower-class whites, who were likewise imprisoned in an oppressed social position. This resemblance is hardly surprising, since both blacks and white servants worked for masters in much the same occupations. Generally speaking, the aims of both groups were satisfactory living conditions and terms of employment and, where possible, advancement in the social hierarchy to a status which allowed them more control over their own lives.

In a seigneurial society, winning the master's favour through loyalty and obedience was the regular means of preferment, and not simply a mark of abject servility. Yet by accepting the master–servant relationship with its prescribed avenues for promotion, the servants had to a degree acquiesced in and internalized their rulers' view of how society should be constructed. Acquiescence in this could lead on to adoption of the masters' other views, a further accommodation which might have sad results where blacks were concerned. Those blacks who adopted their masters' racial opinions could lose their self-respect and come to believe that black people were inferior. Gil Vicente's Furunando who wished to be white had his counterparts in real life: a black woman named Leonor Henriques testified before the Inquisition in 1541 that when a New Christian woman (whom she was denouncing) had asked her if she would like to be white, she had replied that she would.[33] Similarly those blacks who consorted with white women may have done so because they had accepted white ideals of beauty.[34]

Since, however, women were legally subjected to the rule of the men in their family, blacks may have desired to seduce white women so as to undermine the white men's dominance in some way.[35] For the submission of servants, black or white, to their masters was often not a confirmed habit but a conscious tactic. Many servants retained an independent mind which led them to behave in ways damned in blacks as the product of extravagant fantasy but which were, according to playwrights, equally typical of white servants. On the stage, white servants constantly complained about their hard life and bad treatment behind their masters' backs, were rude and offhand to strangers, but nearly always feigned loyalty and obedience in their masters' presence.[36] Occasionally, like Luzia, they talked back to their masters.[37]

If loyalty and giving themselves airs were not unique to blacks as a people, no more were their so-called 'bad habits'. As municipal laws show, both slaves and mancebos de soldada had a proclivity to petty theft. And both slaves and free retainers of powerful men were equally turbulent, relying on their masters' influence to protect them from the full force of the law.

If white or black servants were dissatisfied with their conditions of employment, they might run away.[38] Most often, though, the servants probably employed time-honoured wiles to establish a code of practice in their household. By alternating obedience with grumbling, dilatory work and plain non-cooperation, they could make their master aware of how much he could expect of them and what treatment would encourage the best work. Harsh punishment was not always a spur to action; it could be just the reverse. For instance, the *procuradores* of Santarém to the Cortes of 1461 mentioned that if a master put one of his black slaves in chains, the rest created an uproar, for this punishment was not commonly inflicted upon blacks.[39] Masters might therefore find it advisable to treat servants well, as an incentive for blacks to work well. Hence masters bought pardons for their servants, free or slave; one master who paid to have his slave excused a whipping said he did so because he was afraid that his slave, if whipped, would run away from shame and leave no one to work his farm.[40]

Apart from the Moors, no member of the working classes seems to have thought that violence would cause significant changes in the social structure. No *jacqueries* are recorded in Portugal during this time. For the blacks, organized violence would have been pointless, since they were so heavily outnumbered. Furthermore, except in individual cases, slavery in Portugal was probably not so oppressive as to drive men to take up arms against their masters. Slaves – as all servants – of wealthy and powerful men were better off materially and before the courts than were free wage labourers. If their work was not domestic, they might travel the country or live apart from their masters, as freemen did, and through profit-sharing agreements slavery became a contractual arrangement, like an apprenticeship. And sometimes, if rarely, faithful service was rewarded with preferment, in the form of manumission.

Since blacks' behaviour resembled that of white servants in so many ways, one must ask why the Portuguese regarded blacks as so different from whites that they should be relegated to servitude and were somehow temperamentally adapted to that status. The answer seems to be that the Portuguese thought that, because of their colour, blacks were an entirely different species of human being. Thus though their behaviour might resemble a white's, it was nonetheless not the same thing and did not respond to the same motivations. And in Portuguese eyes, anyone other than a white Catholic European was undoubtedly inferior. Landi could therefore assert that people were slaves in Portugal *because* of their colour (the blacks) or their religion (the Moors), in other words, because they were different from the Portuguese themselves.[41] The Portuguese evidently believed that colour differentiated men so completely that a cross between a white and a black, namely a mulatto, was as different from his parents as a mule (*mulato*) was from an ass and a horse.

Difference in colour was, however, less of an impediment to social (though not sexual) acceptance than difference of religion. The Portuguese regarded themselves pre-eminently as Christians; 'Christian' was the word they used when they wished to distinguish themselves from other, non-European, peoples. Hence blacks, while they were considered an inferior species of man, were trusted because they were Christians. Conversely, even though the Mooresses' whiteness made them sexually desirable, Moors were distrusted and feared. Mulattoes, who were not only Christians but also resembled Europeans in their features – and who often had the advantage of prolonged acquaintance with Portuguese culture – were esteemed. This would explain why the most highly-placed people of African descent in Portugal during the period under study were mulattoes.

Conclusions

The French chronicler Commynes writing between 1489 and 1491 perceived Portugal as a slave-owning society[1] and most Portuguese would probably have accepted this description readily enough. Slaves were, however, a relatively small part of the workforce and supplemented, rather than displaced, free labour even in the most menial jobs. Thus slavery played the same economic role in Portugal as it did in most of the other Mediterranean states where slaves were found. Throughout southern Europe small numbers of slaves were farm-hands, herdsmen and market gardeners;[2] they were rarely organized into gangs to work on plantations, except perhaps on the island colonies of Crete and Cyprus.[3] Most slaves were domestic servants or menial labourers in the towns, and their other urban occupations bear a general resemblance from one end of the Mediterranean to the other: as in Portugal, there were slave ferrymen in Istanbul,[4] slave crew on Genoese vessels,[5] slaves working as stevedores and in the shipyards in Barcelona,[6] and slaves selling vegetables and produce in Genoa and Seville,[7] where they were also involved in garbage disposal.[8] Slavery in Seville was very like slavery in Lisbon and both cities were described (wrongly) as having more slaves than freemen.[9] In both there was a large black population, masters hired out the labour of their slaves and slaves sometimes lived and worked away from their masters on condition that the slaves shared what they earned with their owner.[10] Apart from the size of the black population, conditions were much the same in Valencia and Genoa.[11] In all these cities, slaves were trained as craftsmen, and some guilds took measures to restrict competition from slaves.[12] Yet nowhere in southern and western Europe would the economy have collapsed without slave labour. This absence of any real necessity for servile labour, coupled with the relatively high price of slaves, made slave-ownership a luxury, a symbol of wealth and prestige particularly associated with the crown, nobility and wealthy merchants. The ready availability of slaves in a country heavily involved in the slave-trade made Portugal an exception where even labourers could own slaves. Even so, most slaves there appear to have been in the hands of the wealthy. The geographic distribution of slaves in Portugal resembled that elsewhere in southern Europe: large concentrations in the cities and ports, few slaves in mountains and poorer regions.[13]

Still, if slavery in Portugal corresponded to the Mediterranean pattern, it also foreshadowed the American, and particularly the Brazilian, experience. In this respect the introduction of black slaves into Portugal marks a turning point in the history of slavery. The voyages of the Portuguese caravels were the inauguration of the Atlantic slave-trade and from thenceforward black slavery was to be a typical feature of Atlantic civilization in early modern times. What differentiated slavery in north-east Brazil and other plantation societies of the Americas from slavery in Portugal and the Mediterranean countries was the sheer size of the slave population and its central importance to the economy. Otherwise the nature of the occupations considered suitable for slaves and free blacks were generally the same in the Old World and the New. Urban occupations on both sides of the Atlantic were virtually identical,[14] while rural employments were adapted to the needs of vast or underpopulated new lands: one can trace a line of development associated with the increasing availability of free land from the employment of slaves as farm-hands and gardeners in mainland Portugal to slaves assisting in the small canefields of Madeira and thence to the large gangs of slaves on the sugar plantations of São Tomé and Brazil.

If the organization of slave labour in Brazil was foreshadowed in Portugal, so too were the attitudes toward the blacks who were slaves. The pale-skinned Moors were despised and mistrusted; the blacks accepted; the mulattoes, half-Portuguese as they were, preferred. From this followed the system of prejudice prevalent in colonial and modern Brazil, that is, prejudice on the grounds of colour, with mulattoes distinguished from, and preferred to, blacks.[15]

The same continuity is not found in Portuguese and Brazilian physical and legal treatment of slaves: the Brazilians seem to have been far more suspicious of their black slaves' loyalty and treated them more harshly. Such a response was typical in American plantation colonies where the whites, vastly outnumbered by their slaves, felt threatened by them. Furthermore, in a plantation economy, an interest in profit might lead slaves to be treated as mere human machinery, essential for the production of the export crop, but expendable and easily replaced by the slave-trade.[16] In Portugal, on the other hand, black slaves were never more than a small minority and the nature of their employment, though menial, did not usually balance the life of the slave against a demand for profit. Hence in Portugal the interests of the free population did not require the radical changes in the traditional legal status of the slave which are found in colonial slave codes. In Europe, the slave remained an inferior retainer, subject primarily to his master, while in the plantation colonies slaves were treated more and more as chattels, subject to the entire (if numerically small) white population.

Epilogue

The history of black slaves and freedmen in Portugal during the seventeenth and eighteenth centuries remains to be written; we know a few details, but are not thoroughly familiar with the whole picture.[17] These details, though, suggest that the role of black slavery in the economy and the social attitudes toward blacks remained more or less the same as in the sixteenth century. Probably, as in Castile, there was a decline in the number of blacks imported in the seventeenth century.[18] This decline increased the numerical significance within the slave community of people of mixed blood, who were still called *pretos* and *negros* despite the fact that their skins were sometimes lighter than their masters'. The squandering of human resources caused by the disabilities on these people, Portuguese born and bred, proved offensive to the marquis of Pombal who was likewise opposed to the disabilities placed on another group, also disadvantaged because of what their forefathers had been, the New Christians. Hence, after abolishing all distinctions between Old and New Christians in 1768, on 16 January 1773 Pombal embarked upon a gradual programme of emancipating slaves. He freed and removed all legal disabilities from children born after that date whose parents, grandparents and great grandparents had all been slaves in Portugal.[19] The import of slaves into mainland Portugal had already been banned in 1761,[20] probably to prevent the diminution of colonial slave populations, a consideration which postponed the abolition of the slave-trade in other parts of the empire until 1836. The emancipation of slaves was undertaken at a different pace in the various Portuguese territories and the institution was wholly outlawed throughout the empire only in 1875.[21]

The assimilation of the blacks which, with the slight economic utility of slavery, had favoured emancipation in Portugal has aroused some interest among ethnographers. In the 1930s Portuguese scholars effectively refuted the assertion of some of their German colleagues that the Portuguese physiognomy had been strongly affected by miscegenation. Clearly, the absorption of some 3 per cent of the population would scarcely affect the appearance of succeeding generations.[22] But some negroid features persisted and in some villages, notably São Romão, near Alcácer do Sal, people of distinctly negroid appearance were common as late as 1920, if not later.[23] At that time, however, most of the descendants of slaves would have been indistinguishable from other white Portuguese. Black faces were not again seen in any numbers on the streets of Lisbon until the 1960s, with the influx of Cape Verdians fleeing from the drought in the Sahel.

Notes

Preface

1 A. P. de Carvalho, *Das Origens da Escravidão Moderna em Portugal*; E. Correia Lopes, *A Escravatura*; A. Brásio, *Os Pretos em Portugal*; V. Magalhães Godinho, *Os Descobrimentos e a Economia Mundial*, II, 517–87. See also, P. A. de Azevedo, 'Os Escravos', *Arch. Hist. Port.* I (1903), 289–307 (for abbreviations see pp. xvi–xviii), and J. A. Pires de Lima, *Mouros, Judeus e Negros na História de Portugal*.

2 M. Heleno, *Os Escravos em Portugal*, vol. I (and only); C. Verlinden, *L'Esclavage dans l'Europe médiévale*.

3 Seminal articles have been collected into L. Foner and E. D. Genovese (eds.), *Slavery in the New World*, and A. Weinstein and F. O. Gatell (eds.), *American Negro Slavery*.

4 Reasonably brief overviews are V. Magalhães Godinho, *A Estrutura da Antiga Sociedade Portuguesa*, and A. H. de Oliveira Marques, *History of Portugal*, vol. I. On the discoveries, see J. W. Blake, *West Africa. Quest for God and Gold, 1454–1578*, and C. R. Boxer, *The Portuguese Seaborne Empire*.

5 ANTT, C. C., I. 78. 17, 26 May 1546, published in *Mon. Miss. Af.*, 2a sér., II. 386, referring to mulattoes in the Cape Verde Islands.

6 J. Leite de Vasconcellos, *Antroponímia Portuguesa*, p. 374, suggests that *pardo* was applied to mulattoes; in this period, however, the word is mainly found in connexion with dusky non-negroid peoples, such as the Idzãgen of Mauritania.

7 G. E. de Zurara, *Crónica de Guiné* (many editions; I have used that edited by A. Dias Dinis, as *Crónica dos Feitos de Guiné*, the passages given in *Mon. Hen.* and the French translation of L. Bourdon and R. Ricard, *Chronique de Guinée*), cap. xvi.

8 Álvaro de Caminha, governor of São Tomé, referred to a black who, he feared, would leave the island to become a 'Moor in Mani Kongo', that is, a pagan in the kingdom of Kongo. ANTT, C. C., 3. 1. 34, 24 April 1499, published in *Mon. Miss. Af.*, 1a sér., I. 159.

9 ANTT, Ch. Af. V, 36, f. 240v, 30 Sept. 1459, noted in *Descobs. Ports.*, I, *sup.*, 581. Azevedo, *Arch. Hist. Port.*, I (1903), 290, claimed that the earliest use dated from 1462.

10 'Considerações sôbre o Preconceito Racial no Brasil', *Afro-Ásia*, VIII/IX (1969), 8. On the history of the word *sclavus* and its derivatives, see C. Verlinden, 'L'Origine de sclavus=esclave', *Archivum Latinitatis Medii Aevi*, XVII (1942), 97–128, and his *L'Esclavage*, II. 999–1010.

11 The number of these other slaves in Portugal was never very great. The Amerindians had a tendency to become despondent and to commit suicide (F. Sassetti, *Lettere edite e inedite*, ed. E. Marcucci, p. 125, letter to B. Velori

from Lisbon, 10 Oct. 1578), while the crown limited the importation of Asiatics, since they took up valuable space on the Indiamen which could otherwise be filled with spices and other precious goods. Some important officials were favoured with the privilege of bringing back one or two Asiatic slaves (ANTT, Ctas Miss., I. 79, 28 Feb. 1513, and *Regimento das Cazas das Indias e Mina*, ed. D. Peres, cap. clix, pp. 134–5, 17 Aug. 1517), and slaves could be shipped as crew when there was a manpower shortage on the India fleets (ANTT, Leis, 2. 13, cap. li, 5 Mar. 1505, published in *Docs. Port. Moz.*, I. 226–7), but that, in theory, was all.

12 E.g., in Damião de Goes, *Chronica do Felicissimo Rei D. Emanuel*, pte I, cap. x.

13 As 'fr[ancis]co escrauo preto catiuo de fr[ancis]ca diaz', AHCM Lxa, Ch. Cidade, 924, Fianças dos escravos, I, f. 77, 30 Apr. 1551.

Introduction

1 N. Clenardus, *Correspondance*, ed. and French trans. by A. Roersch, I. 54, 57; III. 32, 36, letter to J. Latomus from Évora, 20 Mar. 1535.

2 'Modern times', because black slaves were perhaps more common in Antiquity than has been supposed; see F. M. Snowden, Jr, *Blacks in Antiquity*, especially pp. 183–6. There were, of course, a few black slaves in mediaeval Europe, for instance in Portugal itself (a black is depicted in the Lisbon Beatus MS. of 1189; see H. W. Janson, *Apes and Ape Lore in the Middle Ages and the Renaissance*, p. 49), in Muslim al-Andalus (E. Lévi-Provençal, *Histoire de l'Espagne musulmane*, III. 74–5, 177–8), and elsewhere in the Mediterranean world (see Verlinden, *L'Esclavage*, vols. I and II, *passim*), but they constituted a small percentage of the slave population.

1 The slave-trade

1 On Portuguese practice in Morocco and the Canaries, see Magalhães Godinho, *Descobrimentos*, II. 520–2.

2 An extensive documentary survey of the slave-trade in the fifteenth and sixteenth centuries is currently being prepared by a team led by Commander A. Teixeira da Mota. When this appears, under the title *Os Portugueses na Guiné*, it should be the definitive treatment.

3 The singular of Idzāgen (Sanhāja in Arabic) is Azenūg, whence the Portuguese *azenegue*, plural *azenegues*; see J. S. Trimingham, *A History of Islam in West Africa*, p. 20, n. 2.

4 *Crón. Guiné*, caps. xii, xiii; J. de Barros, *Asia*, dec. I, liv. I, cap. vi, suggests that the black woman was later recaptured by the Idzāgen, so the first blacks taken in Africa south of Morocco may not have appeared in Portugal until 1443.

5 See R. de Pina, *Chronica d'El-Rei D. Affonso V*, ed. Mello d'Azevedo, *passim*.

6 There is some doubt concerning the exact figure. See V. Magalhães Godinho (ed.), *Documentos sobre a Expansão Portuguesa*, II. 178, n. 19, and D. Leite, *Ácerca da 'Crónica dos Feitos de Guinee'*, p. 162.

7 *Crón. Guiné*, cap. xxv; A. Iria, 'O Algarve no Descobrimento e Cristianização da Guiné no Século xv', in *Congresso Comemorativo do Quinto Centenário do Descobrimento da Guiné*, I. 204.

8 D. Henrique's design in Africa south of Morocco does not seem to have been conquest on the grand scale; rather, the southern voyages were intended to

determine the limits of Muslim power, to seek an ally against Islam, to promote Christianity and to reconnoitre the possibilities of trade (*Crón. Guiné*, cap. vii) in lands whose wealth in gold may well have been known to the Infante from merchants' tales, the study of portolans and the geography book called *El libro del conosçimiento de todos los reynos* (1350–60) (ed. M. Jiménez de la Espada, in *Boletín de la Sociedad Geográfica de Madrid*, II (1877), 7–66, 97–141, 185–210; see especially pp. 99–100, 107–13). Hence the new commercial approach, though it disgusted Zurara (*Crón. Guiné*, cap. xcvi), was not wholly repellent to D. Henrique nor to most Portuguese, least of all as it promised to yield more lucrative results for less effort.

9 *Crón. Guiné*, cap. lxiii. The transaction, involving the redemption of a soul from Muslim or pagan domination, was called a ransom, *resgate*, and eventually the term was extended to describe any exchange of goods in Africa south of the Atlas, even where things such as chickens, eggs ('ransomed' at Malindi, BM Porto, MSS de Sta Cruz de Coimbra, 804, f. 76, 7 Jan. 1499; facsimile in A. de Magalhães Basto (ed.), *Diário da Viagem de Vasco da Gama*, vol. I) and gum arabic were the objects of trade (gum at Arguim: ANTT, Núc. Ant., 888, f. 46, *anno* 1508).

10 Trade after 1448: *Crón. Guiné*, cap. xcvi; status of slaves purchased: V. Fernandes, *Description de la côte occidentale d'Afrique (Sénégal au Cap de Monte, archipels) (1506–1510)*, ed. T. Monod et al., p. 21; T. de Mercado, *Summa de tratos y contratos*, lib. II, cap. xx, ff. 102b, 103; L. de Molina, *De Justitia et Iure* (1st edn, Cuenca, 1593; I have used the edn of Cologne, 1613), tom. I, tract. ii, disp. 33, 34; A. Álvares de Almada, *Tratado Breve dos Rios de Guiné de Cabo Verde* (1594), ed. A. Brásio, cap. iv.

11 The post was founded some time between 1448 and 1455, when A. Ca' da Mosto visited it; see his *Le navigazioni atlantiche*, ed. T. G. Leporace, vol. V of *Il Nuovo Ramusio*, p. 26.

12 Barros, *Asia*, dec. I, liv. III, cap. iii, confirmed by a quittance to Jorge Tenreiro, factor of Mina, 1543–5, who received no slaves, ANTT, Ch. J. III, Doações, I, f. 220v, 24 Jan. 1553. On the trade at Mina, see J. L. Vogt, 'Portuguese Gold Trade: An Account Ledger from Elmina, 1529–1531', in *Transactions of the Historical Society of Ghana*, XIV (1973), 93–103, and his 'Private Trade and Slave Sales at São Jorge da Mina: A Fifteenth-Century Document', in *Transactions of the Historical Society of Ghana*, XV (1974), 103–10.

13 In the area of Guiné–Bissau. Not to be confused with the Slave Rivers (Rios dos Escravos) in Nigeria.

14 Even so, Angolan slave exports to Spanish America surpassed those from Upper Guinea and the Cape Verdes only in 1610: see P. and H. Chaunu, *Séville et l'Atlantique, 1504–1650*, VI. 402–3, and P. D. Curtin, *The Atlantic Slave Trade, a Census*, pp. 106–7.

15 BN Lxa, Fundo Geral, caixa 235, no. 87, 11 Jan. 1458, published in *Mon. Hen.*, XIII. 126–7.

16 Fitting out of vessels in 1453 mentioned in ANTT, Ch. Af. V, 1, f. 82, 2 Mar. 1456; also in Estrem., 8, f. 84v, published in *Mon. Hen.*, XIII. 126–7.

17 Appointment of Fernão Gomes, ANTT, Ch. Af. V, 15, f. 47, 12 Apr. 1455, published in *Descobs. Ports.*, I, *sup.*, 347.

18 *Regimentos e Ordenações da Fazenda* (1516), cap. vi, f. 2, 2v.

19 Armazém in existence before 1480: see ANTT, Ch. Man., 6, f. 56, quittance dated 2 Oct. 1500; also in Estrem. 9, f. 99, published in A. Braamcamp Freire (ed.), 'Cartas de Quitação delRei D. Manuel', *Arch. Hist. Port.* I (1903), 401–2.

20 ANTT, Ch. J. II, 8, f. 35v, published in *Descobs. Ports.*, III. 333–4. The Armazém da Guiné recovered its autonomy in 1501.

21 The Casa da Guiné originally shared a building with the Armazém, but moved to the ground floor of the royal Paços da Ribeira when these were built in 1505; see G. Correa, *Lendas da India*, I. 529.

22 See J. L. Vogt, 'The Lisbon Slave House and African Trade, 1486–1521', *Proceedings of the American Philosophical Society*, CXVII: 1 (1973) 4, referring to A. Vieira da Silva, *As Muralhas de Lisboa*, 2nd edn, 2 vols. (Lisbon, 1940–1), II. 56–70, which I have not seen.

23 Quittance to João do Porto for period 1486–93, ANTT, Estrem., 1, f. 268, published in Freire, 'Cartas de Quitação', *Arch. Hist. Port.*, III (1905), 477.

24 ANTT, C. C., 3. 3. 9, 31 Mar. 1506.

25 For the *quarto*, see Ca' da Mosto, *Navigazioni*, p. 12; for the *vintena*, see ANTT, Mestrados, f. 151, 26 Dec. 1457 (donation of the *vintena* by D. Henrique to the Order of Christ), published in *Descobs. Ports.*, I. 545. The Infante had been granted the *dízima* (10 per cent): (ANTT, Ch. Af. V, 24, f. 61, 22 Oct. 1443, published in *Mon. Miss. Af.*, 2a sér., I. 266–7), but commuted it to the *vintena*.

26 *Crón. Guiné*, cap. xxv.

27 For Santiago de Cabo Verde, see ANTT, Gav. 2. 1. 8, 10 June 1466; São Tomé, Ch. Man., 13, f. 17, 20 Mar. 1500; Príncipe, Ch. Man., 17, f. 22v, 20 Aug. 1500. These charters are published in *Descobs. Ports.*, III. 56, 587–8, 616, respectively.

28 Method followed in Santiago de Cabo Verde, ANTT, Núc. Ant., 528, *passim*.

29 *Regimento das Cazas das Indias e Mina*, cap. clxii, p. 143, 25 Oct. 1530.

30 ANTT, Núc. Ant., 110, ff. 180v–181, 24 Sept. 1534.

31 See F. de Salles Lencastre, *Estudo sobre as Portagens e as Alfandegas em Portugal (Seculos XII a XVI)*, pp. 23, 24.

32 Thus *dízima* was levied at Oporto on slaves shipped from Lisbon; see AD Porto, Originais, liv. 15 (catalogue no. 1673), f. 15, judicial sentence of 27 Mar. 1498.

33 *Dízima* on slaves from the Cape Verdes and on some slaves from the Azores, Madeira and the North African *praças* was collected at the *alfândega*; on slaves from São Tomé and the rest of the African coastline, at the Casa da Sisa: ANTT, Núc. Ant., 110, ff. 180v–181.

34 Ibid., f. 253, 21 Mar. 1564, and ff. 252–254v, 6 Nov. 1564.

35 *Regimentos e Ordenações da Fazenda*, cap. ccxxviii, f. 95v.

36 ANTT, C. C., 1. 69. 8, 10 Jan. 1541; ANTT, C. C., 1. 71. 95, 22 Feb. 1542.

37 ANTT, Ch. Af. V, 9, f. 95v, 23 July 1462, published in *Descobs. Ports.*, III. 31–2. The contractors trading with the coast north of Arguim between 1474 and 1479 had to pay only one-sixth of the goods they imported to the crown and had a licence to send goods to Castile paying only the *sisa* and *portagem*: ANTT, Ch. Af. V, 33, f. 46v, 2 Dec. 1473, noted in H. da Gama Barros, *Historia da Administração Publica em Portugal*, 1st edn, liv. III, tit. iii, cap. v, vol. IV, p. 385, and n.2.

38 ANTT, Leis, 2. 27; *Ord. Man.* (1521), 5. 106; *Regimentos e Ordenações da Fazenda*, cap. ccxxvi, f. 95.

39 Slaves landed in Tavira in 1518: ANTT, Ch. J. III, 13, f. 13v, published in Freire, 'Cartas de Quitação', *Arch. Hist. Port.*, IX (1914), 433–4; in 1530: C. C., 1. 45. 78. Setúbal and the Algarvian ports are mentioned as receiving slaves regularly in F. Mendes da Luz (ed.), 'Relação das Rendas da Coroa de Portugal feita em 1593 por Francisco Carneiro, Provedor de Ementas da Casa dos Contos', *Bol. Bib. Univ. Coimbra*, XIX (1950), 87.

40 E.g., in Setúbal in 1506, ANTT, Ch. Man., 38, f. 55, published in Freire, 'Cartas de Quitação', *Arch. Hist. Port.*, I (1903), 281.

41 *Regimentos e Ordenações da Fazenda*, cap. ccxxvi, f. 95.

42 F. Mauro, *Le Portugal et l'Atlantique au XVIIe siècle (1570–1670)*, pp. 31–8, claims that the *nau* was larger than the *navio*, but during this period the terms seem to have been interchangeable.

43 H. Lopes de Mendonça, *Estudos sobre Navios Portuguezes nos Seculos XV e XVI*, p. 57.

44 ANTT, Núc. Ant., 888, ff. 19–23; 889, ff. 54–72v.

45 Called a *nave* in Italy. See F. C. Lane, *Venetian Ships and Shipbuilders of the Renaissance*, p. 254.

46 ANTT, C. C., 1. 20. 127, 19 Nov. 1516, published in *Mon. Miss. Af.*, 1a sér., I. 372.

47 *Crón. Guiné*, caps. lxxxvi, lxxxix; Barros, *Asia*, dec. I, liv. I, cap. xi; J. Vicens Vives (ed.), *Historia de España y América*, III. 175.

48 ANTT, Núc. Ant., 799, ff. 129–130v.

49 ANTT, Núc. Ant., 16, ff. 34v–35v, 16 Dec. 1517.

50 ANTT, C. C., 2. 161. 27, *c.* 1530; 1. 67. 56, 25 Oct. 1538; 2. 166. 23, 14 Dec. 1530.

51 A. Thevet, *La Cosmographie universelle*, vol. II, liv. xiii, cap. xi, f. 498v. Thevet probably visited Portugal during his travels between 1537 and 1554; see his *Les Singularitez de la France Antarctique* (1558), ed. P. Gaffarel, p. xii.

52 Account of Pedro de Sintra in Ca' da Mosto, *Navigazioni*, pp. 125–6.

53 The passage indicating the method of acquiring slaves is ambiguous, as Professor P. E. Russell has pointed out to me; ibid., p. 77.

54 Fernandes, *Description* (f. 101 in original MS.), pp. 26, 27.

55 *Regimento das Cazas das Indias e Mina*, cap. clv, pp. 123–4, 3 July 1509.

56 *Ord. Af.*, 4. 63; *Ord. Man.* (1521), 5. 81.

57 Horses' tails: ANTT, Ch. Man., 41, f. 67v, 18 Sept. 1511, published in Freire, 'Cartas de Quitação', *Arch. Hist. Port.*, VI (1908), 157.

58 ANTT, Gav., 20. 2. 66, trans. and published in J. W. Blake, *Europeans in West Africa, 1450–1560*, I. 111.

59 Álvares de Almada, *Tratado Breve*, cap. v.

60 See A. Teixeira da Mota (ed.), 'A Viagem do Navio *Santiago* à Serra Leoa e Rio de S. Domingos em 1526 (Livro de Armação)', *Boletim Cultural da Guiné Portuguesa*, XXIV: 95 (1969), 529–79.

61 *Ord. Man.* (1514), 5. 109; (1521), 5. 112.

62 In this period, one *peça de escravo* was equivalent to one slave, or to a slave mother with her suckling child: ANTT, Núc. Ant., 889, ff. 15, 35, 46, and *passim*.

63 *Regimento* in ANTT, Núc. Ant., 16, ff. 83–88v, published in *Mon. Miss. Af.*, 1a sér., IV. 124–33.

64 By 18 Apr. 1532, see ANTT, C. C., 2. 174. 85; see also 2. 188. 40, 2. 188. 120 and 2. 195. 41.

65 'Fruit pits'; A. F. C. Ryder, *Benin and the Europeans, 1485–1897*, p. 64, n. 1, suggests 'palm kernels'.

66 Literally, 'hazelnut biscuit', but a fig-like fruit was called *abellana* on São Tomé (Blake, *Europeans in West Africa*, I. 163), and this may well be what is referred to. Slavers bound for Arguim carried ship's biscuit for both slaves and crew, allowing about 43 kg per man for a month; see ANTT, C. C., 2. 1. 47, 18 Feb. 1489, and 2. 2. 77, 14 Oct. 1494, published in A. Braamcamp Freire, *Expedições e Armadas nos anos de 1488–1489*, pp. 60, 110.

67 E.g., ANTT, C. C., 2. 33. 231, 28 Aug. 1512.
68 Sassetti, *Lettere*, p. 126, letter to B. Velori from Lisbon, 10 Oct. 1578.
69 In Blake, *Europeans in West Africa*, I. 153.
70 ANTT, Núc. Ant., 16, f. 86v, published in *Mon. Miss. Af.*, 1a sér., IV. 129.
71 ANTT, C. C., 3. 4. 98, published in ibid., 1a sér, I. 215–21.
72 ANTT, C. C., 2. 18. 29.
73 ANTT, Livraria, MS. 2664, no. 22, referring to 1525–8, published in A. Baião (ed.), *Documentos Inéditos sôbre João de Barros*, p. 105.
74 *Regimento das Cazas das Indias e Mina*, cap. xxiii, p. 28; cap. cli, p. 119; cap. clv, pp. 124–5; *Ord. Man.* (1514), 5. 109. 12; (1521) 5. 112. 12.
75 *Regimento das Cazas das Indias e Mina*, cap. xxiii, p. 29; cap. cxlviii, p. 117.
76 'Desnudos como Dios los hizo', N. von Popplau, 'Viaje por España y Portugal' (1484–5), in J. Liske (ed.), *Viajes de extranjeros por España y Portugal*, trans. 'F.R.', p. 34; 'sin vestido ninguno como perros', BL, Harl. ms., 3822, D. Cuelbis, 'Thesoro choragraphico de las Espannas' (1599), f. 286.
77 Sassetti, *Lettere*, pp. 126–7; a similar account is in G. Landi, *La descrittione de l'isola de la Madera*, in Latin, with Italian trans. by A. Fini, pp. 42, 83.
78 V. Cortés, *La esclavitud en Valencia durante el reinado de los Reyes Católicos*, p. 58.
79 *Regimento das Cazas das Indias e Mina*, cap. cxlviii, pp. 117–18; and see Vogt, *Proceedings of the American Philosophical Society*, CXVII (1973), 10.
80 *Ord. Man.* (1521), 4. 16. Pr., 1, 2.
81 V. Šašek, *Commentarius Brevis*, ed. K. Hrdina, f. 91, 91v, Engl. trans. and edn, M. Letts, *The Travels of Leo of Rožmital*, p. 118.
82 *Crón. Guiné*, cap. xxvi; E. Falgairolle (ed.), *Jean Nicot*, p. 116, letter of Nicot to Bishop of Limoges from Lisbon, 25 Sept. 1560.
83 See ANTT, Estrem., 1, f. 268, 27 Feb. 1500, published in Freire, 'Cartas de Quitação', *Arch. Hist. Port.*, III (1905), 477.
84 *Regimento das Cazas das Indias e Mina*, cap. cxlix, p. 118.
85 ANTT, Cortes, 5. 6, f. 23, Cortes of Torres Novas, 1525 / Évora, 1535, cap. ger., lxxxiii.
86 From 1488, at least; ANTT, Ch. J. II, 14, f. 73, published in *Descobs. Ports.*, III. 348.
87 ANTT, C. C., 1. 14. 43, 1. 13. 57, 58, mentioned in Vogt, *Proceedings of the American Philosophical Society*, CXVII (1973), 12–13.
88 João Brandão, 'Majestade e Grandezas de Lisboa em 1552', ed. A. Braamcamp Freire and J. J. Gomes de Brito, *Arch. Hist. Port.*, XI (1917), 225.
89 *Livro do Lançamento e Serviço*, I. 105 (original f. 48v); I. 156 (f. 71); II. 105 (f. 224v).
90 AHCM Lxa, Ch. Régia, 29, D. Manuel, 1, no. 70, 10 Feb. 1502; Brandão, 'Majestade e Grandezas', *Arch. Hist. Port.*, XI (1917), 94.
91 *Commentarius brevis*, f. 80, Letts trans., 107.
92 *Ord. Af.*, 4. 35. 3; *Ord. Man.* (1521) 4. 23. 2.
93 *Ord. Af.*, 4. 22; *Ord Man.* (1521), 4. 16. Pr., 1, 2.
94 Numerous bills in Archivo de Protocolos, Badajoz, from 1562.
95 AD Évora CM, Núc. Not., 27, Fernão de Arcos, 2, ff. 143v–144v, and Núc. Not., 20, Diogo Luís, 19, ff. 51–52v, both refer to the sale on 25 Aug. 1548 of the same slave, Guiomar, then in the prison of the Inquisition, by representatives; representative also in sale of 'negro mullato' António, AD Porto, Notas, 3a sér. 6, ff. 147–149v, 18 May 1552. Direct sale in AD Setúbal, Núc. Not., Almada, 1, f. 102, 102v, 10 Mar. 1568.
96 AHCM Lxa, Ch. Cidade, 474, Prov. Ofícios, 1, f. 102, 24 Mar. 1508.

97 Gama Barros, *Historia da Administração Publica*, IV. 183, 184.
98 AHCM Lxa, Ch. Cidade, 474, Prov. Ofícios, 1, f. 55, 55v, 30 Aug. 1490; f. 62, 29 June 1491.
99 'Majestade e Grandezas', *Arch. Hist. Port.*, XI (1917), 102–3.
100 Oliveira, *Sumário*, p. 81; *Livro do Lançamento*, 1. 145–6 (f. 66v), 354 (f. 161v); II. 72 (f. 208), 205 (f. 276), 290 (f. 315), 347 (f. 342).
101 In the early sixteenth century the *corretores* of Lisbon asked the king not to increase their numbers to such an extent that each *corretor* would then make less than 50,000 *rs.* p.a. ANTT, Gav., 15. 9. 1, n. d., considered in Gama Barros, *Historia da Administração Publica*, IV. 185–6; the estates of the six *torretores* in the *Livro do Lançamento* of 1565 ranged in value from 10,000 to 100,000 *rs.*, the mean average value of their real and movable property being 45,000 *rs.*, the median, 40,000 *rs.*
102 *Crón. Guiné*, cap. xcvi; on Zurara's reliability, see references cited above, p. 181, n. 6.
103 Ca' da Mosto's figures vary according to the edition; those here are from the oldest (BN Marciana, Venice, MS. Marciano Italiano, Cl. VI, 454 (= 10701)) Others have 'piu de mille' (ibid., CP VI, 208 (= 5881), cc. 74v–111v) and 'da settecento in ottocento teste' (G. B. Ramusio (ed.), *Delle navigationi et viaggi*, vol. I (Venice, 1550)); see the Leporace edition of Ca' da Mosto, p. 27.
104 D. Pacheco Pereira, *Esmeraldo de Situ Orbis*, ed. A. E. da Silva Dias, liv. I, caps. xxvi, xxxiii.
105 Few black slaves landed at Valencia, 1502–8, V. Cortés, 'La trata de esclavos durante los primeros descubrimientos (1489–1516)', *Anuario de Estudios Atlánticos*, IX (1963), 19; ANTT, Gav., 20. 2. 69, 4 Apr. 1510, complaint that contractors of the trade were going through a lean period.
106 ANTT, Núc. Ant., 889, f. 88v.
107 ANTT, C. C., 3. 15. 87, 8 Jan. 1543. The then captain had 260 *peças* in the fort, but Castilian interlopers were making inroads on the trade.
108 'Livro da receita da renda de Cabo Verde', published in C. J. de Senna Barcelos, *Subsidios para a Historia de Cabo Verde e Guiné*, I. 74; ANTT, Núc. Ant., 528, ff. 2–80.
109 Curtin, *Atlantic Slave Trade*, p. 106.
110 ANTT, Leis, 2. 25, published in *Mon. Miss. Af.*, 1a sér., I. 239–40. Cortés notes that the first slaves from the Kongo arrived in Valencia in 1513, *La esclavitud en Valencia*, p. 58. Around 1500 there had been virtually no trade with the Kongo (Pereira, *Esmeraldo*, liv. III, cap. i).
111 ANTT, C. C., 2. 161. 91, noted in Ryder, *Benin and the Europeans*, p. 65.
112 ANTT, Gav., 20. 5. 24, 28 Mar. 1536; C. C., 1. 80. 105, 12 Nov. 1548, both published in *Mon. Miss. Af.*, 1a sér., II. 58, 200, considered in W. G. L. Randles, *L'Ancien Royaume du Congo*, p. 177.
113 E.g., 300 slaves landed at Madeira in 1552, G. Fructuoso, *Livro das Saudades da Terra*, ed. A. R. de Azevedo, liv. I, cap. xliv, p. 251.
114 'Relação', appendix to P. Peragallo (ed.), *Carta de el-Rei D. Manuel ao Rei Catholico*, pp. 82–3. His estimate of the gold imported from Mina, p. 82, is very close to the figure calculated from the accounts of the Casa da Moeda by V. Magalhães Godinho, *L'Économie de l'empire portugais aux XVe et XVIe siècles*, p. 216.
115 1490–1516: Vogt, *Proceedings of the American Philosophical Society*, CXVII (1973), 8, and Verlinden, *L'Esclavage*, I. 627–8. 1525–8: ANTT, Ch. Seb., 3, f. 93v, published in Baião, *João de Barros*, pp. 3–5.
116 BSG Lxa, Res., 146–B–4, ff. 75v, 76, 2 Aug. 1532.

117 ANTT, Frags., I. I. 16. My thanks to R. B. Smith for allowing me to consult his catalogue of the Fragmentos.

118 See W. Rodney, *A History of the Upper Guinea Coast from 1545 to 1800*, p. 46.

119 Brandão, 'Majestade e Grandezas', *Arch. Hist. Port.*, XI (1917), 44-5.

120 *Lettere*, p. 125. He tended to double the actual figures.

121 ANTT, Ch. Man., 31, f. 97v, 8 Mar. 1498, and Ch. J. III, 13, f. 13v, 15 Mar. 1525, published in Freire, 'Cartas de Quitação', *Arch. Hist. Port.*, III (1905), 396, and IX (1914), 434-5, respectively.

122 Godinho, *L'Économie de l'empire portugais*, pp. 162, 165, 167, 168, 428, 429, 439.

123 BN Lxa, Alcobaça cod. 323, liv. II, f. 476, 15 Dec. 1457; the version used was the transcription in BGU Coimbra, MS. cod. 704, p. 264, where 'xdo' was wrongly transcribed as 'escudo'; Šašek, *Commentarius Brevis*, f. 80, Letts trans., p. 107. Price in Lisbon, ANTT, Estrem., I, f. 268, published in Freire, 'Cartas de Quitação', *Arch. Hist. Port.*, III (1905), 477-8; 4,831 *rs.* in Lagos between 1490 and 1498, Ch. Man., 31, f. 97v, published in Freire, ibid., p. 396; 4,000 *rs.* in Oporto, AD Porto, Originais, liv. XV (catalogue no. 1673), f. 15, 27 Mar. 1498.

124 ANTT, Núc. Ant., 799, ff. 507-508v.

125 ANTT, C. C., 2. 29. 64, f. 1, 10 May 1512: 109 slaves at 763,000 *rs.*

126 ANTT, C. C., 1. 9. 30; 2. 86. 199, f. 2; 2. 87. 48; 2. 88. 49; 2. 91. 31. Prices ranged from 6,000 to 9,000 *rs.*

127 ANTT, Núc. Ant., 548, ff. 22v, 28v, 29v. Average price of male slaves, 7,050 *rs.*; of females, 9,000 *rs.*; of both sexes, 7,781 *rs.*

128 ANTT, C. C., 1. 69. 8, 10 Jan. 1541; Goes, 'Hispania' (20 Dec. 1541), in *Aliquot Opuscula*, no foliation, trans. as 'Descrição da Espanha' in Góis, *Opúsculos Históricos*, p. 119. He gives a range of 10-50 ducats.

129 Confirmed by ANTT, C. C., 1. 85. 118, 26 Dec. 1550.

130 Brandão, 'Majestade e Grandezas', *Arch. Hist. Port.*, XI (1917), 44.

131 Sassetti, *Lettere*, p. 126.

132 Luz, 'Relação das Rendas', *Bol. Bib. Univ. Coimbra*, XIX (1950), 70, 102, 103, 105.

133 AHCM Loulé, Rol dos moradores (1505), and Livro das avaliações das fazendas (1564), summarized in J. A. Romero Magalhães, *Para o Estudo do Algarve Económico durante o Século XVI*, pp. 251-3. In Lisbon 81.2 per cent of the population owned property worth less than 50,000 *rs.*: Rodrigues, 'Travail et société urbaine au Portugal', p. 179.

134 V. Magalhães Godinho, *Introdução a História Económica*, pp. 170-1.

135 ANTT, Ch. Af. V, 9, f. 95v, 23 July 1462, published in *Descobs. Ports.*, III. 31-2.

136 *Commentarius Brevis*, f. 80, Letts trans., pp. 106-7.

137 ANTT, Cortes, 2. 14, f. 60, caps. místicos, IX, published in Lobo, *Historia da Sociedade em Portugal no Seculo XV*, p. 588.

138 In the fifteenth century, exporters of slaves had to buy a permit called an *alvará de saca* from the Casa da Guiné, but this source of revenue was abolished by the Casa's *Regimento* of 1509; ANTT, C. C., 1. 9. 28, 20 June 1510, published in *Mon. Miss. Af.*, 1a sér., IV. 68-9; on *alvarás* and *sisa*, see also Ctas Miss., 4. 372, n. d. (1510-11).

139 *O Livro de Recebimentos de 1470 da Chancelaria da Câmara*, ed. D. Peres, f. 19 (Hernán de Córdoba); ff. 27, 35, 42 (Alfonso de Córdoba); f. 53 ('Joham de Ceja' (Ecija?)); f. 114 (Manuel de Jaén).

140 ANTT, C. C., 1. 9. 28, published in *Mon. Miss. Af.*, 1a sér., IV. 68-9.

141 Overland and seaborne itineraries determined from analysis of documents published in Cortés, *La esclavitud en Valencia*.

142 Archivo del Reino de Valencia, Presentaciones y Confesiones de Cautivos, Baylía General, 198, ff. 73, 74, 1 July 1514, published in Cortés, ibid., p. 443, doc. 1405.

143 A. Domínguez Ortiz, 'La esclavitud en Castilla durante la Edad Moderna', *Estudios de Historia Social de España*, II (1952), 377–8.

144 A. Teixeira da Mota, *Alguns Aspectos da Colonização e do Comércio Marítimo dos Portugueses na África Ocidental nos Séculos XV e XVI*, pp. 8–9; Cortés, *Anuario de Estudios Atlánticos*, IX (1963), 40–1.

145 See prices given in A. Collantes de Terán Sánchez, 'Contribución al estudio de los esclavos en la Sevilla medieval', *Homenaje al profesor Carriazo*, vol. II, pp. 113–16; R. Pike, 'Sevillian Society in the Sixteenth Century: Slaves and Freedmen', *Hispanic American Historical Review*, XLVII (1967), 347–8; Cortés, *La esclavitud en Valencia*, pp. 103–4.

146 J. M. Madurell Marimón (ed.), 'Los seguros de vida de esclavos en Barcelona (1453–1523)', *Anuario de Historia de Derecho Español*, XXV (1955), tables 1 and 2 between pp. 178–9; 40–50 Barcelonese *lliures*.

147 Many of the blacks in Palermo in 1565 were from Bornu, A. Franchina (ed.), 'Un censimento di schiavi nel 1565', *Archivio Storico Siciliano*, NS, XXXII (1907), 383–5.

148 V. R. Rau, 'Notes sur la traite portugaise à la fin du XVe siècle', *Bulletin de l'Institut Historique Belge de Rome*, XLIV (1974), 538; Verlinden, *L'Esclavage*, II. 354–5, 376–7; D. Gioffrè, *Il mercato degli schiavi a Genova nel secolo XV*, p. 34.

149 ANTT, C. C., I. 9. 30, 30 July 1516, 2 slaves to Antwerp. J. Denucé, *L'Afrique au XVIe siècle et le commerce anversois*, pp. 30, 48, claimed that Antwerp had the second largest black population in Europe, after Lisbon; this is simply incorrect, but there were a few black slaves there, see J. A. Goris, 'Slavernij te Antwerpen in de XVIe eeuw', *Bijdragen tot de Geschiedenis*, XV (1923), 541–4.

150 Although there were black slaves in Brazil by the 1530s, the country did not become a big market until after 1550; M. Goulart, *Escravidão Africana no Brasil*, pp. 94–6.

151 For the history of the early trans-Atlantic trade, see G. Scelle, *Histoire politique de la traite négrière aux Indes de Castille*, especially I. 122 seqq., and F. P. Bowser, *The African Slave in Colonial Peru, 1524–1650*, pp. 30 seqq.

152 A direct sailing from São Tomé to Hispaniola occurred in 1526, AGI Seville, Justicia, legajo 7, noted in F. Braudel, *The Mediterranean and the Mediterranean World in the Age of Philip II*, trans. S. Reynolds, I. 146.

153 AGI Seville, Cedulario 2766, lib. II, in R. S. Garcia, 'Contribuição ao Estudo do Aprovisionamento de Escravos Negros da América Espanhola', *Anais do Museu Paulista*, XVI (1962), 23.

154 Scelle, *La Traite négrière*, I. 205.

155 Slaves were smuggled from the Algarve to America by way of the Canaries; see Chaunu, *Séville et l'Atlantique*, II. 567.

156 Prices from J. A. Saco, *Historia de la esclavitud de la raza africana en el Nuevo Mundo*, I. 212.

157 D. Birmingham, *Trade and Conflict in Angola*, pp. 64 seqq.

158 ANTT, Estrem., I, f. 268, quittance dated 27 Feb. 1500 and Ch. Man., 11, f. 69v, quittance dated 17 Dec. 1514, both published in Freire, 'Cartas de Quitação', *Arch. Hist. Port.*, III (1905), 477–8 and II (1904), 440–1, respectively.

159 'Relação', in Peragallo (ed.), *Carta de el-Rei D. Manuel*, p. 94.

160 Barros, *Asia*, dec. I, liv. II, cap. ii.

161 ANTT, Estrem., I, f. 268, published in Freire, 'Cartas de Quitação', *Arch. Hist. Port.*, III (1905), 477–8.

162 ANTT, Ch. Man., 11, f. 69v, published in ibid., 11 (1904), 440–1.
163 ANTT, C. C., 1. 47. 115, published in A. Braamcamp Freire (ed.), 'Os Cadernos dos Assentamentos', *Arch. Hist. Port.*, x (1916), 122–8.
164 Bibliothèque de Carpentras, MS. 499, ff. 337–338v, 'Sommaire du Revenu qu'a le Roy de Portugal', published in L. S. de Matos, *Les Portugais en France au XVIe siècle*, pp. 291–7. The Chevalier's estimates are expressed in ducats and *écus*. I assume that some of his sources gave him values in *cruzados*, which he called ducats, and others in French currency, *écus*. But, as Dr C. J. Challis and Dr H. van der Wee have kindly told me, both the English customs and Netherlandish monetary ordinances during the period 1559–65 considered the *écu* and the *cruzado* in coin to be almost exactly equal in value, so I have taken them both to be worth 469 *rs*, the value of the *cruzado* in coin in 1559: Godinho, *L'Économie de l'empire portugais*, p. 439.
165 'Relação', in Peragallo (ed.), *Carta de el-Rei D. Manuel*, pp. 82, 94.
166 In 1593 Mina yielded only 24,240,000 *rs*. clear of expenses; Luz (ed.), 'Relação das Rendas', *Bol. Bib. Univ. Coimbra*, XIX (1950), 100.
167 28,155,932 *rs*. in 1593, plus 11,170,000 (mainly from the slave trade) from Angola; ibid., p. 98.

2 Legal and philosophical justifications of the slave-trade

1 *Crón. Guiné*, cap. xxv. It may be, however, that the compassion was felt by Zurara's source, Afonso Cerveira (mentioned in caps. xxxii, lvi and lxxxiv), from whom the chronicler copied entire passages.
2 For a summary consideration of the causes of slavery, see J. F. Maxwell, *Slavery and the Catholic Church*, pp. 22–30 and W. W. Buckland, *The Roman Law of Slavery*, pp. 397–436. On rights of infidel states to enslave, see Petrus de Ancharano, *Super sexto Decretalium Acutissima Commentaria*, 'De Regulis Iuris', cap. iv, pp. 528a–529b.
3 See M. Keen, *The Laws of War in the Late Middle Ages*, cap. x.
4 Raimundus de Peniafort, *Summa de Poenitentia et Matrimonio*, lib. 11, cap. v, para. 17; Alvarus Pelagius, *De Planctu Ecclesie*, lib. 11, cap. xlvi, ff. 89v–90. Pelagius (d. 1349), known in Portugal as Álvaro Pais, was bishop of Silves in the Algarve. For theories of just war, see F. H. Russell, *The Just War in the Middle Ages*.
5 Pelagius, *De Planctu Ecclesie*, lib. 11, cap. xlvi, f. 90. This view was held by King Manuel's tutor, Diogo Lopes Rebelo, *Do Governo da República pelo Rei*, facsimile edn (by A. M. de Sá) of his *De Republica Gubernanda per Regem*, pp. 142–3.
6 Innocent IV, *In quinque Libros Decretalium*, in 111 Dec., xxxlv, 8; Augustinus Triumphus, 'Summa de Potestate Ecclesiastica', xxiii, 2, quoted in M. Wilks, *The Problem of Sovereignty in the Later Middle Ages*, p. 415. See also W. Ullman, *Medieval Papalism*, p. 130.
7 E.g., the Canarians, whom King Duarte claimed lived 'like cattle', dressed only in leaves or skins and ignorant of commerce, letters, metal and coinage, Bib. Vat., Cod. lat., 1932, f. 99, 99v, Aug. 1436, published in C.-M. de Witte, 'Les Bulles pontificales et l'expansion portugaise au xve siècle', *Revue d'Histoire Ecclésiastique*, XLVIII (1953), 715–17.
8 Ullman, *Medieval Papalism*, p. 122; Pelagius, *De Planctu Ecclesie*, lib. 1, cap. xxxvii, f. 9v.
9 *Summa Theologiae*, 11. 11ae, q. xii, art. 2 and q. x, art. 8.
10 Wilks, *Problem of Sovereignty*, p. 419, n. 2; Henricus de Bartholomaeis, Cardinal Hostiensis, *Summa Aurea*, v, 'De Sarracenis', 5; Aegidius Romanus, *De Ecclesiastica Potestate*, lib. 11, cap. xi.

11 *Revue d'Histoire Ecclésiastique*, LIII (1958), 455.
12 ANTT, Ordem de Cristo, cod. 234, pte 4, f. 59, 19 Dec. 1442, published in *Mon. Hen.*, VII. 336–7.
13 Also known in abbreviated form as *Divino Amore Communiti*; Arch. Vat., Reg. Vat., vol. 431, ff. 194v–196, 18 June 1452, published in *Mon. Miss. Af.*, 2a sér., I. 269–73.
14 ANTT, Bulas, 7. 29, 8 Jan. 1455, published in *Mon. Miss. Af.*, 2a sér., I. 277–86.
15 Augustine, *Concerning the City of God against the Pagans*, ed. D. Knowles, bk XIX, cap. xvi, pp. 874–5.
16 *De Planctu Ecclesie*, lib. I, cap. xli, f. 19v.
17 *Crón. Guiné*, cap. xvi.
18 Zurara's source, judging from the rest of the chapter, was Alfonso X of Castile's *General estoria*, pte I, lib. II, cap. xxix, p. 53, as was pointed out by D. Leite, *Àcerca da 'Crónica dos Feitos de Guinee'*, p. 94, but Alfonso merely says that the Moors in general are descended from Ham, not the blackamoors specifically. W. D. Jordan, *White over Black*, pp. 18–19, shows that the tradition came from Midrashic and Talmudic sources; for an instance of its adoption by Muslims, see Abu al-Ala al-Ma'arri, in G. B. Wightman and A. Y. al-Udhari (trans. and eds.), *Birds through a Ceiling of Alabaster. Three Abbasid Poets*, p. 116.
19 *Summa Theologiae*, II. IIae, q. lxiv, art. 2, ad 3m.
20 *De Regimine Principum*, lib. II, par. I, cap. i; lib. III, par. II, cap. xxxiv.
21 *Crón. Guiné*, cap. xxvi; mentions Colonna, cap. lvi.
22 Ibid., cap. xxxv.
23 Ibid., caps. xxvi (material benefits), lx (black boy).
24 BGU Coimbra, MS. cod. 491, f. 142, n. d. (between 1579 and 1671), 'Explicação Porque saõ os Negros Negros'.
25 *Navigazioni*, pp. 75–6.
26 R. de Pina, *Crónica de el-Rei D. João II*, ed. A. Martins de Carvalho, cap. lxiii. Pina copied this passage from the captain's own account; see F. Leite de Faria (ed.), 'Uma Relação de Rui de Pina sobre o Congo escrita em 1492', *Stvdia*, XIX (1966), 224.
27 Ed. Mendes dos Remedios, stanza lix, p. 23.
28 *Asia*, dec. I, liv. III, cap. ii.
29 A late description of blacks as bestial may be found in A. Arraes, *Diálogos* (1589), ed. F. de Figueiredo, diál. iv, cap. xxiv, p. 94.
30 ANTT, C. C., I. 2. 58, 16 Sept. 1493 (unbaptized slaves); I. 2. 92, 18 Nov. 1493 ('vestido da vitória').
31 The campaign included the famous embassy with an elephant to Rome in 1514. D. Manuel obtained patronage of the Church in Portugal's overseas colonies but his request for an Inquisition was refused.
32 ANTT, Bulas, 29. 20, 7 Aug. 1513, published in *Mon. Miss. Af.*, 1a sér., I. 275–7.
33 ANTT, Col. S. Vicente, 6, f. 353, noted in Brásio, *Pretos em Portugal*, p. 16.
34 ANTT, Ch. J. III, 48, f. 49, 15 July 1516, confirmed 26 May 1529 and amended 22 June 1559, published in *Mon. Miss. Af.*, 1a sér., II. 436–8.
35 *Ord. Man.* (1514), 5. 98; (1521) 5. 99.
36 *Constitvicoẽs Extravagantes*, 1569, tit. i, const. i, f. 2, 2v.
37 In the diocese of Seville, 1614, Domínguez Ortiz, *Estudios de Historia Social de España*, II (1952), 392–4; in Cádiz, 1628, A. de Castro, 'La esclavitud en España', *La España Moderna*, IV. 38 (Feb. 1892), 141.
38 E.g., João II's black slave, Umar, ANTT, C. C., I. 2. 58, 16 Sept. 1493.

Clothing regulations in ANTT, Cortes, 2. 10, f. iv, Cortes of Santarém, caps. esps. of Santarém, 31 May 1468, and Cortes, 2. 14, ff. 113v–114, Cortes of Coimbra/Évora, 1473, caps. místicos, cix.

39 D. Nunes do Leão (ed.), *Leis Extravagantes* (1569), 4. 5. 8.

40 See Visconde de Santarém, *Alguns Documentos para servirem de Provas à Parte 1a das Memorias para a Historia, e Theoria das Cortes Geraes*, ed. A. Sardinha, p. 59.

41 Carvalho, *Origens da Escravidão Moderna*, pp. 33, 34.

42 ANTT, Ch. J. III, 65, f. 153, 22 Mar. 1556, published in *Mon. Miss. Af.*, 1a sér., II. 383.

43 There was no papal opposition to the slave-trade; see Maxwell, *Slavery and the Catholic Church*, pp. 115–18.

44 So much was recognized by observers of the trade: Ca'da Mosto, *Navigazioni*, p. 42; Fernandes, *Description*, pp. 20–1; Almada, *Tratado Breve*, cap. v.

45 'Como faz o magarefe ao gado no curral', F. de Oliveira, *A Arte da Guerra no Mar* (1st edn Coimbra, 1555), ed. Q. da Fonseca, p. 24.

46 Ibid., pp. 24, 25.

47 As is clear from his *Historia de las Indias*, ed. A. Millares Carlo, with preface by L. Hanke, III, caps. cii, cxxix; but his work was available only for restricted consultation and was not published until 1875 (I, pp. xxxi, xxxiii, xliii).

48 *De Iustitia et Iure*, lib. iv, q. ii, art. 2, conc. 2.

49 *Secunda Quartae [Summae theologiae]* (Coimbra, 1560), f. 225, 225v (which I have not seen); published in J. S. da Silva Dias, *Os Descobrimentos e a Problemática Cultural do Século XVI*, pp. 255, 256.

50 On Mercado, *Summa de tratos y contratos* (1587), lib. II, cap. xx, ff. 102–6, and Albornoz, *Arte de los contratos* (1573), ff. 130–1 (relevant sections published in *Obras escogidas de filósofos*, ed. A. de Castro, vol. LXV of Biblioteca de Autores Españoles, pp. 232–3), see D. B. Davis, *The Problem of Slavery in Western Culture*, pp. 210–13; Arraes, *Diálogos*, diál. iv, cap. xvi, p. 97; Molina, *De Justitia et Iure*, tom. I, tract. ii, disp. 33, 34.

51 *Tratado Breve*, cap. v.

52 ANTT, Mesa de Consciência e Ordens, 26, f. 130, 4 Aug. 1623.

53 V. Fernandes de Lucena, *Ad Innocentium Octauum Pontificem Maximũ de Obedientia Oratio*, f. 6, trans. and ed. by F. M. Rogers as *The Obedience of a King of Portugal*, p. 47.

54 *Asia*, dec. I, liv. I, cap. vi. Gain could be 'legitimized' if sought to a worthy, usually religious, end: thus the Infante D. Henrique and his royal successors could profit from the slave-trade with a quiet conscience. See M. Barradas de Carvalho, 'L'Idéologie religieuse dans la "Crónica dos Feitos de Guiné" de Gomes Eanes de Zurara', *Bulletin des Études Portugaises*, XIX (1955/6), 41–5, 61.

55 *Navigazioni*, p. 12.

56 Arraes, *Diálogos*, diál. iv, cap. xxvi, p. 97; Mercado, *Summa de tratos*, f. 106.

57 'On Winthrop D. Jordan's *White Over Black: American Attitudes Toward the Negro, 1550–1812*', in Weinstein and Gatell (eds.), *American Negro Slavery*, pp. 401–9.

3 The demography of blacks in Portugal

1 R. de Pina, *Crónica do Rei D. Duarte*, cap. xix (D. Pedro); Barros, *Asia*, dec. I, liv. I, cap. iv, f. 8; Cha' Masser, 'Relação', in Peragallo (ed.), *Carta de el-Rei D. Manuel*, p. 96.

2 *Descrittione*, p. 77. The epistle dedicatory indicates that the work was first

written some forty years before it was published, i.e., in the 1530s; see C. Poggiali, *Memorie per la storia letteraria di Piacenza*, II. 206–8.

3 'Dos Remédios para a Falta de Gente' (1655), cap. ii, published in A. Sérgio (ed.), *Antologia dos Economistas Portugueses (Século XVII)*, p. 127.

4 Lobo, *Historia da Sociedade*, p. 48; Magalhães Godinho, *Estrutura*, pp. 42–3.

5 Calculations based on figures for European birth- and death-rates given in R. Mols, 'Population in Europe, 1500–1700', in C. M. Cipolla (ed.), *The Fontana Economic History of Europe*, II. 66, 67.

6 Lobo, *Historia da Sociedade*, p. 49; J. L. de Azevedo, *Épocas de Portugal Económico*, p. 68.

7 Para. vi of a 'Discurso Panegyrico' presented to the Cortes, noted in J. P. Bayaõ, *Portugal Cuidadoso e Lastimado*, liv. I, cap. viii, p. 43.

8 Arraes, *Diálogos*, diál. IV, cap. xxvi, p. 97; Leão, *Descripção do Reino de Portugal*, ed. G. Nunes do Liam (1610), ff. 63v–64.

9 E.g., BGU Coimbra, MS. cod. 695, p. 74, 2 June 1570; 696, p. 394, 16 June 1579. AHCM Lxa, Registro de Provisões Reais, 5, f. 20, 12 Jan. 1599, published in E. Freire d'Oliveira (ed.), *Elementos para a Historia do Municipio de Lisboa*, II. 120.

10 Leão, *Descripção*, ff. 64v, 65; L. Mendes de Vasconcelos, 'Diálogos do Sítio de Lisboa' (1608), diál. ii, in Sérgio, *Antologia*, p. 88.

11 Faria, 'Remédios', caps. ii, v, in Sérgio, *Antologia*, pp. 127–9, 148.

12 Godinho, *Estrutura*.

13 The census enumerated only taxpayers (*moradores* or *vizinhos*), who in most cases were heads of households; see V. R. Rau, 'Para a História da População Portuguesa dos Séculos XV e XVI (Resultados e Problemas de Métodos)', *Do Tempo e da História*, I (1965), 7–46. I have employed the standard multiplier of 4 to convert the number of taxpayers to the number of inhabitants in a city or region.

14 From 1529, to be precise. See E. Felix, 'Les Registres paroissiaux et l'état civil au Portugal', *Archivum*, VIII (1958), 89.

15 The baptismal registers of Santa Cruz do Castelo, Lisbon, and the Sé, Oporto; the funerary lists of the Misericórdias of Elvas and Évora.

16 Nor can they be calculated easily, for there are few parishes with uninterrupted sets of registers, and the registers of deaths do not give the age of the deceased.

17 E.g., white women raped by their masters: BM Elvas, Núc. Par., I (Olivença (Sta Magdalena), liv. I), f. 19.

18 Including the coastal strip which was part of Estremadura for the first half of the sixteenth century.

19 See parish registers listed in Bibliography, Manuscript Sources, under AD Porto, Registo Civil; AD Braga, Registo Civil; AD Viana do Castelo, Registo Civil (now housed in AD Braga); and ANTT, Registo Paroquial, Vila Real. The entries for the first five or ten years in each register were taken as samples, both here and elsewhere.

20 See Pires de Lima, *Mouros, Judeus e Negros*, p. 122. A free black died in Campanhó (Trás-os-Montes) in 1569, for instance: ANTT, Registo Paroquial, Vila Real, Campanhó, óbitos, I, f. 144.

21 See relevant registers listed in Bibliography, Manuscript Sources, under AD Viana do Castelo. Slaves formed about 10 per cent of the Azuraran sample, but it was very small (32 names in all).

22 Šašek, *Commentarius Brevis*, f. 91; Letts trans., p. 118.

23 AD Porto, Originais, Pergaminhos, 15 (catalogue no. 1673), f. 15, 27 Mar. 1498.

24 Total obtained by multiplying the number of *moradores* by 4. Census returns here and elsewhere are taken from those published by A. Braamcamp Freire in *Arch. Hist. Port.*, III (1905), IV (1906), VI (1908), and VII (1909).

25 See parish registers for Oporto listed under AD Porto in Bibliography, Manuscript Sources.

26 Šašek, *Commentarius Brevis*, f. 91v. This town had 105 *moradores* (say 420 inhabitants) in 1527.

27 See parish registers listed under AD Aveiro in Bibliography, Manuscript Sources, and Mis. Aveiro, Receitas e Despesas.

28 See parish registers in Bibliography, Manuscript Sources, under AGU Coimbra, Registo Paroquial, and ANTT, Registo Paroquial, Castelo Branco and Guarda.

29 ANTT, Estrem., 5, ff. 164v–165v, 26 Aug. 1461.

30 Lobo, *Historia da Sociedade*, pp. 13–14, 16; V. R. Rau and G. Zbyszewski, *Estremadura et Ribatejo*, p. 85.

31 ANTT, Cortes, 2. 14, f. 60, caps. místicos, ix, published in Lobo, *Historia da Sociedade*, p. 588.

32 J. M. Cordeiro de Sousa (ed.), *Registo da Freguesia de Nossa Senhora da Encarnação do Lugar da Ameixoeira desde 1540 a 1604*; AD Setúbal, Núc. Par.: Montijo, mistos, 1 (1568–1610). Ten per cent of baptisms and funerals in Benavente between 1565 and 1575 were of slaves: ANTT, Reg. Par., Santarém, Benavente, mistos 1.

33 White slaves are mentioned as working on farms at Quinta da Lagea, near Alenquer (BP Évora, cod. CIII/2–22, f. 40v, 26 Jan. 1531) and at Montijo (*sic*; AHCM Lxa, Ch. Cidade, 924, Fianças dos Escrauos, 1, f. 33v, 13 May 1550). There seems no reason why blacks should not have worked on farms also. For boatmen, see next chapter; for villages along the Tagus where slaves lived, see Map 4.

34 Popplau, 'Viaje', p. 18. He says Lisbon was the size of Cologne or London, which cities had 35,000 and 60,000 people, respectively; see *The New Cambridge Modern History*, I. 42, 43.

35 Oliveira, *Sumário*, p. 95.

36 H. Münzer, 'Itinerarium Hispanicum Hieronymi Monetarii 1494–1495', ed. L. Pfandl, *Revue Hispanique*, XLVIII (1920), 87; C. de Bronseval, *Peregrinatio Hispanica (1531–1533)*, ed. Dom Maur Cocheril, I, 328. For Clenardus, see above, p. 1.

37 *Sumário*, p. 95.

38 E. Prestage and P. d'Azevedo (eds.), *Registos Parochiaes de Lisboa. Registo da Freguesia da Sé desde 1563 até 1610*. Sondage for years 1563–4, 1570–1.

39 E. Prestage and P. d'Azevedo (eds.), *Registos Parochiaes de Lisboa. Registo da Freguesia de Santa Cruz do Castello desde 1536 até 1628*, checked for 1536–40, 1546, 1550–5. For slaves of priests, etc., see pp. 8, 20; for Damião de Gois's slaves, see pp. 24, 32.

40 See Lisbon registers in Bibliography, Manuscript Sources, ANTT, Reg. Par., and J. M. C. de Sousa (ed.), *Registos Paroquiais Quinhentistas de Lisboa. Santa Justa*.

41 BL, Sloane MS., 1572, f. 61. Estimate of Capuchin friar who visited Lisbon in 1633.

42 Šašek, *Commentarius Brevis*, f. 92v; Letts trans., p. 123; G. de Resende, *Chronica de el-Rei D. João II*, cap. ccii.

43 AD Évora, Misericórdia, catalogue no. 761, Livro dos Defuntos (1547–56).

44 AD Évora, Núc. Par.: Évora (S. Pedro), liv. 1 (1546–68); Évora (Sto Antão),

livs. 1 (1535–44), 2 (1545–51), 3 (1551–6); Évora (S. Mamede), baptismos e casamentos, 1 (1537–68) all mention considerable numbers of slaves. Évora (Sé), baptismos, 1 (1535–7) mentions very few.

45 ANTT, Ch. Af. V, 30, f. 161, 14 Mar. 1475.

46 Elvas, Mis. Falecidos, maço 1, liv. 1 (1532); maço 7, liv. 1 (1529–71).

47 AD Évora, Núc. Par.: Borba (Matriz), baptizados, 1 (1550–73); Estremoz (S. Tiago), livs. 1 (1551–1709), 2 (1552–1619); Arraiolos (N. Sra dos Mártires), baptizados, 1 (1549–84); Montemor-o-Novo (N. Sra da Vila), liv. 1 (1533–1678); Montemor-o-Novo (N. Sra do Bispo), baptizados, 1 (1542–50), 2 (1550–6). BM Elvas, Núc. Par., 1, Olivença (Sta Madalena), liv. 1 (1546–74).

48 AD Évora CM, Posturas Antigas, 2, f. 81v, 12 May 1584.

49 ANTT, Confirmações Gerais de D. Filipe III, II, f. 298 (Cortes of Évora, 1475, caps. esps. of Setúbal).

50 AD Setúbal, Núc. Par.: Setúbal (Sta Maria da Graça), baptismos, 1 (1571–95); Alcácer do Sal (Sta Maria do Castelo), mistos, 1 (1570–96). Slaves are mentioned in Setúbal (S. Julião), baptismos, 1 (1564–94), but the folios are hopelessly jumbled, making the dates of entries almost impossible to determine.

51 Popplau, 'Viaje', p. 41.

52 Felix, 'Registres paroissiaux', *Archivum*, VIII (1958), 92.

53 ANTT, Registo Paroquial, Moncarapacho, mistos, 1 (1543–8). Sixty-three male and forty female slaves out of a sample of 1,039 persons.

54 Vila Nova de Portimão, burials (4 July 1596–31 Dec. 1597), considered by Correia Lopes, *Escravatura*, pp. 45–6; Museu Regional de Lagos, Livros de Receita e Despesa do Tesouro da Misericórdia de Lagos, 2 July 1571–2 July 1572 and 2 July 1582–2 July 1583, considered by Romero Magalhães, *Algarve Económico*, p. 231.

55 This is Romero Magalhães's conclusion also; see *Algarve Económico*, p. 231.

56 Godinho estimates that slaves might have formed 5 per cent of the population. *Descobrimentos*, II. 542.

57 50,000 slaves in a total population estimated to have been about 1,220,000 in 1535. See C. Verlinden, 'Schiavitù ed economia nel Mezzogiorno agli inizi dell'età moderna', *Annali del Mezzogiorno*, III (1963), 30–3.

58 *Estudios de Historia Social de España*, II (1952), 377.

59 Twenty-six males to twenty-three females in Elvas summing the years 1529–33, 1541–50 and 1554–5; 122 males to 106 females in Évora, 1547–55; 63 males to 40 females in Moncarapacho in the early 1540s.

60 Anonymous pilot in Blake, *Europeans in West Africa*, I. 153.

61 In Évora, 24 men and 24 women, in Elvas, 12 men and 11 women in the periods stated in n. 59, above.

62 S. B. Schwartz, 'Manumission of Slaves in Colonial Brazil: Bahia, 1684–1745', *Hispanic American Historical Review*, LIV (1974), 611.

4   The occupations of slaves

1 AHCM Lxa, Ch. Régia, 5, Cortes, 1, f. 155, 155v; 167; Cortes of Lisbon, 1498, cap. ger. xxxviii, published in *Livros de Reis*, I. 248.

2 Slave-owning interpreters: ANTT, C. C., 3. I. 34, São Tomé, 24 Apr. 1499; Fragmentos, maço 20, Mina, 12 Jan. 1510, documents published in *Mon. Miss. Af.*, 1a sér., I. 159, IV. 63, respectively.

3 Forbidden by Pope Zachary in 747 or 748: see J. A. Saco, *Historia de la*

esclavitud desde los tiempos más remotos hasta nuestros días, III, 176–7, referring to Anastasius, *Vita Zacchariae Papae*, which I have not seen. *Ord. Af.*, 2. 66. 1, 2; 2. 106.

4 As in Castile: Alfonso X's *Las siete partidas*, IV. xxi. 8 contains much the same provisions with respect to Jewish and Muslim slave-holders and slave-merchants as do the Portuguese laws considered here.

5 The law is not clear, but it seems that infidel slave-merchants could keep Christian slaves even longer: a slave bought by a Jew or Muslim specifically for retail became a free man only if he announced his intention of becoming a Christian within three months after the date of purchase and could produce 12 *xdos* with which to buy his freedom. This provision prevented the slave-merchant from losing his money. BN Lxa, Alcobaça cod. 323, liv. 2, f. 476, copy in BGU Coimbra, cod. 704, pp. 264–5, 15 Dec. 1457, public execution of *Ord Af.*, 4. 51. 184, 185, which it amends.

6 ANTT, Cortes, 3. 5, f. 67, Cortes of Évora, 1490, cap. ger. xlvi.

7 'Itinerarium', *Revue Hispanique*, XLVIII (1920), 88.

8 Dr N. H. Griffin, of Manchester University, tells me that during his researches he encountered a document in which the monks of Plasencia, in Extremadura, expressed surprise at seeing migrant Portuguese builders' labourers with their own slaves in the 1570s.

9 The staff and garrison at Arguim sent back to Portugal eighty of their own slaves in 1517, forty-seven in 1518, forty-eight in 1519 and forty-two in the first eight months of 1520.

10 'Majestade e Grandezas', *Arch. Hist. Port.*, XI (1917), 57.

11 *Correspondance*, I. 58, III. 37–8, letter to Latomus from Évora, 20 Mar. 1535.

12 ANTT, Caps. das Cortes, 4, f. 3, 3v, Cortes of Lisbon, cap. ii.

13 *Ord. Af.*, 4. 26. 1, 4. 28. Pr.; *Ord. Man.* (1514), 4. 21. Pr., 4. 23. Pr.; (1521) 4. 18. Pr., 4. 19. Pr.

14 See Falgairolle, *Jean Nicot*, p. 117, letter to the bishop of Limoges from Lisbon, 25 Sept. 1560.

15 BN Lxa, Fundo Geral, 4354, ff. 213–214v, letter of P. Gonçalo da Silveira to Jesuits in the College of Goa, 9 Aug. 1560, published in *Docs. Port. Moz.*, VII. 502, 503, and by G. McC. Theal (ed.), *Records of South-eastern Africa*, II. 89, whose translation this is.

16 *Crón. Guiné*, cap. xxiv; BM Elvas, 11402, P. H., maço 3 (S. Domingos, 1, f. 57), 29 Oct. 1500, relates how Rui da Gama gave a black slave to the monastery of São Domingos, thereby separating a mother and her child. Santarém: ANTT, C. C., I. 13. 65, 5 Oct. 1513. Setúbal: C. C., I. 18. 37, 15 July 1515; Lisbon (N. Sra da Anunciada): ANTT, C. C., I. 13. 95, 11 Nov. 1513. In the 1550s there were slaves in Lisbon at the nunnery of Santos, the convent of Madre de Deus and the convent of the Penitentes da Paixão de Cristo, for reformed prostitutes: see Oliveira, *Sumário*, pp. 71, 70, 68.

17 'Toda nosa proueza gastamos co moças de soldada', ANTT, Ctas Miss., 3. 13, f. IV, 6 Apr. 15? (no year given).

18 ANTT, Gav., 2. 2. 62, 17 Sept. 1515, published in *As Gavetas da Torre do Tombo*, I. 346–7.

19 *O Regimento do Hospital de Todos-os-Santos* (19 Jan. 1504), ed. F. da Silva Correia, cap. xi, pp. 78, 79; cap. i, p. 23.

20 Participation in commercial transactions involving large sums of money did not detract from a person's respectability. The *Ordenações Manuelinas* considered merchants who had more than 100,000 *rs.* capital to be persons of

quality, and therefore exempt from the degrading punishments meted out to criminals from the lower classes: (1521) 5. 40.

21 *Correspondance*, I. 57, 58, 34; III. 36, 37, 32, letter to Latomus from Évora, 20 Mar. 1535.

22 BL, Sloane MS., 1572, f. 62, *anno* 1633.

23 Brandão, 'Majestade e Grandezas', *Arch. Hist. Port.*, XI (1917), 71. Local holidays may have reduced the length of the working year still further.

24 ANTT, Inq. Lxa, Denúncias, I, f. 87, 3 Feb. 1541; ff. 94v, 95, 15 Feb.; f. 96v, 17 Feb. See also the case of Diogo da Fonseca, another New Christian, who lived on Brava in the Cape Verdes: Inq. Lxa, Denúncias, I, ff. 169v, 170, 19 June 1542. Neither case seems to have come to trial.

25 D. de Goes, 'Hispania', in *Aliquot Opuscula*, no pagination; in *Opúsculos Históricos*, p. 112.

26 BN Lxa, cod. 109, Frei João de São José, 'Corografia do Reyno do Algarve' (1577), f. 130, 130v.

27 Slave herdsmen in AHCM Loulé, Livro dos assentos do gado (1567–9), ff. 71v, 202, noted in Romero Magalhães, *Algarve Económico*, p. 101; AD Évora CM, Originais, I, f. 98, 5 Nov. 1497; ANTT, Ch. J. III, Perdões e Legits., 9, f. 404, 29 Oct. 1544.

28 AHCM Elvas, Provisões, I, f. 604, 11 June 1511; 2, f. 52, 15 June 1528.

29 AHCM Coimbra, Correia, I, 931 (?1514–19), and I, 97 (?1554), published and edited by J. P. Loureiro as 'Arquivo Municipal – Livro I da Correa', *Arquivo Coimbrão*, II (1930/1), 159.

30 BN Lxa, cod. 109, ff. 122–123v.

31 'Compromisso do Hospital das Caldas dado pela Rainha D. Leonor sua Fundadora em 1512', ed. F. da Silva Correia, *O Instituto*, LXXX (1930), 112–13.

32 AHCM Coimbra, Correia, I, 26, 6 Mar. 1554, published by Loureiro, in *Arquivo Coimbrão*, II (1930/1), 139.

33 AHCM Coimbra, Correia, I, 931 (?1514–19), and I, 97 (?1554), published by Loureiro, in *Arquivo Coimbrão*, II (1930/1), 159.

34 AHCM Coimbra, Correia, I, 974, 6 Aug. 1519; I, 100 (?1554), published by Loureiro, in *Arquivo Coimbrão*, V (1940), 87, and II (1930/1), 160, respectively; ANTT, Estrem., 5, f. 165, 26 Aug. 1461; AD Évora CM, Originais, I, f. 98, 5 Nov. 1497; *Ord. Man.* (1514), 5. 93; (1521) 5. 83.

35 ANTT, Conventos, S. Bento de Lisboa, 7, ff. 267–268v, evaluation undertaken between 15 Oct. 1530 and 5 July 1531.

36 E.g., ANTT, Feitos Findos, N. 4, ff. 2v–3, 20 June 1539 (Sintra); Ch. J. III, Perdões e Legits., 8, f. 170v, 9 May 1541 (Óbidos); and see n. 31, above.

37 ANTT, Ch. Dinis, I, f. 176v, 29 Sept. 1286, published in *Descobs. Ports.*, I, *sup.* 16–17.

38 See Gil Vicente, *Auto da Barca do Inferno* (1517), in *Obras Completas*, ed. Marques Braga, II. 50.

39 A. A. Ferreira da Cruz, *Os Mesteres do Pôrto* (1943), I. 36–7.

40 AHCM Lxa, Místicos de Reis, 2, no. 1, 10 June 1284, published in *Descobs. Ports.*, I, *sup.* 14–15.

41 BP Évora, cod. CV / 2–11, f. 157, 14 Aug. 1534.

42 AHCM Lxa, Ch. Cidade, 924, L[iur]o de Fianças de Escrauos. Magalhães Godinho made a preliminary study of this book for the years 1549 to 1552, but my own research, based on a somewhat different sample, indicates that he committed certain errors of fact and, furthermore, seems to have confused the actual owners of the slaves with the guarantors who posted security when the master was unable to do so; *Descobrimentos*, II. 580–1.

43 *Livro dos Regimētos dos Officiaes Mecanicos da Mui Nobre e Sēpre Leal Cidade de Lixboa* (*1572*), 'Do Regimento dos Barqueiros', para. 29, f. 234, ed. V. Correia, p. 197.

44 GHC Porto, Acordãos, 2, f. 35v and f. 39, no. 98, 4 Feb. 1587.

45 E.g., a black youth buried by the Misericórdia of Évora in 1555 was said to have been learning the trade from his shoemaker master: AD Évora, Mis., 761, Defuntos (1547–56), f. 224. For freed shoemakers, see below, p. 145.

46 Verlinden, *L'Esclavage*, I. 145, 146; Heleno, *Escravos em Portugal*, p. 154; G. Pereira, 'O Archivo da Santa Casa da Misericórdia de Évora, 3a Parte', in his *Estudos Eborenses* (1888), p. 17; J. Leite de Vasconcellos, *A Etnografia Portuguesa*, IV. 316.

47 1,119 shoemakers, compared with 976 labourers and 859 tailors. Oliveira, *Sumário*, pp. 88, 90.

48 'Regimento dos Calceteiros e Jubeteiros', 2 Dec. 1575, in F. P. de Almeida Langhans (ed.), *As Corporações dos Ofícios Mecânicos*, I. 393.

49 'Regimento dos Espadeiros', 18 Aug. 1548, in Cruz, *Mesteres do Pôrto* (1943), I. 277.

50 'Do Regto. Dos Ourivezes. De Ouro. e Lapidairos', para 20, f. 5v, in *Livro dos Regimētos dos Officiaes Mecanicos*, pp. 7–8.

51 'Do Regimento dos Pastelleiros', para. 12, f. 255, in ibid., p. 222; AHCM Lxa, Ch. Cidade, 393, Posturas, I, ff. 44v–47, 'Regimento do oficio dos pasteleiros', 5 Sept. 1554, published in Langhans, *Corporações*, II. 426–7.

52 A black slave seaman belonging to a seaman accompanied his master from Portugal to Sofala, in Mozambique, ANTT, C. C., 2. 71. 143, 30 Sept. 1517, *Docs. Port. Moz.*, V. 264, 265; João Velho laboured beside his black slave Pedro at the royal biscuit ovens at Vale de Zebro in 1514, ANTT, Núc. Ant., 817, f. 74; and in 1507 Garcia the slave of Diogo Rodrigues worked as a labourer at the palace of Sintra, where his master was employed as a stone-mason, ANTT, former Casa da Coroa, armário 26, no. 169, now Núc. Ant. 810, published in Conde de Sabugosa, *O Paço de Cintra*, p. 237.

53 See p. 58 above; and also ANTT, Ch. J. III, Perdões e Legits., 10, f. 365, 365v, 6 Nov. 1539, regarding Alexandre, a slave who worked in Elvas while his master lived in Évora.

54 AHCM Lxa, Ch. Cidade, 396, Posturas reformadas, emmendadas e recopiladas no anno de 1610, f. 189, published in Freire d'Oliveira, *Elementos*, I. 464.

55 AD Évora CM, Posturas Antigas, 2, f. 66v, 9 July 1556; AHCM Coimbra, Correia, I, 'Titulo das posturas da limpesa da cidade', 181, 3 May 1556, published in Loureiro, *Arquivo Coimbrão*, II (1930/1), 176.

56 AHCM Coimbra, Vereações, V, f. 6v, 17 Mar. 1526.

57 Brandão, 'Majestade e Grandezas', *Arch. Hist. Port.*, XI (1917), 70.

58 Ibid., and Damião de Gois, *Urbis Olisiponis Descriptio* (1554), with trans. R. Machado as *Lisboa de Quinhentos*, p. 50.

59 AHCM Lxa, Ch. Cidade, 396, Posturas reformadas, liv. 5, tit. 3, post. 10, f. 280, 280v. The slaves were probably displaced because the occupation was connected with the collection of a municipal tax, the *cestaria*, on the baskets used to carry fish from the boats; see Freire d'Oliveira, *Elementos*, I. 138–45.

60 Oliveira, *Sumário*, pp. 82, 83; four 'negros de mariola' brought some boards from Lisbon to Vale de Zebro in October 1526; ANTT, Núc. Ant., 818, f. 84v.

61 AHCM Lxa, Ch. Régia, 31, Manuel, 4, f. 96, 5 Jan. 1517, partly published in *Livros de Reis*, V. 86.

62 The construction accounts for Belém are given in ANTT, Núc. Ant., 811–14. Very few of the king's slaves were placed in the care of royal officers in charge

of construction works at royal palaces. See ANTT, Ch. Man., 39, f. 119, 17 Mar. 1507, quittance to *almoxarife* at Sintra, 1499–1500; Estrem., 1, f. 295v, 12 May 1499, quittance to *vedor das obras* at Tomar for an unstated period; both documents published in Freire, 'Cartas de Quitação', *Arch. Hist. Port.*, II (1904), 350, and V (1907), 78, respectively.

63 Brandão, 'Majestade e Grandezas', *Arch. Hist. Port.*, XI (1917), 233.

64 Ibid., pp. 71, 233.

65 AHCM Lxa, Ch. Régia, 45, Pregos, f. 331v, 10 Dec. 1544, partly published in Freire d'Oliveira, *Elementos*, I. 542.

66 ANTT, Inq. Lxa, Denúncias, 1, f. 59, 59v, 18 Feb. 1538.

67 AHCM, Lxa, Ch. Cidade, 396, Posturas reformadas, liv. 1, tit. 30, post. 2, f. 139.

68 Brandão, 'Majestade e Grandezas', *Arch. Hist. Port.*, XI (1917), 76; Oliveira, *Sumário*, p. 94.

69 Noted without reference in J. de Castilho, *A Ribeira de Lisboa*, 2nd edn, annotated by L. Pastor de Macedo, II. 18–19. Original source is probably in AHCM Lxa, Provimento de Agua, 1, which was (April 1979) unavailable for consultation.

70 'Majestade e Grandezas', *Arch. Hist. Port.*, XI (1917), 59, 60.

71 Ibid., pp. 231, 232.

72 More so in Portugal than in Madeira, where Landi noted that slaves performed all sordid professions and occupations, while in Portugal he observed that free whites also were involved in them; *Descrittione*, pp. 50, 93.

73 BL, Harleian MS., 3822, f. 283 (*anno* 1599); *Relaçam em que se trata, e faz hũa breue descriçao dos arredores mais chegados à Cidade de Lisboa, & seus arrebaldes* (1625), no pagination [p. 10].

74 AHCM Lxa, Livro Carmesim, f. 33, 23 Feb. 1515, partly published in *Livros de Reis*, VI. 17–18.

75 ANTT, Ch. J. III, Doações, 22, ff. 100v–101, 9 Aug. 1529, confirming 22 Mar. 1505 (*sic*: evidently a misreading of 1515).

76 AHCM Elvas, Provisões, 1, f. 500, 12 July 1537, and 1, f. 170, 24 Mar. 1542.

77 AD Évora CM, Posturas Antigas, 2, ff. 81–82v, 12 May 1584; 2, ff. 82v–83, 8 Aug. 1584.

78 Ibid., 2, f. 4, n.d. (late sixteenth century).

79 ANTT, Núc. Ant., 817, ff. 69 seqq., 93 seqq.; 818, 76 seqq., 111 seqq.

80 BL, Sloane MS., 1572, f. 62.

81 Sintra: ANTT, C. C., I. 50. 107, 31 Mar. 1533, published in Freire, 'Cadernos dos Assentamentos', *Arch. Hist. Port.*, X (1916), 135. Muge: C. C., I. 9. 30, 30 July 1516, and see J. A. do A. Frazão de Vasconcelos, 'Subsídios para a História da Vila de Almeirim (Séculos XV a XVIII)', *Ethnos*, IV (1965), 328, who notes that the palace was sometimes called the Paço dos Negros da Ribeira de Muge, because King Manuel sent some black slaves there. Paços da Serra: Inq. Lxa, Denúncias, A, ff. 103v–104, 15 Nov. 1555. Almeirim: C. C., I. 97. 77, 15 Feb. 1556.

82 'Livro de Moradores da Casa de D. João III', published in A. Caetano de Sousa (ed.), *Provas de Historia Genealogica*, IV. 616–17, 623–4.

83 ANTT, MS. 169, f. 143, published in Azevedo, 'Os Escravos', *Arch. Hist. Port.*, I (1903), 305.

84 ANTT, C. C., I. 97. 77, 15 Feb. 1556.

85 Each guardian had to acknowledge receipt of the slaves in writing, and was called upon to account for the expenditure of the moneys allowed to maintain

his or her charges in food and clothing; e.g., ANTT, C. C., 1. 51. 113, 21 Nov. 1533. When a slave died, the guardian was required to confirm the event, in writing; e.g., C. C., 1. 97. 60, 22 Jan. 1556, so that the account could be cleared in the treasury books; C. C., 1. 97. 71, 5 Feb. 1556.

86 E.g., a Moorish slave carpenter, ANTT, C. C., 1. 2. 40, 29 July 1493.

87 At the palace in Évora: ANTT, Extras, f. 2, 10 May 1496, published in Freire, 'Cartas de Quitação', Arch. Hist. Port., IV (1906), 442–3; in the upper and lower gardens of the palace of the Alcáçova in Lisbon: C. C., 1. 27. 19, 17 June 1521.

88 In the orange-groves at Sintra: ANTT, C. C., 1. 50. 107, 31 Mar. 1533, published in Freire, 'Cadernos dos Assentamentos', Arch. Hist. Port., x (1916), 135.

89 Moorish cowherds: ANTT, C. C., 2. 50. 34, 6 Aug. 1514.

90 ANTT, C. C., 1. 52. 101, 28 Mar. 1534; 1. 58. 58, 15 Mar. 1537.

91 ANTT, C. C., 1. 33. 108, 7 Mar. 1526. Slave pastry-cooks were to be a feature of Brazilian life in later centuries, so that Domingos may have been the forerunner of many others; G. Freyre, The Masters and the Slaves, trans. S. Putnam, pp. 459–60.

92 'Livro dos moradores', in Caetano de Sousa, Provas, VI. 624; ANTT, C. C., 1. 56. 138; 1. 56. 163, 26 Feb. 1536; 1. 2. 21, 13 June 1493, which last is published in Mon. Miss. Af., 2a sér., 1. 577–8.

93 ANTT, C. C., 1. 89. 100, 7 Mar. 1553; 1. 93. 74, 22 Aug. 1554; 1. 54. 39, 2 Jan. 1535; 1. 88. 138, 3 Oct. 1552.

94 A mourisca served in the Excelente Senhora's botica in the 1490s; Caetano de Sousa, Provas, II. 79–81, while several slaves, including at least one black, were employed in the botica of D. Manuel's mother, D. Beatriz; see A. Braamcamp Freire (ed.), 'Inventario da Infanta D. Beatriz 1507', Arch. Hist. Port., IX (1914), 82, 84, 103.

95 AHCM Lxa, D. Sebastião, 1, f. 38, 9 Oct. 1565, reply to cap. particular of Lisbon in the Cortes of Lisbon, 1562, published in Freire d'Oliveira, Elementos, I. 572.

96 Freire (ed.), 'Beatriz', Arch. Hist. Port., IX (1914), 81.

97 'Para laa as casarem', ANTT, C. C., 1. 97. 72, 11 Feb. 1556.

98 P. J. Suppico de Moraes, Collecção Politica de Apothegmas, I. 298. Sabugosa, Bobos na Côrte, pp. 94–100, considers and prints Panasco's jokes in modern Portuguese, but fabricates a racially prejudiced myth that Panasco was responsible for Camões's exile. There is no evidence at all for this conclusion.

99 ANTT, Ch. Man., 41, f. 40, 3 Aug. 1510, quittance to the receiver for the treasury of the royal household, 1507–9, published in Freire, 'Cartas de Quitação', Arch. Hist. Port., IV (1906), 474. Regarding treasury of the kingdom, C. C., 1. 56. 106, 16 Dec. 1555.

100 Regimento das Cazas das Indias e Mina, cap. cxvi, pp. 92–3; cap. cxxxviii, pp. 108–9, 3 July 1509. Brandão, 'Majestade e Grandezas', Arch. Hist. Port., XI (1917), 192, n. 124.

101 ANTT, Místicos, 6, f. 117, 28 Feb. 1513, quittance to the almoxarife of the Casa da Pólvora, 1507–12, published in Freire, 'Cartas de Quitação', Arch. Hist. Port., I (1903), 168; Ch. J. III, 50, f. 166, 12 Apr. 1540, quittance to heirs of the almoxarife from 1524 to 1531, published in F. M. de Sousa Viterbo (ed.), 'O Fabrico da Polvora em Portugal – Notas e Documentos para a sua Historia', Revista Militar, XLVIII (1896), 14–16.

102 'Itinerarium', Revue Hispanique, XLVIII (1920), 87.

103 ANTT, Ch. J. III. Perdões e Legits., 3, f. 182, 2 Feb. 1554, quittance to

almoxarife; published in Freire, 'Cartas de Quitação', *Arch. Hist. Port.*, x (1916), 16.

104 ANTT, Ch. Man., 16, f. 99v, 15 Apr. 1499, quittance to *almoxarife*, published in Freire, 'Cartas de Quitação', *Arch. Hist. Port.*, v (1907), 156–7.

105 ANTT, Núc. Ant., 922, f. 196.

106 ANTT, Núc. Ant., 818, f. 85v, 2 Oct. 1526.

107 Information from ANTT, Núc. Ant., 922, 817, 818, the account books of Vale de Zebro for 1513, 1514–15 and 1526, respectively.

108 ANTT, Núc. Ant., 888, f. 118, *anno* 1508.

109 *Correspondance*, I. 54; III. 32, letter to Latomus from Évora, 20 Mar. 1535.

110 E.g., ANTT, Inq. Évora, maço 350, no. 3315, f. 5, 16 Nov. 1551.

111 AHCM Elvas, Provisões, II, f. 204, 9 Nov. 1525.

112 Magalhães, *Algarve Económico*, p. 231. D. João III observed that most of the thieves in Lisbon were youths not only from Beira but also from the Alentejo: AHCM Lxa, Ch. Régia, 40, João III, 3, f. 160, 30 Mar. 1546, partly published in *Livros de Reis*, VII. 160.

113 As little as 10 *rs.* p. d. in Lamego in 1531–2; see R. Fernandes, 'Descripção do Terreno em roda da Cidade de Lamego Duas Leguas', *Collecção de Livros Ineditos de Historia Portugueza*, v. 598.

114 Admittedly a questionable procedure, but unavoidable in the absence of more detailed statistics on the numbers of slaves and unemployed.

115 Oliveira, *Sumário*, pp. 92, 94; Brandão, 'Majestade e Grandezas', *Arch. Hist. Port.*, XI (1917), 80–1.

116 The goldsmiths, piemen, apothecaries, watermen and hosiers, all mentioned above, plus the olive-pressers, the *esparaveleiros* (who made large cloths) and the sellers of old clothes (*adeis*): AHCM Lxa, Casa dos Vinte e Quatro, 35, Liuro dos Regimentos dos Officiaes mecanicos, I, cap. lii, 'Do Regimento dos Esparaveleiros', para. 11, f. 198; cap. lx, 'Do Regimento dos Lagareiros dos Lagares de Azeite', para. 14, f. 226, 226v; 'Do Regimento dos Adeis e Adellas', para. 6, f. 260 (which is published in *Livro dos Regimētos dos Officiaes Mecanicos*, p. 227).

117 From the 1550s the supply of labour began to outrun the demand in most of Southern Europe: Braudel, *The Mediterranean*, I. 403.

118 According to Brandão, a free maidservant's wages were only 2,000 *rs.* p. a., but he may have left out the extra charges for her clothing, which would bring the total costs up to 4,000 *rs.*, which were the wages of a manservant, including clothing, and were also the average annual outlay on maintaining a slave. But employers of free labour were spared the high purchase price of the slave. 'Majestade e Grandezas', *Arch. Hist. Port.*, XI (1917), 57–8.

5   The life of the slave

1 E.g., D. João II's slave, 'O Capitão', The Captain. ANTT, C. C., I. 2. 58, 16 Sept. 1493.

2 A study of slaves' names was made by J. Leite de Vasconcellos in his *Antroponímia Portuguesa*, pp. 361–81.

3 ANTT, C. C., I. 85. 118, 26 Dec. 1550.

4 Guiomar: AD Évora, Núc. Par.: Borba (N. Sra das Neves), baptizados, I, f. 88v, 23 Sept. 1553. Afonso: BM Elvas, Núc. Par.: 8, Olivença (Matriz), baptizados (1561–76), f. 17v, Mar. 1562. Juliana: ibid., f. 17, 4 Mar. 1562. The child's owner was Leonor de Vargas.

5 E.g., Pedro de Madrill (Madrid?), a Benin black who belonged to the musician Diogo de Madrill, ANTT, Ch. J. III, 2, f. 173, 21 Dec. 1547, published in F. M. de Sousa Viterbo (ed.), 'Subsídios para a História da Música em Portugal', *O Instituto*, LXXX (1930), 500.

6 In Oporto, for instance, a person could have one godfather and one god-mother only (*Constituições do Bispado do Porto* (1497), const. liiii, ff. 21v–22), while in the dioceses of Lisbon and Évora four godparents were usual until 1565, though in Lisbon infidels who were converted were allowed as many godparents as they wished (*Constituições do Arcebispado de Lixboa* (1536), tit. i, const. 2, f. 1, 1v). In 1565 the number of godparents was everywhere limited to two (*Constituições Extravagantes do Arcebispado de Lixboa* (1565), const. i, f. 2v, according to Trent, session xxiv, cap. ii).

7 E.g., Joana Rodrigues, a black slave, was godmother to the black slave child Luís; AD Évora, Núc. Par.: Évora (Sé), baptizados, 1, f. 3v, 20 Mar. 1535. Juliana Pires was godmother to her namesake; see n. 4 above.

8 E.g., the master's father; Prestage and Azevedo (eds.), *Santa Cruz do Castello*, p. 34, 4 May 1555.

9 Sousa (ed.), *Ameixoeira*, p. 9 (original f. 1v), 15 July 1540.

10 Though Maria, a black slave baptized in Évora, had a 'courtier' (*cortesão*) as a godfather (AD Évora, Núc. Par.: Évora (Sé), baptizados, 1, f. 1, 3 Mar. 1535) and a white slave had a *cavaleiro* and his wife (Évora (S. Pedro), mistos, 1, f. 2, 11 Apr. 1547).

11 E.g., Inês Fernandes, BM Elvas, Núc. Par.: 1, Olivença (Sta Magdalena), 1, ff. 10v, 19; Isabel Dias, ibid., ff. 10v, 15, 19 (*annis* 1548, 1549, 1550).

12 The terms used were *filho da Igreja* and *expúrio*.

13 ANTT, Ctas Miss., 1. 463, n. d. I am indebted to Dr Peter Bury for bringing this letter to my attention.

14 AD Évora, Mis., 539, Testamentos e Doações, ff. 89–90. Will made in Santarém, 24 Aug. 1546.

15 I found only twenty-five cases in ANTT, Leitura Nova, Legitimações, 1 and 3, which are volumes of some 300 folios each, with several legitimations on a page. Most of the petitions for legitimation came from Lisbon and the provinces south of the Tagus, yet another indication of the distribution of slaves in Portugal.

16 *Correspondance*, 1. 54; III. 32, letter to J. Latomus from Évora, 20 Mar. 1535.

17 Venturino, trans. and ed. A. Herculano as 'Archeologia Portuguesa: Viagem do Cardeal Alexandrino, 1571', in Herculano, *Opúsculos*, VI. 64. Assuming the *scudo* is the Castilian *escudo*, 30–40 *scudi* equal 11,220–14,960 *rs.* in Portuguese currency.

18 But they should be taken seriously; some Castilian masters in Palos appear to have encouraged their slave women to bear a child every year or two years. See V. Cortés Alonso, 'La población negra de Palos de la Frontera, 1568–1579', XXXVI Congreso Internacional de Americanistas, Seville, 1966, III. 614.

19 Clenardus asserted that sex was pandemic in Portugal as a result of slavery and doubted whether there ever was a virgin bridegroom; *Correspondance*, I. 54; III. 32.

20 *Crón. Guiné*, cap. xxv. BM Elvas, 11402, P. H., maço 3 (S. Domingos, 1, f. 57, 19 Oct. 1506).

21 *Crón. Guiné*, cap. xxvi. See also Biblioteca Ajuda, Symmicta Lusitanica, 47, p. 191, 6 July 1569, Pius IV's brief *Qui Terrenis* to the governor of Brazil recommending that he clothe Indian neophytes, published in *Corpo Diplomatico Portuguez*, x. 328–9.

22 A black slave belonging to João da Costa died of cold in Trás-os-Montes while helping his master to buy wheat there in 1522; ANTT, Ctas dos Vice-Reis, 64, f. 2, published in *Docs. Port. Moz.*, VI. 262, 263.

23 *Crón. Guiné*, cap. xxvi.

24 Black was the favoured colour for court dress. See Popplau, 'Viaje', p. 26; A. Herculano (trans. and ed.), 'Archeologia Portuguesa: Viagem a Portugal dos Cavalleiros Tron e Lippomani, 1580', *Opusculos*, VI. 121.

25 Mis. Porto, A, Banco I, no. 1, Enfermos, f. 16v. General information regarding clothing in Portugal may be found in A. H. de Oliveira Marques, *A Sociedade Medieval Portuguesa*, cap. ii.

26 After Diogo Lopes de Sequeira died, his slaves were given a suit of clothes made of *almáfega*, sackcloth, the traditional sign of mourning. ANTT Conventos, S. Bento de Lisboa, 7, f. 176v, and see Marques, *Sociedade Medieval*, pp. 215–16. See also 'Testamento de D. Maria Gramacho', made in Elvas, 1561, published in A. T. Pires (ed.), *Materiaes para a Historia da Vida Urbana Portugueza*, p. 5.

27 *Regimento do Hospital de Todos-os-Santos*, cap. iii, p. 45 (blue livery with 'S' on the chest); 'Compromisso do Hospital das Caldas', *O Instituto*, LXXX (1930), 113.

28 The following information comes from the accounts of the *almoxarife* of Vale de Zebro for the years 1514–15 and 1526, ANTT, Núc. Ant., 817, 818, except where otherwise indicated.

29 ANTT, C. C., 1. 18. 51, 31 July 1515.

30 F. M. Kelly and R. Schwabe, *A Short History of Costume and Armour*, II. 18, 19.

31 ANTT, C. C., 1. 18. 51.

32 Except for hats, with the *barrete redondo*, round bonnet, coming into favour in the reign of D. João III, e.g., ANTT, C. C., 1. 47. 72, 10 Oct. 1531. The exact styles of the hats mentioned in the clothing orders are unknown, since the words used for hats were somewhat imprecise; cf. Marques, *Sociedade Medieval*, p. 47. (But note the pictures of the black huntsman (Plate 2) and the black musicians (Plate 5)).

33 ANTT, C. C., 1. 2. 2, 22 Jan. 1493, published in J. P. Ribeiro, *Dissertações Chronologicas e Criticas sobre a Historia e Jurisprudencia Ecclesiastica e Civil de Portugal*, V. 305; C. C., 1. 2. 3, 30 Jan. 1493; 1. 2. 9, 12 Mar. 1493. Irish or Castilian cloth was sometimes used for the jerkins (*pelotes*); cf. C. C., 1. 2. 58, 16 Sept. 1493.

34 ANTT, C. C., 1. 2. 47, 10 Aug. 1493, published in *Descobs. Ports.*, III. 406 (a *loba* or hooded cape); C. C., 1. 2. 101, 6 Dec. 1493.

35 ANTT, C. C., 1. 2. 15, 20 Apr. 1493; 1. 2. 21, 13 June 1493, published in *Mon. Miss. Af.*, 2a sér., 1. 577–8; C. C., 1. 2. 54, 6 Sept. 1493; 1. 2. 65, 29 Sept. 1493; 1. 2. 92, 18 Nov. 1493.

36 'O negro pregueiro', ANTT, C. C., 1. 2. 95, 25 Nov. 1493.

37 ANTT, C. C., 1. 93. 26, 20 Oct. 1551.

38 Almeida, *Historia de Portugal*, III. 282–5, considers the sumptuary legislation.

39 ANTT, Ch. J. III; Perdões e Legits., 1, f. 99, 99v, 15/16 June 1548; ibid., 4, f. 169v, 2 May 1549.

40 A. Herculano (ed.), 'Archeologia Portuguesa: Aspecto de Lisboa ao ajunctar-se e partir a Armada para a Jornada d'Alcacer-Quibir. 1578', *Opusculos*, VI. 101–2.

41 ANTT, C. C., 1. 91. 8, 9 Sept. 1553.

42 ANTT, C. C., 1. 55. 82, 18 Jan. 1535; 1. 83. 106, 18 Mar. 1550 (57,000 *rs.* allowed for clothing nineteen slaves); 1. 85. 97, 20 Oct. 1550 (4,497 *rs.*).

43 ANTT, C. C., 1. 87. 86, 7 Feb. 1552; 1. 89. 100, 7 Mar. 1553; 1. 97. 127, 20 Mar. 1556; and for a slave of the wardrobe, 1. 87. 88, 8 Feb. 1552.

44 ANTT, C. C., 1. 88. 112, 13 Sept. 1552.

45 ANTT, Ch. Af. V, 35, f. 85, 10 Feb. 1472, 'sob guarda de deus'.

46 ANTT, Reg. Par.: Moncarapacho, mistos, 1, f. 105v.

47 All information on Vale de Zebro from ANTT, Núc. Ant., 817 and 818.

48 ANTT, C. C., 1. 54. 39, 2 Jan. 1535 (two to a bed); 1. 54. 41, 2 Jan. 1535 (separate bed for one of the queen's women).

49 ANTT, C. C., 1. 93. 120, 3 Oct. 1554.

50 *Correspondance*, 1. 139, 140, 142; III. 79, 82, letter to Latomus from Braga, 21 Aug. 1537.

51 Ibid., 1. 58, III. 37–8, letter to Latomus from Évora, 20 Mar. 1535.

52 D. Nunes do Leão (ed.), *Leis Extravagantes*, 4. 13. 1, from Cortes of Évora, 1535, lei xxix.

53 *Regimento do Hospital de Todos-os-Santos*, cap. iii, p. 45. Calculations from wheat allowance of 3.5 *alqueires* a month based on the Lisbon *alqueire* of 13.8 litres (Lobo, *Historia da Sociedade*, p. 268) and 1 litre = 0.725 kg wheat (Braudel, *The Mediterranean*, 1. 570).

54 Data from ANTT, Núc. Ant., 817, ff. 185–192v.

55 Frei Joaquim de Santa Rosa Viterbo, *Elucidário das Palavras, Termos e Frases que em Portugal antigamente se usaram*, ed. M. Fiuza, 'Decimas'. Lamb and kid were the cheapest meats. In 1527 the price of an *arrátel* (0.34 kg) of lamb or kid was pegged at 2⅔ *rs*. in the Alentejo, while mutton, pork and beef cost 4 *rs*. the *arrátel*; see Leão, *Leis Extravagantes*, 4. 8. 1, and also the chart of prices in Lobo, *Historia da Sociedade*, pp. 543–50. Calculations from the wheat allowance of four *alqueires* a month are based on the Alentejan *alqueire* of 14 litres.

56 Seven *rs*.: ANTT, C. C., 1. 40. 53, 6 July 1528, published in Freire, 'Cadernos dos Assentamentos', *Arch. Hist. Port.*, x (1916), 102. 10 *rs*.: Freire, 'Beatriz', *Arch. Hist. Port.*, IX (1914), 81, 7 Jan. 1507. 12 *rs*.: ANTT, C. C., 2. 26. 39, 10 Apr. 1511.

57 10 *rs*. p. d. were allotted to a stable lad who accompanied three slave women on a journey: Freire, 'Beatriz', *Arch. Hist. Port.*, IX (1914), 81.

58 ANTT, C. C., 1. 58. 123, 3 July 1537, published in Freire, 'Cadernos dos Assentamentos', *Arch. Hist. Port.*, x (1916), 145.

59 Braudel, *The Mediterranean*, 1. 420.

60 E.g., 'Jorge boçall', belonging to Queen Catarina, ANTT, C. C., 1. 51. 99, 26 Oct. 1533.

61 S. de Covarrubias, *Tesoro de la lengua castellana* (1611), f. 143, ed. M. de Riquer, p. 233.

62 *Constitvicões Extravagantes do Arcebispado de Lisboa* (30 May 1568), tit. i, const. i, f. 2v.

63 By way of comparison, in eighteenth-century Virginia black slaves imported from Africa took about six months to acquire some grasp of English and two and a half years to speak it at all competently. See G. W. Mullin, *Flight and Rebellion*, p. 46.

64 ANTT, Inq. Lxa, 12086, f. 3. Rome, Archivum Romanum Societatis Iesu, Hisp. 107, f. 26v, 14 Sept. 1567; Dr N. H. Griffin very kindly gave me a transcript of the relevant section of this document.

65 *Gramática da Língua Portuguesa* (1540), ff. 30v, 34; facsimile edn by M. L. Carvalhão Buescu, pp. 116, 123.

66 The earliest use of black Portuguese dates from 1455, when Fernão da

Silveira wrote a poem to accompany a dance performed by a black 'king of Sierra Leone' at the celebrations marking a royal wedding; poem in G. de Resende, *Cancioneiro Geral* (1516), ed. A. J. Gonçalves Guimarãis, I. 204–5. A list of Portuguese and Castilian plays featuring black Portuguese may be found in P. Teyssier, *La Langue de Gil Vicente*, pp. 249–50; and see also J. R. Castellano, 'El negro esclavo en el entremés del Siglo de Oro', *Hispania*, XLIV (1961), 55–65.

67 See F. Weber de Kurlat, 'Sobre el negro como tipo cómico en el teatro español del siglo XVI', *Romance Philology*, XVII (1963), 387–8, and P. E. Russell, 'Towards an Interpretation of Rodrigo de Reinosa's "poesía negra"', in *Studies in Spanish Literature of the Golden Age presented to Edward M. Wilson*, ed. R. O. Jones, pp. 236–7.

68 These salient features are taken from the much fuller accounts given in Teyssier, *La Langue de Gil Vicente*, pp. 227–50, and M. F. Valkhoff, *Studies in Portuguese and Creole with Special Reference to South Africa*, especially pp. 89–93.

69 English-speaking readers may note that some of the same linguistic simplifications occurred in the English spoken by black slaves in the United States, as in 'Sho', massa, me nebber take de 'lasses', for 'Sure, master, I never took the molasses.' See J. L. Dillard, *Black English*.

70 A good summary of these and other relevant arguments may be found in I. F. Hancock, 'Malacca Creole Portuguese: Asian, African or European?', *Anthropological Linguistics*, XVII (1975), 212–18.

71 Cf. *cocoliche*, the hispanized language of Italian immigrants in Buenos Aires: K. Whinnom, 'Linguistic Hybridization and the "Special Case" of Pidgins and Creoles', in D. Hymes (ed.), *Pidginization and Creolization of Languages*, especially p. 99.

72 ANTT, Inq. Lxa, Denúncias, 3, f. 94v, 29 Dec. 1552.

73 H. Lopes, *Cena Policiana*, in A. Prestes et al., *Primeira Parte dos Avtos e Comedias Portvgvesas*, ff. 41v–48; J. F. de Vasconcellos, *Comedia Vlysippo*, ed. B. J. de S. Farinha, act II, sc. v; and his *Comédia Aulegrafia*, ed. A. A. M. de Vilhena, act I, sc. vi.

74 In *Auto de S. Tiago Apostolo* (n. p., n. d.), ff. 1v–2v, facsimile in C. Michaëlis de Vasconcellos, *Autos portugueses de Gil Vicente y de la escuela vicentina*.

75 ANTT, Inq. Lxa, Denúncias, 3, ff. 94v–95v.

76 A black defendant and his interpreter both made less than successful attempts to sign (or copy) their names to append to depositions to the Inquisition; the spirit was willing, at least: ANTT, Inq. Lxa, Processos, 12047, ff. 3v, 4v, 5, May–June, 1553.

77 *Correspondance*, I. 115, III. 67, letter to M. a Vorda, from Évora, 10 Jan. 1537; I. 236, III. 202, Epistola ad Christianos, from Fez, c. 1540–1.

78 Ibid., I. 122, 124, 125, 127, 130, 131, letter to J. Vasaeus, from Évora, 18 July (1537).

79 Ibid., I. 147, III. 89, letter to Fr. Brás de Braga, from Braga (?1537).

80 *Ord. Man.* (1521), 5. 14.

81 *Ord. Af.*, 5. 25; *Ord. Man.* (1521), 5. 21. Action was, however, taken when two slaves, one Christian, the other infidel, were involved: ANTT, Ch. J. II, 3, f. 84, 20 Nov. 1482, published in F. M. de Sousa Viterbo (ed.), 'Notícia sobre alguns Médicos Portugueses ou que exerceram a sua Profissão em Portugal. Quinta Série', *Archivos de Historia da Medicina Portugueza*, IV (1913), 85–6.

82 *Ord. Man.* (1521), 5. 18. 2; 'escrava branca de guarda', 5. 23. Not in *Ord. Af.* or *Ord. Man.* (1514), this law was probably a belated legalization of the

punishment which D. Álvaro de Castro had inflicted on a man who had slept
with one of Castro's white slave women in 1512: see D. de Goes, *Chronica do
Felicissimo Rei D. Emanuel*, III, cap. xl, f. 75.

83 *Constituições do Bispado Deuora* (1534), tit. x, const. xvi, ff. 23v–24; *Constituições
do Arcebispado de Lixboa* (1536), tit. x, const. xvi, f. 25, 25v.

84 *Vlysippo*, act II, sc. vi, p. 145; *Comedia Eufrosina*, ed. A. F. G. Bell, act v, sc. i,
p. 242.

85 ANTT, Ch. Man., 35, f. 112, 13 Aug. 1520, published in P. A. de Azevedo,
'Costumes do Tempo d'el-Rei D. Manuel', *Revista Lusitana*, IV (1896), 5–6.

86 *Auto da Sibila Cassandra*, in *Obras Completas*, I. 54.

87 D. Francisco, count of Vimioso, in *Auto das Fadas* (1511); an esquire, in
Auto Pastoril Portugues (1523), in *Obras Completas*, v. 183, and I. 168–9,
respectively.

88 ANTT, Ch. J. III, Perdões e Legits., 13, f. 43v, 12 Feb. 1543. A similar case
in São Tomé, ibid., 9, f. 299v, 20 Aug. 1533.

89 *Fragoa d'Amor* (1524), in *Obras Completas*, IV. 107–9; *Nao d'Amores* (1527), in
ibid., IV. 80.

90 BM Porto, MS. 553, f. 26v (sometime between 1548 and 1583), published as
F. Dias, *Memórias Quinhentistas dum Procurador del-Rei no Porto*, ed. A. de
Magalhães Basto, pp. 45–6.

91 *Descrittione*, pp. 41, 82.

92 AHCM Elvas, Posturas, I (6 Aug. 1617), f. 45; II (16 Sept. 1672), f. 21.

93 See R. Naz, 'Esclave', in *Dictionnaire de droit canonique*, vol. v, cols. 451–3.

94 AD Évora, Núc. Par.: Évora (Sto Antão), mistos, 2, f. 166v, 3 Apr. 1548;
f. 169, 23 Sept. 1548 (marriages involving blacks). Prestage and Azevedo
(eds.), *Santa Cruz do Castello*, p. 163, 19 Apr. 1546 (marriage between blacks).
AD Setúbal, Núc. Par.: Montijo (formerly Aldeia Galega do Ribatejo),
mistos, 1, ff. 163, 164, 167 (blacks not mentioned specifically); Alcácer do Sal
(Sta Maria do Castelo), mistos, 1, f. 122, 20 Apr. 1573 (marriage of blacks);
ff. 117, 121v, 122, 126, 127, 132v, 135v (between 1570 and 1575; black
slaves not mentioned specifically in these marriages).

95 Vicente, *Floresta de Enganos* (1536), in *Obras Completas*, III. 197.

96 AD Setúbal, Núc. Par.: Alcácer do Sal (Sta Maria do Castelo), f. 117, 28 Oct.
1571 (slave and free mulatta); f. 127, 27 June 1574 (slave and free black
woman).

97 See Marques, *Sociedade Medieval*, pp. 115–17, and P. A. de Azevedo, 'O
Antigo Casamento Português', *Arch. Hist. Port.*, III (1905), 107–10.

98 *Constitvições Extravagantes do Arcebispado de Lisboa* (30 May 1568), tit. v, const. i,
f. 9, 9v.

99 Masters objected to no fewer than six out of the eight slave marriages performed between 1570 and 1575. Reference in n. 94 above.

100 E.g., an order that Moors and Jews of the Alentejo attend the royal wedding
at Évora, BGU Coimbra, MS. cod. 629, pp. 51–2, 6 Aug. 1490; Pina,
Crónica de el-Rei D. João II, cap. xliv, p. 120.

101 D. João III had a group of Moors at court especially to dance and accompany
the *mourisca*, a Moorish dance: ANTT, C. C., 1. 53. 53, 23 Nov. 1535; 1. 56.
112, 19 Dec. 1535; 1. 56. 114, 22 Dec. 1535.

102 Valckenstein, 'Historia Desponsationis', in Caetano de Sousa, *Provas*, vol. I,
liv. III, pp. 608, 611, 613.

103 Freire d'Oliveira, *Elementos*, I. 516n.

104 The later dances are considered by R. Gallop, 'The Fado (The Portuguese
Song of Fate)', *The Musical Quarterly*, XIX: 2 (1933), 199–213. He claims on

p. 204 that D. Manuel forbade the *batuque*, *lundum* and *charamba*, but gives no reference, and on p. 205 shows that the *lundum* could only have been of much later date, since it was a dance imported from Africa via Brazil.

105 *Fragoa d'Amor*, in *Obras Completas*, IV. 106.

106 N. Pereira, 'A Fernam Gomez da Myna', in Resende, *Cancioneiro Geral*, IV. 249.

107 L. V. de Camões (attrib.), 'Carta IV', in *Obras Completas*, ed. Hernâni Cidade, III. 262.

108 Russell, 'Rodrigo de Reinosa', in *Studies in Spanish Literature*, p. 234, provides a good short exposition, with references. The Castilian form was *maagana*.

109 Covarrubias, *Tesoro*, f. 457v / p. 670.

110 But note BL Sloane MS. 1572, ff. 61–2 (*anno* 1633), where a Capuchin observed that blacks played 'instrumentos al vso de su tierra'.

111 Venturino, 'Cardeal Alexandrino', in Herculano, *Opusculos*, VI. 56, 57.

112 Flute players at Mosselbaai, South Africa: Magalhães Basto (ed.), *Diário da Viagem de Vasco da Gama*, I. f. 8; in Angola: BL, Add. MS., 20: 876, ff. 48–9, 23 Aug. 1578, published in *Mon. Miss. Af.*, 1a sér., IV. 302; in Kongo: D. Lopez and F. Pigafetta, *Relação do Reino de Congo*, trans. R. Capeans, II, cap. vii, pp. 126–7.

113 'Gajta de negros', ANTT, Ch. Man., 35, f. 112, published in Azevedo, 'Costumes', *Revista Lusitana*, IV (1896), 6.

114 E.g., order that two blacks be taught to play the drum and fife, ANTT, Ctas Miss., I. 127, n. d.

115 E.g., frontispiece to A. Ribeiro Chiado, *Auto da Natural Invençam*, in his *Autos*, ed. Berardinelli and Menegaz, vol. I.

116 ANTT, Estrem., 5, ff. 164v, 165, caps. esps. of Santarém, 26 Aug. 1461; adjudged by J. Leitão, *Côrtes do Reino de Portugal*, p. 227, to be from the Cortes of Évora, 1461.

117 Leão, *Leis Extravagantes*, 4. 5. 10.

118 ANTT, Ch. Seb., Perdões e Legits., 38, f. 17v, 16 Dec. 1563, published in Azevedo, 'Os Escravos', *Arch. Hist. Port.*, I (1903), 306. The custom of having a ceremonial king or queen persisted in the Portuguese black community until the late nineteenth century, by which time the office appears to have become hereditary: J. Ribeiro Guimarães, 'O Congo em Lisboa', *Summario de Varia Historia*, v. 147–9.

119 AHCM Lxa, Ch. Cidade, 396, Posturas, ff. 224v, 225 (liv. 4, tit. 1, postura 3), n. d.

120 AD Évora CM, Posturas Antigas, 2, f. 66, 13 Apr. 1555.

121 BP Évora, cod. cv / 2–11, f. 223, 28 May 1536. Stable lads: ANTT, Inq. Lxa, Denúncias, 4, ff. 129v, 130, 26 Aug. 1556.

122 *Ord. Man.* (1521), 5. 11. 3.

123 *Ord. Af.*, 5. 92. 6; *Ord. Man.* (1514), 5. 75. 3; (1521) 5. 68. 3.

124 J. Leite de Vasconcellos, 'Língua de Preto num Texto de Henrique da Mota', *Revue Hispanique*, LXXXI: 1 (1933), 243, note to lines 3–4; Vicente, *Barca do Inferno* (1517), in *Obras Completas*, II. 60, and his *Historia de Deus* (1527), in ibid., II. 206; ANTT, Ch. J. II, 24, f. 81v, 9 Nov. 1489, published in P. M. Laranjo Coelho, *Documentos Inéditos de Marrocos*, I, 303–4.

125 Unlike in Castile: Alfonso X of Castile, *Las siete partidas*, IV. xxi. 6.

126 ANTT, Inq. Lxa, Denúncias, 2, ff. 32v–33, 22 Apr. 1544. Even the Mani Kongo and his ambassador were called dogs by Fernão de Melo, the captain of São Tomé: ANTT, C. C., I. 16. 28, published in *Mon. Miss. Af.*, 1a sér., I. 311.

127 Arch. Prots., Badajoz, 1, f. 478, 478v, 10 Sept. 1562.

128 *Os Estrangeiros*, in his *Obras Completas*, ed. M. Rodrigues Lapa, II. 125: act I, sc. ii.

129 *Crón. Guiné*, cap. xxvi. In 1461 blacks at Santarém believed being chained was an exceptional imposition: ANTT, Estrem., 5, f. 165, 165v, caps. esps. of Santarém, 26 Aug. 1461. At Vale de Zebro, the *bragas de ferro*, foot shackles linked to a chain around the waist, listed in the inventory were said to be specifically 'for punishment of the blacks': ANTT, Núc. Ant., 818, f. 65, 15 Jan. 1526.

130 *Descrittione*, pp. 41, 83.

131 ANTT, Núc. Ant., 817, f. 55, 22 June 1515; 818, f. 65, 15 Jan. 1526, f. 86, Oct. 1526.

132 ANTT, Conventos, S. Bento de Lisboa, 7, f. 178; ANTT, C. C., I. 89. 27, 30 Nov. 1552.

133 AD Évora, Mis., 276, Registo de Entradas no Hospital e Falecimentos (22 July 1554–18 June 1562), ff. 26v, 27, 39v, 61, with six blacks being admitted in 1555 (out of 196 admissions) but only two (out of 217) in 1556 and none (out of 138) in 1554; and see also Mis. Porto, A, Banco I, no. 1, ff. 6v, 7, 12v, 42v, 52v.

134 E.g., the Misericórdia of Oporto admitted one slave whose master lived in Guimarães, about 45 km away, A, banco I, no. 1, f. 16v, 28 Sept. 1596. The doctors of Todos-os-Santos examined and admitted one of the king's slaves who was suffering from asthma and back pain; ANTT, C. C., I. 41. 76, 12 Oct. 1528, partly published in A. da Silva Carvalho, *Crónica do Hospital de Todos-os-Santos*, p. 193. The slave, used for paying a debt, had been evaluated as worth 11,000 *rs.*, which casts some suspicion on royal evaluation practices.

135 *Regimento do Hospital de Todos-os-Santos*, cap. iii, p. 41.

136 AD Évora CM, Originais, 1, f. 105, 24 Jan. 1506.

137 AHCM Lxa, Prov. Saúde, 1, ff. 65–66, 23 July 1520; f. 86, 3 Aug. 1523; f. 89, 13 Aug. 1523. For further precautions, see Freire d'Oliveira, *Elementos*, I. 453–5 (being 452 n. 1).

138 AHCM Lxa, Prov. Saúde, 1, f. 51, 13 Nov. 1515, published in Freire d'Oliveira, *Elementos*, I. 509–10 (being 452 n. 1).

139 See G. de Matos Sequeira, *Depois do Terremoto*, II. 44–6. *Poço dos Negros* as a street name first appeared in 1681.

140 A. Thomaz Pires, *Estudos e Notas Elvenses*, XII. 105–9.

141 ANTT, Núc. Ant., 922, f. 217v, 5 June 1513.

142 Alms in AD Évora, Mis., 761, Livro dos Defuntos, 1547–56, *passim*.

143 AHCM Coimbra, Vereações, v, f. 82 (?3 Nov. 1526) and f. 84v, 10 Nov. 1526.

144 Churchyards: Mis. Elvas, maço 7, liv. 1 (1529–71), *passim*. In church: ANTT, Reg. Par., Castelo Branco, Covilhã (Sta Maria do Castelo), mistos, 1, f. 10v, 5 June 1598.

145 Symmicta Lusitanica, tomo XXXII, doc. 38, para. 32 (*c.* 1535–43), published in A. G. da Rocha Madahil, 'Para a História da Inquisição no Século XVI', *Arquivo do Distrito de Aveiro*, X (1944), 89.

146 *The Mediterranean*, I. 460.

6 *Slaves and the law*

1 The variety in the treatment of slaves in different municipalities is noted in Verlinden, *L'Esclavage*, I. 139–47.

2 Justinian, *Institutes*, I. 3. 1.

3 *Institutiones cum commentariis Accursii et aliorum*, I. 3. 1.

4 *Ord. Af.*, 4. 25; *Ord. Man.* (1514), 4. 20; (1521) 4. 17.

5 ANTT, Ch. Man., 45, f. 37, 8 Aug. 1500. Ransom: AG Simancas, Registro del Sello, 20 Mar. 1480, published in A. de la Torre and L. Suárez Fernández (eds.), *Documentos referentes a las relaciones con Portugal durante el reinado de los Reyes Católicos*, II. 33.

6 AD Évora, Núc. Not., 6, Diogo Luís, 5, ff. 44–5. For other examples, see ANTT, C. C., I. 19. 134, 4 Mar. 1516; I. 46. 3, 20 Oct. 1530.

7 *Digest*, 48. 8. I. 2; *Codex*, 3. 35. 3, noted in Buckland, *Roman Law of Slavery*, pp. 31, 37. Death confirmed as penalty in Portuguese law: AD Évora CM, Registo, I, ff. 50–51v, 7 Oct. 1516.

8 Neighbours denounced murderer: in ANTT, Ch. Af. V, 22, f. 19v, 7 Sept. 1471, published in Azevedo, 'Os Escravos', *Arch. Hist. Port.*, I (1903), 299; and in cases recorded below, in notes 9 and 12. Inquiries: ANTT, C. C., I. 22. 135, 26 Dec. 1517; BP Évora, cod. cv/2–11, f. 111, 28 Mar. 1533.

9 In the Cape Verde Islands, however, a woman convicted of murdering her slaves through excessive punishment was sentenced to a considerable term in gaol, long enough for her to be afraid that she would die there: ANTT, Ch. Seb. e Hen., Perdões e Legits., 8, f. 54, 18 Apr. 1560, published in P. A. de Azevedo, 'Superstições Portuguesas no Seculo XVI', *Revista Lusitana*, VI (1900), 219. She obtained a pardon.

10 See Almeida, *Historia de Portugal*, III. 233; Magalhães Godinho, *Descobrimentos*, II. 561.

11 ANTT, Ch. Af. V, 11, f. 41, 15 Apr. 1451; he was completely pardoned in ibid., f. 102, 20 May 1451. Both documents published in P. A. de Azevedo, *Documentos das Chancelarias Reais anteriores a 1531 relativos a Marrocos*, II. 22–3.

12 ANTT, Ch. J. II, 24, f. 81v, 9 Nov. 1489; 17, f. 35v, 6 Feb. 1490. Both documents published in Coelho, *Documentos Inéditos de Marrocos*, I. 303–4, 311–12.

13 ANTT, Ch. J. II, 26, f. 121v, 23 May 1483 (murder of *criado*), published in Coelho, *Documentos Inéditos de Marrocos*, I. 86.

14 *Ord. Af.*, 2. 30. 2; *Ord. Man.* (1521), 2. 21.

15 *Ord. Af.*, 3. 61. 12, 14; *Ord. Man.* (1514), 3. 50. 11, 13; (1521) 3. 42. 13, 15.

16 *Ord. Af.*, 4. 82, 83; *Ord. Man.* (1521), 1. 67. 20; 4. 76. Pr.

17 Justinian, *Institutes*, 2. 9. 1; *Digest*, 41. 2. 49. 1, 1. 40. 5; and see Buckland, *Roman Law of Slavery*, p. 187.

18 *Ord. Af.*, 3. 36. 6; *Ord. Man.* (1514), 3. 31. 8; (1521) 3. 28. 8.

19 BP Évora, cod. cv/2–11, f. 222v, 28 May 1536.

20 Ibid., f. 223v.

21 ANTT, Ctas Miss., 2. 64, f. 5v. Undated, but the style of writing indicates the period assigned.

22 Theft, sorcery, pandering and counterfeiting.

23 *Ord. Man.* (1521), 5. 40.

24 ANTT, Ch. Af. V, 30, f. 161, 14 Mar. 1475.

25 ANTT, Ch. J. III, Perdões e Legits., 10, ff. 352v–353, 26 Nov. 1539.

26 Mentioned in 1262: AHCM Lxa, Ch. Régia, 45, Pregos, f. 30.

27 v. 197–9.

28 Leão, *Leis Extravagantes*, 4. 22. 21.

29 ANTT, Ch. Af. V, 18, f. 73, 28 Apr. 1439, published in Azevedo, *Chancelarias*, I. 68–9.

30 *Livro de Recebimentos de 1470 da Chancelaria da Câmara*, pp. 35, 36, 38, 51, 84, 90, 99.

31 ANTT, Ch. Af. V, 28, f. 16v, 27 Apr. 1468. A similar pardon (ibid., 15, f. 105, 13 Feb. 1456) is published in Azevedo, *Chancelarias*, II. 323–4.

32 ANTT, Ch. J. I, 5, f. 90v, 25 Sept. 1402; 'Fragmentos de Legislação Portugueza', in *Collecção de Livros Ineditos de Historia Portugueza*, III. 561, no. 16.

33 ANTT, Leitura Nova, Odiana, 5, f. 294, Cortes of Lisbon, caps. esps. of Beja. The definition of black slaves as foreigners was probably influenced by attitudes toward Moorish slaves (the bulk of the slave population at this time) who were usually prisoners of war and, when ransomed, returned to their homes in North Africa.

34 GHC Porto, Vereações, 4, f. 9v, 29 July 1475; 6, f. 9, 2 Aug. 1497; Leão, *Leis Extravagantes*, 4. 5. 1, 8 July 1521; 4. 5. 2, 12 Apr. 1559.

35 *Ord. Man.* (1514), I. 44. Pr.; (1521) I. 57. 1, 2.

36 Leão, *Leis Extravagantes*, 4. 5. 1.

37 Ibid., 4. 2. 11, 3 Aug. 1557.

38 AD Évora CM, Registos, 1, f. 153v, 23 Nov. 1527.

39 Cortes of Lisbon, cap. ger., xi, 12 July 1459, published in M. J. da Cunha Brito, 'Os Pergaminhos da Câmara de Ponte de Lima', *O Archeologo Português*, xv (1910), 24.

40 *Ord. Man.* (1521), I. 57. 2, law of 22 Oct. 1460.

41 Leão, *Leis Extravagantes*, 4. 5. 3, 8 July 1521; AD Évora CM, Originais, 1, f. 99, 3 June 1528; AHCM Elvas, Provizões, 1, f. 504, 12 July 1537.

42 Leão, *Leis Extravagantes*, 4. 5. 7, 7 May 1525.

43 Leão, *Repertorio dos Cinquo Livros das Ordenações*, f. iv.

44 *Ord. Af.*, 5. 65. 1.

45 ANTT, Cortes, 2. 14, f. 114v, Cortes of Coimbra/Évora, caps. místicos, iii, 1472–3; ibid., f. 135, Cortes of Évora, cap. xxxii (caps. ger. of the Algarve), 1475; *Regimēto dos Ofiçiaaes das Çidades Villas e Lugares destes Regnos* (1504), cap. xii, f. 5v. See also *Ord. Man.* (1514), I. 35. 40; (1521) I. 44. 44.

46 *Ord. Man.* (1521), 5. 37. 2.

47 Ibid., 5. 37. Pr., 1.

48 E.g., ANTT, Ch. J. III, Perdões e Legits., 25, ff. 117v, 118, slave pardoned for grand larceny 22 Apr. 1554.

49 AHCM Coimbra, Correia, 1, 'Titulo de outras posturas', c. 1514–23; art. 973, 6 Aug. 1519; art. 160, c. 1514–23; published by J. Pinto Loureiro in *Arquivo Coimbrão*, IV (1938/9), 170–1; V (1940), 86–7; and II (1930/1), 173, respectively.

50 AD Évora CM, Posturas Antigas, 2, f. 29, 29v (slaves and *mancebos* treated alike); f. 37, 37v; 79v, 25 Aug. 1572 (slaves selling grapes); ff. 80v–81, 9 Mar. 1584. AHCM Elvas, Posturas, 1, ff. 41v–42 (in force 1617). For Lisbon, see *Livro dos Regimētos dos Officiaes Mecanicos*, 'Regimento dos Sombreireiros', para. xvii (original f. 209), p. 169 (slaves selling stolen hats).

51 ANTT, Estrem., 5, f. 165v, 26 Aug. 1461; probably from Cortes of Évora.

52 AHCM Lxa, Ch. Régia, 45, Pregos, f. 23v, 17 Jan. 1449, published in Freire d'Oliveira, *Elementos*, I. 245 (being p. 244, n. 3).

53 ANTT, Leis, 2. 3, 22 Mar. 1502.

54 Santarém: n. 51, above. Lisbon: *Livro dos Regimētos dos Officiaes Mecanicos* (*1572*), 'Do Regimento dos Taverneiros', para. x (original f. 228), p. 188; 'Do Regimento dos Pastelleiros', para. xxii (f. 256), p. 223. GHC Porto, Vereações, 12, f. 7v, 11 Apr. 1534; Acordãos, 2, f. 42v, 4 Feb. 1587. Prosecution: ANTT, Inq. Lxa, Reconciliações, 1, ff. 114–7, 15 June 1555.

55 AD Évora CM, Posturas Antigas, 2, f. 29, 29v; GHC Porto, Vereações, 12, f. 7v, 11 Apr. 1534.

56 ANTT, Confirmações Gerais de D. Filipe III, 11, f. 298, 8 Oct. 1635, confirming law of 11 Feb. 1475, from Cortes of Évora.
57 AHCM Loulé, Vereações, 1530, f. 44, 44v; repeated in 1561, f. 38v; published in Romero Magalhães, *Algarve Económico*, pp. 134–5; AD Évora CM, Posturas Antigas, 2, f. 29, n. d. (late sixteenth century); AHCM Elvas, Posturas, 1, ff. 43v–44v (in force 1617).
58 AHCM Lxa, Ch. Régia, 40, D. João III, 3, f. 29, 12 Sept. 1544; ff. 33, 36, 37, 1 Feb. 1545; documents noted in *Livros de Reis*, VII. 138, 141. Leão, *Leis Extravagantes*, 4. 5. 9.
59 AHCM Beja, Vereações, 1542, f. 31, 31v. Partly published in A. Viana (ed.) 'Livro das Vereações da Câmara de Beja – 1542', *Arquivo de Beja*, 1 (1944), 190.
60 ANTT, Estrem., 7, f. 155, 16 Mar. 1477, caps. esps. of Lisbon; *Ord. Man.* (1514), 5. 9. 3; (1521) 5. 11. 3; ANTT, Forais Novos, *passim*.
61 ANTT, Ch. J. III, Perdões e Legits., 9, f. 188, 13 May 1533; f. 379, 2 Oct. 1533.
62 ANTT, Estrem., 5, f. 165, 26 Aug. 1461. Similar response to *procuradores* of Setúbal: ANTT, Confirmações Gerais de D. Filipe III, 11, f. 298, 8 Oct. 1635, confirming 11 Feb. 1475.
63 *Ord. Man.* (1521), 5. 10. 2, 3.
64 ANTT, Ch. J. III, Perdões e Legits., 8, f. 52, 52v, 16 Feb. 1540. Other examples in ibid., 10, f. 367v, 12 Dec. 1539; 8, ff. 175v–176, 18 May 1541; 16, f. 277, 277v, n. d. (1550).
65 ANTT, Ch. J. II, 16, f. 133, 28 Dec. 1492, published in Coelho, *Documentos Inéditos de Marrocos*, I. 396–7. Another case: Ch. J. III, Perdões e Legits., 9, f. 325, 325v, 5 Sept. 1533.
66 ANTT, Ch. J. III, Perdões e Legits., 27, ff. 247v–248, 31 Mar. 1557. *Ord. Man.* (1514), 5. 30. Pr.; (1521) 5. 35. Pr., 1; 5. 36.
67 *Ord. Af.*, 5. 32. 4; *Ord. Man.* (1514), 5. 9. Pr.; (1521) 5. 10. Pr.
68 Slave sentenced to be sold in Spain: ANTT, Ch. J. III, Perdões e Legits., 25, f. 387, 387v, 25 Sept. 1555.
69 *Ord. Man.* (1521), 5. 10. 6.
70 AHCM Elvas, Receita e Despeza, II. (1504), f. 16, 16v.
71 According to Tacitus, *Annals*, 13. 32, 14. 42; see Buckland, *Roman Law of Slavery*, p. 94.
72 ANTT, Ch. J. III, Perdões e Legits., 10, f. 309, 3 Oct. 1539.
73 AHCM Lxa, Ch. Cidade, 393, Registro de Posturas, 1, f. 24, 24v, 15 June 1551; another copy (Livro de D. Filipe I, 1, f. 206v), published in Freire d'Oliveira, *Elementos*, I. 562. AD Évora CM, Originais, 12, f. 244, 12 Jan. 1544; Posturas Antigas, 2, f. 79v, 25 Aug. 1572.
74 AHCM Coimbra, Correia, 1, art. 102, *c.* 1554, published by Loureiro in *Arquivo Coimbrão*, II (1930/1), 160, 161; AHCM Elvas, Provisões, 1, f. 504, 12 July 1537: both of these laws gave the option of a 1,000 *rs.* fine or thirty days in gaol.
75 AD Évora, Mis., Livro de Privilegios, f. 361, 361v, 21 Aug. 1503 (based on provision of Lisbon Misericórdia, 12 Feb. 1503), published in G. Pereira (ed.), *Documentos Historicos da Cidade de Evora*, II. 91–2; Leão, *Leis Extravagantes*, 4. 21. 3, 27 Feb. 1520.
76 AD Évora, Mis., Privilegios, f. 46, 27 Feb. 1520.
77 Ibid., ff. 19v–20, 10 Oct. 1501, published in Pereira, *Documentos*, II. 89–90.
78 AD Évora, Mis., Compromissos, cap. viii (*c.* 1516–9), published in Pereira, *Documentos*, II. 117–8.

79 AD Évora, Mis., Privilegios, f. 361, 361v, published in Pereira, *Documentos*, II. 91–2; BP Évora, cod. cv/2–11, f. 180v, 24 May 1535.
80 ANTT, Ch. J. III, Perdões e Legits., 1, f. 266v, 12 July 1548, published in F. M. de Sousa Viterbo, *Trabalhos Nauticos dos Portuguezes nos Seculos XVI e XVII*, I. 239–41.
81 ANTT, Ch. J. III, Perdões e Legits., 15, f. 269v, 11 April 1551.
82 AHCM Loulé, Vereações, 1530, f. 44, 44v, 15 July 1530; published in Romero Magalhães, *Algarve Económico*, p. 134.
83 BP Évora, cod. cv/2–11, ff. 179–82, 24 May 1535; ff. 216–19, 28 Apr. 1536; ff. 222–227v, 28 May 1536. On the Casa do Cível's purview in criminal cases, see the glossary, p. 267.
84 ANTT, C. C., 2. 72. 133, 6 Dec. 1516.
85 Leão, *Leis Extravagantes*, I. 17. 6.
86 AHCM Lxa, Ch. Cidade, 178, Livro 1 de Vereações dos annos de 1515. 1551. 1552, f. 201v, 1 Oct. 1552.
87 Leão, *Leis Extravagantes*, I. 4. 4, para. xxv.
88 It may be noted that free inhabitants of a village without a *câmara* were likewise subject to summary trials before a layman similar to a justice of the peace from whose verdict they had no right of recourse or appeal: *Ord. Man.* (1514), I. 35. 55; (1521) I. 44. 64–9.

7 Fugitives, freedom and freedmen

1 See Heleno, *Escravos em Portugal*, pp. 157–8, for examples.
2 *Ord. Af.*, 2. 113.
3 *Ord. Af.*, 5. 54. 7, decree of 2 Mar. 1459.
4 *Ord. Man.* (1521), 5. 41. 1.
5 *Ord. Af.*, 2. 114. 1; 5. 113. 1.
6 The restitution of the value of the slave to the master, and similar sums to the crown and to the person who revealed the name of the fugitive's assistant.
7 *Ord. Af.*, 2. 114. 2; 5. 113. 2, 3.
8 *Ord. Man.* (1521), 5. 77.
9 E.g., ANTT, Ch. J. III, Perdões e Legits., 3, ff. 172v–173, 26 Jan. 1547, where a black slave was stopped on suspicion, near his residence in Beja; 15, ff. 169v–170, 19 Aug. 1550, and 27, ff. 91v–92, 16 Mar. 1556: runaways picked up in small towns.
10 *Ord. Man.* (1514), 5. 33. 1; (1521) 5. 41. 1, 2; ANTT, Cortes, 4. 3, f. 15, 15v, Cortes of Lisbon, 1498, cap. ger. xxxi.
11 ANTT, Núc. Ant., 1, Livro das Leis e Posturas Antigas, ff. 167v–168.
12 *Ord. Af.*, 2. 8; *Ord. Man.* (1514), 2. 2; (1521) 2. 4. E.g., a Brazilian Indian slave was ejected from a sanctuary into which he had been dragged by a fellow gaol-breaker to whom he was chained: ANTT, Ch. J. III, Perdões e Legits., 21, ff. 245v–246, 18 Oct., n. d. (1552).
13 *Ord. Af.*, 5. 61; *Ord. Man.* (1514), 5. 55; (1521) 5. 52.
14 AHCM Elvas, Provisões, 1, f. 611, 27 Jan. 1517; ANTT, C. C., 1. 86. 116, 23 Aug. 1551.
15 On treaties, see H. Baquero Moreno, 'Alguns Acordos de Extradição entre Portugal e Castela nos Séculos XIII a XV', *Portugaliae Historica*, 1 (1973), 81–101, which publishes several treaties; and *Concordia entre estos reynos de Castilla y el de Portugal, acerca de la remission de los delinquentes*, 29 June 1569. Orders and warrants of D. Fernando and Da Isabel noted in Simancas, Archivo General, *Catálogo XIII. Registro general, anno* 1486, 20 Mar., f. 107;

1489, 26 Jan., f. 138; 1490, Sept., f. 236 and 5 Nov., f. 213. On slaves as thieves: Alfonso X, *Siete partidas*, VII. xiv. 23.

16 Arch. Prots. Badajoz, legajo 1, f. 478, 478v, 10 Sept. 1562; ibid., f. 566, 566v, 1 Oct. 1562.

17 ANTT, Núc. Ant., 893, f. 46v, 4 June 1565.

18 Arch. Prots. Badajoz, legajo 1, f. 478, 478v.

19 Portuguese law, rather than forcing anyone to guard the boats, merely made it advisable to do so, by penalizing the masters of slave boatmen who escaped with their boats from Lisbon, as we have seen, and, in the Algarve, by requiring the owners of boats in which slaves escaped to make good the value of the slaves to the slaves' masters: ANTT, Estrem., 1, f. 108, 22 Sept. 1351, confirmed 18 April 1367, published in *Descobs. Ports.*, I. 92.

20 ANTT, Ch. Man., 46, f. 146, 19 Jan. 1517.

21 Both men were released within three months: ANTT, Inq. Lxa, Processos, 12047 and 12086.

22 Simancas, Archivo General. *Catálogo XIII. Registro general del Sello, anno* 1491, f. 231; 1492, 4 June, f. 147; the original law is in Alfonso X, *Siete partidas*, VII. xiv. 23.

23 ANTT, Ch. Man, 17, f. 64, 6 June 1501, published in Azevedo, 'Os Escravos', *Arch. Hist. Port.*, I (1903), 300–1.

24 ANTT, Ch. Man., 29, f. 31, 14 July 1495.

25 ANTT, Ordem de Santiago, Cartório de Palmela, 1, f. 64, published in Sousa Viterbo, *Trabalhos Nauticos*, II. 280–1.

26 The Infante D. Fernando freed four *mouriscos* 'for the honour of Christianity', Caetano de Sousa, *Provas*, I. 508, will of D. Fernando, 18 Apr. 1437. The count of Arraiolos in his will thought freeing his Christian slaves a 'service to God' and to the good of his own soul, ibid., III. 558–9, 6 Aug. 1453.

27 But the heirs did not always comply with the testator's wishes. See Chapter 8, p. 140.

28 See F. Basas, 'Un caso de esclavitud en el siglo XVI', *Anuario de Historia Económica y Social*, I (1968), 614–18.

29 The *cartas* requested the magistrates of Portugal and of all other kingdoms and lordships to enforce the acceptance of the bearer's free status; e.g., AD Évora, Núc. Not., no. 17, f. 83v, 24 Feb. 1548; 13, f. 66v, 12 Jan. 1547. Courts in the Castilian empire did enforce Portuguese *cartas de alforria*; see V. Cortés Alonso, 'La liberación del esclavo', *Anuario de Estudios Americanos*, XXII (1965), 533–68. The Portuguese, in turn, honoured the letters of manumission issued in other countries, e.g., D. João II confirmed a letter granted to one Pedro Álvares, a black, by the king of England: ANTT, Ch. J. II, 16, f. 61, 17 Mar. 1490, published in Azevedo, 'Os Escravos', *Arch. Hist. Port.*, I (1903), 300.

30 AD Porto, Notas, 3. 5, f. 51, 51v, 13 Feb. 1552; BP Évora, cod. CLXIX / 1–26, no. 7, 21 Oct. 1577.

31 They also had to pay 10 per cent of the 10 per cent to the *alcaide* of the town in which they were ransomed: *Ord. Af.*, I. 62. 16; *Ord. Man.* (1514), I. 42. 11; (1521) I. 55. 17.

32 Leão, *Leis Extravagantes*, 5. 3. 10, 16 Apr. 1529. Lisbon: ANTT, Forais Novos, Estrem., ff. 7v–8, 7 Aug. 1500; Santarém: f. 22, 1 Feb. 1506, both in published edn (*Forais Manuelinos*), pp. 8, 22. Silves: Forais Novos, Entre-Tejo-e-Odiana, f. 14, 20 Aug. 1514. Évora: ANTT, Forais Novos, Entre-Tejo-e-Odiana, f. 4, 1 Sept. 1501; also Abrantes: Forais Novos, Estrem., f. 55v, 1 June 1510, in published edn (*Forais Manuelinos*), p. 61; Guarda: Forais Novos, Beira, f. 4,

1 June 1510, in published edn (*Forais Manuelinos*), p. 4; Miranda do Douro: Forais Novos, Trás-os-Montes, f. 3, 1 June 1510, in published edn (*Forais Manuelinos*), p. 4, etc.

33 AD Évora, Núc. Not., 17, f. 83, 83v, 24 Feb. 1548: purchase of the freedom of a 23- or 24-year-old *mourisca* by her mother for 18,000 *rs*. Purchase of freedom by husband: BM Elvas, 11402 P. H., maço 6, 20 Apr. 1553 (Tombo do Salvador, 3, f. 129).

34 AD Évora, Núc. Not., 2, ff. 84v–86, 30 July 1544: purchase of the freedom of a 4-year-old mulatto child for 2,000 *rs*. by the father, a tailor.

35 BM Elvas, 11402 P. H., maço 6, 20 Apr. 1553 (Tombo do Salvador, 3, f. 129).

36 Mentioned in ANTT, Ch. J. II, 21, f. 11, 28 July 1487; *Ord. Man.* (1514), 5. 46. 3; (1521) 5. 81. 5.

37 AD Évora, Núc. Not., 10, ff. 63–4, 4 Jan. 1546.

38 ANTT, Gav., 16. 2. 1, will of 26 July 1516, published in *As Gavetas da Torre do Tombo*, VI. 107.

39 Arquivo da Casa de Bragança, 'Apontamentos que fez D. Fernando II, 1478–1483', published in Caetano de Sousa, *Provas*, III. 626.

40 E.g., the customs of Garvão (thirteenth/fourteenth century), in *Portugaliae Monumenta Historica, Leges et Consuetudines* (Lisbon, 1856), II. 80. Thus the 'treasurer of captives', who received ransom money and Moorish prisoners to exchange for Christians could receive 'a third of a Moor': ANTT, Extras, f. 245, 245v, 11 June 1494.

41 E.g., multiple ownership of a Moor: ANTT, Ch. Af. V, 13, f. 13v, 10 July 1456, published in Azevedo, *Chancelarias*, II. 394–5.

42 BM Elvas, 11402 P. H., maço 6 (Tombo do Salvador, 3, f. 129), will of Estêvão da Gama, 20 Apr. 1553, permitting a *meia forra* freed by Gama's wife to buy her complete freedom; AD Évora, Núc. Not., 2, ff. 65v–66, 21 July 1544, wherein D. Mecia de Andrade confirmed her late husband's manumission of a *mourisco*.

43 ANTT, Ch. Man., 37, ff. 59v–60, 29 Dec. 1501 (1502 in the document, *anno nativitatis*).

44 Domínguez Ortiz, 'La esclavitud en Castilla', *Estudios de Historia Social de España*, II (1952), 390.

45 ANTT, Ch. Af. V, 20, f. 83, 13 Feb. 1440, published in *Mon. Hen.*, VII. 57; 5, f. 69v, 11 Aug. 1446; Caetano de Sousa, *Provas*, II. 81–2, will of Infanta D. Joana, 19 Mar. 1490; ANTT, MS. 169, f. 143, published in Azevedo, 'Os Escravos', *Arch. Hist. Port.*, I (1903), 305–6. J. P. Ribeiro, *Dissertações Chronologicas*, II. 263, will of Dr Diogo Afonso, 9 Dec. 1447, conditionally freeing two slaves named Ahmed and one called 'Daguila'.

46 BM Elvas, 11402 P. H., maço 3 (Tombo do Salvador, 3, f. 55v), 20 July 1490.

47 AHCM Loulé, Avaliações (1564), noted in Romero Magalhães, *Algarve Económico*, p. 230.

48 AD Évora, Mis., 476, Receita e Despeza do An. D. 537; 761, Defuntos, 1547–56; Mis. Elvas, Falecidos, maço 7. liv. 1 (1529–71).

49 AD Évora, Mis., 276, Registo de Entradas no Hospital (1554–62), f. 39v, 16 July 1555; f. 26v, 25 Jan. 1555; f. 27, 15 Feb. 1555.

50 *Ord. Af.*, 2. 30. 2; *Ord. Man.* (1514 and 1521), 2. 21. Citizenship was perhaps not so valuable for the right it gave to take part in the political direction of the town, because this was normally in the hands of an oligarchy, as for the exemption from certain municipal taxes, such as the *portagem* and *passagem*, which people from other places had to pay on goods which they sold or brought through the town in question.

51 *Ord. Af.*, 3. 9. 6, 7; *Ord. Man.* (1521), 3. 8. 7, 8.
52 E.g., sale of a house by a *mourisco* and his free black wife, AD Évora, Núc. Not., 20, ff. 1-13, 18 June 1548.
53 ANTT, Reg. Par.: Lisboa (Sto Estêvão), mistos, 1, f. 149v, 24 July 1566, where it is noted that an old black woman had made a will before she died; AD Évora, Mis., 537, Testamentos e Doações, 1515 a 1738, ff. 82-3, 27 June 1585: execution of the will of Pedro Touregão, a freed black; and Núc. Par.: Évora (S. Pedro), mistos, 1, f. 33 *bis*, 30 June 1555, which mentions the executor of the will of João Gomes, a free black, buried in that church.
54 *Ord. Af.*, 3. 9. 2; *Ord. Man.* (1514 and 1521), 3. 8. 1.
55 *Ord. Af.*, 4. 70. 7-9; *Ord. Man.* (1514 and 1521), 4. 55. 7-9.
56 *Ord. Man.* (1514 and 1521), 4. 55. 10. Alfonso X, *Siete partidas*, IV. xxii. 11, includes a similar law; there are in fact many similarities between Portuguese and Castilian laws regarding manumission: see ibid., IV. xxii, *passim*.
57 AHCM Lxa, Ch. Régia, 45, Pregos, f. 331v, 10 Dec. 1544, published in Freire d'Oliveira, *Elementos*, I. 542.
58 BP Évora, cod. CV/2-11, f. 226, 28 May 1536.
59 *Ord. Af.*, C. C., 3. 25. 2.
60 ANTT, C. C., 1. 59. 110, 25 Oct. 1537; and J. A. de Figueiredo, *Synopsis Chronologica de Subsidios ainda os Mais Raros para a Historia e Estudo Critico da Legislação Portugueza*, I. 345-6.
61 BP Évora, cod. CV/2-11, f. 218v, 28 Apr. 1536: gift of 300 *rs.* to a mulatta held for debt to her landlord; f. 224, 28 May 1536: partial pardon to Gaspar Gomes, a black, for carrying a lump of lead as a weapon: he was relieved of the necessity to pay the part of the fine due to the city, but not the part due to the *alcaide* who had arrested him; he was also released from gaol; f. 227, 28 May 1536, Leonor Nunes, a black, was given 1,200 *rs.* toward payment of her fine of 1,400 *rs.* for assault; measures were also taken to provide her with sureties for the remaining 200 *rs.*
62 Freire, 'Beatriz', *Arch. Hist. Port.*, IX (1914), 104, 25 Nov. 1506.
63 BM Elvas, 11402 P. H., maço 6 (Tombo da Alcáçova, 150), 17 Nov. 1545, will of Diogo da Gama, o Velho; and ibid. (Tombo do Salvador, 3, f. 129), 20 Apr. 1553, will of Estêvão da Gama. Money: Mis. Elvas, Testamentos (C-J), 28 Feb. 1545, will of Estêvão de Sequeira, giving 30 *xdos* (12,000 *rs.*) to Maria, a freedwoman; AD Évora, Mis., 539, Testamentos e Doações, f. 180v, 23 Oct. 1562, will of D. Maria de Vilhena, leaving various sums of money ranging from 10,000 to 20,000 *rs.* to seven freed persons.
64 E.g., Caetano de Sousa, *Provas*, II. 414, will of Queen D. Maria, 26 July 1516 (conditional gift); ibid., I. 437, 440, will of Infanta D. Filipa, 9 Jan. 1493; AD Évora, Mis., 99, Escrituras (1540-50), f. 44, will of Diogo da Silveira, 1 Apr. 1549, giving 20,000 *rs.* and a bed.
65 AD Évora, Mis., 539, ff. 146, 146v, 6 Nov. 1538.
66 BM Elvas, 11402 P. H., maço 4 (S. Domingos, 1, f. 53; 2, f. 145v), 17 Nov. 1510. The houses were in the Rua dos Hortelães (Gardeners' Street).
67 ANTT, Estrem., 13, f. 22v, 2 June 1510: royal grant of half of a deceased black freedman's property at Castanheira; by law the other half of the property had to be sold to ransom prisoners of the Moors. See also *Ord. Af.*, 2. 28. 15. On escheat or *maninhádego*, see Almeida, *Historia de Portugal*, I. 413, 424.
68 ANTT, Feitos Findos, N. 4, 20 June 1539.
69 E.g., to a *criado*, BM Elvas, 11402 P. H., maço 4 (S. Domingos, 1, f. 53; 2, f. 145v), 17 Nov. 1510

70 AHCM Loulé, Avaliações (1564), noted in Romero Magalhães, *Algarve Económico*, p. 230.

71 ANTT, Núc. Ant., 817, f. 124.

72 AHCM Lxa, Ch. Régia, 40, D. João III, 3, ff. 36-7, 1 Feb. 1545, summarized in *Livros de Reis*, VII. 141, and being the reply to Lisbon's requests at the Cortes of Almeirim, 1544.

73 ANTT, Reg. Par.: Lisboa (S. Pedro de Alfama), baptismos, 1, f. 14, 13 Mar. 1561, child of a black seaman and his wife; Lisboa (Sto Estêvão), mistos, 1, f. 43, 18 Feb. 1567: child of a black boatman (*companheiro*) and his wife.

74 *Livro do Lançamento*, II. 313 (f. 326v); III. 266 (f. 483v). Professor Boxer suggests that these women may have been laundresses or prostitutes, or both (personal communication).

75 AD Évora, Mis., 99, Escrituras (1540–50), f. 36, 28 Nov. 1545: will of Cecília Falcoa; ibid., 539, Testamentos e Doações, f. 30, will of Tristão Homem, 8 May 1541.

76 *Livro do Lançamento*, I. 149 (f. 68: locksmith, 30,000 *rs*.); II. 280 (f. 311: cushion-maker, 30,000 *rs*.); 310 (f. 325: tailor, 40,000 *rs*.).

77 Popplau, 'Viaje', p. 81.

78 AD Évora CM, Originais, 12, f. 294 (agravo ix, Cortes of Torres Novas, 1525); f. 255v (agravo vii, Cortes of Évora, 1535).

79 *Sumário*, p. 8, 'The Alley of the Black Woman's Hostelry'.

80 BL, Harleian MS., 3822, ff. 243v, 315, 332v, 337 (the last was called 'Las Ventas de Ginea [*sic*]': 'The Guinea Inn').

81 ANTT, Ch. J. III, 5, f. 111, 16 Sept. 1544, noted in Sousa Viterbo, 'Notícia sobre alguns Médicos', *Archivos de Historia da Medicina Portugueza*, III (1912), 114. See also fictitious Mestre Tomé, p. 171.

82 According to Almeida Lucas in his 'Prefácio' to Álvares, *Auto de Santo António* (Lisbon, 1948), pp. 12–13, but the evidence is slight.

83 D. B. Machado, *Bibliotheca Lusitana Historica, Critica e Cronologica*, I. 374.

84 L. Stegagno Picchio, *História do Teatro Português*, trans. M. de Lucena, p. 98; Almeida Lucas, 'Prefácio' to Álvares, *Auto de Santo António*, pp. 22–3.

85 Black to a white's house to pass the time chatting: ANTT, Inq. Lxa, Denúncias, A, ff. 78v–79, 2 Mar. 1555; members of two races playing cards together: ibid., 4, ff. 129v–130, 26 Aug. 1556. Sharing bed: ANTT, Inq. Lxa, Processos, 13190, 2 Aug. 1557. Hospitality: BN Lxa, Fundo Geral, cod. 4388, Obras de D. João de Castro, tomo XVIII: 'Tratado dos Portugueses de Veneza', liv. 5, cap. iii, published in J. L. de Azevedo, *A Evolução do Sebastianismo*, p. 137, where Castro relates how he stayed in Évora with João Pinto, a black student from the Kongo in 1567.

86 E.g., ANTT, Reg. Par.: Lisboa (S. Pedro de Alfama), baptismos, 1, f. 14, 13 Mar. 1561. The wives of a white seaman and a fisherman were godmothers to a black seaman's child.

87 ANTT, Inq. Évora, maço 350, no. 3315, f. 5v, 16 Nov. 1551: a black woman held by the Inquisition mentioned another free black woman married (by common law, apparently) to a *ratinho*, a migrant labourer from Beira. Mis. Elvas, Falecidos, maço 7, liv. 1, f. 115v, 8 May 1543, and (no foliation) 22 Aug. 1555: two white men married to blacks could not afford alms for their own funerals. AD Setúbal, Núc. Par.: Setúbal (Sta Maria da Graça), casamentos, 1, f. 5, 10 Jan. 1575: labourer and black woman – but f. 5v, 3 May 1575, miller and *parda* (dusky) woman. Perhaps lighter-skinned women were more acceptable to wealthier Portuguese?

88 AD Évora, Núc. Par.: Estremoz (S. Tiago), mistos, 2, f. 282v: 20 Feb. 1554,

marriage of Domingos Fernandes and Isabel Fernandes, before many witnesses.

89 E.g., Prestage and Azevedo (eds.), *Registos Parochiaes. Sé.*, I. 95, 23 Apr. 1569; AD Évora, Mis., 761, Defuntos, f. 73, 30 Oct. 1548, and f. 81, 21 Feb. 1549.

90 Magalhães Godinho, *Descobrimentos*, II. 564, 577. Source not indicated.

91 Oliveira, *Arte da Guerra no Mar*, cap. iv, p. 24; A. B. Gromicho (ed.), 'O Testamento de Garcia de Resende', *A Cidade de Évora*, V: 13/14 (1947), 17: will dated 8 Sept. 1523.

92 M. Harris, *Patterns of Race in the Americas*, pp. 84–6; C. N. Degler, *Neither Black nor White*, pp. 44–5.

8 Blacks and Christianity

1 Zurara, *Crón. Guiné*, cap. lv.

2 Ibid., cap. xxiv, where he is called a 'frade de Sam Framcisquo'.

3 Ibid., cap. lxxxviii.

4 In Leo of Rožmital, *Travels*, trans. and ed. M. Letts, p. 113.

5 BL, Sloane MS., 1572, ff. 61–2.

6 For a good short account of the origins of the Misericórdia, see A. J. R. Russell-Wood, *Fidalgos and Philanthropists*, pp. 14–23.

7 AD Évora, Mis., 49, Registo de Confrades, 1, ff. 15, 16, 16v, 18, 18v.

8 Ibid., ff. 16, 51, 52v, 116.

9 Russell-Wood, *Fidalgos and Philanthropists*, pp. 143–4. None of the brothers of the Misericórdia of Oporto in 1575 can be identified certainly as blacks or slaves, but there is one 'Paulo preto', in Mis. Porto, Irmãos (1575–1605), D, banco 5, no. 7, f. 170.

10 The Rodrigues Pretos, of whom one member, Brás, was a *mordomo* in 1548 (AD Évora, Mis., 761, Defuntos, f. 61v) appear to have been an important white family (AD Évora, Núc. Par.: Évora (S. Pedro), mistos, 1, f. 26v).

11 BN Lxa, Iluminado 151, Compromisso da Irmandade de Nossa Senhora do Rosário dos Homens Pretos, 2 Dec. 1565, published in I. da R. Pereira, 'Dois Compromissos de Irmandades de Homens Pretos', *Arqueologia e História*, IV (1972), 27–8.

12 L. de Cacegas, *Historia de S. Domingos*, ed. and expanded by L. de Sousa, pte I, liv. III, cap xxv, p. 337.

13 AHCM Lxa, D. João II, 2, f. 35, 28 Sept. 1494. The description of this document at the head of the folio attributes it to 1484 and may thus have confused Cacegas or Sousa (see n. 12 above), but the document itself is clearly dated, in Arabic numerals, 1494.

14 Évora: ANTT, Ch. Man., 9, f. 61, 26 Mar. 1518, confirmed in Ch. J. III, 45, f. 10, 10v, 6 Aug. 1529; a modernized transcription may be found in Brásio, *Pretos em Portugal*, p. 100. Lagos: ANTT, Ch. J. III, 3, f. 308v, 5 Feb. 1555, published in Azevedo, 'Os Escravos', *Arch. Hist. Port.*, I (1903), 305; São Tomé: ANTT, Ch. J. III, 12, f. 134, 134v, 9 July 1526, published in *Mon. Miss. Af.*, 1a sér., I. 472–4.

15 Elvas: São Domingos, 7, Tomo da Hirmandade de N. Sa do Rosario dos Hommens Pretos, ff. 12v–14v, 10 Feb. 1562. Leiria: ANTT, Ch. Seb., 8, f. 251, 10 Feb. 1571. Mugem: ANTT, Ch. Fil. I, 5, f. 43, 21 Nov. 1583. Funchal: ANTT, Sé do Funchal, maço 21, doc. 10, 20 Aug. 1583. Setúbal: ANTT, Ch. Fil. I, 5, f. 50, 21 Jan. 1584. Alcácer: ANTT, Ch. Fil. I, 5, f. 220, 22 Oct. 1588.

16 E. Carneiro, 'As Irmandades do Rosário', in his *Ladinos e Crioulos*, p. 90.

17 A. D. de Sousa Costa, 'Dominicanos', *Dicionário de História de Portugal*, i. 849; Cacegas, *Historia de S. Domingos*, 1st edn, pte ii, liv. vi, cap. vi, f. 238.

18 *Graças e Indulgencias Concedidas aa confraria de nossa Senhora do Rosayro* (1572), f. lv: privileges given by Innocent VIII in 1484.

19 Azevedo, 'Superstições Portuguesas no Seculo xvi', *Revista Lusitana*, v (1897/9), 2.

20 See AHCM Lxa, Ch. Régia, 24, D. João II, 2, f. 35, 28 Sept. 1494, where the king spoke highly of the spiritual works of the black brothers, and forbade that the fraternity be taken away from their control, as was threatened.

21 The following information about the brotherhood in Lisbon comes from BN Lxa, Iluminado 151, ff. 1–10v, published in Pereira, 'Dois Compromissos', *Arqueologia e História*, iv (1972), 27–34. (References hereafter are only to the chapter, folio and page in Pereira.)

22 Cap. ii, f. 2, 2v, Pereira, p. 29. Pereira in his introduction, p. 14, claims that the presence of a white clerk in a black fraternity indicates the absence of racial prejudice in Portugal, which it obviously does not.

23 Cap. vii, f. 4, 4v, Pereira, p. 30. On discrimination by colour as developed in Brazil, see Degler, *Neither Black nor White*, pp. 207–64.

24 ANTT, Ch. Seb., 11, f. 175, 18 Oct. 1578, noted in Brásio, *Pretos em Portugal*, p. 85.

25 Cap. vi, f. 4, Pereira, p. 30; cap. viii, f. 4v, p. 30; cap. xiii, ff. 5v–6, p. 31; cap. xx, ff. 7v–8, p. 32; cap. xxvii, f. 10, p. 33. The sheer number of chapters on the subject suggests that the standard of honesty, or at least of financial ability, of the officers was often not very high.

26 ANTT, Ch. J. III, 4, f. 132v, 21 June 1550, published in Pereira, pp. 22–3 .

27 Brandão, 'Majestade e Grandezas', *Arch. Hist. Port.*, xi (1917), 135; the editors observe (n. 320) that there is no record of this donation in D. João's will, nor in the ANTT, but that it could have been recorded in one of the missing chancery books for 1485, 1493, 1494 or 1495. The gift was confirmed in ANTT, Ch. J. III, 22, f. 100, 8 Aug. 1529 (confirming a previous confirmation by D. Manuel, 18 Apr. 1518), published in Pereira, p. 19.

28 ANTT, Ch. J. III, 22, f. 100v, confirming 21 June 1518, confirming 14 July 1496, published in Brásio, *Pretos em Portugal*, pp. 76–7; cap. xxiv, f. 9, 9v, Pereira, pp. 32–3. Most of the ships bound for São Tomé left in February: anonymous pilot in Blake, *Europeans in West Africa*, i. 146.

29 Cap. xxv, f. 9v, Pereira, p. 33. The date of the feast does not seem to have been 7 Oct., as it is now, in commemoration of the battle of Lepanto (see 'Maria', *Enciclopedia Cattolica*, viii. 102), but was apparently shortly before Sta Isabel (8 July) (see cap. xvi, f. 6v, p. 31). Probably it was celebrated on 2 July, the feast of the Visitation of Our Lady, or on the first Sunday in July. Until 1573 the festival of Our Lady of the Rosary was exclusive to the Dominicans.

30 ANTT, Ch. J. III, 22, f. 101, 2 Oct. 1529, confirming 16 Dec. 1521, published in Brásio, *Pretos em Portugal*, pp. 82–3, and Pereira, pp. 19–20 (being p. 17, n. 6).

31 ANTT, Ch. J. III, 12, f. 134, 134v, 9 July 1526, in *Mon. Miss. Af.*, 1a sér., i. 473.

32 ANTT, Ch. J. III, 17, f. 44v, 6 Mar. 1529, confirming 24 May 1513, which stated that an earlier order by D. João II had been lost.

33 Ibid., confirming 20 Mar. 1518.

34 See Brásio, *Pretos em Portugal*, pp. 90 seqq., for the story of the fight to prevent

218   NOTES TO PP. 156-9

masters from selling slaves whom the brotherhood wished to redeem out of the country.

35 On the subject, see S. Leite, *História da Companhia de Jesus no Brasil*, II. 324; Carneiro, *Ladinos e Crioulos*, pp. 87–8; A. J. R. Russell-Wood, 'Black and Mulatto Brotherhoods in Colonial Brazil', *Hispanic American Historical Review*, LIV (1974), 567–602.

36 On slaves and the priesthood in general, see *Dictionnaire de droit canonique*, IV. cc. 453, 454.

37 The requirement is evident from the description of one of those who received his first tonsure in the cathedral of Évora in 1480: Évora, Arquivo da Sé, CEC-5-II, f. 5v, 'Alfomsum filiũ Aluari Egidij mouro . . . de legitimo matrimonjo procreatum.'

38 ANTT, Bulas, 21. 9, *Etsi ea que a nobis*, 3 May 1518; Arch. Vat., Acta Vice Cancelarii, vol. 2, f. 70, 5 May 1518; published in *Mon. Miss Af.*, 1a sér., I. 414–15 and 416, respectively.

39 ANTT, Bulas, 20. 17, 12 June 1518, published in *Mon. Miss. Af.*, 1a sér., I. 421–2.

40 Francisco de Santa Maria, *O Ceo aberto na Terra* (Lisbon, 1697), caps. xviii, xx, published in *Mon. Miss. Af.*, 1a sér., I. 91, 99–100, 102. Black at Jesuit University of Évora: BN Lxa, Fundo Geral, cod. 4388, tomo XVIII, liv. 5, cap. iii, published in Azevedo, *Evolução do Sebastianismo*, p. 137.

41 Évora, Arquivo da Sé, CEC-5-III, f. 4v.

42 André: ibid., f. 68, 24 Feb. 1535. João: f. 23, 29 Mar. 1533. Manuel: f. 127v, 21 Sept. 1538.

43 1533: ibid., ff. 20–52. 1538: ff. 127v–141.

44 Évora, Arquivo da Sé, CEC-5-IV.

45 I was not able to gain admittance to the cathedral archives of Lisbon, since they were being catalogued at the time (June, 1976).

46 Will of D. Filipa, 9 Jan. 1493, published in Caetano de Sousa, *Provas*, I. 440.

47 ANTT, Feitos Findos, cela 7, 1600, Livro da Fundaçam do Convento do Carmo de Beja, ff. 29v–32v, 14 Sept. 1553. I am indebted to R. B. Smith for drawing this document to my attention (see his *Diogo Fernandes de Beja*). He tells me it has been published by M. Ribeiro in *Diário do Alentejo*, nos. 1982–9 (5–14 Nov. 1938).

48 ANTT, Inq. Lxa, Denúncias, A, f. 82, 8 Apr. 1555.

49 It is not impossible that Mendes was a mulatto. For a parallel case elsewhere in Europe, see the story of St Benedetto (Benedict the Black), a dark-skinned Nubian lay brother whom the Franciscans of Palermo, in Sicily, chose to be their superior in 1578: see D. Attwater, *The Penguin Dictionary of Saints*, pp. 62–3. Benedetto was revered in later days by the black brothers of the Rosary of Elvas; a statue of him still exists in the sacristy of the church of S. Domingos in that town.

50 For the story of the establishment of the Inquisition and its organization, see A. Herculano, *História da Origem e Estabelecimento da Inquisição em Portugal*, ed. J. B. de Macedo; A. J. Saraiva, *Inquisição e Cristãos-Novos*; and A. Baião, 'A Inquisição em Portugal e no Brasil. Subsídios para a sua História. A Inquisição no Século XVI', *Arch. Hist. Port.*, IV–X (1906–16). Baião provides a chronological list of nearly all persons denounced to the Inquisition, but unfortunately does not give references to the Livros de Denúncias.

51 ANTT, Inq. Lxa, Denúncias, 1, f. 108, 108v, 14 Mar. 1541, confirming ff. 107v–108, 14 Mar. 1541; noted in Baião, *Arch. Hist. Port.*, VI (1908), 96–7.

52 ANTT, Inq. Lxa, Denúncias, 1, ff. 81–2, 12 Jan. 1541, noted in Baião, *Arch. Hist. Port.*, vi (1908), 91.

53 ANTT, Inq. Lxa, Denúncias, A, f. 6a, 6b.

54 ANTT, Sto Ofício, cod. 976, Livro dos Acordos e Determinações, f. 4, question iii, 11 Mar. 1572, published in Baião, *Arch. Hist. Port.*, iv (1906), 404.

55 Bastião: ANTT, Inq. Lxa, Denúncias, A, ff. 99–100v; 147, 147v; 148, 148v; 148v–149; 149–150, from 26 Sept. to 2 Oct. 1555. White man: ANTT, Inq. Lxa, Processos, 5549, 26 Jan. 1563, published in Azevedo, 'O Antigo Casamento Português', *Arch. Hist. Port.*, iii (1905), 109–10. Lopes: Denúncias, A, ff. 82v–83, 27 May 1555.

56 ANTT, Inq. Lxa, Processos, 13190, *anno* 1557.

57 *Ord. Af.*, 5. 17; ANTT, C. C., 3. 2. 17, 17 Apr. 1506; *Ord. Man.* (1514), 5. 10; (1521) 5. 12.

58 ANTT, Inq. Lxa, Processos, 1621, *anno* 1565.

59 See the evidence of Fernão de Oliveira, p. 43 above, and also ANTT, Inq. Lxa, Denúncias, 3, f. 100v, 2 Jan. 1553, where a neighbour testified that he could not see that a black slave was being instructed in Christianity by his master.

60 ANTT, Inq. Lxa, Denúncias, A, f. 43, 30 Jan. 1553.

61 Fernandes, *Description*, pp. 10, 11, 28, 29; Pereira, *Esmeraldo*, liv. i, caps. xxvii, xxxi.

62 ANTT, Inq. Lxa, Denúncias, 2, ff. 124v–125v, 22 Mar. 1549; 3, ff. 94v–95v, 29 Dec. 1552; 4, f. 18, 18v, 10 Nov. 1554.

63 ANTT, Inq. Lxa, Denúncias, 4, f. 18, 18v, 10 Nov. 1554.

64 ANTT, Inq. Lxa, Denúncias, 3, ff. 94v, 95, 29 Dec. 1552.

65 Francisco is mentioned as an interpreter in the trial of the would-be fugitives: ANTT, Inq. Lxa, Processos, 12086, f. 3, 3v, 26 May 1553.

66 ANTT, Inq. Lxa, Processos, 10832, 4 Aug.–20 Nov. 1553.

67 ANTT, Inq. Lxa, Processos, 12047 and 12086.

68 *Ord. Man.* (1514), 5. 28; (1521) 5. 33. Black sorcerers mentioned in ANTT, Ch. J. III, Perdões, 22, f. 370v, 18 Oct. 1555; Ch. Seb. e Hen., Legits., 3, f. 44, 20 Apr. 1562 and 34, f. 100v, 19 Dec. 1578; all three documents published in Azevedo, 'Superstições Portuguesas no Século xvi', *Revista Lusitana*, vi (1900), 217, 220 and 225.

69 ANTT, Bulas, 2. 6, bull *Cum ad nichil*, 17 Dec. 1531, published in *Corpo Diplomatico Portuguez*, ii. 336; Livraria, cod. 979, f. 7v, 'Carta do edicto e tempo da graça', 20 Oct. 1536, published in Baião, *Arch. Hist. Port.*, iv (1906), 229–31.

70 ANTT, Inq. Lxa, Denúncias, A, ff. 78v–79, 2 Mar. 1555.

71 ANTT, Inq. Évora, Processos, maço 350, no. 3315.

72 This spell was also known in the district of Toledo; cf. Inq. Toledo, legajo 82, no. 24, *annis* 1530–7, mentioned in S. Cirac Estopañán, *Aportación a la historia de la Inquisición española. Los procesos de hechicería en la Inquisición de Castilla la Nueva (Tribunales de Toledo y Cuenca)*, pp. 157, 260–1. The fundamental ideas seem to have been that the knot tied the man to the woman, and the star was symbolic of the constancy of the union: see J. G. Frazer, *The Golden Bough*, pp. 240–2.

73 AD Évora, Mis., 761, Defuntos (1547–56), f. 148v, 14 May 1552.

74 *Ord. Man.* (1514), 5. 28. 2; (1521) 5. 33. 2. Of course, the inquisitorial clerk may have written *encruzilhada* as the nearest Portuguese equivalent to some form of African magic circle.

75 Ca' da Mosto, *Navigazioni*, pp. 44–5, 57, 102; Pina, *Crónica de el-Rei D. João II*, cap. lviii, p. 159, Mar.–Apr., 1491.
76 J. V. Blassingame, *The Slave Community. Plantation Life in the Antebellum South*, p. 17.

9   Race relations

1 Songs: L. Chaves, 'O Preto da Guiné no nosso Folclore', in *Congresso Comemorativo do Quinto Centenário do Descobrimento da Guiné*, ii. 558; Leite de Vasconcellos, *Etnografia Portuguesa*, iv. 42–3; A. Thomaz Pires, 'Investigações Ethnographicas', *Revista Lusitana*, xii (1909), 61–92; and A. Pires de Lima, *Mouros, Judeus e Negros, passim*. Giants: C. Pedroso (ed.), 'The Seven Iron Slippers', in *Portuguese Folk-Tales*, trans. H. Monteiro, p. 89. Blacks: 'The Maid and the Negress', and 'The Three Citrons of Love', in *Portuguese Folk-Tales*, pp. 6–9, 11–13 respectively. For a white child burnt all over with an iron and called a mulatta: 'The Maiden with the Rose on her Forehead', in *Portuguese Folk-Tales*, p. 65. The general incoherence of these tales suggests their antiquity.
2 Leite de Vasconcellos, *Etnografia Portuguesa*, iv. 43; A. Ribeiro Chiado, 'Parvoices que acontecem muitas vezes', in *Obras*, pp. 155, 157, 167.
3 BGU Coimbra, MS. cod. 348, f. 53v, 'Das Tenções das Cores'; unfavourable meaning of 'black' in Gil Vicente, *Obras Completas*, ii. 73, 76, 118, 226; iii. 193; iv. 200; v. 46, 109, 286, 293; and in Chiado, *Obras*, pp. 26, 42, 98, 110, 121. References to black devils in: F. M. Esteves Pereira (ed.), 'Visão de Tundalo' (from twelfth century), *Revista Lusitana*, iii (1895), 110; B. Gomes de Brito, *História Trágico-Marítima*, i. 51: 'Naufrágio da Nau São Bento, 1554'. See also the painting of the Last Judgement (Portuguese school, mid-sixteenth century) in Lisbon, Museu Nacional de Arte Antiga, reproduced in *A Thousand Years of Portuguese Art*, p. 18.
4 *Auto dos Reis Magos*, in *Obras Completas*, i. 42; *Dom Duardos*, iii. 278; contrasting ugly black women with pretty whites in *Fragoa d'Amor*, iv. 113.
5 *Crón. Guiné*, cap. xxv.
6 Lopez and Pigafetta, *Relação do Reino de Congo*, liv. i, cap. ii, p. 26.
7 *Crón. Guiné*, cap. xxvi; Ca' da Mosto, *Navigazioni*, p. 27.
8 *Asia*, dec. i, liv. iii, cap. xii, f. 39v.
9 'Trabalhar é bom para o Preto', Leite de Vasconcellos, *Etnografia Portuguesa*, iv. 43.
10 This preference for Asiatics seems to contradict Godinho's assertion that the Iberian peoples recognized the illegality of enslaving white or yellow races untouched by the curse of Ham: *Descobrimentos*, ii. 561.
11 Sassetti, *Lettere*, pp. 125–6, to Baccio Velori from Lisbon, 10 Oct. 1578; Landi, *Descrittione*, pp. 41, 83.
12 *Asia*, dec. i, liv. iii, cap. xii, f. 39v. By the seventeenth century, however, when there were no longer enough Moorish slaves to pose a serious threat to law and order, some Portuguese began to consider the blacks rascally and treacherous and even idealized the Moors. See F. Rodrigues Lobo, *Corte na Aldeia e Noites de Inverno* (1619), ed. A. Lopes Vieira, diál. iv, pp. 94–6.
13 As I have noticed in my visits to art galleries and churches in Portugal, and in my researches in the Arquivo Fotográfico of the Museu Nacional de Arte Antiga, Lisbon, where I was kindly helped by Sr Francisco Marques.
14 On black magi, see H. L. Kehrer, *Die Heiligen drei Könige in Literatur und Kunst*, ii. 223–5. Possibly the depiction of black magi in Portugal may have

begun under the influence of Flemish art, where black kings were portrayed with far less reluctance than in southern Europe, where the presence of black slaves often inhibited their portrayal as people of rank: I. Sachs, 'L'Image du Noir dans l'art européen', *Annales. Economies. Sociétés. Civilisations,* XXIV (1969), 887.

15 Resende, *Cancioneiro Geral,* I. 204–5, and see C. Michaëlis de Vasconcellos, 'Contribuições para o Futuro Diccionário Etimológico das Línguas Hispánicas', *Revista Lusitana,* XI (1908), 15.

16 Blacks also appeared with some frequency in Castilian literature, but I have chosen to study the Portuguese literary image of the black in order to detect any unique features. One difference appears to be that the woman slave was the more common type in Castile: see F. Weber de Kurlat, 'El tipo del negro en el teatro de Lope de Vega: tradición y creación', 2º Congreso Internacional de Hispanistas, Nijmegen, 1965, *Actas,* II. 695. For further information on blacks in Castilian literature, see the same author's 'El tipo cómico del negro en el teatro prelopesco: fonética', *Filología,* VIII (1962), 139–68, and 'Sobre el negro como tipo cómico en el teatro español del siglo XVI', *Romance Philology,* XVII (1963), 380–91; J. Brooks, 'Slavery and the Slave Trade in the Works of Lope de Vega', *Romanic Review,* XIX (1928), 232–42; J. R. Castellano, 'El negro esclavo en el entremés del Siglo de Oro', *Hispania,* XLIV (1961), 55–65; Russell, 'Rodrigo de Reinosa', in *Studies in Spanish Literature,* pp. 225–45; W. E. Wilson, 'Some Notes on Slavery During the Golden Age', *Hispanic Review,* VII (1939), 171–4.

17 Ff. 11–12v, published in Michaëlis de Vasconcellos, *Autos portugueses.*

18 F. 11v, in Michaëlis de Vasconcellos, *Autos portugueses.*

19 Moor in A. Álvares, *Auto de Santiago,* in Michaëlis de Vasconcellos, *Autos portugueses.*

20 In Henrique Lopes, *Cena Policiana,* in Prestes et al., *Primeira Parte dos Avtos,* f. 45, the mulatto, Solis, is told that 'Os õmes da vossa cor / ser musicos derda [*sic*: ? de herdade] o tẽ.' ('Men of your colour / are musical [? by inheritance].')

21 The apparently easy transformation of a black man to a white suggests that the part was played by a white in blackface – as does the scene in Vicente's *Floresta de Enganos* where a judge disguises himself as a black slave woman and speaks in *fala de Guiné.*

22 Chiado, *Pratica de Oito Figuras,* in *Obras,* p. 11. The black in the anonymous *Auto de Dom Fernando,* f. 12, in Michaëlis de Vasconcellos, *Autos portugueses,* is also accused of being a thief. Rodrigues Soropita, 'Carta. que escreueo a instancia do negro do abadinho Manuel soares. a filha do Marques de Villa real de quem o negro se namorou e estaua auzente.', in *Cancioneiro Fernandes Tomás,* f. 95v.

23 Also in *Clerigo da Beyra,* in *Obras,* VI. 24–7.

24 F. 11.

25 Resende, *Cancioneiro Geral,* V. 197–9.

26 As pointed out in A. Pimentel's 'Prefacio' to Chiado, *Obras,* p. 87.

27 In *Autos,* I. 168.

28 In *Obras Completas,* IV. 80, 81.

29 In ibid., VI. 23–30.

30 Ed. C. Berardinelli, pp. 73–80.

31 Chains: *Clerigo da Beyra,* in Vicente, *Obras Completas,* VI. 24. Whippings: *Dom Fernando,* f. 12, in Michaëlis de Vasconcellos, *Autos portugueses;* Chiado, *Auto das Regateiras,* in *Autos,* I. 107. Hot fat: Resende, *Cancioneiro Geral,* V. 197;

Dom Fernando, f. 12; Chiado, *Auto da Natural Invençam* and *Auto das Regateiras*, in *Autos*, I. 36, 108. Called 'dogs': Vicente, *Floresta de Enganos* and *Nao d'Amores*, in *Obras Completas*, III. 195; IV. 80; Chiado, *Pratica de Oito Figuras*, in *Obras*, p. 13; *Auto de Vicente Anes Joeira*, p. 80; Lopes, *Cena Policiana*, in Prestes et al., *Primeira Parte dos Avtos*, f. 45v; J. F. de Vasconcellos, *Vlysippo*, act II, sc. v, pp. 130, 133, 136.

32 In Prestes et al., *Primeira Parte dos Avtos*, f. 45.

33 ANTT, Inq. Lxa, Denúncias, I, f. 129, 26 Apr. 1541.

34 It is understandable that mulattoes might be even more uncertain of the value of *négritude* and indeed the playwright Afonso Álvares wrote paeans to white beauty into his *Auto de Santa Babora*, ff. 6, 10.

35 Cf. C. C. Hernton, *Sex and Racism*, pp. 63–6, 77.

36 Chiado, *Pratica de Oito Figuras*, in *Obras*, pp. 4–5, 10–11, 19–20; Vicente, *Quem tem Farelos* and *Velho da Horta*, in *Obras Completas*, v. 58, 152–4.

37 Vicente, *Farsa dos Almocreves*, in *Obras Completas*, v. 345–6.

38 For a humorous look at this phenomenon, see F. Sá de Miranda, 'A António de Sá na fugida de uns seus criados', in *Obras Completas*, I. 61–2.

39 ANTT, Estrem., 5, f. 165, 165v, caps. esps. of Santarém, 26 Aug. 1461.

40 ANTT, Ch. J. III, Perdões e Legits., 8, f. 170v, 9 May 1541. That black slaves were shamed by a public whipping was also noted by the *procuradores* of Lagos, see above, p. 118. If what these whites said was true, then the blacks' feelings of self-esteem had mingled with Portuguese notions of honour to produce a state of mind wherein the shame of being whipped in public rather than in private was as much feared as the pain of punishment itself. The blacks would then appear to have held the same values as the lower-class whites with whom they worked.

41 *Descrittione*, pp. 40, 82. He also says that some people, namely the mulattoes, were slaves because of heredity, but this was the mechanism by which almost everybody was assigned a place in society.

Conclusions

1 'Les Portugoys, que maint esclave ont eu et ont tous les jours', P. de Commynes, *Mémoires*, ed. J. L. A. Calmette, liv. v, cap. xviii (II. 210–11).

2 Gardeners in Genoa: Gioffrè, *Mercato*, p. 90; agricultural employment of slaves in the kingdom of Naples: Verlinden, 'Schiavitù', *Annali del Mezzogiorno*, III (1963), 36; a few in Castile: Domínguez Ortiz, *Estudios de Historia Social de España*, II (1952), 387.

3 C. Verlinden, 'Some Aspects of Slavery in Medieval Italian Colonies', in his *The Beginnings of Modern Colonization*, trans. Y. Freccero, pp. 79–97.

4 On the *perames*, Bibliothèque de la Faculté de Médecine, Montpellier, MS. H. 385, f. 35, 'Voyage faict par moy Pierre Lescalopier', noted in Braudel, *The Mediterranean*, I. 348.

5 Gioffrè, *Mercato*, p. 89.

6 C. Verlinden, 'Précédents et parallèles européens de l'esclavage colonial' *O Instituto*, CXIII (1949), 132.

7 Gioffrè, *Mercato*, p. 92; BN Madrid, MS. 18.735, 'Informe sobre los moros esclavos y libres de Sevilla' (*c.* 1624), published in Domínguez Ortiz, *Estudios de Historia Social de España*, II (1952), 425–6.

8 Archivo Municipal, Seville, Actas capitulares, 1461, 18 Sept., noted in A. Collantes de Terán Sánchez, 'Contribución al estudio de los esclavos en la Sevilla medieval', in *Homenaje al profesor Carriazo*, II. 121.

9 Damasio de Frias, 'Diálogo en alabanza de Valladolid', published by N. Alonso Cortés in *Miscelanea Vallisoletana*, 2a ser. (n. d. given), p. 23, which I have only seen noted in Domínguez Ortiz, *Estudios de Historia Social de España*, II (1952), 377.

10 Apart from Domínguez Ortiz, *Estudios de Historia Social de España*, II (1952), p. 386, see also Pike, 'Slaves and Freedmen', *Hispanic American Historical Review*, XLVII (1967), 353–5.

11 M. Gual Camarena, 'Un seguro contra crímenes de esclavos en el siglo xv', *Anuario de Historia del Derecho Español*, XXIII (1953), 252, 253; Gioffrè, *Mercato*, pp. 94, 102.

12 There appear to have been more guilds which banned slaves in Genoa (Gioffrè, *Mercato*, p. 91) than in Spanish cities (Domínguez Ortiz, *Estudios de Historia Social de España*, II (1952), 386, n. 40).

13 Domínguez Ortiz, *Estudios de Historia Social de España*, II (1952), pp. 380–4; R. Livi, *La schiavitù domestica nei tempi di mezzo e nei moderni*, p. 31.

14 See F. P. Bowser, *The African Slave in Colonial Peru, 1524–1650*, pp. 103–5, 318–19; A. J. R. Russell-Wood, 'Colonial Brazil', in D. W. Cohen and J. P. Greene (eds.), *Neither Slave nor Free*, pp. 100–4.

15 Compare the situation in the United States: since the overwhelming majority of slaves there were black, American slave-holders lacked a tradition which distinguished between slaves of different colours and cultures and thus saw blacks and mulattoes simply as slaves and the descendants of slaves. The logical consequence of this vision was prejudice on the grounds of racial descent. See Degler, *Neither Black nor White*, p. 111, and O. Nogueira, 'Skin Color and Social Class', in *Plantation Systems of the New World*, pp. 164–79.

16 C. R. Boxer, *Race Relations in the Portuguese Colonial Empire*, pp. 111–13; Elsa Goveia, 'The West Indian Slave Laws of the Eighteenth Century', in Foner and Genovese (eds.), *Slavery in the New World*, pp. 113–37.

17 See Brásio, *Pretos em Portugal*; Verlinden, *L'Esclavage*, I. 835–40; and Almeida, *Historia de Portugal*, v. 128–57.

18 Domínguez Ortiz, *Estudios de Historia Social de España*, II (1952), 400, 404.

19 Published in Marquês de Rio Maior, 'O Marquês de Pombal e a Repressão da Escravatura – A Obra e o Homem', in *Congresso do Mundo Português*, VIII (1940), 109–11.

20 Ibid., pp. 107–8. The law appears to have been enforced: W. J. Simon drew my attention to ANTT, Intendência de Polícia, maço 10, ff. 366 seqq., concerning the punishment of a man for the crime of importing a black slave into Portugal in 1798.

21 See J. Capela, *Escravatura*, pp. 244, 256–62, and *Memoria ácerca da Extincção da Escravidão*, pp. 22–38.

22 A. A. Mendes Corrêa, 'A Propôsito do "Homo Taganus". Africanos em Portugal', *Boletim da Junta Geral do Distrito de Santarém*, VI: 43 (1936), 37–55; more recently, E. dos Santos, 'Escravatura e Antropologia dos Portugueses', *Ultramar*, nova sér., II: 5/6 (1973), 51–98. The possibility of the nearly complete absorption of a minority of blacks into a white population is considered by H. L. Shapiro, *Race Mixture*, pp. 18, 26, and C. Stern, 'The Biology of the Negro', *Scientific American*, CXCI: 4 (1954), 83, 85.

23 J. Leite de Vasconcellos, 'Espécime Português da Raça Negra', *Boletim de Etnografia*, I (1920), 40–1. There were people with negroid features until much more recently in southern Spain: A. de Larrea Palacín, 'Los negros en la provincia de Huelva', *Archivos del Instituto de Estudios Africanos*, VI: 20 (1952), 39–57.

Bibliography

Manuscript sources

Portugal

The fundamental guide to archives, archival catalogues and manuscript collections (as well as to printed works) relevant to the period under study is

Marques, António Henrique de Oliveira. *Guia do Estudante de História Medieval Portuguesa*. Lisbon, 1964

The following works on more specialized subjects may also be consulted with profit:

Andrade, António Alberto Banha de. 'Arquivos Municipais', in *Papel das Áreas Regionais na Formação Histórica de Portugal. Actas do Colóquio*, pp. 143–84. Academia Portuguesa da História. Lisbon, 1975

Felix, Emília. 'Les Registres paroissiaux et l'état civil au Portugal', *Archivum*, VIII (1958), 89–94

Leitão, Joaquim. *Côrtes do Reino de Portugal. Inventário de documentação servindo de Catálogo da Exposição documental e biblio-iconográfica*. Lisbon, 1940

Roteiro dos Arquivos Municipais Portugueses. Vol. I– . Academia Portuguesa da História. Lisbon, 1976– (in progress)

Ryder, Alan F. C. *Materials for West African History in Portuguese Archives*. London, 1965

Aveiro

Arquivo Distrital

This is in the Biblioteca Municipal. The collection of parish registers (Livros Paroquiais) is catalogued, but individual volumes are not identified by contents or number; only the terminal dates of the holdings for each parish are given. I used the first volume in each holding and have described the contents in the titles below.

Arouca, baptizados, 1 (1581–96)
Arrifana, mistos, 1 (1587–1656)
Aveiro (Espírito Santo), mistos, 1 (1589–1616)
Aveiro (Vera Cruz), mistos, 1 (1572–91)

Esgueira, mistos, 1 (1594–1696)
Oliveira do Bairro, baptizados e óbitos, 1 (1544–1631)
Ovar, mistos, 1 (1588–1605)
Pessegueiro (S. Martinho), mistos, 1 (1565–?)
Sta Eulália, mistos, 1 (1564–1632)
Silva Escura, baptizados e óbitos, 1 (1566–1611)
Tropeço (Sta Marinha), mistos, 1 (1564–1617)
Vila Nova de Monsarros, mistos, 1 (1551–1734)

Santa Casa da Misericórdia

This archive is attached to the Hospital.
5A. Receitas e Despesas, 1593–4
6. Receitas e Despesas, 1597–8
7. Receitas e Despesas, 1598–9
9. Receitas e Despesas, 1599–1600
38. Doentes entrados no Hospital, from 1618
167. Liuro das dívidas, 1560

Braga

Arquivo Distrital

The archive of Braga also houses the district archives of Viana do Castelo.
The following documents from the collection Registo Civil were consulted:
Concelho de Barcelos: Vilar de Figos (S. Paio), mistos, 1
Concelho de Braga: Braga, Souto (S. João), mistos, 1
    Crespo (Sta Eulália), mistos, 1
And from the Arquivo Distrital de Viana do Castelo, Registo Civil:
Concelho de Arcos de Valdevez: Proselo (Sta Marinha), mistos, 1
Concelho de Monção: Monção (Sta Maria dos Anjos), mistos, 1

Coimbra

Arquivo Geral da Universidade

This is also the district archive. Documents consulted were from the
Registo Paroquial, Diocese de Coimbra.
Bobadela (Sta Maria), mistos, 1
Coimbra (S. João de Sta Cruz), baptizados, tomo 1, livro 1 (1546–68);
    defuntos, tomo 1, livro 1 (1558–91)
Coimbra (Sé Nova), baptizados, livro 1 (1546–67); baptizados, casados e
    defuntos, livro 1 (1568–87)
Condeixa a Nova, baptismos (1546–1747); defuntos (1546–1768); casa-
    mentos (1563–1725)
Montemor-o-Velho (Alcáçova), mistos, 1 (1546–1782)
Penela (Sta Eufémia), baptismos, casamentos e defuntos, livros 1, 2
Vila Cova de Sub Avô, baptismos, casamentos e defuntos, tomo 1 (1530–
    1743)
Vilarinho da Lousã, baptizados, tomo 1 (1545–1758); casados e defuntos,
    tomo 1 (1547–1742)

Arquivo Histórico da Câmara Municipal

Livros de Vereações, II (anno 1515); III (1518); IV (1520); V (1526); VI (1533); VII (1535–6); VIII (1550)

Biblioteca Geral da Universidade: Secção de Manuscritos

Códices 348, 491, 629, 695, 696, 704

Santa Casa da Misericórdia

A visit to the Misericórdia archive (Rua Sobre-Ribas, 49), which has no catalogue, did not reveal any documents from the period under study.

Elvas

Arquivo da Igreja de São Domingos

There is a small archive in the sacristy, and various relics of the brother-hood of the Rosary (meeting-table of the chapter and statue of San Benedetto) remain in the church.

7. Tomo da Hirmandade de N. Sa. do Rosario dos Hommens Pretos sita no Convento de San Domingos desta Çidade delvas donde esta a Fazenda que tem nossa sª. Contem em sî 375 meyas folhas, foi Renouado aos 19 de faureiº de 1652

9. Livro dos Escravos de N. S. do Rosario de Elvas. 1706

10. Libro da Irmandade de nossa s'nora do Rosario situada no çonuento de saõ dominguos da çidade deluas na hera de mil e quinhẽtos e nouenta annos

Arquivo Histórico da Câmara Municipal

The *fonds* of documents consulted were:

Pergaminhos. 1 small chest; 86 documents

Posturas. Vols. I (6 Aug. 1617), II (1672)

Proprias Provizões, Alvaras, Cartas e Ordens Regias (called Provisões in the notes). Vols. I (1501–1629), II (1449–1615), III (1434–1629)

Receita e Despeza. Vols. I (1432–5), II (1504)

Biblioteca Municipal

This contains the parish registers of Elvas and its district (including Olivença) and other manuscript documents.

Núcleo Paroquial:

1. Liv. 1, Olivença (Sta Magdalena), baptizados (1546–74), casados (1566–74), e óbitos (1546–74)

8. Liv. 1, Olivença (Matriz), baptizados (1561–76), casados (1560–76) e defuntos (1560–76)

37. Loose fascicle, Elvas (Sé), baptizados (1532–8)
    Liv. 1, baptizados (1548–54)

Other documents:

11402 P. H., maços 2–6. Almada, Vitorino de Sant'Anna Pereira de. 'Elementos para um Diccionario de Geographia e Historia Portugueza. Concelho d'Elvas e extinctos de Barbacena, Villa-Boim e Villa

Fernando'. (This is an extremely important collection; it comprises the *fiches* on which Almada took notes of documents which were in the individual archives of the churches of Elvas and district in the later nineteenth century, and may still be there (though my personal experience of the archive of the church of São Domingos, the only one to which I gained access, leads me to believe the contrary). Almada's sources are noted in parentheses in the text.)

1000 T. P. Documentos.

Colegiada de Sta Maria de Alcáçova. Documents nos. 35, 42, 46 and 47, being wills from 1489, 1502 (two wills) and 1504, respectively

Santa Casa da Misericórdia

Maço 1, livro 1. Titulo de Defuntos, 1532–3
Maço 7, livro 1. Falecidos (actually Despesas), 1529–71
Testamentos. 4 maços in alphabetical order by first name of testator

Évora

Arquivo Distrital

a) Câmara Municipal
Documents consulted (with catalogue numbers):
66. Livro Pequeno de Pergaminho
68–70. Livros de Pergaminho. Livros 2, 3, 4
71–5. Colecção de Originais da Câmara. Livros 1–5 (abbreviated Originais in the notes)
79, 80, 82. Colecção de Originais da Câmara. Livros 9, 10, 12 (abbreviated Originais in the notes)
135–6. Colecção de Registos. Livros 1, 2
206–7. Posturas, Licenças e Aforamentos. Livros 1 (Posturas Antigas, to 1395), 2 (1466–1588)
226. Sentenças de 1530 a 1640
230. Testamento de Gaspar de Sequeira e de Catarina Borges (1552)

b) Núcleo Notarial
11–1–1–1, no. 1, Livro de Francisco Fernandes, 1533
nos. 2–20, Livros 1–19 de Diogo Luís, 1544–8
nos. 26–32, Livros 1–7 de Fernão de Arcos, 1546–52

c) Núcleo Paroquial
Arraiolos (N. Sra dos Mártires), baptizados, 1 (1549–84)
Borba (N. Sra das Neves; Matriz), baptizados, 1 (1550–73); defuntos, 13 (1551–1724)
Estremoz (S. Tiago), 1, baptizados (1551–5), óbitos (1600–1709); 2, baptizados (1557–99), casamentos (1552–1619), óbitos (1552–80)
Évora (Sto Antão), 1, baptizados (1535–41), defuntos (1535–44); 2, baptizados (1545–51), casamentos (1545–51), defuntos (1545–51); 3, baptizados (1551–6), casamentos (1552–6), defuntos (1549–56)
Évora (S. Mamede), 1, baptizados (1537–57), casamentos (1541–68)
Évora (S. Pedro), 1, baptizados (1546–65), casamentos (1546–68), óbitos (1547–65)

Évora (Sé), 1, baptizados (1535–7)

Montemor-o-Novo (N. Sra da Vila), 1, baptizados (1533–1678), casamentos (1556–1664), óbitos (1556–1651)

Montemor-o-Novo (N. Sra do Bispo), 1, baptizados (1542–50); 2, baptizados (1550–6)

d) Santa Casa da Misericórdia

Documents consulted (with numbers of maços):

1. Acordãos (1531–1635)
48. Livro de Privilegios da Mizericordia de Evora
49. Registo de Confrades (1499–1556)
99. Escrituras (1540–50)
276. Registo de Entradas no Hospital e Falecimentos (1554–62)
389. Receita e Despesa (Rendas, Pitanças, Esmolas, Consumo de Cereais). Livro 1 (1569–70)
476. Receita e Despesa com Defuntos (Livº de Receita e Despeza da Mizericordia de Evora do An. D. 537)
524. Livro de Dotes de D. Álvaro da Costa, 1540–60. 2 vols.
537. Livº de Testamentos e Doações (Originais Traslados), 1515 a 1738
538. Testamentos e Doações, 1529–1699
539. Testamentos e Doações (Originais Traslados), 1507–62
761. Livro dos Defuntos de 1547 ate 1556

Arquivo do Cabido da Sé

The documents housed in this archive may be consulted in the Manuscript Room of the Biblioteca Pública.

Catalogued documents consulted (with catalogue numbers):

CEC–4–II. Livro Novo dos Estatutos do Cabido da Sé de Évora de 1476
CEC–4–IV. Estatutos Reformados do Cardeal D. Henrique de 1548
CEC–4–VI. Constituições do Bispado de Évora, 27 May 1534
CEC–5–I. Matrículas das Ordenações, 1472
CEC–5–II. Matrículas das Ordenações, 1480–3
CEC–5–III. Matrículas das Ordenações, 1532–40
CEC–5–IV. Matrículas das Ordenações, 1541–58
CEC–6–VIII. Livro das Escripturas da Letra B
CEC–10–XI, XII, XIII, XIV, XV. Livros dos Originais
CEC–13–I, II. Livros dos Acordos do Cabido, 1 (1469–78) and II (1539–55)

Uncatalogued documents consulted (with number of *estante* (shelf) in tower room above main archive):

A I. Registo do R[everem]do C[abi]do 1550 ate 1556
A IV. Livro de lembranca dos aRemdamentos & côtratos q[ue] se fazem este año de 1548
A IV. Liuro dos ẽçassamẽtos e dos contos do Rev[erem]do cabyda [*sic*] ssee deu[or]a
A IV. Rendas, 1519–32

Biblioteca Pública Municipal

Manuscript codices checked (with catalogue numbers of codices):

CIII/2–21

CIII/2–22

CV/2–11. Cartas del rej Dom João o Terc[ei]ro ao S[enh]or Governador Dom Fernando de Castro, 12 Sept. 1530–19 Nov. 1536

CXII/1–37, ff. 399–412v. Writings of António Ribeiro Chiado and Afonso Álvares

CLXVII/1–4. Convento da Graça. Livro da Despeza do Convento 1573 a 1599

CLXVIII/2–1. Convento do Espinheiro, Évora. Cartas régias, alvarás e provisões, 1458–1768

CLXIX/1–26

Lisbon

Arquivo Histórico da Câmara Municipal

Casa dos Vinte e Quatro:

35. Liuro dos Regimentos dos Offiçiaes mecanicos da mui excelente e Semp[re] leal Cidade de lix[bo]a reformados per ordenãça do Illustrissimo Senado della. pello. L[icencia]do D[ua]rte Nunez do Liam Ano. MDLXXij

89. Livro do Regimento dos Corretores (1433–1760)

Chancelaria da Cidade:

178. Livro 1 de Vereações dos Annos de 1515. 1551. 1552

391. Posturas. 1 (1430–1606)

393. L[iur]o 1º de Registro de posturas, regimentos, taxas, priuilegios e officios dos annos de 1495 – te 1591 – e Acordos

395. Posturas da Cidade (1531–1665)

396. Posturas de mui excelente, e sempre leal Cidade de Lisboa reformadas emmendadas, e recopiladas, pello Ill[ustrissi]mo Senado della. Anno 1610

413. 1º Registo de Posturas da Almotaçaria (1470–1719)

415. Almotaçaria. 1 (1491–1745)

416. Almotaçaria. 2 (1515–1706)

474. Provimento de Ofícios. 1

924. L[iur]o 1º de Fianças de Escrauos

Chancelaria Régia:

1. Místicos de Reis. 1
2. Místicos. 1
5. Cortes. 1
17. D. Afonso V. 1, 2
18. D. Duarte e D. Afonso V. 2
23. Livro das Ordenações de D. Afonso V
24. D. João II. 2
25. D. João II. 3
29. D. Manuel. 1
30. D. Manuel. 3
31. D. Manuel. 4
36. Provisões de D. Manuel. 1, 2, 3, 4, 5

37. Livro Carmesim
39. D. João III. 2
40. D. João III. 3
42. Provisões de D. João III. 1, 2, 3, 4, 5
45. Liuro dos Pregos, e tambem intitulado da Gralha
78. Festas (1486–1632)
Provimento da Saúde:
   1. Provimento da Saúde. 1 (1484–1625)
Santo António:
14/228. Contratos. 1 (1294–1620)
14/230. Contratos. 3 (1496–1665)
14/256. Compras e Vendas (1369–1620)
14/292. Sentenças. 1 (1399–1511)
14/294. Sentenças. 3 (1517–76)
Maps. Tinoco, João Nunes. 'Planta da Cidade de L[i]x[bo]a', 1650

Arquivo Nacional da Torre do Tombo
The following list gives those collections of documents which were
thoroughly checked in the relevant catalogues or else, where no catalogue
was available, by going through them, document by document. Exact
references to the documents consulted will be found in the notes.
Cartas Missivas. 3 Partes
Chancelarias: D. Afonso V, D. João II, D. Manuel I and D. João III
Colecção de São Vicente. Vols. 5, 8
Confirmações Gerais de D. Filipe III. Vol. II
Conventos. S. Bento de Lisboa. Livro 7
Corpo Cronológico:
   Parte 1: maços 1–97
   Parte 2: maços 1–158
   Parte 3
Cortes. The Cortes from 1439 to 1562 were checked first of all in the books
   of Capítulos de Cortes, and then the relevant documents were con-
   sulted in the original maços of the Cortes.
Feitos Findos. Cela 7 (Gabinete do Conservador), pasta N. 4, Documentos
   dos seculos XV e XVI
   Cela 7, 1600: Convento do Carmo de Beja
Fragmentos. Caixas 1, 2, 3
Gavetas
Leis. Maços 1, 2
Leitura Nova:
   Além Douro. Livros 1–5
   Beira. Livros 1–3
   Direitos Reais. Livros 1, 2
   Estremadura. Livros 1–13
   Extras
   Forais Novos. Livros de Beira, Entre-Douro-e-Minho, Entre-Tejo-
   e-Odiana, Estremadura, Trás-os-Montes

Forais Velhos
Ilhas
Legitimações. Livros 1, 3
Mestrados
Místicos. Livros 1–6
Odiana. Livros 1–8
Reis. Livros 1, 2

Manuscritos:
166–9. Collecção dos Autos da Fe e listas das pessoas que foram peni-
tenciadas pela Inquisição de Portugal
186. Capítulos dos Cónegos Azuis
959. Auto da Fe da Cidade de Lisboa, 1543
Mesa de Consciência e Ordens. Livro 26

Núcleo Antigo:
1. Livro das Leis e Posturas Antigas, 1249–1393
16. Livro de Registo de Leys, Regimentos e outras Mercês do Señor
Rey D. Manuel. Desde o Anno de 1516, té 1520
110. Registo da Alfândega do Porto
528. Livro dos quartos e vintenas dos Escravos q[ue] se pagaraõ na
Alfandega de Lisboa no anno de 1529. (Actually the duties paid at
Ribeira Grande, on Santiago in the Cape Verdes.)
548. L[iv]ro dos aforam[en]tos das erdades do ano de bc xxx da diz[im]a
e sysa (the duties paid to the Casa da Sisa e Herdades in Lisbon,
1530)
799. Rec[ei]tas e despesas do tesouro de Guyné. 1504–5
810. L[iv]ro da R[ecei]ta e desp[es]a de Andre G[onça]ll[ve]z R[ece-
bed]or e V[ea]dor das obras dos pacos de Simtra q[ue] comecou em
anno de bc.biij. p[er] diamte
811–14. Despesas com obras no convento de Belém
817. Livro da Receita e despeza do Almox[arif]e dos fornos delRey Anno
de 1514 té 1515
818. Liuro da comta de Fernam do Cassall Almoxarife dos fornos de Vall
de Zebro de sua recepta e despesa do Anno de quinhemtos e vimte e
seis de Janeiro por diamte
888. Arguim. Livro dos conhecim[en]tos daz couzas q[ue] o Cap[it]am
G[on]c[al]o da Fon[se]ca entregou a Rodr[ig]o Affonso Piloto do
Navio S[an]ta M[ari]a da Mizericordia. Anno de 1508. Truncado.
Resgate de pretos e outras cousas
889. Arguim. Livro do Resgate dos Escravos (truncado), 1519
893. (kept in Sala dos Índices, where numbered 487) Collecção dos
documentos Pertencentes ao Regno do Algarve, que se achão no
Real Archivo da Torre do Tombo. 1774
922. Livro dos Fornos de Vale de Zebro (truncado), 1512–13
Ordem de Cristo

Registo Paroquial:
Castelo Branco. Concelho de Castelo Branco

Castelo Branco (Sta Maria), mistos, 1 (1540–1612)
Monforte da Beira, mistos, 1 (1558–84)
Castelo Branco. Concelho de Covilhã
    Covilhã (Sta Maria do Castelo), mistos, 1 (1596–1629)
    Covilhã (S. João de Malta), mistos, 1 (1566–1648)
    Covilhã (S. João Mártir), mistos, 1 (1551–1626)
    Covilhã (S. Pedro), baptizados, 1 (1565–1698)
Castelo Branco. Concelho de Sertã
    Sernache de Bomjardim, óbitos, 1 (1560–1605)
Faro. Concelho de Lagos
    Odiáxere (N. Sra da Conceição), mistos, 2 (1566–1612,
Faro. Concelho de Loulé
    Loulé (S. Clemente), mistos, 1 (1540–75)
Faro. Concelho de Olhão
    Moncarapacho (N. Sra da Graça), mistos, 1 (1543–8)
Faro. Concelho de Tavira
    Tavira (Sta Maria), baptizados, 1 (1562–3)
Faro. Concelho de Vila Real de Sto António
    Cacela, mistos, 1 (1570–86)
Guarda. Concelho de Castelo Rodrigo
    Figueira de Castelo Rodrigo, mistos, 1 (1563–1603)
Guarda. Concelho de Celorico da Beira
    Celorico da Beira (S. Martinho), mistos, 1 (1558–1620)
    Linhares, mistos, 1 (1566–1677)
Guarda. Concelho de Gouveia
    Paços da Serra (S. Miguel), mistos, 1 (1534–1731)
Guarda. Concelho de Manteigas
    Manteigas (Sta Maria), mistos, 1 (1559–1652)
Lisboa. Concelho de Lisboa
    Lisboa (N. Sra da Conceição, the Conceição Nova), mistos, 1 (1568–78)
    Lisboa (Santiago), mistos, 1 (1557–1601)
    Lisboa (Sto Estêvão), mistos, 1 (1561–70)
    Lisboa (S. Pedro de Alfama, called de Alcântara), baptismos, 1 (1559–1622)
    Lisboa (S. Vicente de Fora), mistos, 1 (1550–69)
Lisboa. Concelho de Lourinhã
    Lourinhã (N. Sra da Anunciação), mistos, 2 (1547–56)
Lisboa. Concelho de Sintra
    Colares, mistos, 1 (1559–76)
    Sintra (Sta Maria e S. Miguel), mistos, 1 (1557–1705)
    Sintra (S. João das Lampas), mistos, 1 (1569–1631)
Lisboa. Concelho de Vila Franca de Xira
    Alhandra, mistos, 1 (1567–96)
Santarém. Concelho de Benavente
    Benavente (N. Sra da Graça), mistos, 1 (1563–1605)
Santarém. Concelho de Cartaxo
    Pontevel, mistos, 1 (1541–1777)

Santarém. Concelho de Sardoal
  Sardoal (Santiago), mistos, 1 (1558–71)
Santarém. Concelho de Tomar
  Tomar (Sta Maria dos Olivaes), mistos, 1 (1554–1613)
Santarém. Concelho de Torres Novas
  Torres Novas (S. Pedro da Vila), óbitos, 1 (1543–1638)
  Torres Novas (Santiago), mistos, 1 (1531–67)
Vila Real. Concelho de Mondim de Basto
  Atei, óbitos, 1 (1551–63)
  Campanhó, óbitos, 1 (1563–73)
  Ermelo (S. Vicente), mistos, 1 (1550–77)
Santo Ofício:
  Inquisição de Coimbra. Processos
  Inquisição de Évora. Processos
  Inquisição de Lisboa:
    141–7–16: Denúncias, 1 (1537–43)
    144–2–54: Denúncias, A (1542–55)
    141–6–1: Denúncias, 2 (1544–50)
    141–6–2: Denúncias, 3 (1550–4)
    141–6–3: Denúncias, 4 (1554–9)
    144–2–56: Denúncias (1556)
    Processos
    141–6–7: Reconciliações, 1 (1544–59)

Biblioteca Nacional de Lisboa: Secção dos Reservados
Manuscritos:
Cod. 109: Frei João de São José, 'Corografia do Reyno do Algarve
  dividida em quatro livros' (1577)
679–80: Lisboa: Estatística de 1552
9164: Ordenações delRei D. Duarte

Sociedade de Geografia de Lisboa, Biblioteca: Secção de Reservados
One important manuscript codex was consulted in this library:
Reservados, 146–B–4. Regimentos da Cidade de Sam Jorge da Mina,
  S. Thome, e obras Pias, Por onde se handem reger o Cap[it]am,
  Feytor e mais Officias [sic] e varias Leys e Aluaras del Rey concer-
  nentes â mesma materia (1529–32)
Of the other archives which I visited in Lisbon, that of the Santa Casa da
Misericórdia was largely destroyed in the earthquake of 1755, while that
of the church of São Domingos suffered the same fate in a fire during the
1960s.

Oporto

Arquivo Distrital
Documents consulted (with catalogue numbers where applicable):
Cabido da Sé:
  106. Liuro do Recebim[en]to da Redizima: desta alfãdegua do Porto

del Rey nosso S[enh]or: q[ue] se pagua ao B[is]po e Cabido desta
See do Porto: do anno q[ue] Começa em dia de Jan[ei]ro de 1573,
& ha daCabar em o mesmo dia de 1574
1673. Livro dos Originais (Pergaminhos), 15
Notas. 3a sér. Livros 1–7 (21 Jan. 1548–23 Jan. 1553)

Registo Civil:
Concelho de Amarante. Gondar (Sta Maria), mistos, 1 (1537–88)
S. Gonçalo de Amarante, mistos, 1 (1549–65)
Concelho de Canavezes. Sto Isidoro de Riba Tâmega, mistos, 1 (1536–89)
Concelho de Felgueiras. Rande (S. Tiago), mistos, 1 (1537–58)
Concelho de Matosinhos. Leça de Palmeiro (S. Miguel), mistos, 1
(1553–74)
Concelho do Porto. Miragaia (S. Pedro), mistos, 1 (1569–1610)
Porto (Sé: N. Sra da Assunção), baptismos, 1 (1540–72)
Concelho de Póvoa de Varzim. Póvoa de Varzim (N. Sra da Conceição),
mistos, 1 (1540–1610)
Concelho de Vila do Conde. Azurara (Sta Maria), mistos, 1 (1561–98)
Vila do Conde, baptismos, 1 (1535–95); óbitos, 1 (1595–1637)

Biblioteca Pública Municipal

Manuscripts consulted (with new catalogue numbers):
807. Index dos Livros das Provizoens e Cartas (a Camara do Porto)
(from the reign of D. Afonso V to 1784)
1298. Index dos Documentos transcriptos nos Livros *Rerum Memorabilium*
(existentes no Archivo debaixo da Sta Se Primaz. 1834)

Gabinete de História da Cidade

Acordãos. Livros 1, 2
Pergaminhos. Livros 1–5
Vereações. Livros 4–12

Santa Casa da Misericórdia

Documents consulted (with shelf numbers):
A. Banco 1, no. 1: Liuro dos enfermos q[ue] se hentrão a se curar neste
sp[ri]tal hos qua[e]s se hasentarão ha sy como entrarẽ e se por a sua
cota quando se forẽ e se falecerẽ ho mesmo hoie 7 de Julho de 96
(1596)
C. Banco 1, no. 1: Receitas e Despesas, 1 (1585–6)
D. Banco 5, no. 1: Eleiçõẽs antigas da Meza (1536–a–1646)
D. Banco 5, no. 7: Irmãos da Misericordia (1575)
E. Banco 1, no. 1: Receita e Despesa (1555)

Setúbal

Arquivo Distrital

Núcleo Notarial, Almada, 1: Bernardo Arrelho, 1567–9
Núcleo Paroquial:

Concelho de Alcácer do Sal. Alcácer do Sal (Sta Maria do Castelo), mistos, 1 (1570–96)
Concelho de Grândola. Grândola (N. Sra da Assunção), baptizados, 1 (1573–81)
Concelho de Montijo (antiga Aldeia Galega do Ribatejo), Montijo, mistos, 1 (1568–1610)
Concelho de Setúbal. Setúbal (Sta Maria da Graça), baptizados, 1 (1571–95); casamentos, 1 (1572–1632)
Setúbal (S. Julião), baptizados, 1 (1564–94); casamentos, 1 (1566–1607; includes óbitos, 1568–82, but the foliation before 1580 is very confused)

Museu da Cidade

This houses the Misericórdia archive, which is unfortunately uncatalogued and incomplete for the sixteenth century.
The Arquivo Histórico da Câmara Municipal has no documents prior to 1910, when the town hall was destroyed by a fire.

Spain

Badajoz

Archivo del Ayuntamiento

I could find no documents relevant to slaves in the sixteenth century in this archive.

Archivo de Protocolos

Legajo 1 (1560–2). Escribano: Marcos de Herrera
Legajo 18 (1575). Escribano: Marcos de Herrera
Legajo 32 (1590). Escribano: Marcos de Herrera

United Kingdom

London

British Library, Department of Manuscripts
Additional MSS.:
20:922, Memorias dos successos de Portugal
20:959, Census of Portugal
Harleian MSS. 3822: Cuelbis (called Cuelvis in the catalogue), Diego. 'Thesoro choragraphico de las Espannas' (1599), in 5 parts (nos. A6–A10)
Sloane MSS. 1572: Jornalero del año de 1633 y 34 (Itinerary of a Capuchin friar)

Printed sources

These lists of primary and secondary printed sources do not contain all the works consulted during the course of research but only those mentioned in the notes to the text plus a few others of outstanding interest. I have retained here, as in the notes, the Portuguese spellings of authors and titles as they appeared on the title-pages or jackets of the books consulted, since this is the form in which they appear in most library catalogues in English-speaking countries. In Portuguese libraries the catalogues amend both name and title according to the latest orthographic convention.

Primary sources

Accursius (glossator). *Institutiones cum commentariis Accursii et aliorum.* Paris, 1576.

Institutiones libri IV. glossis Franc. Accursii. Lyon, 1607

Adler, Elkan Nathan (ed.). *Jewish Travellers.* London, 1930

Aegidius Romanus. See Colonna, Egidio

Alberi, Eugenio (ed.). *Relazioni degli ambasciatori veneti al Senato durante il secolo decimosesto.* 15 vols. Florence, 1839–63

Albornoz, Bartolomé de. 'De la esclavitud' (extract from his *Arte de los contratos,* Barcelona, 1573), in *Obras escogidas de filósofos,* ed. Adolfo de Castro. Madrid, 1873 (Biblioteca de Autores Españoles, vol. LXV, pp. 232–3)

Alfonso X of Castile. *General estoria.* Vol. I, ed. A. G. Solalinde. Madrid, 1930

(called Alfonso IX on title-page). *Las siete partidas.* Lyon, 1550

Almada, André Alvares d'. *Tratado Breve dos Rios de Guiné do Cabo-Verde Desde o Rio de Sanagá ate aos Baixos de Sta Anna; de todas as Nações de Negros que ha na dita Costa, e de seus Costumes, Armas, Trajes, Juramentos e Guerras* (1594), ed. Diogo Köpke. Oporto, 1841

Almada, André Álvares de. *Tratado Breve dos Rios de Guiné de Cabo Verde,* ed. António Brásio. Lisbon, 1964

Almeida, Fernando de. *Ad Alexandrū. VI. Pont[ificem]. Max[imum]. Ferd[inandi]: de Almeida electi Eccl[es]ie Septin[ensis]: & Sereniss[imi]: Io[annis]. II. Regis Portugallie Oratio.* Rome, 1493

Alvares, Afonso or Affonso. *Auto de Santa Babora.* Lisbon, 1634

Auto de S. Tiago Apostolo [Lisbon, 1639]; facsimile edn in Carolina Michaëlis de Vasconcellos, *Autos portugueses.* Madrid, 1922

Auto de Sto Antonio. Lisbon, 1642

Auto de Santo António, ed. Almeida Lucas. Lisbon, 1948

'Édition de l'*Auto de Sam Vicente* d'Afonso Alvares', ed. I. S. Revah, *Bulletin d'Histoire du Théâtre Portugais,* II (1951), 213–53

Ancharano (or Ancharanus), Petrus Joannes de. *Super sexto Decretalium Acutissima Commentaria.* Bologna, 1583

Aquinas, Thomas. *Summa Theologiae,* with Eng. trans. by Dominicans from the English-speaking provinces. 60 vols. London, 1963–76

Aristotle. *The Ethics of Aristotle. The Nicomachean Ethics translated*, trans. and ed. J. A. K. Thomson. Harmondsworth, Middx, 1955

Politics, trans. and ed. T. A. Sinclair. Harmondsworth, Middx, 1962

Arraes, Amador. *Diálogos*, selected and ed. Fidelino de Figueiredo. Lisbon, 1944

Artijgos das Sysas. Lisbon, 1542

Augustine. *Concerning the City of God against the Pagans*, ed. David Knowles, trans. Henry Bettenson. Harmondsworth, Middx, 1972

Auto de Dom Fernando, facsimile in Carolina Michaëlis de Vasconcellos, *Autos portugueses*. Madrid, 1922

Auto de Vicente Anes Joeira, ed. Cleonice Berardinelli. Rio de Janeiro, 1963

Azevedo, Pedro A. de (ed.). 'Benzedores e Feiticeiros do tempo del-Rei D. Manuel', *Revista Lusitana*, III (1895), 329–47

(ed.). 'Costumes do tempo d'el-Rei D. Manuel', *Revista Lusitana*, IV (1896), 5–12

(ed.). 'Superstições Portuguesas no Seculo xv (Documentos)', *Revista Lusitana*, IV (1896), 197–215, 315–24

(ed.). 'Superstições Portuguesas no Seculo xvi', *Revista Lusitana*, V (1897/9), 1–21, 198–207, 261–70; VI (1900/1), 211–25

(ed.). 'Os Escravos', *Archivo Historico Portuguez*, I (1903), 289–307

(ed.). 'O Testamento da Excelente Senhora', *Archivo Historico Portuguez*, I (1903), 8–11

(ed.). 'A Marinha Mercante do Norte de Portugal em 1552', *Archivo Historico Portuguez*, II (1904), 241–53

(ed.). 'O Antigo Casamento Português', *Archivo Historico Portuguez*, III (1905), 107–10

(ed.). *Documentos das Chancelarias Reais anteriores a 1531 relativos a Marrocos*. 2 vols. Lisbon, 1915–34

Baião, Antonio (ed.). 'A Inquisição em Portugal e no Brasil. Subsídios para a sua História. A Inquisição no Século xvi', *Archivo Historico Portuguez*, IV (1906), 205–36, 389–424; V (1907), 1–17, 94–102, 192–215, 272–306, 411–25; VI (1908), 42–56, 81–117, 169–85, 463–80; VII (1909), 1–16, 140–60, 227–40, 441–8; VIII (1910), 47–61, 415–40, 470–80; IX (1914), 471–80; X (1916), 474–80

(ed.). *Documentos Ineditos sôbre João de Barros, sôbre o Escritor seu Homónimo Contemporâneo, sôbre a Familia do Historiador e sôbre os Continuadores das suas 'Decadas'*. Coimbra, 1917

(ed.). *Documentos do Corpo Chronologico relativos a Marrocos (1488 a 1514)*. Coimbra, 1925

Baquero Moreno, H. (ed.). 'Alguns Acordos de Extradição entre Portugal e Castela nos Séculos xiii a xv', *Portugaliae Historica*, I (1973), 81–101

Barcelos, Christiano Jose de Senna (ed.). *Subsidios para a Historia de Cabo Verde e Guiné*. 7 vols. Lisbon, 1900–12

Barreiros, Gaspar. *Corographia de algvns lvgares que stam em num caminho, que fez G. Barreiros ó anno de M. D. xxxxvi. começãdo na cidade de Badajoz em Castella, te á de Milam em Italia*. Coimbra, 1561

Barros, João de. *Gramática de Língua Portuguesa. Cartinha, Gramática, Diálogo em Louvor da Nossa Linguagem e Diálogo da Viciosa Vergonha.* Lisbon, 1540; facsimile, ed. Maria Leonor Carvalhão Buescu. Lisbon, 1971
Asia de Joam de Barros, dos fectos que os Portugueses fizeram no descobrimento & conquista dos mares & terras do Oriente. 4 decades. Lisbon, 1552–1615
Bartolus (of Sassoferrato; glossator). *In Institutiones et Authenticas, Commentaria.* Basle, 1562
Basas, Fernando (ed.). 'Un caso de esclavitud en el siglo XVI', *Anuario de Historia Económica y Social,* 1 (Madrid, 1968), 614–18
Basto, Artur de Magalhães (ed.). *Diário da Viagem de Vasco da Gama.* 2 vols. Oporto, 1945
Bayaõ, Jozé Pereira. *Portugal Cuidadoso, e Lastimado com a Vida, e Perda do Senhor Rey Dom Sebastiaõ, O Desejado de Saudosa memoria. Historia chronologica de suas acçoens, e successos desta Monarquia em seu tempo; suas jornadas a Africa, batalha, perda, circunstancias, e consequencias notaveis della.* Lisbon, 1737
Blake, John William (ed.). *Europeans in West Africa (1450–1560).* 2 vols. London, 1942 (Hakluyt Society, 2nd series, vols. LXXXVI, LXXXVII)
Book of the Knowledge of all the Kingdoms, Lands, and Lordships that are in the World, and the Arms and Devices of each Land and Lordship, or of the Kings and Lords who Possess them. Written by a Spanish Franciscan in the Middle of the XIV Century, trans. and ed. Clements Robert Markham. London, 1912 (Hakluyt Society, 2nd series, vol. XXIX)
Botero, Giovanni. *Relationi universali.* 4 parts in 1 vol. Revised edn. Brescia, 1599
Brandão, João. 'Majestade e Grandezas de Lisboa em 1552', ed. Anselmo Braamcamp Freire and J. J. Gomes de Brito, *Archivo Historico Portuguez,* XI (1917), 8–241
Brásio, António (ed.). *Monumenta Missionaria Africana. África Ocidental,* in two series. 1a sér.: vols. I–VI used. Lisbon, 1952–5. 2a sér.; vols. I and II used. Lisbon, 1958–63
Braun Agrippinensis, Georgius. *Civitates orbis terrarum.* 5 vols. in 2, Cologne, 1575–99
Brito, Bernardo Gomes de. *História Trágico-Marítima.* 6 vols. Oporto, 1942–3
Bronseval, Frère Claude de. *Peregrinatio Hispanica (1531–1533). Voyage de Dom Edme de Saulieu, Abbé de Clairvaux, en Espagne et au Portugal,* ed. Dom Maur Cocheril. 2 vols. Paris, 1970
Bullarium patronatus Portugalliae regum in ecclesiis Africae, Asiae atque Oceaniae, bullas, brevia, epistolas, decreta actaque ab Alexandro III ad hoc usque tempus amplectens, ed. Levi Maria Jordão, visconde de Paiva Manso and João A. de Graça Barreto. 3 vols. Lisbon, 1868–79

Cacegas, Luís de. *Historia de S. Domingos, particular do Reino, e Conquistas de Portugal,* ed. and expanded by Luís de Sousa [Manuel de Sousa Coutinho]. *Parte* I, 2nd edn, Lisbon, 1767. *Partes* II, III, 1st edn, Lisbon, 1662, 1678

Ca' da Mosto, Alvise da. *The Voyages of Cadamosto and Other Documents*, trans. and ed. G. R. Crone. London, 1937 (Hakluyt Society, 2nd series, vol. LXXX)

Le navigazioni atlantiche del veneziano Alvise da Mosto, ed. Tullia G. Leporace. Rome, 1966 (Il Nuovo Ramusio, vol. v)

Camões, Luís Vaz de. *Obras Completas*, ed. Hernâni Cidade. 5 vols. Lisbon, 1946–7

Cancioneiro Fernandes Tomás, facsimile edn by the Museu Nacional de Arqueologia e Etnologia. Lisbon, 1971

Carneiro, Pero de Alcáçova. *Relações de Pero de Alcáçova Carneiro, Conde da Idanha do Tempo que êle e seu pai, António Carneiro, serviram de secretários (1515 a 1568)*, ed. Ernesto de Campos de Andrade. Lisbon, 1937

Carvalho, José Branquinho de (ed.). 'Cartas Originais dos Reis (1480–1571)', *Arquivo Coimbrão*, VI (1942), 39–118; VII (1943), 77–128; VIII (1945), 49–133

(ed.). 'Câmara de Coimbra. O Mais Antigo Livro de Vereações – 1491', *Arquivo Coimbrão*, XII (1954), 53–68

(ed.). 'Livro II da Correia', *Arquivo Coimbrão*, XII (1954), 172–240; XIII (1955), 64–125; XIV (1956), 65–128; XV (1957), 134–229; XVI (1958), 230–339

(ed.). 'Tombo Antigo 1532', *Arquivo Coimbrão*, XVIII (1963), 36–83, 192–230

Casas, Bartolomé de las. *Historia de las Indias*, ed. Agustín Millares Carlo, with preface by Lewis Hanke. 3 vols. México, DF, and Buenos Aires, 1951

Chiado, António Ribeiro. *Obras do Poeta Chiado*, ed. Alberto Pimentel. Lisbon, n.d. [1889]

Pratica dOito Figuras, ed. M. de L. Belchior Pontes. Lisbon, 1961

Pratica dos Compadres, ed. Luciana Stegagno Picchio. Lisbon, 1964

Autos de Antônio Ribeiro Chiado. Vol. I: *Auto da Natural Invençam* and *Auto das Regateiras*, ed. Cleonice Berardinelli and R. Menegaz. Rio de Janeiro, 1968

Clenardus, Nicolaus. *Correspondance*, ed. and French trans. A. Roersch. 3 vols. Brussels, 1940

Coelho, Possidónio Mateus Laranjo (ed.). *Documentos Inéditos de Marrocos. Chancelaria de D. João II*. Vol. I. Lisbon, 1943

Collaço, João Maria Tello de Magalhães (ed.). *Cadastro da População do Reino (1527). Actas das Comarcas Damtre Tejo e Odiana e da Beira*. Lisbon, 1929

Collecção Chronologica de varias Leis, Provisões e Regimentos delRei D. Sebastião. Coimbra, 1819

Collecção de Livros Ineditos de Historia Portugueza dos Reinados de D. João I. D. Duarte. D. Affonso V., e D. João II. Academia Real das Sciencias. 5 vols. Lisbon, 1790–1824

Colonna, Egidio. *De Regimine Principum*. Rome, 1556

(called Aegidius Romanus). *De Ecclesiastica Potestate*. Weimar, 1929

Commynes, Philippe de. *Mémoires*, ed. J. L. A. Calmette. 3 vols. Paris, 1924–5

'Compromisso do Hospital das Caldas dado pela Rainha D. Leonor sua Fundadora em 1512', ed. Fernando da Silva Correia, *O Instituto*, LXXX (1930), 107–23, 241–65

Concordia entre estos reynos de Castilla y el de Portugal, acerca de la remission de los delinquentes que de un reyno a otro se acogen: y de los delictos y casos y en la forma que han de ser remitidos al reyno y parte donde los ouiessen cometido. Madrid, 1569

Constituições do Arcebispado de Lixboa. 25 Aug. 1536. N.p., n.d. [Lisbon, 1536]

Constituições do Bispado Deuora. Lisbon, 1534

Constuições do Bispado do Porto: Full title: *Constituições que fez ho Senhor dom Diogo de Sousa b[is]po do Porto. As quaaes forom pobricados no Sinado que çelebrou na dita çidade. a vinte e quatro dagosto de mil e quatroçentos e nouenta e seys annos*. Oporto, 1497

Constituições Extravagantes do Arcebispado de Lixboa. 6 June 1565. Lisbon, 1565

Constituições Extravagantes do Arcebispado de Lisboa. 30 May 1568. Lisbon, 1569

Corpo Diplomatico Portuguez, ed. Luiz Augusto Rebello da Silva, Jose da Silva Mendes Leal and Jayme Constantino de Freitas Moniz. 14 vols. Lisbon, 1862–1910

Correa, Gaspar. *Lendas da India*. Lisbon, 1858–64 (Collecção dos Monumentos Ineditos para a Historia das Conquistas dos Portuguezes em Africa, Asia e America. 1a serie: Historia da Asia, vols. i–iv)

Covarrubias, Sebastián de. *Tesoro de la lengua castellana o española, según la impresión de 1611, con las adiciones de Benito Remigio Noydens publicadas en la de 1674*, ed. Martín de Riquer. Barcelona, 1943

Cruz, António Augusto Ferreira da (ed.). *Forais Manuelinos da Cidade e Têrmo do Pôrto*. Oporto, 1940

(ed.). *Os Mesteres do Pôrto*. Vol. i. Oporto, 1943

Dias, Francisco. *Memórias Quinhentistas dum Procurador del-Rei no Porto*, ed. A. de Magalhães Basto. Oporto, 1936

Documentos do Arquivo Histórico da Câmara Municipal de Lisboa. Livros de Reis. Arquivo Histórico da Câmara Municipal, Lisbon. Lisbon, 1957– (in progress)

Documentos sobre os Portugueses em Moçambique e na África Central, 1497–1840 / Documents on the Portuguese in Mozambique and Central Africa, 1497–1840. National Archives of Rhodesia (and Nyasaland) and Centro de Estudos Históricos Ultramarinos. Vols. i–vii. Lisbon, 1962–71

Donnan, Elizabeth (ed.). *Documents illustrative of the History of the Slave Trade to America*. Vol. i. Washington, DC, 1930

Duarte, King of Portugal. *O Leal Conselheiro o qual fez Dom Eduarte Rey de Portugal e do Algarve e Senhor de Cepta*, ed. Joseph M. Piel. Lisbon, 1942

Ehingen, Jörg von. *The Diary of Jörg von Ehingen*, trans. and ed. M. Letts. London, 1929

Falgairolle, Edmond (ed.). *Le Chevalier de Seure ambassadeur de France en Portugal au XVIe siècle*. Paris, 1896

(ed.). *Jean Nicot, ambassadeur de France en Portugal au XVIe siècle. Sa correspondance diplomatique inédite*. Paris, 1897

Fantoni, Raffael. 'Relatione del Regno di Portigallo fatta da Raffael Fantoni Fiorentino', in Louis Demoulin (ed.), 'Le Portugal, son économie et son trafic d'outre-mer vers 1600, vus par le Florentin Raffael Fantoni', *Bulletin de L'Institut Historique Belge de Rome*, XLIV (1974), 157–73

Faria, Francisco Leite de (ed.). 'Uma Relação de Rui de Pina sobre o Congo escrita em 1492', *Studia*, XIX (1966), 223–303

Faria, Manuel Severim de. 'Dos Remédios para a Falta de Gente' (1655), in António Sérgio (ed.), *Antologia dos Economistas Portugueses (Século XVII)*, pp. 117–63. Lisbon, 1974

Faria y Sousa, Manuel de. *Asia Portuguesa*. 3 vols. Lisbon, 1666–75

Fernandes, Rui. 'Descripção do Terreno em roda da Cidade de Lamego Duas Leguas' (1531–1532), in *Collecção de Livros Ineditos de Historia Portugueza*, vol. V, pp. 546–613. Lisbon, 1824

Fernandes, Valentim. *Description de la côte d'Afrique de Ceuta au Sénégal, par V. Fernandes (1506–1507)*, ed. P. de Cenival and Théodore Monod. Paris, 1938

O Manuscrito 'Valentim Fernandes', ed. A. Baião. Lisbon, 1940

Description de la côte occidentale d'Afrique (Sénégal au Cap de Monte, archipels) par Valentim Fernandes (1506–1510), ed. T. Monod, A. Teixeira da Mota and R. Mauny. Bissau, 1951

Fernandes de Lucena, Vasco. *Ad Innocentium Octauum Pontificem Maximũ de Obedientia Oratio*, trans. and ed. by Francis Millet Rogers as *The Obedience of a King of Portugal*. Minneapolis, Minn., 1958

Forais Manuelinos do Reino de Portugal e do Algarve – Beira, ed. Luiz Fernando de Carvalho Dias. Lisbon, 1961

Forais Manuelinos do Reino de Portugal e do Algarve – Estremadura, ed. Luiz Fernando de Carvalho Dias. Lisbon, 1962

Forais Manuelinos do Reino de Portugal e do Algarve – Trás-os-Montes, ed. Luiz Fernando de Carvalho Dias. Lisbon, 1961

Ford, Jeremiah Denis Matthias (ed.). *Letters of John III., King of Portugal, 1521–1557*. Cambridge, Mass., 1931

and Lucius Gaston Moffatt (eds.). *Letters of the Court of John III, King of Portugal*. Cambridge, Mass., 1933

Fosse, Eustache de la. 'Eustache de la Fosse. Voyage à la côte occidentale d'Afrique, en Portugal et en Espagne (1479–1480)', ed. R. Foulché-Delbosc, *Revue Hispanique*, IV (1897), 174–201

'Fragmentos de Legislaçaõ Portugueza, extrahidos do Livro das Posses da Casa da Supplicaçaõ', in *Collecção de Livros Ineditos de Historia Portugueza*. Vol. III, pp. 543–615. Lisbon, 1793

Franchina, Antonio (ed.). 'Un censimento di schiavi nel 1565', *Archivio Storico Siciliano*, NS, XXXII (1907), 374–420

Freire, Anselmo Braamcamp (ed.). 'Cartas de Quitação delRei D.

Manuel', *Archivo Historico Portuguez*, I (1903), 94–6, 163–8, 200–8, 240–8, 276–88, 328, 356–68, 398–408, 447–8; II (1904), 34–40, 74–80, 158–60, 232–40, 349–60, 421–42; III (1905), 75–80, 155–60, 237–40, 313–20, 385–400, 471–80; IV (1906), 72–80, 237–40, 282–8, 364–8, 439–48, 474–80; V (1907), 73–80, 156–60, 235–40, 321–6, 442–6, 472–80; VI (1908), 76–80, 155–60; VIII (1910/1912), 76–86, 391–414; IX (1914), 433–70; X (1916), 1–16

(ed.). 'Povoação de Entre Douro e Minho no XVI Seculo', *Archivo Historico Portuguez*, III (1905), 241–73

(ed.). 'Povoação de Entre Tejo e Guadiana no XVI Seculo', *Archivo Historico Portuguez*, IV (1906), 93–105, 330–63

(ed.). 'Povoação da Estremadura no XVI Seculo', *Archivo Historico Portuguez*, VI (1908), 241–84

(ed.). 'Povoação de Tras os Montes no XVI Seculo', *Archivo Historico Portuguez*, VII (1909), 241–90

(ed.). 'Os Cadernos dos Assentamentos', *Archivo Historico Portuguez*, VI (1908), 233–40, 443–4; VII (1909), 220–6, 291–2, 376, 478; VIII (1910), 70–5; X (1916), 60–208

(ed.). 'Inventario da Infanta D. Beatriz 1507', *Archivo Historico Portuguez*, IX (1914), 64–110

Fructuoso, Gaspar. *Livro das Saudades da Terra*. Vol. I, ed. Álvaro Rodrigues de Azevedo. Funchal, 1873

As Gavetas da Torre do Tombo. Edition of the Centro de Estudos Históricos Ultramarinos. Lisbon, 1960– (in progress)

Gioffrè, Domenico (ed.). 'Documenti sulle relazioni fra Genova ed il Portogallo dal 1493 al 1539', *Bulletin de l'Institut Historique Belge de Rome*, XXXIII (1961), 179–316

Godinho, Vitorino Magalhães (ed.). *Documentos sobre a Expansão Portuguesa*. 3 vols. Lisbon, 1943–56

Goes, Damianus a. *Aliquot Opuscula (de Rebus Aethiopicis, Lappicis Indicis Lusitenicis & Hispanicis) ab Ipso Autore Recognita*. Louvain, 1544

Goes, Damião de. *Chronica do Felicissimo Rei D. Emanuel*. 4 parts. Lisbon, 1566

Góis, Damião de. *Urbis Olisiponis Descriptio* (1554), trans. Raul Machado as *Lisboa de Quinhentos*. Lisbon, 1937

Opúsculos Históricos, trans. D. de Carvalho. Oporto, 1945

Graças e Indulgencias Concedidas aa confraria de nossa Senhora do Rosayro pelo muy sancto padre Pio quinto Anno de M. D. lxix. E. acrecentadas pelo Papa Gregorio. xiij. Lisbon, 1572

Gromicho, António Bartolomeu (ed.). 'O Testamento de Garcia de Resende', *A Cidade de Évora*, V: 13/14 (1947), 3–23

Gual Camarena, Miguel (ed.). 'Un seguro contra crímenes de esclavos en el siglo xv', *Anuario de Historia del Derecho Español*, XXIII (1953), 247–58

Herculano, Alexandre (trans. and ed.). 'Archeologia Portuguesa: Aspecto de Lisboa ao ajunctar-se e partir a Armada para a Jornada d'Alcacer-Quibir. 1578', in his *Opusculos*, vol. VI, pp. 91–112. Lisbon, 1907 (ed.). 'Archeologia Portuguesa: Viagem a Portugal dos Cavalleiros Tron e Lippomani, 1580', in his *Opusculos*, vol. vi, pp. 113–26. Lisbon, 1907

Hostiensis, Henricus de Bartholomaeis, cardinal. *Summa Aurea super titulis Decretalium*. Lyons, 1588

Index das Notas de Varios Tabelhiães de Lisboa, entre os annos de 1580 a 1747. Vols. i, iii. Lisbon, 1930, 1934

Innocent IV, Pope. *In quinque Libros Decretalium*. Venice, 1578

Iria Júnior, Joaquim Alberto (ed.). 'Novas Cartas Régias Afonsinas acerca dos Descobrimentos e Privilégios do Infante D. Henrique', *Stvdia*, xxv (1968), 51–115

Justinian, *The Institutes of Justinian*, trans. T. C. Sandars. London, 1956

Landi, Giulio. *La descrittione de l'isola de la Madera*, in Latin, with Italian trans. by Alemanio Fini. Piacenza, 1574

Langhans, Franz Paul de Almeida (ed.). *As Corporações dos Ofícios Mecânicos. Subsídios para a sua História*. 2 vols. Lisbon, 1943–6

Leão, Duarte Nunes do. *Repertorio dos Cinquo Livros das Ordenações, com Addições das Lejs Extrauagantes*. Lisbon, 1560

Annotações sobre as Ordenações dos Cinqvo Livros, que pelas Leis Extrauagantes são Reuogadas ou Interpretadas. Lisbon, 1569

(ed.). *Leis Extravagantes Collegidas e Relatadas*, 2nd edn. Lisbon, 1569

Descripção do Reino de Portugal, ed. Gil Nunes do Liam. Lisbon, 1610

Legnano, Joannes de. *De Amicitia*. N.p., 1584

(called here John of Legnano). *Tractatus de Bello, de Represaliis et de Duello*, ed. T. E. Holland. Oxford, 1917

Leys, e Provisões qve ElRey Dom Sebastião Nosso Senhor Fez depois qve Começou a Governar. Lisbon, 1570

'El libro del conocimiento de todos los reinos, tierras y señoríos que son por el mundo, que escribio un franciscano español á mediados del siglo xiv', ed. Marcos Jiménez de la Espada, *Boletín de la Sociedad Geográfica de Madrid* (continued as *Boletín de la Real Sociedad Geográfica*), ii (1877), 7–66, 97–141, 185–210

Lisbon, Arquivo Histórico da Câmara Municipal. See *Documentos do Arquivo Histórico da Câmara Municipal*

O Livro de Recebimentos de 1470 da Chancelaria da Câmara, ed. Damião Peres. Lisbon, 1974

Livro do Lançamento e Serviço que a Cidade de Lisboa fez a El Rei Nosso Senhor no ano de 1565. Edition of the Arquivo Histórico da Câmara Municipal. 4 vols. Lisbon, 1947–8

Livro dos Regimētos dos Officiaes Mecanicos da Mui Nobre e Sēpre Leal Cidade de Lixboa (1572), ed. Vergilio Correia. Coimbra, 1926

'Livro Vermelho do Senhor Rey D. Affonso V', in *Collecção de Livros Ineditos de Historia Portugueza*, vol. iii, pp. 387–541. Lisbon, 1793

Lobo, Francisco Rodrigues. *Corte na Aldeia e Noites de Inverno (1619)*, ed. A. Lopes Vieira. 3rd edn. Lisbon, 1972

Lopes, Henrique (called here Anrrique Lopez). *Cena Policiana*, in António Prestes et al., *Primeira Parte dos Avtos e Comedias Portvgvesas*, ff. 41v–48. N.p. [?Lisbon], 1587

Lopez, Duarte and Filippo Pigafetta. *Relação do Reino de Congo e das Terras Circunvizinhas*. Port. trans. by Rosa Capeans. Lisbon, 1951

Loureiro, José Pinto (ed.). 'Arquivo Municipal – Livro I da Correa', *Arquivo Coimbrão*, II (1930/1), 127–78; III (1936/7), 49–128; IV (1938/9), 115–84; V (1940), 49–157

Luz, Francisco Mendes da (ed.). 'Relação das Rendas da Coroa de Portugal feita em 1593 por Francisco Carneiro, Provedor de Ementas da Casa dos Contos', *Boletim da Biblioteca da Universidade de Coimbra*, XIX (1950), 45–108

Madahil, António Gomes da Rocha (ed.). 'Para a História da Inquisição no Século XVI', *Arquivo do Distrito de Aveiro*, X (1944), 81–91

Madurell Marimón, José María (ed.). 'Los seguros de vida de esclavos en Barcelona (1453–1523). Documentos para su estudio', *Anuario de Historia del Derecho Español*, XXV (1955), 123–88

Marques, João Martins da Silva (ed.). *Descobrimentos Portugueses*. Vol. I, *Suplemento* to vol. I, and vol. III. Lisbon, 1944–71

Mercado, Tomás de. *Summa de tratos y contratos*. Seville, 1587

Molina, Luis de. *De Justitia et Iure*. Tome I. Cologne–Mainz, 1613

Monumenta Henricina. Comissão Executiva das Comemorações do V. Centenário da Morte do Infante D. Henrique. 14 vols. Coimbra, 1960–73

Moraes, Pedro Jozé Suppico de. *Collecçaõ Politica de Apothegmas, ou ditos agudos, e sentenciosos*. 2 parts. Coimbra, 1761

Mota, Avelino Teixeira da (ed.). 'A Viagem do Navio *Santiago* à Serra Leoa e Rio de S. Domingos em 1526 (Livro de Armação)', *Boletim Cultural da Guiné Portuguesa*, XXIV: 95 (1969), 529–79

Münster, Sebastian. *La Cosmographie universelle*. Basle, 1552

Münzer, Hieronymus (here called Jeronymo Monetario). 'Carta do Dr. Jeronymo Monetario a D. João II, 1493', in *Archivo dos Açores*, I (1878/80), 444–7

'Itinerarium Hispanicum Hieronymi Monetarii 1494–1495', ed. Ludwig Pfandl, *Revue Hispanique*, XLVIII (1920), 1–179

Oliveira, Christovão Rodrigues de. *Sumário em que brevemente se contém Algumas Coisas (assim Ecclesiásticas como Seculares) que há na Cidade de Lisboa (c. 1554–5)*, ed. A. Vieira da Silva. Lisbon, 1938 [1939 on cover]

Oliveira, Eduardo Freire d' (ed.). *Elementos para a Historia do Municipio de Lisboa*. 17 vols. Lisbon, 1882–1911. Index separately published by Arquivo Histórico da Câmara Municipal, Lisbon, as *Indice dos Elementos para a História do Município de Lisboa*. 2 vols. Lisbon, 1942–3

Oliveira, Fernão de. *A Arte da Guerra no Mar (1555)*, ed. Quirino da Fonseca. Lisbon, 1937

Oliveira, Nicolao d'. *Livro das Grandezas de Lisboa* (1620). Lisbon, 1804

Ordenaçoens do Senhor Rey D. Affonso V. 5 vols. Coimbra, 1792

Ordenaçoens do Senhor Rey D. Manuel. 3 vols. Coimbra, 1797

Ordenações Manuelinas. 1st edn. Lisbon, 1514. 2nd edn. Évora and Lisbon, 1521. 4th edn. Lisbon, 1565

Pacheco, Diogo. 'Dieghi Pacecchi Jur. Consult. In prestanda Obedientia pro Emanuele Lusitanorum Rege Invictiss. Leoni X. Pont. Opt. Max. dicta Oratio.', in G. Roscoe, *Vita e pontificato di Leone X*, with notes and documents added by L. Bossi, vol. VI, pp. 184–96. Milan, 1816

Obedientia Potentissimi Emanuelis Lusitaniae Regis [et]c & per clarissimum Iuriscōsultum Dieghum Pacettum Oratorem ad Iulium II Ponti[ficem] Max[imum] Anno D[omi]ni MDV Pridie No[nis] Iunii. Facsimile edn by Eugénio do Canto. Lisbon, 1906

Pais, Álvaro (here called Alvarus Pelagius). *De Planctu Ecclesie.* Venice, 1560

Espelho dos Reis, being the *Speculum Regum,* trans. Miguel Pinto de Meneses. 2 vols. Lisbon, 1955–63

Paiva Manso, Levy Maria Jordão, visconde de (ed.). *Historia do Congo (Documentos).* Lisbon, 1877

Pelagius, Alvarus. See Pais, Álvaro

Peragallo, Prospero (ed.). *Carta de el-Rei D. Manuel ao Rei Catholico Narrando-lhe as Viagens Portuguezas á India desde 1500 ate 1505. . . . seguem em Appendice a Relação analoga de Lunardo Cha Masser e dois Documentos de Cantino e Pasqualigo.* Lisbon, 1892

Pereira, Duarte Pacheco. *Esmeraldo de Situ Orbis,* ed. Augusto Epiphanio da Silva Dias. Lisbon, 1905; facsimile edn, 1975

Esmeraldo de Situ Orbis, trans. and ed. G. H. T. Kimble. London, 1937 (Hakluyt Society, 2nd series, vol. LXXIX)

Pereira, F. M. Esteves (ed.). 'Visão de Tundalo', *Revista Lusitana,* III (1895), 97–120

Pereira, Gabriel Victor do Monte (ed.). *Documentos Historicos da Cidade de Evora.* 3 parts. Évora, 1887–91

Pereira, Isaías da Rosa (ed.). 'Dois Compromissos de Irmandades de Homens Pretos', *Arqueologia e História,* IV (1972), 9–47

Pérez de Guzmán, Fernando. *Cronica del serenissimo rey don Juan el segundo deste nõbre,* ed. Lorenzo Galíndez de Carvajal. Logroño, 1517

Piloto Anónimo. 'Nauigatione da Lisbona all'isola di san Thomè, posta sotto la linea dell'equinottiale', in Giovanni Baptista Ramusio (ed.), *Delle navigationi et viaggi,* vol. I, ff. 124–9. Venice, 1554

Viagem de Lisboa à Ilha de S. Tomé escrita por um Pilôto Português (Século XVI), trans. Sebastião Francisco de Mendo Trigoso, ed. Augusto Reis Machado. Lisbon, n.d.

Pina, Rui de. *Crónica de el-Rei D. João II,* ed. Alberto Martins de Carvalho. Coimbra, 1950

Crónica do Rei D. Duarte, ed. António Borges Coelho. Lisbon, 1966

Pina, Ruy de. *Chronica d'El-Rei D. Affonso V*, ed. Mello d'Azevedo. 3 vols. Lisbon, 1901–2

Pires, Antonio Thomaz (ed.). *Materiaes para a Historia da Vida Urbana Portugueza. A Mobilia, o Vestuario e a Sumptuosidade nos Seculos XVI a XVIII. Ineditos.* Lisbon, 1899

Pires, Sebastião. *Auto da Bella Menina*, facsimile edn in Carolina Michaëlis de Vasconcellos, *Autos portugueses*. Madrid, 1922

Popplau, Nicolaus von. 'Viaje de Nicolas de Popielovo por España y Portugal', in Javier Liske (ed.), *Viajes de extranjeros por España y Portugal en los siglos XV, XVI y XVII*, trans. 'F. R.', pp. 9–65. Madrid, 1878

Portugaliae Monumenta Historica a Saeculo Octavo post Christum usque ad Quintumdecimum iussu Academiae Scientiarum Olisiponensis edita. Leges et Consuetudines. 2 fascicles. Lisbon, 1856

Prestage, Edgar and Pedro d'Azevedo (eds.). *Registos Parochiaes de Lisboa. Registo da Freguesia de Santa Cruz do Castello desde 1536 até 1628.* Coimbra, 1913

(eds.). *Registos Parochiaes de Lisboa. Registo da Freguesia da Sé desde 1563 até 1610.* 2 vols. Coimbra, 1924–7

Prestes, António, et al. *Primeira Parte dos Avtos e Comedias Portvgvesas*, compiled by Afonso Lopes. N.p. [?Lisbon], 1587

Ramón de Penyafort (Raimundus de Peniafort on title-page), *Summa de Poenitentia et Matrimonio*, glossed by Ioannes de Friburgo. Rome, 1603

Ramos-Coelho, José (ed.). *Alguns Documentos do Archivo Nacional da Torre do Tombo acerca das Conquistas e Navegações Portuguezas.* Lisbon, 1892

Rebelo, Diogo Lopes. *Do Governo da República pelo Rei*, being a fascimile of his *De Republica Gubernanda per Regem*, Paris, 1496, with trans. by M. Pinto de Meneses and notes by A. Moreira de Sá. Lisbon, 1951

Regimento das Cazas das Indias e Mina (1509), ed. Damião Peres. Coimbra, 1947

O Regimento do Hospital de Todos-os-Santos (19 Jan. 1504), ed. Fernando da Silva Correia. Lisbon, 1946

Regiméto dos Ofiçiaaes das Çidades Villas e Lugares destes Regnos. Lisbon, 1504; facsimile edn by Marcelo Caetano, 1955

Regimentos e Ordenações da Fazenda de el Rey nosso Senhor. Lisbon, 1516

Relaçam em que se trata, e faz hũa breue descriçao dos arredores mais chegados à Cidade de Lisboa, & seus arrebaldes, das partes notaueis, Igrejas, Hermidas, & Conuentos que tem, começando logo da barra, vindo corredo por toda a praya atè Enxobregas, & dahi pella parte de cima atè Saõ Bento o nouo. Lisbon, 1625; facsimile edn, 1934

Resende, Garcia de (ed.). *Cancioneiro Geral* (1516), ed. A. J. Gonçalves Guimarãis. 5 vols. Coimbra, 1910–17

Miscellanea (1554), ed. Mendes dos Remedios. Coimbra, 1917

Chronica de el-Rei D. João II. 3 vols. Coimbra, 1798

Reubeni, David. 'Diary', in Elkan Nathan Adler (ed.), *Jewish Travellers*, pp. 251–328. London, 1930

Ribeiro Chiado, António. See Chiado, António Ribeiro.

Rožmitalu a Blatne a na Přimdě, Baron Lev. 'Des böhmischen Herrn Leo's von Rožmital Ritter-, Hof- und Pilger-Reise durch die Abendlande 1465–1467', ed. J. A. Schmeller, in *Bibliothek des literarischen Vereins*, vol. vii. Stuttgart, 1844 (called here Leo of Rožmital). *The Travels of Leo of Rožmital through Germany, Flanders, England, France, Spain, Portugal and Italy, 1465–1467*, trans. and ed. Malcolm Letts. Cambridge, 1957 (Hakluyt Society, 2nd series, vol. cviii)
See also Šašek, Vaclav

Ryder, Alan Frederick C. (ed.). 'An Early Portuguese Trading Voyage to the Forcados River', *Journal of the Historical Society of Nigeria*, i (1959), 294–321

Sá de Miranda, Francisco de. *Obras Completas*, ed. M. Rodrigues Lapa. 2 vols. Lisbon, 1937

Santarém, Manuel Francisco de Barros e Sousa de Mesquita de Macedo Leitão e Carvalhosa, visconde de. *Memorias para a Historia, e Theoria das Cortes Geraes, que em Portugal se celebrárão pelos Tres Estados do Reino*. 2 parts. Lisbon, 1827–8; with *Alguns Documentos para servirem de Provas à parte 1a* (and *2a*). Lisbon, 1828; bound together with an introduction by António Sardinha. Lisbon, 1924

Šašek, Vaclav. *Commentarius Brevis, et iucundus itineris atquè peregrinationis, pietatis & religionis causa susceptae, ab illustri & Magnifico Domino, Domino Leone libero Barone de Rosmital et Blatna, Iohanne Regine Bohemie fratre germano, Proauo Illustris ac Magnifici Domini, Domini Zdenco Leonis liberi Baronis de Rosmital & Blatna, nunc supremi Marchionatus Morauiae Capitanei: Ante centũ annos Bohemicè cõscriptus, & nunc primùm in latinã linguam translatus & editus*. Olomouc, 1577; facsimile edn by Karolus Hrdina. Prague, 1951

Sassetti, Filippo. *Lettere edite e inedite*, ed. Ettore Marcucci. Florence, 1855

Sérgio, António (ed.). *Antologia dos Economistas Portugueses (Século XVII)*. Lisbon, 1974

Serra Ràfols, Elías and Alejandro Cioranescu (eds.). *Le Canarien. Crónicas francesas de la conquista de Canarias*. 3 vols. La Laguna and Las Palmas, 1959, 1960, 1965 (Fontes Rerum Canariarum, vols. viii, ix, xi)

Sintra, Pedro de. 'La navigazione del portoghese Pedro de Cintra (1462) scritta da Alvise da Mosto', ed. Tullia G. Leporace. Rome, 1966 (Il Nuovo Ramusio, vol. v)

Soto, Domingo de (Dominicus de Soto on title-page). *De Iustitia et Iure*. Antwerp, 1568

Sousa, Antonio Caetano de (ed.). *Provas de Historia Genealogica da Casa Real Portugueza*. 6 vols. Lisbon, 1739–48

Sousa, J. M. Cordeiro de (ed.). *Registo da Freguesia de Nossa Senhora da Encarnação do Lugar da Ameixoeira desde 1540 a 1604*. Lisbon, 1930 (1931 on cover)

(ed.). *Registos Paroquiais Quinhentistas de Lisboa. Santa Justa*. Lisbon, 1949

Sousa, Frei Luis de. *Anais da Vida, Reinado e Governo do Prudentíssimo Rei D. João III*, ed. M. Rodrigues Lapa. 2 vols. Lisbon, 1951

Sprenger, Balthasar. See Vespuccius, Albericus

Suárez Fernández, Luis (ed.). *Relaciones entre Portugal y Castilla en la época del Infante D. Enrique, 1393–1460*. Madrid, 1960

Theal, George McCall (ed.). *Records of South-eastern Africa. Collected in Various Libraries and Archive Departments in Europe*. 9 vols. London, 1898–1903

Thevet, André. *La Cosmographie universelle*. 2 vols. Paris, 1575
Les Singularitez de la France Antarctique (1558), ed. Paul Gaffarel. Paris, 1878

Torre y del Cerro, Antonio de la, and Luis Suárez Fernández (eds.). *Documentos referentes a las relaciones con Portugal durante el reinado de los Reyes Católicos*. 3 vols. Valladolid, 1958–63

Tron and Lippomani. See Herculano, Alexandre.

Usodimare, Antoniotto. 'Itinerarium Antonii Ususmaris Civis Januensis', in Youssouf Kamal (ed.), *Monumenta Cartographica Africae et Aegypti*, vol. IV, fascicle I, f. 1102. N.p., 1936

Valckenstein, Nicolaus Lanckmann von. 'Historia Desponsationis Frederici III. cum Eleonora Lusitanica', in Antonio Caetano de Sousa (ed.), *Provas da Historia Genealogica da Casa Real Portugueza*, vol. I, pp. 601–33. Lisbon, 1739

Vasconcellos, Carolina Michaëlis de (ed.). *Autos portugueses de Gil Vicente y de la escuela vicentina*. Madrid, 1922

Vasconcellos, Jorge Ferreira de. *Comedia Eufrosina* (1555), ed. Aubrey F. G. Bell. Lisbon, 1918 (1919 on cover)
Comedia Vlysippo (pre 1561), ed. B. J. de Sousa Farinha. Lisbon, 1787
Comedia Aulegrafia (1619), ed. António A. Machado de Vilhena. Oporto, n.d. [*c*. 1969]

Vasconcelos, Luiz Mendes de. *Do Sitio de Lisboa. Dialogo*. Lisbon, 1608

Venturino, Giambattista. 'Archeologia Portuguesa: Viagem do Cardeal Alexandrino', trans. and ed. Alexandre Herculano, in *Opusculos*, vol. VI, pp. 43–90. Lisbon, 1907

Vespucci, Alberico. *Paesi Nouamente retrouati. Et Nouo Mondo*. Vicenza, 1507

Vespuccius, Albericus (actually written by Balthasar Sprenger). *The Voyage from Lisbon to India 1505–6*, trans. and ed. C. H. Coote. London, 1894

Viana, Abel (ed.). 'Livro das Vereações da Câmara de Beja – 1542', *Arquivo de Beja*, I (1944), 85–96, 188–98, 269–79, 380–91

Vicente, Gil. *Obras Completas*, ed. Marques Braga. 6 vols. Lisbon, 1942–4

Viterbo, Francisco Marques de Sousa (ed.). 'Notícia sobre alguns Médicos Portuguezes ou que exerceram a Clinica em Portugal. 3a sér.', *Jornal da Sociedade das Ciências Médicas*, LIX (1895), 107–25, 163–91, 215–41 (ed.). 'O Fabrico da Polvora em Portugal – Notas e Documentos para a sua Historia', *Revista Militar*, XLVIII (1896), 12–20, 46–54, 77–84, 118–26, 151–6, 213–53, 283–8, 306–12, 346–51

(ed.). *Os Portugueses e o Gentio*. Coimbra, 1896

(ed.). *Trabalhos Nauticos dos Portuguezes nos Seculos XVI e XVII*. 2 parts. Lisbon, 1898–1900

(ed.). 'Artes Industriaes e Industrias Portuguezas. A Tapeçaria', *O Instituto*, XLIX (1902), 361–7, 418–24, 485–7, 557–60, 619–25, 674–7

(ed.). 'Artes Industriaes e Industrias Portuguezas. O Vidro e o Papel', *O Instituto*, XLIX (1902), 747–53; L (1903), 38–43, 104–8, 236–41, 294–9, 360–3, 415–19, 487–94, 555–63, 631–3

(ed.). 'Artes e Industrias Metallicas em Portugal. Minas e Mineiros', *O Instituto*, L (1903), 696–702, 756–65; LI (1904), 33–40, 107–13, 179–86, 236–9

(ed.). 'Artes Industriaes e Industrias Portuguezas. Industrias Textis e Congeneres', *O Instituto*, LI (1904), 283–9, 375–82, 442–8, 504–10, 568–74, 637–40, 686–91

(ed.). 'Relações de Portugal com alguns Potentados Africanos e Asiaticos', *Archivo Historico Portuguez*, II (1904), 441–62

(ed.). 'Noticia de alguns Arabistas e Interpretes de Linguas Africanas e Orientaes', *O Instituto*, LII (1905), 367–74, 417–25, 491–8, 547–50, 683–93, 749–56; LIII (1906), 48–53, 107–14, 237–41, 315–20

(ed.). 'Artes e Industrias Metallicas em Portugal. Serralheiros e Ferreiros', *O Instituto*, LV (1908), 38–59, 126–41, 191–5

(ed.). 'Artes Industriaes e Industrias Portuguesas. A Industria Sacharina', *O Instituto*, LV (1908), 248–55, 298–308, 348–57, 403–16, 432–45, 475–84, 538–49; (2a sér.), LVI (1909), 650–6, 726–37

(ed.). 'Artes e Industrias Metálicas em Portugal. Moedeiros', *O Archeologo Português*, XVI (1911), 29–47; XVII (1912), 1–22; XVIII (1913), 82–93, 191–201; XIX (1914), 4–12

(ed.). 'Notícia sobre alguns Médicos Portuguêses ou que exerceram a sua Profissão em Portugal. Quinta Série', *Archivos de Historia da Medicina Portugueza*, III (1912), 33–9, 65–74, 107–14, 140–8, 170–7; IV (1913), 17–24, 49–56, 82–9, 111–18, 129–36, 161–76; V (1914), 22–32, 65–80, 129–36, 143–52, 196; VI (1915), 13–22, 44–55, 65–78

(ed.). 'Artes e Indústrias Portuguesas – Ourivesaria, Quinquilharia e Bijuteria', *O Instituto*, LXI (1914), 20–5, 76–80, 138–44

(ed.). 'Subsídios para a História da Música em Portugal', *O Instituto*, LXXII (1925), 292–306, 466–80; LXXIII (1926), 91–111, 262–70, 381–98, 494–510, 715–34; LXXIV (1927), 106–17, 632–9; LXXV (1928), 178–89, 510–21; LXXVI (1928), 217–36, 580–97; LXXVII (1929), 248–55, 367–76, 495–502, 603–18; LXXVIII (1929), 115–22, 373–90, 573–90; LXXIX (1930), 400–18, 511–28, 645–55; LXXX (1930), 141–52, 223–40, 370–85, 498–512, 655–70; LXXXI (1931), 147–63, 288–96, 366–80, 516–27; 641–57; LXXXII (1931), 236–52, 385–404,

517-32, 649-64; LXXXIII (1932), 70-86, 232-47, 393-402, 528-38; LXXXIV (1932), 103-17, 246-50, 351-7

Vitoria, Francisco de. 'De los indios', being 'De Indis recenter Inventis', trans. and ed. T. Urdanoz, in *Obras*. Madrid, 1960

Wightman, George B. H., and Abdullah Y. al-Udhari (trans. and eds.). *Birds through a Ceiling of Alabaster. Three Abbasid Poets*. Harmondsworth, Middx, 1975

Zurara, Gomes Eanes de. *Vida e Obras de Gomes Eanes de Zurara*, ed. A. J. Dias Dinis. Vol. I: *Introdução à Crónica dos Feitos de Guiné*. Vol. II: *Crónica dos Feitos de Guiné*. Lisbon, 1949
Chronique de Guinée, ed. Léon Bourdon and Robert Ricard. Dakar, 1960
Crónica de Guiné, ed. J. de Bragança. 2nd edn. Barcelos, 1973

Secondary sources

Actas. Congresso Internacional de História dos Descobrimentos. 6 vols. Lisbon, 1961
Alcoforado, M. da Maia. 'A Indústria do Sal', *Museu Technologico*, I (1877), 29-124
Almeida, Fortunato de. *Historia de Portugal*. 6 vols. Coimbra, 1922-9
História da Igreja em Portugal, ed. Damião Peres. 4 vols. Oporto, 1967-71
Aragão, Augusto Carlos Teixeira de. *Descripção Geral e Historica das Moedas cunhadas em nome dos Reis, Regentes e Governadores de Portugal*. 3 vols. Lisbon, 1874-80
Attwater, Donald. *The Penguin Dictionary of Saints*. Harmondsworth, Middx, 1965
Azevedo, João Lúcio de. *A Evolução do Sebastianismo*. 2nd edn. Lisbon, 1947
Épocas de Portugal Económico. Esboços de História, 3rd edn. Lisbon, 1973
Azevedo, Pedro A. de (ed.). 'Catálogo dos Manuscritos do Museo Etnológico', *O Archeologo Português*, XVII (1912), 196-204, 299-303; XVIII (1913), 108-29; XIX (1914), 46-83

Baião, António. 'A Villa e Concelho de Ferreira do Zezere. VI. O Morgado e a Villa de Aguas Bellas até fins do Seculo XVII', *O Archeologo Português*, XVI (1911), 60-84
Episodios Dramaticos da Inquisição Portuguesa. 3 vols. Lisbon, 1936-8
Hernani Cidade and Manuel Múrias (eds.). *História da Expansão Portuguesa no Mundo*, 3 vols. Lisbon, 1937-42
Barcia, J. A. 'Lisboa Antiga'. *Indice Alfabético e Remissivo dos Oito Volumes desta Obra*. Lisbon, 1915; and see Castilho, Júlio
Barros, Henrique da Gama. *Historia da Administração Publica em Portugal nos Seculos XII a XV*. 4 vols. Lisbon, 1885-1922; for index, see Machado, Augusto Reis (edn used, unless otherwise indicated)
História da Administração Pública em Portugal. Revised edn. 11 vols. Lisbon, 1945-54

Baxter, Paul, and Basil Sansom (eds.). *Race and Social Difference*. Harmondsworth, Middx, 1972

Bennassar, Bartolomé. *Valladolid au Siècle d'Or. Une ville de Castille et sa campagne au XVIe siècle*. Paris and the Hague, 1967

Birmingham, David B. *Trade and Conflict in Angola. The Mbundu and their Neighbours under the Influence of the Portuguese, 1483–1790*. Oxford, 1966

Blake, John William. 'The Organisation of Portuguese Trade with West Africa during the Sixteenth Century', in *Congresso do Mundo Português*, vol. v, pp. 31–53. Lisbon, 1940

West Africa. Quest for God and Gold, 1454–1578 (being the 2nd, revised and expanded edn of *European Beginnings in West Africa, 1454–1578*, London, 1937). London and Totowa, NJ, 1977

Blassingame, John W. *The Slave Community. Plantation Life in the Antebellum South*. New York, 1972

Bluteau, Rafael. *Supplemento ao Vocabulario Portuguez, e Latino*. 2 vols. Lisbon, 1727–8

Raphael. *Vocabulario Portuguez e Latino*. 8 vols. Coimbra and Lisbon, 1712–21

Bourdon, Léon. *Episodes inconnus de la vie de Fernando Oliveira*. Coimbra, 1955. Offprint from *Revista Portuguesa de História*, v (1955)

Bowser, Frederick P. *The African Slave in Colonial Peru, 1524–1650*. Stanford, Calif., 1974

Boxer, Charles Ralph. *The Golden Age of Brazil, 1695–1750: Growing Pains of a Colonial Society*. Berkeley, Calif., 1962

Race Relations in the Portuguese Colonial Empire, 1415–1825. Oxford, 1963

The Portuguese Seaborne Empire, 1415–1825. London, 1969

Brásio, António. *Os Pretos em Portugal*. Lisbon, 1944

'A Iconografia do Negro na Arte Portuguesa', *Portugal em África*, 2a sér., IV: 21 (1947), 152–4

Braudel, Fernand. *The Mediterranean and the Mediterranean World in the Age of Philip II*, trans. Siân Reynolds. 2 vols. London, 1972–3

Brito, J. J. Gomes de. *Ruas de Lisboa*. Vols. I, II. Lisbon, 1935

Brito, Manoel J. da Cunha. 'Os Pergaminhos da Câmara de Ponte de Lima', *O Archeologo Português*, XIV (1909), 60–73; XV (1910), 5–25

Brochado, Costa. 'A Espiritualidade dos Descobrimentos e Conquistas dos Portugueses', *Portugal em África*, 2a sér., III (1946), 232–40

'O Problema da Guerra Justa em Portugal', *Rumo*, I (1946), 41–59

Brooks, John. 'Slavery and the Slave Trade in the Works of Lope de Vega', *Romanic Review*, XIX (1928), 232–42

Brunschvig, R. ''Abd', in *The Encyclopaedia of Islam*, vol. I, pp. 24–40. Leiden, 1954

Buckland, William Warwick. *The Roman Law of Slavery: The Condition of the Slave in Private Law from Augustus to Justinian*. Cambridge, 1908, reprinted 1970

Capela, José. *Escravatura. A Empresa de Saque. O Abolicionismo (1810–1875)*. Oporto, 1974

Carlyle, R. W. and A. J. *A History of Mediaeval Political Theory in the West.* 6 vols. Edinburgh, 1903–36

Carneiro, Edison. *Ladinos e Crioulos (Estudos sôbre o Negro no Brasil).* Rio de Janeiro, 1964

Carreira, Antonio. *Notas sobre o Tráfico Português de Escravos.* Lisbon, 1978

Carvalho, António Pedro de. *Das Origens da Escravidão Moderna em Portugal.* Lisbon, 1877

Carvalho, Augusto da Silva [de]. *Crónica do Hospital de Todos-os-Santos.* Lisbon, 1949

Carvalho, Joaquim de. *Estudos sobre a Cultura Portuguesa do Século XV.* Coimbra, 1949

Carvalho, Margarida Barradas de. 'L'Idéologie religieuse dans la "Crónica dos Feitos de Guiné" de Gomes Eanes de Zurara', *Bulletin des Études Portugaises et de l'Institut Français au Portugal,* XIX (1955/6), 34–63

Castellano, Juan R. 'El negro esclavo en el entremés del Siglo de Oro', *Hispania,* XLIV (1961), 55–65

Castelo-Branco, Fernando. 'Escravatura e o Pretenso Racismo dos Portugueses', in *Anais,* Academia Portuguesa da História, 2a sér., XIX (1970), 241–52
  'A Navegação da Metrópole para S. Tomé nos meados do Século XVI', *Stvdia,* XXX/XXXI (1970), 71–80

Castilho, Júlio de. *Lisboa Antiga.* Parte I: *O Bairro Alto.* Parte II: *Bairros Orientaes.* Lisbon, 1879–90; for index, see Barcia, J. A.
  A Ribeira de Lisboa. Descrição Historica da Margem do Tejo desde a Madre-de-Deus até Santos-o-Velho. 2nd edn annotated by L. Pastor de Macedo. 5 vols. Lisbon, 1941–68

Castro, Adolfo de. 'La esclavitud en España', *La España Moderna,* IV: 38 (Feb. 1892), 128–49

Cerejeira, M. Gonçalves. *O Renascimento em Portugal.* Vol. I: *Clenardo e a Sociedade Portuguesa do seu Tempo.* 4th edn. Coimbra, 1974

Chasca, Edmund Villela de. 'The Phonology of the Speech of the Negroes in the Early Spanish Drama', *Hispanic Review,* XIV (1946), 322–39

Chaunu, Pierre. *L'Expansion européenne du XIIIe au XVe siècle.* Paris, 1969
  and Huguette. *Séville et l'Atlantique, 1504–1650.* 8 vols. Paris, 1955–6 (Part VI of the series Ports. Routes. Trafics)

Chaves, Luiz. 'O Preto da Guiné no nosso Folclore', in *Congresso Comemorativo do Quinto Centenário do Descobrimento da Guiné,* vol. II, pp. 557–71. Lisbon, 1946

Cirac Estopañán, Sebastián. *Aportación a la historia de la Inquisición española. Los procesos de hechicería en la Inquisición de Castilla la Nueva (Tribunales de Toledo y Cuenca).* Madrid, 1942

Cohen, David W., and Jack P. Greene (eds.). *Neither Slave nor Free. The Freedmen of African Descent in the Slave Societies of the New World.* Baltimore and London, 1972

Collantes de Terán Sánchez, Antonio. 'Contribución al estudio de los esclavos en la Sevilla medieval', in *Homenaje al profesor Carriazo*, vol. II, pp. 109–21. Seville, 1972

Congresso Comemorativo do Quinto Centenário do Descobrimento da Guiné. 2 vols. Lisbon, 1946

Congresso do Mundo Português. 19 vols. Lisbon, 1940

Corrêa, Antonio Augusto Esteves Mendes. 'A Propôsito do "Homo Taganus". Africanos em Portugal', *Boletim da Junta Geral do Distrito de Santarém*, VI: 43 (1936), 37–55

(spelt Correia). 'Escravos Africanos em Portugal e no Brasil – Conferência', *Anais*, Faculdade das Ciências, Universidade do Porto, XXIII (1938), 185–91, and *Boletim Geral das Colónias*, CLVII (1938), 3–30

Correia, Fernando da Silva. *Estudos sobre a Historia da Assistência. Origens e Formação das Misericórdias Portuguesas.* Lisbon, 1944

Cortés Alonso, Vicenta. 'La trata de esclavos durante los primeros descubrimientos (1489–1516)', *Anuario de Estudios Atlánticos*, IX (1963), 23–46

La esclavitud en Valencia durante el reinado de los Reyes Católicos (1479–1516). Valencia, 1964

'La liberación del esclavo', *Anuario de Estudios Americanos*, XXII (1965), 533–68

'La población negra de Palos de la Frontera, 1568–1579', *Actas*, XXXVI Congreso Internacional de Americanistas, vol. III, pp. 609–18. Seville, 1966

'Los esclavos domésticos en América', *Anuario de Estudios Americanos*, XXIV (1967), 955–83

'Algunas ideas sobre la esclavitud y su investigación', *Bulletin de l'Institut Historique Belge de Rome*, XLIV (1974), 127–44

Costa, Américo. *Diccionario Chorographico de Portugal Continental e Insular.* 12 vols. Oporto, 1929–49

Costa, António Domingues de Sousa. 'O Factor Religioso, Razão Jurídica dos Descobrimentos Portugueses', in *Actas*, Congresso Internacional de História dos Descobrimentos, vol. IV, pp. 99–139. Lisbon, 1961

'A Expansão Portuguesa a Luz do Direito', *Revista da Universidade de Coimbra*, XX (1962), 1–243

Couto, Gustavo. *História da antiga Casa da Índia em Lisboa.* Lisbon, 1932

Cruz, António Augusto Ferreira da. 'A Antiga Organização dos Mesteres no Pôrto', *Congresso do Mundo Português*, vol. XVIII, pp. 835–48. Lisbon, 1940

Os Mesteres do Pôrto no Século XV. Aspectos da sua Actividade e Taxas de Ofícios Mecânicos. Offprint from *Boletim Cultural da Câmara Municipal do Pôrto*, III (1940)

Curtin, Philip D. *The Atlantic Slave Trade, a Census.* Madison, Wis., 1969

David, Paul A. et al. *Reckoning with Slavery. A Critical Study in the Quantitative History of American Negro Slavery.* New York, 1976

Davidson, Basil. *Black Mother. Africa: The Years of Trial.* London, 1970

Davis, David Brion. *The Problem of Slavery in Western Culture*. Harmondsworth, Middx, 1970

Deerr, Noël. *The History of Sugar*. 2 vols. London, 1949–50

Degler, Carl N. *Neither Black nor White. Slavery and Race Relations in Brazil and the United States*. New York and London, 1971

Denucé, Jean. *L'Afrique au XVIe siècle et le commerce anversois. Avec reproduction de la carte murale de Blaeu-Verbist de 1644*. Collection de Documents pour l'Histoire du Commerce, Chambre de Commerce d'Anvers, vol. II. Antwerp, 1937

De Witte, Charles-Martial. 'Les Bulles pontificales et l'expansion portugaise au XVe siècle', *Revue d'Histoire Ecclésiastique*, XLVIII (1953), 683–718; XLIX (1954), 438–61; LI (1956), 413–53, 809–36; LIII (1958), 5–46, 443–71

Dias, José Sebastião da Silva. *Os Descobrimentos e a Problemática Cultural do Século XVI*. Coimbra, 1973

Dias, Manuel Nunes. *O Capitalismo Monárquico Português (1415–1549)*. 2 vols. Coimbra, 1963–4

O Dicionário de História de Portugal, ed. Joel Serrão. 4 vols. Lisbon, 1971

Dictionnaire de droit canonique, ed. R. Naz. 7 vols. Paris, 1935–65

Dillard, J. L. *Black English. Its History and Usage in the United States*. New York, 1972

Dinis, António Joaquim Dias. *Estudos Henriquinos*. Vol. I. Coimbra, 1960

Domínguez Ortiz, Antonio. 'La esclavitud en Castilla durante la Edad Moderna', *Estudios de Historia Social de España*, II (1952), 369–428

Donnet, Fernand. 'Quelques Notes sur le commerce des esclaves', *Bulletin de la Société Royale de Géographie de Anvers*, XLVI: 1/2 (1926), 6–37

Duncan, R. M. 'Adjetivos de color en el español medieval', *Anuario de Estudios Medievales*, V (1968), 463–72

Enciclopedia Cattolica. 12 vols. Vatican City, 1948–54

The Encyclopaedia of Islam. New edn, ed. J. H. Kramers, H. A. R. Gibb and E. Lévi-Provençal, Leiden, 1954– (in progress)

Exposição Henriquina. Comissão Executiva das Comemorações do v. Centenário da Morte do Infante D. Henrique. Lisbon, 1960

Farinha, Bento José de Souza. *Summario da Bibliotheca Lusitana*. 4 vols. Lisbon, 1786–88; see also Machado, Diogo Barbosa

Felix, Emília. See p. 224

Figanier, Joaquim. *História de Santa Cruz do Cabo de Gué (Agadir), 1505–1541*. Lisbon, 1945

Figueiredo, Jozé Anastásio de. *Synopsis Chronologica de Subsidios ainda os Mais Raros para a Historia e Estudo Critico da Legislação Portugueza, 1143–1603*. 2 vols. Lisbon, 1790

Foner, Laura, and Eugene D. Genovese (eds.). *Slavery in the New World. A Reader in Comparative History*. Englewood Cliffs, NJ, 1969

Fonseca, Quirino da. *Os Navios do Infante D. Henrique*. 2nd edn. Lisbon, 1958

A Caravela Portuguesa e a Prioridade Técnica das Navegações Henriquinas. Coimbra, 1934
Frazer, James George. *The Golden Bough. A Study in Magic and Religion.* Abridged edn. London, 1922
Freire, Anselmo Braamcamp. *Expedições e Armadas nos anos de 1488–1489.* Lisbon, 1915
Freyre, Gilberto. *The Masters and the Slaves*, trans. Samuel Putnam. 2nd edn. New York, 1963
Fyfe, Christopher. *A History of Sierra Leone.* London, 1962

Gallop, Rodney. 'The Fado (The Portuguese Song of Fate)', *The Musical Quarterly*, XIX: 2 (1933), 199–213
Gamble, David P. *The Wolof of Senegambia. Together with Notes on the Lebu and the Serer.* London, 1957
Garcia, Rozendo Sampaio. 'Contribuição ao Estudo do Aprovisionamento de Escravos Negros da América Espanhola (1580–1640)', *Anais do Museu Paulista*, XVI (1962), 7–195
García Gallo, Alfonso. 'Las bulas de Alejandro VI y el ordenamiento jurídico de la expansión portuguesa y castellana en África e Indias', *Archivo de Historia del Derecho Español*, XXVII/XXVIII (1957/8), 461–829
Garfield, Robert. *A History of São Tomé Island, 1470–1655* (Ph.D. thesis, Northwestern Univ., Evanston, Ill., 1971), Ann Arbor, Mich.: Univ. of Michigan Microfilms printout, 1974
Genovese, Eugene D. *Esclavitud y capitalismo*, trans. Angel Abad. Barcelona, 1971
Roll, Jordan, Roll. The World the Slaves Made. London, 1975
Giese, W. 'Notas sobre a Fala dos Negros em Lisboa no princípio do Século XVI', *Revista Lusitana*, XXX (1932), 251–7
Gioffrè, Domenico. *Il mercato degli schiavi a Genova nel secolo XV.* Genoa, 1971
Godinho, Vitorino Magalhães. *A Economia dos Descobrimentos Henriquinos.* Lisbon, 1962
Os Descobrimentos e a Economia Mundial. 2 vols. Lisbon, 1963–5
L'Économie de l'empire portugais aux XVe et XVIe siècles. Paris, 1969
A Estrutura da Antiga Sociedade Portuguesa. Lisbon, 1971
Introdução a História Económica. Lisbon, n.d.
Goodolphim, Costa. *As Misericordias.* Lisbon, 1897
Goris, Johannes Albertus. 'Slavernij te Antwerpen in de XVIe eeuw', *Bijdragen tot de Geschiedenis*, XV (Antwerp, 1923), 541–4
Étude sur les colonies marchandes méridionales (portugais, espagnols, italiens) à Anvers de 1488 à 1567. Contribution à l'histoire des débuts du capitalisme moderne. Louvain, 1925
Goulart, Maurício. *Escravidão Africana no Brasil.* 2nd edn. São Paulo, 1950
Gouveia, Maurílio de. *História da Escravidão.* Rio de Janeiro, 1955
Granda, Germán de. 'Materiales para el estudio sociohistórico de los elementos lingüísticos afroamericanos en el área hispánica', *Thesaurus*, XXIII (Bogotá, 1968), 547–73

'Sobre el estudio de las hablas "criollas" en el área hispánica', *Thesaurus*, XXIII (Bogotá, 1968), 64–74

'Posibles vías directas de introducción de africanismos en el "habla de negro" literaria castellana', *Thesaurus*, XXIV (Bogotá, 1969), 459–69

'Materiales complementarios para el estudio sociohistórico de los elementos lingüísticos afroamericanos en el área hispánica', *Thesaurus*, XXVI (Bogotá, 1971), 118–33, 400–22

'Sobre el origen del "habla de negro" en la literatura peninsular del Siglo de Oro', *Prohemio*, II: 1 (1971), 95–109

'Socio-historical Approach to the Problem of Portuguese Creole in West Africa', *Linguistics*, CLXXVII (23 May 1976), 11–22

Grande Enciclopédia Portuguesa e Brasileira (Portugal). 40 vols. Lisbon and Rio de Janeiro, n.d.

Guimarães, J. Ribeiro. *Summario de Varia Historia*. 5 vols. Lisbon, 1872

Hair, P. E. H. 'The Use of African Languages in Afro-European Contacts in Guinea, 1440–1560', *Sierra Leone Language Review*, V (1966), 5–26

The Atlantic Slave Trade and Black Africa. London, 1978

Hale, J. R. *Renaissance Europe, 1480–1520*. London, 1971

Hancock, Ian F. 'Malacca Creole Portuguese: Asian, African or European?', *Anthropological Linguistics*, XVII (1975), 211–36

Harris, Marvin. *Patterns of Race in the Americas*. New York, 1964

Heleno, Manuel. *Os Escravos em Portugal*. Vol. I (and only). Lisbon, 1933

Helps, Arthur. *The Spanish Conquest in America and its Relation to the History of Slavery and to the Government of Colonies*, ed. M. Oppenheim. 4 vols. London and New York, 1900–4

Herculano, Alexandre. *História da Origem e Estabelecimento da Inquisição em Portugal*, ed. Jorge Borges de Macedo. 3 vols. Lisbon, 1975–6

Hernton, Calvin C. *Sex and Racism*. London, 1969

Hoffman, R. C., and H. B. Johnson. 'Un Village portugais en mutation. Póvoa d'El Rey à la fin du quatorzième siècle', *Annales. Economies. Sociétés. Civilisations*, XXVI (1971), 917–40

Iria Júnior, Alberto. 'O Algarve no Descobrimento e Cristianização da Guiné no Século XV', in *Congresso Comemorativo do Quinto Centenário do Descobrimento da Guiné*, vol. I, pp. 193–206. Lisbon, 1946

O Algarve e os Descobrimentos. 2 tomes, forming vol. II of João Martins da Silva Marques, *Descobrimentos Portugueses*. Lisbon, 1956

Iung, Nicolas. *Un Franciscain, théologien du pouvoir pontifical au XIVe siècle. Álvaro Pelayo, évêque et pénitencier de Jean XXII*. Paris, 1931

Janson, Horst Woldemar. *Apes and Ape Lore in the Middle Ages and the Renaissance*. London, 1952

Johnson, Harold B. 'A Portuguese Estate of the Late Fifteenth Century', *Luso-Brazilian Review*, X: 2 (1973), 149–62

Jordan, Winthrop D. 'American Chiaroscuro: The Status and Definition

of Mulattoes in the British Colonies', *William and Mary College Quarterly Historical Magazine*, 3rd ser., xix (1962), 183–200
White over Black: American Attitudes toward the Negro, 1550–1812. Baltimore, Md, 1969

Kahn, Zadoc. *L'Esclavage selon la Bible et le Talmud*. Paris, 1867
Keen, Maurice. *The Laws of War in the Late Middle Ages*. Oxford, 1965
Kehrer, Hugo Ludwig. *Die Heiligen drei Könige in Literatur und Kunst*. 2 vols. Leipzig, 1909
Kelly, Francis M., and Randolph Schwabe. *A Short History of Costume and Armour*. 2 vols. in 1. London, 1931; reprinted Newton Abbot, Devon, 1972
Kurlat, Frida Weber de. 'El tipo cómico del negro en el teatro prelopesco: fonética', *Filología*, viii (1962), 139–68
'Sobre el negro como tipo cómico en el teatro español del siglo xvi', *Romance Philology*, xvii (1963), 380–91
'El tipo del negro en el teatro de Lope de Vega: tradición y creación', *Actas*, 2⁰ Congreso Internacional de Hispanistas, vol. ii, pp. 695–704. Nijmegen, 1965

Lane, Frederic Chapin. *Venetian Ships and Shipbuilders of the Renaissance*. Baltimore, Md, 1934
Larrea Palacín, Arcadio de. 'Los negros en la provincia de Huelva', *Archivos del Instituto de Estudios Africanos*, vi: 20 (1952), 39–57
Lawrence, Arnold Walter. *Trade Castles and Forts of West Africa*. Stanford, Calif., 1964
Leal, Augusto Soares d'Azevedo Barbosa de Pinho. *Portugal Antigo e Moderno. Diccionario Geographico, Estatistico, Chorographico, Heraldico, Archeologico, Historico, Biographico e Etymologico de Todas as Cidades, Villas e Freguezias de Portugal e de Grande Numero de Aldeias*. 12 vols. Lisbon, 1873–90
Leitão, Joaquim. See p. 224
Leite, Duarte. *Ácerca da 'Crónica dos Feitos de Guinee'*. Lisbon, 1941
Leite, Serafim. *História da Companhia de Jesus no Brasil*. Vols. i and ii. Lisbon and Rio de Janeiro, 1938
Lencastre, Francisco de Salles. *Estudo sobre as Portagens e as Alfandegas em Portugal (Seculos XII a XVI)*. Lisbon, 1891
Lévi-Provençal, Evariste. *Histoire de l'Espagne musulmane*. New edn. Vol. iii. Paris, 1953
Livi, Ridolfo. *La schiavitù domestica nei tempi di mezzo e nei moderni*. Padua, 1928
Lobo, A. de Sousa Silva Costa. *Historia da Sociedade em Portugal no Seculo XV*. Secção i (and only). Lisbon, 1903
Logan, R. W. 'The Attitude of the Church toward Slavery prior to 1500', *Journal of Negro History*, xvii (1932), 466–80
Lopes, Edmundo Correia. *A Escravatura: Subsídios para a sua História*. Lisbon, 1944

Lucena, Armando. 'A Iconografia do Negro na Arte Portuguesa', *O Mundo Português*, 2a sér., XIII (1946), 3–7

Luttrell, Anthony. 'Slavery and Slaving in the Portuguese Atlantic (to about 1500)', in C. Fyfe (ed.), *The Transatlantic Slave Trade from West Africa*. Mimeographed copy of seminar held in the Centre of African Studies, University of Edinburgh, 1965

Luz, Francisco Paulo Mendes da. *O Conselho da Índia*. Lisbon, 1952

Machado, Augusto Reis. *Índice Analítico da História da Administração Pública em Portugal nos Séculos XII a XV de H. da Gama Barros*. Lisbon, 1934

Machado, Diogo Barbosa. *Bibliotheca Lusitana Historica, Critica e Cronologica*. 4 vols. Lisbon, 1741–59; reprinted, ed. by M. Lopes de Almeida. Coimbra, 1965–7

Magalhães, Joaquim Antero Romero. *Para o Estudo do Algarve Económico durante o Século XVI*. Lisbon, 1970

Marques, António Henrique (Rodrigo) de Oliveira. 'Notas para a História da Feitoria Portuguesa na Flandres, no Século XV', in *Studi in onore di Amintore Fanfani*, vol. II, pp. 439–76. Milan, 1962

Introdução à História da Agricultura em Portugal (A Questão Cerealífera durante a Idade Média). Lisbon, 1962

A Sociedade Medieval Portuguesa. Aspectos de Vida Quotidiana. Lisbon, 1964

Ensaios de História Medieval Portuguesa. Lisbon, 1965

História de Portugal desde os Tempos Mais Antigos até ao Governo do Sr Marcelo Caetano. 2 vols. Lisbon, 1972–3

History of Portugal, 2nd edn. 2 vols. in 1. New York, 1976

Matos, Luís Salgado de. *Les Portugais en France au XVIe siècle*. Coimbra, 1952

Mauro, Frédéric. *Le Portugal et l'Atlantique au XVIIe siècle (1570–1670)*. Paris, 1960

Maxwell, John Francis. *Slavery and the Catholic Church*. Chichester, Sussex, 1976

Memoria ácerca da Extincção da Escravidão e do Trafico de Escravatura no Territorio Portuguez. Ministerio da Marinha, Portugal. Lisbon, 1889

Mendes, M. Maia. 'Escravatura no Brasil (1500–1700)', in *Congresso do Mundo Português*, vol. X, pp. 31–55. Lisbon, 1940

Mendonça, Henrique Lopes de. *Estudos sobre Navios Portuguezes nos Seculos XV e XVI*. Lisbon, 1892

Merêa, (Manuel) Paulo. 'A Guerra Justa segundo Alvaro Pais', *O Instituto*, LXIV (1917), 351–3

Miret i Sans, J. 'La esclavitud en Cataluña en los últimos tiempos de la Edad Media', *Revue Hispanique*, XLI (1917), 1–109

Mols, Roger. 'Population in Europe 1500–1700', in Carlo M. Cipolla (ed.), *The Fontana Economic History of Europe*. Vol. II: *The Sixteenth and Seventeenth Centuries*, pp. 15–82. Glasgow, 1974

Mörner, Magnus. 'The History of Race Relations in Latin America:

Comments on the State of Research', *Latin American Research Review*, I: 3 (1966), 17–44

Mota, Avelino Teixeira da. *Guiné Portuguesa*. 2 vols. Lisbon, 1954

Alguns Aspectos da Colonização e do Comércio Marítimo dos Portugueses na África Ocidental nos Séculos XV e XVI. Lisbon, 1976. Offprint from *Anais do Clube Militar Naval*, CVI: 10/12 (1976), 677–710

Frédéric Mauro and Jorge Borges de Macedo, 'Les Routes portugaises de l'Atlantique', *Anuario de Estudios Americanos*, XXV (1968), 129–51

Mullin, Gerald W. *Flight and Rebellion: Slave Resistance in Eighteenth Century Virginia*. New York, 1972

Múrias, Manuel. *Portugal e o Tráfico da Escravatura*. Lisbon, 1938

Naro, Anthony J. 'The Origin of West African Pidgin', in C. Corum et al. (eds.), *Papers from the Ninth Regional Meeting, Chicago Linguistic Society* (April 13–15, 1973), pp. 442–9. Chicago, 1973

Naz, R. 'Esclave', in *Dictionnaire de droit canonique*, vol. V, cols. 448–54. Paris, 1953

The New Cambridge Modern History. Vol. I: *The Renaissance*, ed. Denys Hay; paperback edn, Cambridge, 1975. Vol. II: *The Reformation*, ed. G. R. Elton; paperback edn, Cambridge, 1976

Nogueira, Oracy. 'Skin Color and Social Class', in *Plantation Systems of the New World*, pp. 164–79, with comments by James G. Leyburn, pp. 179–82, and Lloyd Braithwaite, pp. 182–3. Pan American Union, Washington, DC, 1959

Oliveira, Waldir Freitas. 'Considerações sôbre o Preconceito Racial no Brasil', *Afro-Ásia*, VIII/IX (Salvador, 1969), 5–19

Ortiz, Fernando. 'La leyenda negra contra Fray Bartolomé de las Casas', *Cuadernos Americanos*, V (Mexico, DF, 1952), 146–84

Parreira, Henrique Gomes de Amorim. 'História do Açúcar em Portugal', *Anais da Junta das Missões Geográficas e de Investigações do Ultramar*, VII: 1 (1952), 1–321

Parrinder, (Edward) Geoffrey S. *Witchcraft, European and African*. London, 1963

Parry, J. H. *The Age of Reconnaissance*. New York, 1964

Pedroso, Consiglieri. *Portuguese Folk-Tales*, trans. Henriqueta Monteiro, London, 1882 (Publications of the Folk-Lore Society, vol. IX)

Pereira, Gabriel (Victor do Monte). *Estudos Eborenses*. 3 vols. 1st edn. Évora, 1888; 2nd edn. Évora, 1947–51

Pereira, João Manuel Esteves. *A Industria Portugueza (Seculos XII a XIX)* com uma Introdução sobre as Corporações Operarias em Portugal. Lisbon, 1900

Peres, Damião (António) (ed.). *História de Portugal*. 9 vols. Barcelos, 1928–58

'A Actividade Agrícola em Portugal nos Séculos XII a XIV', in *Congresso do Mundo Português*, vol. II, pp. 463–80. Lisbon, 1940

Pérez Embid, Francisco. *Los descubrimientos en el Atlántico y la rivalidad castellano–portuguesa hasta el tratado de Tordesillas.* Seville, 1948

Pike, Ruth. *Enterprise and Adventure. The Genoese in Seville and the Opening of the New World.* Ithaca, NY State, 1966

'Sevillian Society in the Sixteenth Century: Slaves and Freedmen', *Hispanic American Historical Review*, XLVII (1967), 344–59

Piper, Anson C. 'The Lisbon of J. F. de Vasconcelos', *Luso-Brazilian Review*, IV: 1 (1967), 17–25

Pires, A. Thomaz. 'Investigações Ethnographicas', *Revista Lusitana*, XII (1909), 61–92

Estudos e Notas Elvenses. Vol. XII: *As Ruas d'Elvas.* Vol. XIII: *Excerptos de um Estudo sobre a Toponymia Elvense.* Elvas, 1924, 1931

Pires de Lima, Augusto César. 'Descobertas Portuguesas (Antropofagia e Alimentação)', *Archivos de Historia da Medicina Portugueza*, nova sér., II (1911), 165–78

'Tradições Populares do Concelho de Santo Tirso (3a série)', *Revista Lusitana*, XXII (1919), 35–90

Pires de Lima, Joaquim Alberto. 'Influência dos Mouros, Judeus e Negros na Etnografia Portuguesa', *Congresso do Mundo Portugues*, vol. XVIII, pp. 63–102. Lisbon, 1940

Mouros, Judeus e Negros na História de Portugal. Oporto, 1940

Plantation Systems of the New World. Papers and Discussion Summaries of the Seminar held in San Juan, Puerto Rico (Nov. 1957). Pan American Union, Division of Science Development (Social Sciences), Dept of Cultural Affairs, Washington, DC, 1959

Poggiali, Cristoforo. *Memorie per la storia letteraria di Piacenza.* 2 vols. Piacenza, 1789

Pope-Hennessy, James. *Sins of the Fathers: A Study of the Atlantic Slave Traders, 1441–1807.* London, 1970

Poppino, Rollie E. *Brazil. The Land and People.* 2nd edn. New York, 1973

Prestage, Edgar. *The Portuguese Pioneers.* London, 1933

Ramos, Arthur. *O Negro Brasileiro.* Rio de Janeiro, 1934

As Culturas Negras do Novo Mundo. Rio de Janeiro, 1937 (Coleção A. Ramos, vol. III)

Ramos y Loscertales, José María. *El cautiverio en la Corona de Aragón durante los siglos XIII, XIV, y XV.* Saragossa, 1915

Randles, W. G. L. *L'Image du Sud-est africain dans la littérature européenne au XVIe siècle.* Lisbon, 1959

L'Ancien Royaume du Congo des origines à la fin du XIXe siècle. The Hague and Paris, 1968

Rau, Virgínia Roberts. *A Exploração e o Comércio do Sal de Setúbal. Estudo de História Económica.* Lisbon, 1951

'Para a História da População Portuguesa dos Séculos XV e XVI (Resultados e Problemas de Métodos)', *Do Tempo e da História*, I (1965), 7–46

'Notes sur la traite portugaise à la fin du XVe siècle et le florentin

Bartolomeo di Domenico Marchionni', *Bulletin de l'Institut Historique Belge de Rome*, XLIV (1974), 535–43

and Jorge Borges de Macedo. *O Açúcar da Madeira nos fins do Século XV. Problemas de Produçao e Comércio*. Funchal, 1962

and Georges Zbyszewski. *Estremadura et Ribatejo*. Lisbon, 1949

Ribeiro, João Pedro. *Dissertações Chronologicas e Criticas sobre a Historia e Jurisprudencia Ecclesiastica e Civil de Portugal*. 5 vols. Lisbon, 1810–81 *Additamentos e Retoques a Synopse Chronologica*. Lisbon, 1829

Ribeiro, Orlando. *Portugal, o Mediterrâneo e o Atlântico*. 3rd edn. Lisbon, 1967

Ribeiro, Victor Maximiano. *A Santa Casa da Misericordia de Lisboa (Subsidios para a sua Historia) 1498–1898*. Lisbon, 1902

Ricard, Robert. *Études sur l'histoire des portugais au Maroc*. Coimbra, 1955

Rio Maior, João de Saldanha Oliveira e Sousa, marquês de. 'O Marquês de Pombal e a Repressão da Escravatura – A Obra e o Homem', *Congresso do Mundo Português*, vol. VIII, pp. 93–120. Lisbon, 1940

Rodney, Walter. *A History of the Upper Guinea Coast 1545 to 1800*. Oxford, 1970

Rodrigues, José Albertino R. 'Travail et société urbaine au Portugal dans la seconde moitié du XVIe siècle', thèse du 3e cycle, Faculté de Lettres, Université de Paris, 1968

Rout, Jr, Leslie B. *The African Experience in Spanish America 1502 to the Present Day*. Cambridge, 1976

Rumeu de Armas, Antonio. *España en el África atlántica*. Madrid, 1956 'Los problemas derivados del contacto de razas en los albores del Renacimiento', *Cuadernos de Historia*, I (Madrid, 1967), 61–104

Russell, Frederick H. *The Just War in the Middle Ages*. Cambridge, 1975

Russell, Josiah Cox. 'Late Ancient and Medieval Population', in American Philosophical Society, *Transactions of the American Philosophical Society*, NS, XLVIII: 3 (1958)

Russell, Peter Edward Lionel. *Prince Henry the Navigator*. London, 1960 'Towards an Interpretation of Rodrigo de Reinosa's "poesía negra"', in R. O. Jones (ed.), *Studies in Spanish Literature of the Golden Age presented to Edward M. Wilson*, pp. 225–45. London, 1973 '*Congregatio Fidelium* or *Communitas Mortalium*: the Portuguese Crown and the Problem of the Legitimacy of Black African States (1444–1521)' (article forthcoming)

Russell-Wood, Anthony John R. *Fidalgos and Philanthropists. The Santa Casa da Misericórdia of Bahia, 1550–1755*. London, 1968 'Black and Mulatto Brotherhoods in Colonial Brazil: A Study in Collective Behavior', *Hispanic American Historical Review*, LIV (1974), 567–602 'Iberian Expansion and the Issue of Black Slavery: Changing Portuguese Attitudes, 1440–1770', *American Historical Review*, LXXXIII (1978), 16–42

Ryder, Alan Frederick C. *Benin and the Europeans, 1485–1897*. London, 1969

Sabugosa, António Maria Vasco de Melo Silva César e Meneses, 9th conde de. *O Paço de Cintra*. Lisbon, 1903

Bobos na Côrte, ed. Ayres d'Ornellas. 2nd edn. Lisbon, n.d. [1923]

Sachs, Ignacy. 'L'Image du Noir dans l'art européen', *Annales. Economies. Sociétés. Civilisations*, xxiv (1969), 883–93

Saco, José Antonio. *Historia de la esclavitud desde los tiempos más remotos hasta nuestros días*. 3 vols. Barcelona, 1875–7

Historia de la esclavitud de la raza africana en el Nuevo Mundo y en especial en los países américo-hispanos. Vol. 1. Barcelona, 1879

Santarém, Manuel Francisco de Barros e Sousa de Mesquita de Macedo Leitão e Carvalhosa, visconde de. *Quadro Elementar das Relações Politicas e Diplomaticas de Portugal com as diversas Potencias do Mundo, desde o principio da Monarquia Portugueza ate aos Nossos Dias*. Vols. I–VIII. Paris, 1842–53. Continued by L. A. Rebello da Silva (vols. IX–XI) and J. da Silva Mendes Leal (vols. XII, XIII). Lisbon, 1864–76

Santos, Eduardo dos. 'Escravatura e Antropologia dos Portugueses', *Ultramar*, nova sér., II: 5/6 (1973), 51–98

Santos Júnior, J. R. dos. *Nota de Coreografia Popular Transmontana. A Dança dos Pretos (Moncorvo)*. Oporto, 1935

Nota de Coreografia Popular Transmontana. A Dança dos Pretos (Carviçais). Oporto, 1936

Saraiva, António José. *História da Cultura em Portugal*. 3 vols. Lisbon, 1950–62

Inquisição e Cristãos-Novos. 4th edn. Oporto, 1969

and Óscar Lopes. *História da Literatura Portuguesa*. 7th edn. Oporto and Lisbon, n.d.

Saraiva, Francisco de São Luiz, cardinal. 'Nota sobre a Origem da Escravidão e Trafico dos Negros', in *Obras Completas do Cardeal Saraiva*, vol. V, pp. 323–47. Lisbon, 1875

'Glossario de Vocabulos Portuguezes derivados das Linguas Orientaes e Africanas, excepto a Arabe', in *Obras Completas do Cardeal Saraiva*, vol. VIII, pp. 209–317. Lisbon, 1878

Sarmento, Alberto Artur. *Os Escravos na Madeira*. Funchal, 1938

Scelle, Georges. *Histoire politique de la traite négrière aux Indes de Castille. Contrats et traités d'Assiento*. 2 vols. Paris, 1906

Schwartz, Stuart B. 'Manumission of Slaves in Colonial Brazil: Bahia, 1684–1745', *Hispanic American Historical Review*, LIV (1974), 603–35

Sequeira, Gustavo de Matos. *Depois do Terremoto. Subsídios para a História dos Bairros Ocidentais de Lisboa*. 4 vols. Lisbon, 1916–34

Serrão, Joaquim Veríssimo. 'Uma Estimativa da População Portuguesa em 1640'. Offprint from *Memórias da Academia das Ciências*, XVI (1975), 213–303

Shapiro, Harry Lionel. *Race Mixture*. Paris, 1953

Sherwin-White, Adrian Nicholas. *Racial Prejudice in Imperial Rome*. Cambridge, 1967

Shyllon, Folarin. *Black Slaves in Britain*. London, 1974

Black People in Britain 1555–1833. London, 1977

Silva, António de Morais. *Grande Dicionário da Língua Portuguesa,* ed. and revised by Augusto Moreno et al. 10th edn. 11 vols. Lisbon, 1949–58
Silva, Augusto Vieira da. *A População de Lisboa.* Lisbon, 1919
As Freguesias de Lisboa (Estudo Histórico). Lisbon, 1943
Silva, Baltasar Lopes da. *O Dialecto Crioulo de Cabo Verde.* Lisbon, 1957
Silva, Fernando Augusto da, and Carlos Azevedo de Menezes, *Elucidário Madeirense.* 3 vols. Funchal, 1965–6
Silva, Inocêncio Francisco da. *Diccionario Bibliographico Portuguez,* continued by Pedro Venceslau de Brito Aranha. 22 vols. Lisbon, 1858–1923
Silva, Luís Augusto Rebello. *Memoria sobre a População e Agricultura de Portugal desde a Fundação da Monarchia até 1865.* Parte 1. Lisbon, 1868
Simancas, Archivo General. *Catálogo* XIII. *Registro general del Sello.* 11 vols. Valladolid and Madrid, 1950–70
Smith, Ronald Bishop. *Diogo Lopes de Sequeira.* Lisbon, 1975
Diogo Fernandes de Beja. Lisbon, 1977
Snowden, Jr, Frank Martin. *Blacks in Antiquity.* Cambridge, Mass., 1970
Sousa, Antonio Caetano de. *Historia Genealogica da Casa Real Portugueza.* 14 vols. Lisbon, 1735–48
Stegagno Picchio, Luciana. *História do Teatro Português,* trans. Manuel de Lucena. Lisbon, 1969
Stern, C. 'The Biology of the Negro', *Scientific American,* CXCI: 4 (1954), 80–5

Tannenbaum, Frank. *Slave and Citizen. The Negro in the Americas.* New York, 1946
Taunay, Affonso de Escragnolle. 'Subsídios para a História do Tráfico Africano no Brasil Colonial', *Anais,* 3° Congresso de História Nacional, vol. III, pp. 519–676. Rio de Janeiro, 1941
Teyssier, Paul. *La Langue de Gil Vicente.* Paris, 1959
A Thousand Years of Portuguese Art. Portuguese Art 800–1800. Royal Academy of Arts. London, 1955
Trimingham, J. Spencer. *A History of Islam in West Africa.* London, 1970

Ullmann, Walter. *Medieval Papalism.* London, 1949

Valkhoff, Marius F. *Studies in Portuguese and Creole with Special Reference to South Africa.* Johannesburg, 1966
Vasconcellos, Carolina Michaëlis de. 'Contribuições para o Futuro Diccionário Etimológico das Línguas Hispánicas', *Revista Lusitana,* XI (1908), 1–62
Notas Vicentinas. Lisbon, 1949
Vasconcellos, José Leite de. *Tradições Populares de Portugal.* Oporto, 1882
'Espécime Português de Raça Negra', *Boletim de Etnografia,* 1 (1920), 40–1
Antroponímia Portuguesa. Lisbon, 1928
'Língua de Preto num texto de Henrique da Mota', *Revue Hispanique,* LXXXI: 1 (1933), 241–5

A Etnografia Portuguesa. Tentame de Sistematização. 5 vols. published. Lisbon, 1933–67

Vasconcelos, José Augusto do Amaral Frazão de. 'Subsídios para a História da Vila de Almeirim (Séculos XV a XVIII)', *Ethnos*, IV (Lisbon, 1965), 321–36

Verlinden, Charles. 'L'Origine de sclavus=esclave', *Archivum Latinitatis Medii Aevi* (=*Bulletin du Cange*), XVII (1942), 97–128

'Précédents et parallèles européens de l'esclavage colonial', *O Instituto*, CXIII (1949), 113–53

L'Esclavage dans l'Europe médiévale. 2 vols. published. Bruges, 1955–77. (Werken uitgegeven door de Faculteit van de Letteren en Wijsbegeerte, Rijksuniversiteit te Gent, vols. CXIX, CLXII)

'La Crete, débouché et plaque tournante de la traite des esclaves aux XIVe et XVe siècles', in *Studi in onore di Amintore Fanfani*, vol. III, pp. 591–669. Milan, 1962

'L'Esclavage en Sicile au Bas Moyen Age', *Bulletin de l'Institut Historique Belge de Rome*, XXXV (1963), 13–113

'Schiavitù ed economia nel Mezzogiorno agli inizi dell'età moderna', *Annali del Mezzogiorno*, III (1963), 11–38

'Esclavage noir en France méridionale et courants de traite en Afrique', *Annales du Midi*, LXXVIII (1966), 335–43

'Les Débuts de la traite portugaise en Afrique (1433–1448)', in *Miscellanea Medievalia in Memoriam Jan Frederik Niemeyer*, pp. 365–77. Groningen, 1967

'L'Esclavage dans le royaume de Naples à la fin du Moyen Age et la participation des marchands espagnols à la traite', *Anuario de Historia Económica y Social*, I: 1 (1968), 345–401

Beginnings of Modern Colonization, trans. Yvonne Freccero. Ithaca, NY State, 1970

Vicens Vives, Jaime (ed.). *Historia de España y América*. 2nd edn. Vol. III. Barcelona, 1961

Vila, Isidro. *Elementos de la gramática Ambú ó de Annobón*. Madrid, 1891

Viterbo, Frei Joaquim de Santa Rosa de. *Elucidário das Palavras, Termos e Frases que em Portugal antigamente se usaram e que hoje regularmente se ignoram*, ed. M. Fiuza. 2 vols. Oporto, 1962–6

Vogt, John L. 'The Early São Tomé – Príncipe Slave Trade with Mina, 1500–1540', *International Journal of African Historical Studies*, VI (1973), 453–67

'Portuguese Gold Trade: An Account Ledger from Elmina, 1529–1531', *Transactions of the Historical Society of Ghana*, XIV (1973), 93–103

'The Lisbon Slave House and African Trade, 1486–1521', *Proceedings of the American Philosophical Society*, CXVII: 1 (1973), 1–16

'Private Trade and Slave Sales at São Jorge da Mina: A Fifteenth-Century Document', *Transactions of the Historical Society of Ghana*, XV (1974), 103–10

'Notes on the Portuguese Cloth Trade in West Africa, 1480–1540', *International Journal of African Historical Studies*, VIII (1975), 623–51

Wade, Richard C. *Slavery in the Cities. The South 1820–1860.* New York, 1967

Walvin, James. *The Black Presence. A Documentary History of the Negro in England, 1555–1860.* London, 1971

Black and White. The Negro and English Society, 1555–1945. London, 1973

Weinstein, Allen, and Frank Otto Gatell (eds.). *American Negro Slavery. A Modern Reader.* 2nd edn. New York, 1973

Whinnom, Keith. 'The Origin of the European-based Pidgins and Creoles', *Orbis*, XIV (1965), 509–27

'Linguistic Hybridization and the "Special Case" of Pidgins and Creoles', in Dell Hymes (ed.), *Pidginization and Creolization of Languages*, pp. 91–115. Cambridge, 1971

'The Context and Origins of Lingua Franca', in Jürgen M. Meisel (ed.), *Langues en contact – Pidgins – Creoles*, pp. 1–18. Tübingen, 1975

Wilks, Michael. *The Problem of Sovereignty in the Later Middle Ages. The Papal Monarchy with Augustinus Triumphus and the Publicists.* Cambridge, 1963

Wilson, W. A. A. *The Crioulo of Guiné.* Johannesburg, 1962

Wilson, William E. 'Some Notes on Slavery during the Golden Age', *Hispanic Review*, VII (1939), 171–4

Zelinsky, Wilbur. 'The Historical Geography of the Negro Population of Latin America', *Journal of Negro History*, XXXIV (1949), 153–221

Addenda

Two recent works came to my attention too late for their findings to be incorporated in the present work. They are:

Franco Silva, Alfonso. *La esclavitud en Sevilla y su tierra a fines de la Edad Media.* Seville, 1979

Vogt, John L. *Portuguese Rule on the Gold Coast, 1469–1682.* Athens, Ga, 1979

Glossary

alcaide: military commander of a fortress or town and, by virtue of his office, having administrative and judicial functions. By the fifteenth century, the actual command of the troops in a town or fortress was entrusted to the *alcaide-mor*, while the civil functions, especially the enforcement of police regulations, were delegated to his deputy, the *alcaide-menor* or *alcaide-pequeno*.

alfândega: customs house; see p. 9.

almoxarife: fundamentally, a fiscal agent entrusted with the collection of certain rents and taxes for the crown. By the fifteenth century, the term designated an official in charge of a royal enterprise and was virtually interchangeable with *recebedor*.

armazém: warehouse. Armazém da Guiné: royal institution entrusted with fitting out, and with signing and paying the crew for, vessels bound for Guinea and subsequently for Mina and India (whence the later titles of Armazém da Mina e Índia, Armazém da Índia). The institution was under the direction of an *almoxarife* (after 1501, of a *provedor*) and its warehouse and other buildings were on the riverside in Lisbon.

baraço: noose of rope hung around the neck of a convicted criminal while his sentence, such as a whipping, was being carried out; usually in conjunction with *pregão* (*q. v.*).

batlle: bailiff; royal representative in a district (Catalan).

besteiro: a cross-bow man. A certain number of citizens of reasonable means in every town were required to serve as *besteiros*, thus forming a militia.

câmara: town council.

carta de alforria: letter of manumission.

Casa da Guiné; Casa da Mina e Tratos de Guiné; Casa da Mina e Índia; Casa da Guiné e Índia; Casa da Índia: royal institution originally entrusted with overseeing and collecting duties on the trade with Guinea and Mina, and subsequently with similar tasks with respect to the trade with India and Asia. From 1509 two separate sections headed by treasurers oversaw the African and Asian trades, respectively, though the whole enterprise remained under the general direction of the factor, *feitor*. The names of this mercantile complex varied; in this book Casa da Guiné is the preferred term used to designate the whole institution and, in particular, that section of it that was concerned with the African trades; see p. 8.

Casa do Cível: court of appeal, with its seat in Lisbon, and entrusted with the hearing of all appeals in civil cases that occurred throughout the kingdom except within 5 leagues (22.5 km) of the royal court. It also heard appeals in criminal cases that occurred within the city limits (*termo*) of Lisbon. Roughly equivalent to the Court of Common Pleas.

Casa dos Escravos: department of the Casa da Guiné entrusted with over-seeing and collecting duties on the slave-trade; see p. 8.

cavaleiro: gentleman; a gentleman descended from three generations of gentlemen was considered to have acquired a noble lineage and was called a *cavaleiro fidalgo*.

compromisso: rule to which brothers of a religious fraternity swore adherence.

contador: auditor of accounts.

corregedor: royal magistrate in charge of the administration of justice in a certain district, which was called a *correição*.

Cortes: assembly of representatives of the three estates (nobility, clergy and commons) meeting on the king's command to vote taxes, propose laws for royal approval and seek redress for grievances.

criado: literally, someone brought up in another man's household. The term is met with in two senses. Sons of noblemen were often brought up in another noble's house, in which case they were his *criados* and owed him loyalty, but otherwise their status carried few juridical disabilities in practice. Most *criados*, however, were free servants who formed part of their master's extended family. *Criados a bem fazer* served for board, lodging and clothing only; other *criados* served for wages as well. *Criados'* contracts were not passed before a notary but were enforceable at law.

dízima: 10 per cent customs duty on all goods entering or leaving seaports or frontier towns; see p. 9.

fala de Guiné: hybrid form of Portuguese spoken by some blacks in Portugal; see p. 99.

Fazenda: department of a royal or aristocratic household entrusted with the receipt and expenditure of revenue.

fidalgo: person of noble blood.

Infante, Infanta: title given to the legitimate children of the king. The heir apparent was called the Príncipe, prince.

inquiridor: official entrusted with inquiring into the state of crown lands and rights.

Juiz da Guiné: judge attached to the Casa da Guiné and empowered to hear cases involving the infringement of regulations concerning over-seas trade.

juiz de fora: judge who was not a citizen of the town which the king placed under his jurisdiction.

mancebo de soldada: wage-labourer.

meio forro: slave who was half-free; see p. 140.

meirinho: officer of justice who was charged with the execution of court orders; the *meirinho*'s men performed police functions in the towns.

mordomo: (of the Misericórdia and other religious brotherhoods) an elected official charged with carrying out the decisions of the brotherhood's governing body (*mesa*) during his term of office.

mourisco: term applied to Muslims who had been converted to Christianity; also applied to their descendants.

New Christian (*cristão novo*): term applied to Portuguese Jews compelled to embrace Christianity in 1497; also applied to their descendants.

ouvidor: royal judge, especially in the Casa do Cível or Suplicação.

peça: item; *peça de escravo*: one slave, or a slave mother with suckling child.

pelourinho: column, usually made of stone, where criminals were punished; akin to a whipping post. Occasionally called a *picota*.

pingar: punishment for slaves that consisted of letting drops of hot molten fat or wax fall upon a slave's naked flesh.

portagem: municipal tax paid by a merchant who was not a citizen (*vizinho*) of a town on goods which he brought into and sold in the town.

praça: (in North Africa) one of the towns held by the Portuguese on the coast of Morocco.

pregão: public proclamation of a convicted criminal's crime and sentence, often at the same time as punishment was being carried out, such as when a criminal was being whipped through the streets of a town.

procurador: representative, especially of a town to the Cortes.

provedor: superintendent.

quarto: 25 per cent duty levied on goods brought directly to Portugal from Portuguese possessions or trading posts overseas in Africa and Asia; see p. 9.

recebedor: literally, receiver, especially of royal revenue; similar to an *almoxarife* (*q. v.*).

Relação: court of appeals in the Suplicação (*q. v.*).

sisa: sales tax. See p. 10.

Suplicação (or Casa da Corte): the highest appeal court in the land, roughly equivalent to the Court of King's Bench. It followed the royal court in the king's progresses and heard appeals in criminal cases that occurred everywhere in the kingdom except within the city limits of Lisbon; it also heard appeals in civil cases that occurred within 5 leagues (22.5 km) of the royal court. The court of Suplicação was after the 1470s divided into three sections (*mesas*) and was composed of judges with various functions. Some of these judges, the *desembargadores do paço*, were chiefly concerned with vetting appeals; if three *desembargadores* could not reach a unanimous decision regarding an appeal, the case was referred to the first, principal, *mesa* of the *Suplicação*, sitting in *Relação*. The *desembargadores* were also entrusted with hearing petitions to the king and with granting pardons and commutations of sentences.

termo: rural area under jurisdiction of a municipal council.

vedor: superintendent, overseer.

vintena: 5 per cent duty levied on goods brought directly to Portugal from Portuguese possessions or trading posts in Africa or Asia; see p. 9.

Index

abolition of slavery and slave-trade, 3, 178–9, 223 n20

Abrantes, 54, 72, 212 n32

accommodation: of freedmen, 125, 143, 144, 146, 160; of slaves (in Portugal) 15, 16, 89, 124, (on ship) 13, 14, (supervision of) 124–5, 132, (in West Africa) 13, 38–9

Accursius, Franciscus, 113, 114

Afonso V, king of Portugal: and freedmen, 142; and infidel masters, 63; and slave law, 113, 118, 120, 122, 125, 126; and slave-trade, 16, 28

Afonso, slave child called, 90

Afonso, Álvaro, 102–3, 106

Afonso, Maria, 139

Afonso de Portugal, bishop of Évora, 146

Africa: central, 29; East, 7; North (escape to), 72, 134, 137, 147, (exile to) 116, 118, (Islamic centre) 161, (ransoms from) 172, 209 n33, (source of slaves) 29, 45, 183 n33; West (freedmen in) 62, 145, 155, (language) 98, 100, (source of slaves), 1–46 passim, 156, 157

age: of freedmen, 141, 143; of slaves, 24, 25, 26, 139, 141

agriculture: freedmen in, 144; slaves in, 2, 28, 49, 54, 58, 66, 69–71, 80, 85, 86, 87, 123, 174, 176, 177, 193 n33

al-Andalus, 181 n2 to Introduction

Alandroal, 70

Albornoz, Bartolomé de, 44

Alcácer do Sal, 58, 126, 152, 179

Alcáçova, Palácio da, Lisbon, 55, 199 n87

alcaide, 131, 155, 212 n31, 214 n61, 266

Alcântara, Lisbon, 109–10

Alcochete, 158

alcoholism, among blacks, 83, 100, 124

Aldeia Galega de Ribatejo (Montijo), 54, 193 n33

Alentejo (Entre-Tejo-e-Odiana), province: demography, 49, 57–8, 59, 60; economy, 48, 79, 86, 87, 203 n55; fugitives in, 137, 211 n9; Moors and Jews in, 205 n100; slavery in, 71, 79; thieves from, 200 n112

Alexandre, slave called, 197 n53

Alexandrino, Cardinal, 106

Alfama, 17, 55, 169

alfândega, 9, 10, 15, 22, 183 n33, 266

Alfonso X, king of Castile, 190 n118

Algarve, kingdom: demography, 49, 58, 59, 60; fugitives, 137, 212 n19; punishment in, 119, 123, 160; slavery in, 69, 70, 86, 87, 125; slave-trade, 5, 8, 10, 149, 188 n155

Almada, 72, 120

Almeirim, 80

almoxarife, 8, 83, 266; dos escravos, 8, 9, 15, 16, 17, 31; see also Fornos Reais, Vale de Zebro

alvará de saca, 187 n138

Álvares, Afonso, 101, 146, 147, 222 n34

Álvares, Pedro, freedman, 212 n29

Álvares de Almada, André, 44

Ameixoeira, 54

America; slavery in, 42, 177; slave-trade with, 7, 10, 20, 23, 28, 30, 31, 32, 33, 42, 47, 182 n14, 188 nn152 and 155

Andrade, Mecia de, 213 n42

Angola, 7, 31, 33, 34, 182 n14, 189 n167, 206 n112

Antilles, 4, 23, 28, 31

Antónia, slave, 139

António, slaves and freedmen called, 90, 119, 126, 130, 131, 140, 146, 161–2, 164, 185 n95

Antwerp, 188 n149

apothecary's store, slaves in, 69, 82, 199 n94, 200 n116

appeals, judicial, 117, 122, 123, 211 n88, 268

Arguim: slave-trade, 5, 13, 14, 20–5, 32, 61, 184 n66, 195 n9; other trade, 182 n9, 183 n37

aristocracy: arm slaves, 120, 121, 127; breed slaves, 92; clothe slaves, 93; employ slaves, 62, 80, 85, (in agriculture) 70–1, 85, 86, (hire out) 67, (domestic servants) 63, 64–6, 85, 86; influence legal treatment of slaves, 114, 124, 125, 132, 133; legitimize

aristocracy(*cont.*)
children by slaves, 91; own slaves, 2, 55, 57, 65, 80, 111, 177; sexual intercourse with slaves, 91
Aristotle, 35, 38, 44
Armazém da Guiné, 8, 17, 183 nn20 and 21, 266
arms, bearing of, 120–2, 126, 127, 150, 214 n61
Arraiolos, 57
Arraiolos, count of, 212 n26
Arrais, Amador, 44, 46, 48, 50
Arrifana, 53
art depicting blacks, *see* literature; painting
artisans, *see* guilds
Asia, trade with, 7, 8; *see also* India; Asiatics, 168, 172, 180 n11, 220 n10
Asilah, Morocco, 118
assault: by freedmen, 214 n61; on master, 128, 132; by slaves, 43, 75, 77, 119, 121, 125–8, 130, 131, 132
asylum, 136, 211 n12
Atlantic islands, 47; *see also* Azores; Canary Islands; Cape Verde Islands; Madeira; São Tomé
Atlantic slave-trade, *see* America; re-export
attitudes of blacks to Portuguese: in literature, 169–71; in reality, 171–5, 222 n34
attitudes of Portuguese to blacks, regarding: appearance, 1, 166–7, 170; cleanliness, 77; conceit, 168, 169, 170, 171, 172, (reasons for attitude) 173; criminality, 122, 130, 147, 169, 170, 171, (reasons) 173; good humour, 3, 169; honour and shame, 118, 174, 222 n40; loyalty, 167, 169, (reasons) 173; musicality, 168, 169–172, 221 n20, *see also* music; obedience, 167, 169, (reasons) 173; rudeness, 169–70, (reasons) 172–3; sexuality, 102, 167; stupidity, 39, 167–8, 170, 171, (reasons) 172; trustworthiness, 82, 120, 121, 122, 133; unreasonableness, 78; warlikeness, 3, 167, 168, (reasons) 172, 173; *see also* justification
attitudes of Portuguese to blacks and Moors, compared: favourable to blacks, 108–9, 111, 120–2, 130, 133; favourable to Moors, 82, 102, 135, 220 n12
attitudes of Portuguese to Idzãgen, 39, 108, 167
attitudes of Portuguese to Moors, regarding: appearance, 82, 102, 175, 204 n82; criminality, 76–7, 120–3, 130–1, 168, 169; proclivity to escape, 72, 168; untrustworthiness, 72, 74–5, 76, 120–3, 133, 143, 168, 177; *see also* justification; Moors
attitudes, seigneurial, to slaves, 119, 127, 132–3, 178

Augustine, Saint, 38
Augustinus Triumphus of Ancona, 37
Auto de Dom Fernando, 169, 170, 221 n22
Auto de Vicente Anes Joeira, 171
Aveiro, 53, 60, 110
Avis, 130
Azenegues, Azenũg, *see* Idzãgen
Azevedo, João Lúcio de, 48
Azevedo, Pedro A. de, 152
Azores, 21, 183 n33
Azurara, town, 53, 192 n21; chronicler, *see* Zurara

baço, xiii, 138, 160
Badajoz, 29, 136, 185 n94
Bahia (Baía), Brazil, 61, 151
BaKongo, *see* Kongo, Kongolese
ball games, 107
Balthasar, mage, 168
baptism of blacks, 40–2, 45, 52, 53, 54, 55, 58, 64, 90–1, 111, 149, 150, 161
baraço, 118, 266, 268
Barbacins, African people, 39
Barbary, 16, 28, 172
Barcelona, 29, 176
Barcelos, 127
Barreira, Alonso, 68
Barros, João de, 40, 45, 99, 167, 168
Bartolus of Sassoferrato, 113
Bastião, slaves and freedmen called, 137, 143, 160, 169, 170
batlle of Valencia, 29, 266
Baybry, slave, 40
Beatriz, Infanta, 82, 143, 199 n94
Beatriz, slave charged with witchcraft, 163–4
Beca da Estalagem da Negra, Lisbon, 145
beds: for freedmen, 143; for slaves, 96–7
beggars and vagrants, 48, 87, 88, 97; freedmen as, 147; slaves as, 97, 111
Beira, province: demography, 49, 52, 53–4, 60; slavery in, 86, 87, 131; thieves from, 200 n112; witchcraft in, 163; Beirans, *see* ratinhos
Beja, 120, 125, 158, 211 n9
Belém, 76
Benavente, 193 n32
Benedetto, Saint, 218 n49, 226
Benin, 5–6, 11, 13, 170
bigamy, 159, 160
biscuits for ships, *see* Fornos Reais
blasphemy, 140, 159, 161
boatmen: freedmen, 72, 142, 145, 215 n73; Portuguese, 71–2, 200 n116; slaves, 2, 54, 71–3, 176, 196 n42, 212 n19
boçal, 99
Bojador, Cape, 5, 38
Borba, 57

Borges, Isabel, 158
Bornu, African kingdom, 188 n147
Braga, 97, 102
Bragança, Fernando II, duke of, 140
Bragança, João I, duke of, 92
Brandão, João, 17, 19, 23, 27, 31, 63, 68, 77–8, 79, 83, 87, 88, 145
branding, 13, 108
Braudel, Fernand, 98, 110
brawling, 126, 127, 130, 132–3
Brazil: dances from, 205 n104; discrimination in, 61, 151, 177; emigration to, 47, 48; exile to, 118; Indians, 201 n21, 211 n12; manumission in, 147; Misericórdia in, 151; Rosary in, 156; slavery in, 177, 199 n91; slaves from Portugal married in, 82; slave-trade to, 7, 188 n150
breeding of slaves, 92, 111, 201 n18
Bronseval, Frère Claude de, 54
brotherhoods, religious, see Misericórdia; Rosary
building trades, blacks in, 76, 197 n62; see also carpenters; stone-masons
burials of blacks: at sea, 14; in Portugal, 50, 52, 99, 110, 111, 150, (freedmen) 61, 142, 154–5, (numbers) 53, 54, 55, 57, 58, 60, 61, 65, 66

Ca' da Mosto, Alvise da, 12, 19, 39, 45, 164, 167
Caldas da Rainha, hospital at, 69, 93
câmaras municipais, 266; appoint corretores, 18; control festivities, 106–7; control occupations, 70, 75, 76; control watch, 131; slave law, 69–70, 113, (arms and curfew) 121–3, (assault) 126, (execution of sentence) 128, 130, (gaols) 129, (receiving stolen goods) 123–5
Caminha, Álvaro de, 180 n8
Canaan, see Ham, curse of
Canarians, 105, 119, 189 n7
Canary Islands, 4, 21, 181 n1 to Chapter 1, 188 n155
Cantor, on Gambia, 11
Cape Verde Islands; murder of slaves in, 208 n9; New Christian slave-holder, 196 n24; slave-trade, 5, 9, 10, 11, 15, 20, 21, 23, 30, 182 n14, 183 n33; Cape Verdians, 179
cards, 107
Carneiro, António, 91
Carneiro, Pedro de Alcáçova, 41
Carnero, Juan Antonio, 91
carpenters, slaves as, 80, 199 n86
Carrança, António de, 131
carta de alforria, 138, 139, 140, 141, 142, 158, 212 n29, 266
Cartagena, 29

Carvalho, Fernão, 127
Casa da Guiné e Índia, 8, 9, 15, 17, 19, 83, 183 n21, 266
Casa da Pólvora, 83
Casa da Saúde, in Alcântara, 110
Casa da Sisa, 10, 183 n33
Casa de Ceuta, 8
Casa do Cível, 130, 267, 268
Casa dos Escravos, 8, 9, 15–19, 21, 22, 25, 27, 31, 33, 63, 267
Casas, Bartolomé de las, 42, 44
Castanheira, 214 n67
Castelo Branco, 54
Castile: African dances in, 105–6; breeding of slaves, 201 n18; demography of slaves in, 60, 63; employment of slaves in, 176; freedmen, 145, 212 n29; fugitives in, 134, 136, 147; manumission in, 138, 141, 212 n29; notaries in, 18, 141; penal sale of slaves to, 119, 127, 128, 136, 159; religious knowledge of blacks in, 42; slave-trade to, 4, 10, 22, 23, 28, 29, 30, 178, 183 n37, 186 n107; Castilians, 28, 69, 115, 136
Castro, Álvaro de, 205 n82
Castro, Fernando de, 71, 130
Castro Marim, 119
Catarina, queen of Portugal, 80, 82, 90, 109, 203 n60
cativo, xiii, 134, 181 n13
caulker of ships, freedman, 154
censuses, 19, 50, 55, 57, 87, 192 n13
Cerveira, Afonso, 189 n1
Ceuta, 8, 36, 115, 116
Chafariz del-Rei, 77
chains for slaves, 14, 108, 134, 171, 174, 207 n129
Cha' Masser, Lunardo, 21, 23, 31, 32, 186 n114
Charles V, Holy Roman Emperor and king of Spain, 30
chattel slavery, 17–18, 114, 115, 178
Chiado, António Ribeiro, 170
children, Moorish, 84
children, Portuguese, 77, 108; legal status (similar to freedmen's) 142, (similar to slaves) 116, 125, 126, 131
children, slave: baptism, 41, 55, 90–1; education, 39, 91, 149; illegitimacy, 52, 91, 111, 157; legitimation, 91, 210 n15; manumission, 92, 139, 141; separation from mother, 92, 195 n16; slaves by heredity, 35, 43; slave-trade, 14, 16, 24–5, 39, 92
Chinese, 168
Christ, Order of, 183 n25
Christianity, see Church; clergy; conversion of blacks; papacy and slavery; religion of

Christianity (*cont.*)
blacks; religious education; religious institutions
Church: accepts blacks, 2, 40–1, 50–61, 90–1, 110, 149–65; accepts slavery, 35–8, 45, 149; burials, 110; owns slaves, 2, 63, *see also* religious institutions; policy (towards manumission) 138, 146, (towards marriages of slaves) 104–5; priests' servants, 102; *see also* clergy; conversion; papacy and slavery; religion of blacks; religious education; religious institutions
citizenship: of freedmen, 142, 213 n50; of slaves, 116
Clenardus (? Cleynaerts), Nicolaus, 1, 54–5, 63–4, 68, 86, 91, 92, 96–7, 101–2, 201 n19
clergy, own slaves, 63, 65, 91, 102, 144, 170
cloth: for bedding, 96; for clothing, 92, 93, 94, 95, 142, 202 n33
clothing, 89, 92–6, 111, 201 n21; African, 150; 'clothes of victory', 40; cost, 95–6, 202 n42; at court, 82, 94–6, 202 nn24 and 32; freedmen's, 142, 143; infidels', 42; lack of, 15, 39–40, 185 n76; livery, 92, 93, 202 n27; mourning, 93, 202 n26; sumptuary laws affecting, 95; workclothes, 93–4, 95
Coimbra, 44, 53, 69, 70, 75, 87, 123, 129, 159
Colares, 106–7
Colonna, Egidio (Aegidius Romanus), 37, 38, 39
community of blacks, 2, 89, 90, 111, 112, 148, 155, 206 n118
Commynes, Philippe de, 176
compromisso, 151, 152, 153, 156, 267
Conceição, Nossa Senhora da, Lisbon, 40–1, 55
Condeixa-a-Nova, 54
confirmation, 150
confraternities, religious, *see* Misericórdia; Rosary
contador, auditor, accountant, 8, 13, 267
contraband trade in slaves, 10–11, 30, 188 n155
contractors: of sale of slaves in Lisbon, 17, 22, 23; of slave-trade, 9, 15, 16, 17, 18–19, 22, 29, 30, 31, 32, 33, 183 n37
conversion of blacks: in Africa, 7, 40, 44, 157; appreciated, 167, 168; justification of slavery from, 35, 39; in Portugal, 40–2, 43, 44, 45, 90, 119–20, 141, 149, 152
cooks, slaves as, 69, 80, 84, 95, 99, 146, 199 n91
Correia, Ambrósio, 115
corretores, brokers of slaves and livestock, 18, 19, 186 n101

Cortes, 267, 268; positions regarding: employment of slaves, 28, 54, 64, 131; freedmen, 125, 145; ownership of slaves, 63, 174; slave crime, 69–70, 106, 117, 120, 122, 124, 126, 222 n40; slave-trade, 28, 48, 54
coutos, see asylum
Covilhã, 54, 207 n144
creole languages in West Africa, 100
Crete, 176
criados, 66, 70, 85, 96, 115, 116, 127, 144, 148, 151, 267; *criados a bem fazer*, 85, 86, 267
crier (*pregueiro*) in treasury, black, 94–5
crime, committed by blacks, 117–31, 142; incidence of, 130–1; *see also* attitudes, and under individual crimes
critics of slave-trade and enslavement, 3, 36, 42–4, 45–6, 168; governmental response to, 44
crown: owns slaves, 2, 62, 76, 80–4, 92, 93, 94, 95, 96, 111, 141, 177, 197 n62, 198 nn81 and 85; participation in slave-trade, 4–34, *passim*
Cruz, Filipe da, 162–3, 164
Cubelos, Pedro, 126
Cuelbis, Jakob, 145
culture, African, 2, 89, 94, 150, 160, 162–4, 165
Cumba, slave, 116
Cunha, Maria da, freedwoman, 158
curfew, 120, 121, 122
customs clearance of slaves, 9, 10, 15, 16, 21, 22, 28, 31–2, 183 nn32, 33 and 37
Cyprus, 176

dances, 168, 203 n66; African, 2, 89, 105–7, 112, 205 n104; in churches, 150; law against, 106–7, 112, 142, 205 n104; Moorish and Jewish, 105, 205 n101
death penalty, 115, 119, 121, 122, 127, 128, 131, 160
debt incurred by blacks, 143, 214 n61
demography: of blacks, 2, 47–61, 177, 178, 194 n56, 201 n15, (in Antiquity and Middle Ages) 181 n2 to Introduction, (freedmen) 144–5, 148, (ratio of men to women), 60, 61, 194 nn59 and 61; comparison with America, 147, 177–8; of Moors, 1, 52, 57, 72, 113–14, 166; of other peoples, 180 n11; *see also* Antwerp; Sicily; Spain
de Witte, Charles-Martial, 37
discrimination: by colour, 174, 175, (in America) 151, 177–8, 223 n15, (in confraternities), 151, 152, 153, 217 n22, (in fugitive rewards), 135, (in holy orders) 157–8, (in marriage) 147, 148, 215 n87,

(in wages) 84; by juridical status: freedmen (in jobs) 11, 72, 125, 145, 148, 176, (in law) 2, 125, 142, 143, 148, (in manumission) 147; by juridical status: slaves (baptism) 55, 90, 91, (in law) 103, 113–33, 136; by religion, 62–3, 75–6, 120–2, 135, 136, 174, 175, 195 nn4 and 5; by sex, 102–5, 126, 215 n87
disease, of slaves, 16, 18, 109–10, 141, 154; see also hospitals; medical care of blacks
dízima, 9, 10, 15, 183 nn32 and 33, 267
Domingos, slave, 139
Domínguez Ortiz, Antonio, 59
Dominicans, 152
Douro, river, boatmen on, 71, 72
Duarte, king of Portugal, 135, 189 n7
Dum Diversas, bull (1452; also known as Divino Amore Communiti), 37, 40

Eça, Rodrigo de, 128
education of blacks, 39, 91, 101–2, 146, 157, 215 n85; see also literacy; religious education
Elmina, see São Jorge da Mina
Elvas: baptism of blacks, 55, 192 n15; bigamist from, 160; burials of blacks, 110; demography, 57, 60, 61; employment of blacks, 67, 69, 78, 86, 197 n53; freedmen in, 61, 141, 144; free labourers in, 69, 87; law affecting blacks, 78, 86, 103, 118, 121, 125, 128; manumission in, 139; slave-trade from, 29
emancipation, see abolition of slavery and slave-trade; manumission
embroiderer, freedman, 154
emigration from Portugal, 2, 47, 48, 49, 50, 87, 88
employment of slaves, reasons for, 2, 47–50, 61, 62, 68, 85–8, 98, 176–7; see also occupations of blacks
England, 212 n29
English corsairs, 12, 33
Engrácia, freedwoman, 144
enslavement for crime, 135, 143
Entre-Douro-e-Minho, province: demography, 49, 52, 53, 60; slavery in, 87
Entre-Tejo-e-Odiana, see Alentejo
escape, see fugitives
escheat of property belonging to blacks, 144, 214 n67
escravo, xiii, 114; escravo branco, xiii; escravo forro, xiii, 142
esparto industry, 69
Estremadura, province: demography, 49, 54, 59, 60; slavery in, 70; see also Lisbon; Ribatejo
Estremoz, 57
'Ethiopians' (i.e., blacks), 26, 157

evaluation of slaves, 15, 16, 25, 26, 28, 119, 207 n134; see also prices
Évora, 47, 97; baptisms, 55, 201 nn6 and 10; burials, 65, 66; demography, 1, 57, 58, 59, 60, 61, 194 nn59 and 61; education of blacks, 101–2, 215 n85; employment of blacks, 58, 63, 64, 75, 78, 79, 80, 86, 197 nn45 and 53, 199 n87; freedmen in, 127, 141, 142, 146; fugitives from, 108; games, 107; Inquisition, 159, 163; law affecting blacks, 75, 79, 107, 121, 124, 125, 129, 130; manumission, 138, 139; Misericórdia, 151; music, 106; pawn of slave, 115; plague regulations, 109; religious education, 157, 158, 218 n37; Rosary, 151, 154; sexual relations in, 102, 103, 104; witchcraft in, 163
Excelente Senhora, see Juana de Castilla
exile as punishment, 115–16, 118, 119, 121, 127, 131, 135, 143
Eximiae Devotionis, bull (1513), 41
Exponi Nobis, brief (1518), 157
extradition of fugitives from Castile, 134, 136

factors (feitores): in Africa, 13; of Casa da Guiné, 8, 15, 83
fala de Guiné, de negros, see language of blacks
Falcoa, Justa, 115
families of blacks, see children, slave; marriages; sexual relations
Faria, Manuel Severim de, 47, 48–50, 61
Fazenda, royal, 8, 267
feitores, see factors
Fernandes, Bastião, criado, 127
Fernandes, Domingos, freedman, 215 n88
Fernandes, João, mulatto priest, 158
Fernandes, Jorge, slave, 131
Fernando, Infante, 212 n26
Fernando, Infante, Grand Master of Order of Santiago, 125
Fernando, slaves and freedmen called, 90, 169, 170, 171, 173
festivities of blacks, 105–7, 112, 142, 203 n66; religious, 2, 150, 152, 206 n118
feuds, involving slaves, 127, 132
Fieis de Deus, 14
Filipa, Infanta, 158, 214 n64
Filipe III, king of Portugal (Felipe IV of Spain), 44
fines, 124, 131; on abettors of fugitives, 135; on freedmen, 143, 214 n61; on slaves, 118, 121, 125–6, 128, 129, 130
fiscalization of slave-trade, see customs clearance of slaves
fishermen, 215 n86; and slaves, 53, 71, 72
Flanders, 30, 220 n14

Florence, 30; Florentines, 18, 23, 29
folklore, blacks in 166, 168, 220 n1
Fonseca, Diogo da, 196 n24
food for blacks: in Africa, 38–9; on ship, 13, 14, 184 n66; in Portugal, 69, 89, 97–8, 106, 111, 124, 129, 163, (cost of) 97–8, 129, 203 n55, (general insufficiency) 48
Fornos Reais, 8; Vale de Zebro (burial of slaves) 110, (employment of slaves), 83–4, 85, 197 nn. 52 and 60, (maintenance of slaves) 93–4, 95, 96, 97, 98, 109, (punishment of slaves), 207 n. 129, (wood from freedman for), 144
forro, xiii, 140, 142
foundry, naval, slaves in, 83
France, free soil, 134, 136
Francisco, slaves called, 126, 161
Francisco de Cor Baço, East Indian, 138–9
fraud, 76, 123, 143
freedmen, 134, 141–7, 148; clothing, 142, 143; crime, 130, 143, 147; demography, 52–61 passim; education, 101; housing, 125, 143–6, 160; laws affecting, 76, 78, 79, 106; literary depiction of, 170–1; marriage and sexual relations, 55, 104, 146–7, 160, 215 n87; medical care, 109; Misericórdia, 151; music and dance, 106; occupations, 11, 12, 52, 70, 72, 74–9 passim, 82, 137, 144–6, 215 n86; poverty, 2, 141–2, 143, 147–8, 153, 154; religion, 3, 150, 151–8, 161, 165; Rosary, 3, 78, 151–8, 165; as slave-holders, 62; witches, 162; word for, xiii; see also citizenship; discrimination; property rights; status; testimony; wills
free labour, in relation to slave: same occupations, 66, 69, 70, 71, 72, 78, 80, 82, 85, 176, (displace slaves) 72, 82, (displaced by slaves) 48, 86, (slaves affect working conditions) 67, 84, 87, 198 n72; similar behaviour, 127, 172–4, 222 n40; status, 114–15, 132; treatment compared, 52, 72, 82, 87, 89, 94, 95, 108, 110, 115, 118, 123, 126, 131–3; wages, 84, 200 n118
Freire, André, 157
French corsairs, 12, 33
Frois (? Flores), Beira, 131
Frorença (? Florença), Domingos de, slave, 80, 199 n91
fugitives, 71–2, 106, 134–8, 147, 148, 155, 162, 167, 173, 212 n19
Fula, African people, 161
Funchal, Madeira, 116, 152, 157
Furnando, Furunando, see Fernando

Galicians, 78
galleys, 119, 121, 127, 160

Gama, Diogo da, 214 n63
Gama, Estêvão da, 139, 213 n42, 214 n63
Gama, Rui da, 195 n16
Gambia, river, 11, 12
gaols, 71, 122, 123, 127, 128–30, 135, 208 n9; escape from, 118, 129–30, 211 n12; of Inquisition, 162; private, 108
garbage and excrement, slaves in removal of 75, 78, 81, 176
Garcia, slave, 197 n52
gardeners: freedmen, 144; slaves, 69, 80, 176, 177, 199 nn 87 and 88
Garrido, João, 137–8
Genoa, 28, 30, 176, 222 n2, 223 n12
gifts: to freedmen, 143–4, 148, 154–5, 156, 214 nn61, 63 and 64; to religious fraternities, 154; to slaves for freedom, 139
Gil, Lopo, 141
Godinho, Vitorino Magalhães, 28, 50, 194 n56, 196 n42, 220 n10
godparents, 90, 91, 146, 201 nn6, 7 and 10, 215 n86
Góis, Damião de, humanist, 27
gold trade in West Africa, see São Jorge da Mina
Gomes, António, slave, 127
Gomes, Gaspar, freedman, 214 n61
Gomes, João, freedman, 214 n53
Gomes, Manuel, 126
Gomes da Mina, Fernão, 32, 105
Graciosa, fort in Morocco, 116
grammar-teacher, freedman, 146
Grammatica Aethiopica, 102
Guadalquivir, river, 28, 29
Guarda, 212 n32
guilds, 2, 71–2, 74, 145, 197nn 45 and 47, 200 n116; attitude (to freedmen) 145, (to slaves) 74–5, 87, 88, 176, 200 n116, 223 n12
Guimarães, 207 n134
Guinea: fugitive in, 137; slaves from, 28, 63, 163, 167; slave-trade from, 5–33 passim 40, 45, 108, 154
Guiomar, slaves called, 90, 185 n95

Ham, curse of, 38, 39, 190 n18, 220 n10
Henrique, bishop of Utica, 157
Henrique, Infante, administrator of the Order of Christ, 45, 66–7, 152; regulates slave-trade, 7, 8, 9, 183 n25; religious attitudes, 37, 191 n54; sponsors voyages to West Africa, 1, 2, 4, 37, 181 n8
Henriques, Leonor, freedwoman, 173
Henry the Navigator, see Henrique, Infante
herbalist doctor, black stage character, 171
herdsmen, 86; own slaves, 63; slaves as, 69, 70, 80, 95, 176, 199 n89

hiring out slaves, 11, 12, 58, 67, 75, 84, 176, 197 n53
Hispaniola, 31, 188 n152
holy orders, blacks in, 140, 143, 149, 156–8, 135
homosexuality among blacks, 159, 160
horse-racing, 107, 143
hospitals: freedmen in, 142, 143, 207 nn133 and 134; slaves in, 67, 69, 93, 97, 98, 111; treatment in, 109, 142
Hostiensis, Henricus de Segusio, 37

Idzāgen: clothing, 39, 92; enslavement justified, 35, 36, 39; good slaves, 167; good treatment, 108; own blacks, 5, 38; raided by Portuguese, 5, 9; trade with Portuguese, 5, 12; words for, 180 n6, 181 n3; see also attitudes of Portuguese to
illegitimacy, see children
Illius qui, bull (1442), 37
Imbangala, African people, 31, 34
India: breeding of slaves in, 92; emigration to, 47; trade with, 8, 32–3, 34, 88
Indians: American, 42, 46, 180 n11, 201 n21, 211 n12; East Indians, 72, 75, 77, 135, 138, 153, 157, 168, 172
Inês, slave, 103
informers: blacks, 101, 159, 161, 164; whites, 115, 116, 160
Innocent IV, pope, 37
inns: blacks in, 97, 124; free blacks keep, 145
Inquisition, 68, 99, 101, 137, 150, 158–64, 170, 204 n76
Institutes of Justinian, 114
insubordination, 128, 159, 174
interpreters, black, 12, 62, 99, 100, 137–8, 145, 155, 219 n65
insurrections, lack of in Portugal, 107, 126, 127, 132–3, 174; in São Tomé, 107; on ship, 14–15
Istanbul, 176
Italy, slave-trade to, 29–30

Japanese slaves, 168
Jerónimo, slaves called, 29, 127
jester, black, 82–3, 199 n98
Jews: abused, 108; attitudes to, 108, 143; curse of Ham, 38, 190 n18; denounced to Inquisition, 159; expelled, 42; legal discrimination against, 63, 120, 124, 135, 136; music and dance, 105; own slaves, 62–3, 195 nn4 and 5
Joana, Infanta, 168
João I, king of Portugal, 120
João II, king of Portugal: appoints corretores, 18; legislation (on Jewish slave-

holders) 63, (on slaves) 114, 125–6; policy (toward manumission) 137–8, 155, 212 n29, (toward Rosary) 152, 154, 155; slaves at court, 40, 94
João III, king of Portugal: correspondence with Fernando de Castro, 71, 130; Inquisition, 159; legislation (on infidels' clothing) 42, (on slaves) 107, 117, 119, 121, 122, 125; Moorish dancers at court, 205 n101; policy (toward freedmen) 125, 148, (toward Rosary) 155; slaves at court, 80, 82, 94; slaves in royal industry, 83, 84; slave-trade, 7, 23, 30
João, Mestre, surgeon, 146
João, slaves and freedmen called, 117, 118, 144, 157
Jorge, freedman, 141
Juana de Castilla, the Excelente Senhora, 199 n94
Juiz da Guiné, 8, 15, 267
Juliana, slave and freedwoman called, 90
justification: acquisition of slaves, 35–46 (by trade) 3, 7, 38, 40, 45, 46, 191 n54, (by war) 36–7, 43, 45, 46; of enslavement of Africans (bestiality), 3, 37, 38–9, 40, 45, 189 n7, 190 n29, (curse of Ham) 38–9, 190 n18, 220 n10, (in literature) 3, 166, 167, 169, (natural slaves) 3, 38, 39, 40, 44, 167, 168, (result of sin) 38–9

Kayor, Damel of, 164
Kongo, 39, 167, 180 n8, 206 n112; evangelized, 7, 40, 157; in slave-trade, 7, 13, 21, 31, 33, 186 n110; Kongolese, 101, 157, 167, 170, 215 n85

labour conditions, for slaves, 68; see also free labour
labourers, 88, 197 n47; blacks as, 2, 76, 79, 84, 85, 141, 148, 154, 176, 197 n52; as slave-holders, 62, 63, 75, 84, 177, 195 n8, 197 n52
ladinhos, 101
Lagos, Algarve: demography, 58; procuradores' view of blacks, 117, 222 n40; Rosary 151; slave-trade, 5, 25, 35, 45, 92, 149, 167
Lamego, 200 n113
Landi, Giulio, count, 47, 103, 108, 167–8, 174, 198 n72
language of blacks, 2, 89, 98–102, 146; comparison with United States, 203 n63, 204 n69; fala de Guiné, 99–101, 105, 111–12, 168, 169, 203 n66, 267
Larache, Morocco, 116
law: canon, on slavery, 35, 37, 43, 113, 156; Portuguese, on slaves and freedmen, 2, 113–33, 142–3, 177–8, see also under

law (cont.)
  individual crimes; Roman on slavery, 35,
    43, 113, 115, 116, 128
lay piety, 150–6, 158
Leão, Duarte Nunes do, 48, 50, 114, 122
Ledesma, Martín de, 44, 168
legitimation, see children
Leiria, 152
Leis Extravagantes, 114
Lemos, Francisco de, 91
Leo X, pope, 40, 157
Leonor, Infanta, 105
Leonor, queen of Portugal, 82, 151
lezírias, 54, 86
licencia de libertad, 138
Lisbon, 179; administration of slave law,
  115, 121, 124, 125, 129, 130, 131; archbishop of, 19, 41–2, 99, 102, 104; baptism of blacks, 40, 201 n6; burials of
  blacks, 110; Cortes, 48, 50, 88; dances
  and gatherings, 106–7; demography, 1,
  54–7, 59, 60, 61, 188 n149, 201 n15;
  employment of blacks, 2, 48, 49, 63, 67,
  68, 71–80, 81, 83, 84, 87, 88, 195 n16,
  197 n60, 199 n87, 200 n116; freedmen,
  125, 130, 141–6, 148; fugitives from, 71,
  137; grain supply, 49, 54; Inquisition,
  159–61; Jewish slave-holders, 63; language of blacks, 99; literary depiction of
  blacks, 169; manumission, 139; Misericórdia, 151; Moors, 42, plague control,
  109–10; religious education, 157; religious festivities, 150, 154; Rosary, 152–6;
  slavery, 176; slave-trade, 8–34 passim,
  40, 41, 53, 88, 108, 183 n32; thieves,
  200 n112; wealth of property-owners, 88,
  187 n133
literacy of blacks, 39, 91, 101, 146, 204 n76
literature, depiction of blacks in, 99, 100,
  101, 105, 166–72, 203 n66, 221 nn16 and
  21
livre, 140
Lobo, A. de Sousa Silva Costa, 48
Lopes, António, freedman, 160
Lopes, Duarte, 167
Lopes, Henrique, 171
Loreto, Nossa Senhora do, Lisbon, 144
Loulé, 27, 125, 130, 131, 141, 144
Lourenço, Isabel, 144
Lourenço, Pedro, freedman, 144
Luís, Infante, 80
Luís, slave, 201 n7
Luís, Álvaro, 144
Luzia, literary character, 170, 171, 173

Madeira, 21, 116, 163, 177, 183 n33,
  186 n113, 198 n72
Madre de Deus, convent, Lisbon, 195 n16

Magalhães, Joaquim Antero Romero, 87,
  194 n55
Magi, adoration of, 168, 220 n14
magic, 152; see also witchcraft
maintenance of slaves, 110–11, 129,
  198 n85; cost, 80–1, 83, 95–6, 97–8, 109,
  118; see also accommodation; clothing;
  food for blacks; medical care of blacks
Málaga, 91
Malindi, Kenya, 182 n9
Mane, African people, 23, 34
Mani Kongo, 7, 20, 157, 164–5, 206 n126
Manuel, freedman, 158
Manuel I, king of Portugal, 105; gives
  slaves to hospitals, 67; Inquisition, 158;
  legislation (on freedmen), 142, (on
  fugitives) 135, (on slaves) 114, 118, 121,
  124, 126, 205 n104; plague control, 109,
  110; policy towards Rosary, 154, 155;
  promotes Christianity, 40, 41, 45, 149,
  157, 190 n31; provides for burial of slaves,
  110; regulates regateiras, 78; slaves at
  court, 94; slaves in royal industry, 83, 84;
  slave-trade, 10, 13
manumission, 2, 3, 134, 138–41, 214 n56;
  by carta de alforria, 138–41; conditional,
  138–41; by court action, 116–17, 155–6;
  by flight and return, 137; frequency of,
  147; opposition to, 130, 134, 140, 147,
  155–6; by promise of service, 139; by
  purchase, 91, 116, 138–9, 169, 195 n5,
  213 n33; reasons for, 12, 61, 63, 92, 174,
  212 n26; revocable, 142; Rosary promotes, 155–6, 165, 217 n34; unconditional, 138, 140–1; by will, 138, 139,
  140, 144, 147, 155–6; see also carta de
  alforria
Marchionni, Bartolomeo, 18, 29, 32
Margarida, freedwoman, 138, 139
Maria, queen of Portugal, 140, 214 n64
Maria, slaves and freedwomen called, 90,
  115, 201 n10, 214 n63
marketwomen, see regateiras
marriages: of blacks, 55, 103–5, 111, 144,
  147, 148, 150, (arranged) 82, (common
  law) 104, 215 n87, (with mourisco) 214 n52
  (with whites) 103, 146, 147, 148, 215 n88;
  condition of freedom, 140, 143; status of
  African marriage, 156
Mauritania, 5, 19, 20, 33, 36, 45, 180 n6
medical care of blacks, 16, 89, 109–10,
  207 n134; see also disease; hospitals
Medina del Campo, 29
Mediterranean countries, 1, 35, 98, 176,
  177, 181 n2 to Introduction
meios forros, 140, 156, 213 n42, 268
meirinho, 131, 268
Melo, Fernão de, 206 n126

Mendes, António, mulatto prior of Alcochete, 158, 218 n49
Mendonça, António de, 127
Mercado, Tomás de, 44, 46
merchants: of slaves, 17, 22, 43, 44, 62, 63, 195 nn4 and 5, (African) 5, 44; own slaves, 63, 64, 65
migrant labour, see ratinhos
mill, slaves in, 84, 94, 97, 110
Mina, see São Jorge da Mina
Miragaia, Oporto, 53
Miranda do Douro, 213 n32
Misericórdia, Santa Casa da: black members, 151, 216 nn9, 10; blacks treated in hospital, 142; buries blacks, 50, 52, 55, 57, 59, 61, 110, 141, 163, 197 n45; feeds slaves in gaol, 129
Molina, Luis de, 44, 46
Monção, 53
Moncarapacho, 58, 61, 70, 85, 96, 194 n59
Monchique, Serra do, 58
Mondego, river, 70, 75
Montargil, 97
Montemor-o-Novo, 57, 125
Montijo, see Aldeia Galega
Moors: badly treated, 108–9, 111, 165; crime, 75, 120, 121, 122, 128, 130, 131, 174; curse of Ham, 38, 190 n18; distrusted, 2, 72, 74–5, 120, 121, 122, 133, 143, 168, 177; fugitives, 71–2, 134, 135, 137, 168; language, 101, 169; in Middle Ages, 5, 62, 74, 113, 138, 166; multiple owners of, 213 n41; music and dance, 105, 205 n100; in North Africa, 45, 118, 137, 147; not Christians, 59, 164; occupations, 12, 28, 71, 74, 78, 199 nn86 and 89; priests, 157; prisoners of war, 5, 36, 37, 172, 209 n33; word for, xiii, 8, 114, 149, 180 n8; see also attitudes; demography; discrimination; ransoms
mordomos, 152, 153, 154, 268
Morocco, 4, 95, 115, 116, 137, 181 n1 to Chapter 1; Sharif of, 167
mortality of blacks, 14, 52
Mosselbaai, South Africa, 206 n112
Mota, Henrique da, 170
mouriscos: discrimination against, 75, 122; employment of, 75, 76, 199 n94; fugitives, 137; manumission of, 213 n42; and Rosary, 153; status in society, 143, 148
mouro, xiii, 113, 114
Mozambique, 66, 197 n52
Mugem, 152; see also Ribeira de Muge
mulato, xiii, 175
mulattoes: attitudes of, to Portuguese, 222 n34; attitudes of Portuguese to, 168, 172, 174–5, 220 n1, 221 n20, 222 n41; crime, 130, 159; discrimination against,

153, 177; language of, 101; literary depiction of, 101, 171; in modern times, 178, 179, 223 n23; occupations, 49, 75, 77, 146; poverty, 142, 214 n61; religion, 153, 157, 158, 218 n49; sale of, 185 n95; sexual relations, 91, 102, 103, 160, 163, 215 n87; word for, xiii, 180 n6
municipalities, see câmaras municipais
Münzer, Hieronymus, 54, 63, 83
Murcia, 29
murder: by slaves, 43, 121, 127, 130, (of master) 128; of slaves, 14, 108, 115, 116, 117, 127, 131, 159, 208 n9
music, 150, 168, 169, 201 n5; African, 2, 89, 105–6, 150
musical instruments, 106, 150, 168, 169, 206 nn110 and 114
Muslims, see Idzãgen; Moors; religion of blacks
mutilation: of ears, 122, 123, 135; of hands, 128

names of blacks, 89, 90; abusive, 108, 170–1; indicating colour and status, xii–xiii; see also under individual words
Naples, kingdom of, 222 n2
negro, xii, 167, 178
New Christians, 63, 68, 143, 148, 159, 178, 196 n24
Nicholas V, pope, 5, 38
Noronha, Maria de, slave, 95, 96, 98
notaries public: in manumission, 141; own slaves, 65, 80; in sale of slaves, 18, 185 n95
Nubia, 167; Nubians, 218 n49
Nūn, Cape, 38
Nunes, Fernão, 116
Nunes, Leonor, freedwoman, 214 n61
Nunes, Simão, 139

obstruction of justice, 120, 124–5, 127, 132
occupations of blacks, 2, 62–88, 144–5, 177; see also agriculture and under individual occupations
old people, see age of slaves
olive industry, slaves in, 54, 69, 70, 77, 81, 200 n116
Oliveira, Cristóvão Rodrigues de, 19, 55, 74, 87, 88, 145
Oliveira, Fernão de, 43–4, 46, 68, 147
Oliveira, W. F., xiii
Olivença, 49, 57, 90
Oporto: baptism of slaves, 53, 201 n6; bigamy, 160; demography, 53, 59, 60; freedmen, 53, 146; Misericórdia, 93, 207 n134, 216 n9; occupations of slaves, 71–2, 74; sexual relations between races, 103; slave-holders, 53, 64; slave law, 121,

Oporto (cont.)
124; slave-trade, 16, 183 n32
Ordenações Afonsinas, 113, 114, 122
Ordenações Manuelinas, 114, 123, 126, 162
ownership of slaves, 2, 27, 53, 57, 62–88
passim, 114, 120, 132, 195 n9; numbers
owned, 66, 67, 70, 80; and see under individual entries of occupations

paintings depicting blacks, 166, 168,
220 n14
Pais, Álvaro, bishop of Silves, 38, 189 n4
palaces, royal, slaves in, 80, 82, 83, 94–6,
198 n81, 199 nn87, 88
Palermo, 188 n147, 218 n49
Palhais, 160
Palos, 201 n18
papacy and slavery, 5, 36, 37, 38, 40–1,
191 n43
pardo, xiii, 180 n6, 215 n87
pardons: to freedmen, 140, 143, 214 n61;
to masters, 115–16, 208 n9; to slaves,
117, 119–20, 126–32 passim, 162, 174
pastimes, 106–7, 112, 146; see also festivities
patronage aids freedmen, 145–6, 148
pawn, slaves left in, 115
peça de escravo, 24, 25, 184 n62, 268
peculium, 116, 138
Pedro, Infante, 47
Pedro, Kongolese, 157
Pedro, slaves and freedmen called, 137,
139, 197 n52
Pedro de Madrill (? Madrid), slave,
201 n5
Pelagius, Alvarus, see Pais, Álvaro
Pelourinho Velho, 17
pena de armas, 125–6
Peña Guillén, 136
Penela, 54
Peniche, 137
Penitentes da Paixão de Cristo, convent,
Lisbon, 195 n16
Pereira, Duarte Pacheco, 19
Peru, 31, 33
Piacenza, 47
pingar, 108, 116, 171, 268
Pinto, João, informer, 101, 161
Pinto, João, Kongolese, 215 n85
Pires, Gomes, 5
Pires, Juliana, freedwoman, 90, 201 n7
Pires, Sebastião, 169
plague, control of, 109–10
plantations, 13, 70–1, 176, 177, 178
Plasencia, 195 n8
Plumb, J. H., 46
Poço dos Negros, Poço Novo, Poço Seco, 110
police: molest freedwomen, 155; slaves
assist, 131; police legislation, 120–2, 142–3

Pombal, Sebastião José de Carvalho e
Melo, marquês de, 178
population of Portugal, 2, 49, 200 n117;
considered ample, 48, 88; considered
insufficient, 47–8; growth of, 84, 88;
see also demography
portagem, 183 n37, 213 n50, 268
Porto Pisano, 30
ports of landing for slaves in Portugal, 10,
15, 21, 22, 23, 25, 28, 53
Portugal, northern, 48, 49, 50, 52–4, 59,
61, 87; southern, 2, 48, 49, 50, 54–8, 59,
61, 69, 86, 88, 201 n15
Póvoa das Paredes, 71
Póvoa de Varzim, 53
Praça dos Escravos, Lisbon, 17
pregão, 118, 268
preto, xii, 178
prices of slaves, 16, 24–7, 28, 29, 31, 33–4,
63, 88, 92, 95, 138, 187 nn123 and 125–8,
189 n164, 201 n17; in relation to disposable income, 26, 27, 34, 187 n133
priests, black, see holy orders
procuradores, see Cortes
profit from slave-labour, 77, 79–80, 98
profit-sharing by masters and slaves, 67,
74, 77, 176
property rights: of freedmen, 142, 144,
214 n52; of slaves, 116
prostitutes: black, 215 n74; own slaves, 62,
195 n16; rape of, 102
provedor, 268; dos Armazens da Guiné, 119;
of Vale de Zebro, 96
provenance of slaves: blacks, 5, 7, 15–16,
19, 20, 21, 23, 33, 182 n14, 186 n110,
188 n147; others, 1, 4, 5, 180 n11; see also
Asiatics; Idzāgen; Indians; Moors
proverbs, 166, 168
punishment: of abettors of fugitives, 135;
of freedmen, 143; by law, 118–19, 121,
122, 123, 125, 126, 127, 128, 131, 132,
222 n40; by masters, 89, 107–9, 111, 117,
132, 174, 208 n9

quarto, 9, 16, 268
Quinta da Lagea, near Alenquer, 193 n33
Quiroz, Lionel, meirinho, 131

race relations, 166–75; see also attitudes;
discrimination; justification; treatment
ransoms: blacks, 182 n9; Moors, 5, 138,
140, 172, 182 n9, 209 n33, 212 n31,
213 n40
rape and sexual violation, 52, 89, 102–3,
111, 192 n17; see also sexual relations
ratinhos, migrant workers from Beira, 78,
86, 87, 215 n87
Reboredo, António and Diogo, 127

recebedor da vintena, see almoxarife dos escravos
Receiver of 'Moors, Mooresses, parrots and other things', 8
receiving stolen goods, 123–5, 155
re-export of slaves, 2, 4, 10, 20, 22, 23, 28–31, 34, 42, 136, 187 n138, 188 nn152 and 155
regateiras, regatões: blacks as, 2, 58, 76–9, 80, 81, 85, 86, 143, 155, 160, 200 n116; restrictions on, 78–9; slaves as, in Southern Europe, 176
regulation of trade, *see* slave-trade
religion of blacks; Christianity, 2, 3, 35, 39, 40–6, 50, 52, 59, 62–3, 68, 74–5, 90, 93, 101, 104, 110, 111, 116, 119–20, 124, 137, 139, 140, 141, 149–65, 167, 169, 172, 195 n5, (apostasy) 137, 180 n8, (heterodoxy) 150, 152, 159, 161, 162, 164; Islam, 42, 137, 161, 164, 190 n38; paganism, 3, 37, 40, 45, 50, 90, 102, 124, 152, 157, 162, 164, 165, 180 n8
religious education and knowledge, of blacks, 41–2, 43, 46, 90, 91, 149, 157, 160, 161, 162, 169, 170, 171, 219 n59
religious institutions, own slaves, 2, 17, 63, 64, 65, 67, 139, 149, 195 n16; *see also* hospitals
Resende, André de, 147
Resende, Garcia de, 4, 40, 57, 119, 147
resgate, 182 n9; *see also* ransoms
retainers, slaves as, *see* aristocracy
Ribatejo, land on either side of the middle Tagus, 71, 86, 87
Ribeira das Naus, *see* shipyards
Ribeira de Muge, Paços da, 80, 198 n81; *see also* Mugem
Río de Oro, 5, 23
Rio dos Escravos, *see* Slave Rivers
Rios da Guiné, 7, 13
Rodrigues, Bastião, freedman, 160
Rodrigues, Joana, slave, 201 n7
Rodrigues Soropita, Fernão, 170
Romanus Pontifex, bull (1455), 5, 38
Rosary, confraternity of Our Lady of the (Nossa Senhora do Rosário), 2, 78, 105, 148, 151–6, 165, 217 nn20, 25 and 27, 217 n34, 218 n49, 226
Rossio, Lisbon, 107

Sá, João de, called Panasco, 82–3, 199 n98
Sá de Miranda, Francisco de, 108
Sado, river, 10, 58, 86, 124
Sagres, 7, 66
Sahara, 29, 59
Sahel, 19, 179
sailors, *see* boatmen; seamen
Saint John Evangelist, order of, 157

Salamanca, 29
sale of slaves, 17–19, 22, 43, 162, 185 n95; by *almoxarife dos escravos,* 9, 16, 17; at auction, 5, 17, 35, 129; by contractors in Lisbon, 17, 22, 23; laws regarding, 17, 18, 35; markets, 53, 136; taxes on (*portagem*) 183 n37, 213 n50, 260, (*sisa*) 9, 10, 15, 28, 183 n37, 268; *see also corretores*
saltpans, slaves work in, 58, 86, 124
Santa Cruz do Castelo, Lisbon, 55, 57, 192 n15
Santa Justa, Lisbon, 55, 145
Santa Maria da Graça, Setúbal, 58
Santa Maria das Neves, 11
Santa Maria do Castelo, Alcácer do Sal, 58, 104–5
Santarém: bigamist from, 160; blacks protest at, 174, 207 n129; employment of blacks, 54, 67, 70; law affecting slaves, 70, 106, 107, 124, 126; manumission, 139, 140
Santiago, Cape Verde Islands, 5, 20, 183 n28
Santiago, order of, 82, 125
Santo Eloi, house of order of Saint John Evangelist, Lisbon, 157
Santo Estêvão, Lisbon, 55
Santos, suburb of Lisbon, 68, 195 n16
São Domingos: Dominican houses (Elvas) 195 n16, 218 n49, (Lisbon) 153, 154
São Fins, Jesuit house, Lisbon, 99
São Francisco da Cidade, Franciscan house, Lisbon, 150
São João, house of order of Saint John Evangelist, Xabregas, 157
São Jorge da Mina, gold trade at, 5, 7, 32, 33, 34, 154, 186 n114, 189 n166; Lisbon blacks at, 154, 215 n74
São Pedro: (Évora) 57, (Lisbon) 55
São Romão, Alentejo, 179
São Tiago, Lisbon, 55
São Tomé, island, 180 n8; exile to, 135; plantations on, 13, 177; Rosary in, 152, 155; slave revolts on, 107; slave-trade from, 7, 9, 11, 13, 14, 15, 21, 23, 30, 32, 183 n33, 184 n66, 188 n152, 217 n28
São Vicente de Fora, Lisbon, 55, 146
São Vicente do Cabo, monastery, Algarve, 66, 149
Saracens, 37; *see also* Moors
Šašek, Vaclav, 16, 17, 26, 28, 53, 57
Sassetti, Filippo, 23, 167–8, 187 n120
seamen: black, 2, 11, 12, 145, 154, 155, 197 n52, 215 n73, (affect naval tactics) 12, (similar to slave seamen elsewhere) 176, 180 n11; white, 63, 75, 126, 197 n52, 215 n86
Sebastião king of Portugal, xiii–xiv, 10, 95

Senegal, river, 5, 19
Senegambia, 7, 16, 161
Sequeira, Diogo Lopes de, 70, 109, 202 n26
Serers, African people, 39
Serpa, 102
Serra, Paços da, 80, 95
servants, domestic, 80, 88; blacks as, 2, 43, 62, 63, 64–71, 82, 85, 86, 92, 93, 94, 95, 132, 141, 166, 176; slave-holders, 63, 65; whites as, 64, 67, 108, 132
servo, xiii
Setúbal: demography, 58; employment of slaves, 67; feud in, 127; Inquisition, 152, 159, 161, 162; law affecting slaves, 124, 125; Rosary, 152; slave-trade, 10
Seure, chevalier du, 32, 189 n164
Seville, 22, 23, 29, 30, 176
sexual relations, extramarital: bigamy, 159, 160; of blacks, 92, 103–5, 111, 170, (with whites) 91, 92, 102–5, 159, 160, 163, 170, 171, 173, 201 n19, 215 n87; breeding of slaves, 92, 111, 201 n18; homosexuality, 159, 160; involving Moors, 102, 204 n82; rape and violation, 52, 89, 102–3, 111, 192 n17; see also marriages (common law)
ships in slave-trade, 5, 11, 14, 149, 154, 184 n42
shipyards: freedmen in, 154; slaves in 83, 176
Sicily, slaves in, 59, 188 n147, 194 n57, 218 n49
Sierra Leone, 23, 32, 168, 204 n66
Silveira, Fernão da, 203 n66
Silves, 139, 189 n4
Sintra, 80, 144, 197 n52, 198 n62, 199 n88
sisa, 9, 10, 15, 28, 183 n37, 268
slave, words for, xiii
slave-catchers, 135, 136
slave-merchants, see merchants
Slave Rivers, 7, 13, 32, 182 n13
slavery: in Antiquity, 181 n2 to Introduction; in Iberia after 1555, 178, 206 n118; mediaeval (in Europe), 1, 28, 29, 35, 36, 181 n2 to Introduction, (in Portugal), 5, 62, 74, 113, 138, 166, 181 n2 to Introduction; in Renaissance Europe, 7, 30, 59, 63, 110, 176, 177, 178, 188 n149, 220 n14
slave-trade from West Africa, 1, 2, 3, 4–34, 149; end of, 178, 223 n20; numbers, 5, 19–25, 27, 29, 30, 31, 33, 48, 178, 180 n11, 182 n14, 186 nn103, 105, 107 and 113, 195 n9; revenue from, 31–4, 45, 189 n167; see also prices of slaves; re-export of slaves; sale of slaves
social mobility for blacks, 146, 148, 165, 172, 175
Sofala, Mozambique, 197 n52

Solis, freedman in play, 171, 221 n20
Soto, Domingo de, 44
Souto Redondo, Alentejo, 137
Spain: blacks in contemporary period, 223 n23; slave population in, 29, 60, 176, 223 n12; see also Castile; re-export of slaves; Seville; Valencia
Spanish legists and theologians, 42, 44, 46
stable-lads, slaves as, 82
status, juridical: of freedmen, 2, 134, 142–3, 148; of slaves, 2, 17–18, 89, 102, 108, 113–17, 131–3
stereotype of black in literature, 3, 169–71; see also attitudes
stevedores, slaves as, 76, 81, 176, 197 nn59 and 60
stone-masons: freedman, 154; own slaves, 75, 197 n52
sugar, 7, 177
suicide, 180 n11
surgeon, freedman, 146
sweepers, slaves as, 80, 83, 95, 96

Tagus, river, 15, 29, 54, 61, 83; boatmen on, 71–3, 142; valley, see Ribatejo
tailor, freedman, 154
Tanba, slave, 40
Tancos, 71, 72
tangos maos, tangos maus, 13, 14
Tapeçaria, slaves in, 98
taverns, slaves in, 124, 132
Tavira, 58, 96, 137, 183 n39
Tenreiro, Jorge, 182 n12
Terreiro do Paço, square in Lisbon, 77
testimony: of freedmen, 142; of slaves, 116, 158, 163
Tetzel, Gabriel, 150
theft: by freedmen, 147; by slaves, 106, 107, 111, 117, 119, 120, 121, 122–3, 124, 130, 131, 142, (of produce), 70, 97, 117, 123, 130, 169, 170; considered typical of blacks, 122, 130, 169, 170, 172, 221 n22, (judgement assessed) 130–1, 173
Thomas Aquinas, Saint, 37, 38
Todos-os-Santos, hospital, Lisbon, 67, 86, 93, 97, 98, 207 n134
Toledo, 29, 136, 219 n72
Tomar, 60, 198 n62
Tomé, freedman, 144
Tomé, Mestre, character in play, 171
Tonba, slave, 40
Tordesillas, 169
Torres Novas, 131
Touregão, Pedro, freedman, 214 n53
trade-goods for slave-trade, 12, 13
tradesmen, own slaves, 63, 64, 65–6; see also guilds, merchants
trading posts, 5, 7, 13, 42

Trás-os-Montes, province: demography, 49, 52, 53; blacks in, 202 n22
treasurers: of Casa da Guiné e Índia, 8, 10, 15, 83; of Infante D. Henrique's household, 8
treatment, harsh: on ship, 14; in literature, 171; in Portugal, 82, 107–9, 111
Trent, Council of, 41, 42, 104, 111, 149
trespass, by slaves, 70, 117, 130
trials: of freedmen, 140, 142, 143; of freemen, 87, 211 n88; of slaves, 87, 117–20, 122–3, 131, 132

Ughoton, port of Benin, 13
Umar, slave, 190 n38
unemployment, 48, 87, 88
United States of America, 204 n69, 223 n15

Valarinho, Diogo, 28
Vale de Zebro, see Fornos Reais, Vale de Zebro
Valencia, 15, 22, 29, 30, 176, 186 n110
Valladolid, 29
Vasconcellos, Jorge Ferreira de, 102, 134
Vaz, Pedro, archdeacon of Elvas, 118
vendors, see regateiras
Venice, 28
Las Ventas de Ginea (sic), 215 n80
Venturino, Giambattista, 92, 106
Verde, Cape, 168
Vicente, slave, 159
Vicente, Gil, 100, 103, 105, 146, 167, 169, 170, 171, 173, 221 n21
Vila do Conde, 53
Vila Nova de Portimão, 58, 103
Vila Viçosa, 92, 106
vineyards: freedmen in, 144; slaves in, 69
vintena, 9, 16, 183 n25, 269
Virginia, 203 n63
Vitoria, Francisco de, 42

voyages to West Africa, 1, 5, 8, 9, 11–14; reasons for, 181 n8

wages: of criados, 85; of free labour, 84, 88, 89, 200 nn113 and 118, 203 n57; paid to slaves, 11, 77, 79, 84, 89, 131
war, acquisition of slaves by, 4, 5, 7, 25, 26, 43, 44, 181 n4 to Chapter 1
washerwomen, 88; freedwomen as, 163, 215 n74; slaves as, 75–6, 81
watch, see police
whipping: by law, 77, 117, 118, 119, 121, 122, 123, 129, 135, 174, 222 n40; in literature, 171; by masters, 108, 132
white slaves, see Moors
whitewashers, slaves as, 76, 81
wills: of freedmen, 142, 214 n53; of slaves, 116
witchcraft, 152, 160, 162–4, 165, 219 nn72 and 74
Wolofs, African people, 16, 29, 99, 137, 161, 164
women (when treatment distinct from men): legal status, 102, 125, 126; literary depiction, 169, 170; manumission, 61, 143; occupations, 67, 68, 69, 70, 71–2, 75–80, 81, 82, 93, 94, 95, 145, 215 n74; ratio of sexes (in slave-trade) 24–5, (in society) 60, 61, 194 nn59 and 61; in slave-trade, 14, 16, 39, 60–1; wives of interpreters and seamen, 155; see also marriages; sexual relations
woodcutter, freedman, 144

Xabregas, Lisbon, 157

Zurara, Gomes Eanes de, 19, 35, 38, 39, 45, 92, 108, 149, 167, 182 n8, 189 n1, 190 n18

Made in the USA
Monee, IL
08 October 2020

44357755R00184